James Allen

Daily Meditations
For Every Day in the Year

This edition is a combination of two books: 'Morning and Evening Thoughts' by James Allen, published 1909 and 'James Allen's Book of Meditations' published 1913.

Copyright 2014 by Thinking Anew Media, Los Angeles, Calif.

James Allen

(1864 – 1912)

EDITOR'S PREFACE

(From 'James Allen's Book of Meditations', 1913)

James Allen may truly be called the Prophet of Meditation. In an age of strife, hurry, religious controversy, heated arguments, ritual and ceremony, he came with his message of Meditation, calling men away from the din and strife of tongues into the peaceful paths of stillness within their own souls, where the Light that lighteth every man that cometh into the world ever burns steadily and surely for all who will turn their weary eyes from the strife *without* to the quiet *within*. Many of the Meditations were written as he came down from the Cairn in the early morning, where he spent those precious hours alone with God while the world slept. Others are gleaned from his many writings, published and *unpublished*, and are arranged for daily readings at his request, and, we believe, under his spiritual guidance. The book must ever be a stronghold of Spiritual Truth and blessing to all who read it, and especially to those who use it for daily meditation. Its great power lies in that it is the very heart of a good man *who lived every word he wrote.* The beautiful half-tone portrait is a speaking likeness of the Author. It was taken only six weeks before his translation, and has not been published before.

We are indebted to Messrs. Putnam's Sons (London and New York), and to Messrs. Wm. Rider and Son, Limited (London), for their cordial expressions of pleasure that some of the Meditations should be culled from the books published by them, viz., *The Mastery of Destiny,* and *Above Life's Turmoil* (Putnam), and *From Passion to Peace,* and *Man : King of Mind, Body, and Circumstance* (Rider).

LILY L. ALLEN

"BRYNGOLEU",
ILFRACOMBE, ENGLAND.

He who does not find
*   The way of Meditation cannot reach*
*   Emancipation and enlightenment.*
*   But thou wilt find the way of Holy Thought;*
*   With mind made calm and steadfast, thou will see*
*   The Permanent amid the mutable,*
*   The Truth eternal in the things that change:*
*   Thou wilt behold the Perfect Law: Cosmos*
*   From Chaos rises when the conquered self*
*   Lies underneath man's heel: Love be thy strength;*
*   Look on the passion-tortured multitudes,*
*   And have compassion on them; know their pain*
*   By thy long sorrow ended. Thou wilt come*
*   To perfect peace, and so wilt bless the world,*
*   Leading unto the High and Holy Way*
*   The feet of them that seek.—And now I go*
*   To my Abode; go thou unto thy work.*

By Thought we rise, by Thought we fall; by Thought
We stand or go; all destiny is wrought
By its swift potency; and he who stands
Master of Thought, and his desires commands,
Willing and weaving thoughts of Love and Might,
Shapes his high end in Truths unerring Light.

January First

Thought for the Morning

In aiming at the life of blessedness, one of the simplest beginnings to be considered, and rightly made, is that which we all make every day—namely, the beginning of each day's life. There is a sense in which every day may be regarded as the beginning of a new life, in which one can think, act, and live newly, and in a wiser and better spirit. The right beginning of the day will be followed by a cheerfulness permeating the household with a sunny influence, and the tasks and duties of the day will be undertaken in a strong and confident spirit, and the whole day will be well lived.

Meditation for the Day

*The way from passion to peace
is by overcoming one's self.*

FREQUENTLY the man of passion is most eager to put others right; but the man of wisdom puts himself right. If one is anxious to reform the world, let him begin by reforming himself. The reformation of self does not end with the elimination of the sensual elements only; that is its beginning. It ends only when every vain thought and selfish aim is overcome. Short of perfect purity and wisdom, there is still some form of self-slavery or folly which needs to be conquered.

On the wings of aspiration man rises from earth to heaven, from ignorance to knowledge, from the under darkness to the upper light. Without it he remains a grovelling animal, earthly, sensual, unenlightened, and uninspired.

Aspiration is the longing for heavenly things.

Thought for the Evening

There can be no progress, no achievement, without sacrifice, and a man's worldly success will be in the measure that he sacrifices his confused animal thoughts, and fixes his mind on the development of his plans, and the strengthening of his resolution and self-reliance. And the higher he lifts his thoughts, the more manly, upright, and righteous he becomes, the greater will be his success, the more blessed and enduring will be his achievements.

January Second

Thought for the Morning

None but right acts can follow right thoughts; none but a right life can follow right acts; and by living a right life all blessedness is achieved. Mind is the Master-power that moulds and makes. And Man is Mind, and evermore he takes the tool of thought, and, shaping what he wills, brings forth a thousand joys, a thousand ills;—He thinks in secret, and it comes to pass: environment is but his looking-glass.

Meditation for the Day

Where is peace to be found! Where is the hiding-place of truth!

LET first things be put first; work before play; duty before enjoyment; and others before self: this is an excellent rule which cannot lead astray. To make a right beginning is half-way to victory. The athlete who makes a bad start may lose his prize; the merchant who makes a false start may lose his reputation; and the Truth-seeker who makes a wrong start may forego the crown of Righteousness. To begin with pure thoughts, sterling rectitude, unselfish purpose, noble aims, and an incorruptible conscience this is to start right; this it is to put first things first, so that all other things will follow in harmonious order, making life simple, beautiful, successful, and peaceful.

The soul will cry out for its lost heritage.

Thought for the Evening

Calmness of mind is one of the beautiful jewels of wisdom. A man becomes calm in the measure that he understands himself as a thought-evolved being... and he as he develops a right understanding, and sees more and more clearly the internal relations of things by the action of cause and effect, he ceases to fret and fume, and worry and grieve, and remains poised, steadfast, serene.

January Third

Thought for the Morning

To follow, under all circumstances, the highest promptings within you; to be always true to the divine self; to reply upon the inward voice, the inward light, and to pursue your purpose with a fearless and restful heart, believing that the future will yield unto you the need of every thought and effort; knowing that the laws of the universe can never fail, and that your own will come back to you with mathematical exactitude—this is faith and the living of faith.

Meditation for the Day

If one would find peace, he must come out of passion.

So long as animal conditions taste sweet to a man, he cannot aspire: he is so far satisfied; but when their sweetness turns to bitterness, then in his sorrow he thinks of nobler things. When he is deprived of earthly joy, he aspires to the joy which is heavenly. It is when impurity turns to suffering that purity is sought. Truly aspiration rises, phoenix-like, from the dead ashes of repentance, but on its powerful pinions man can reach the heaven of heavens.

The man of aspiration has entered the way which leads to peace; and surely he will reach that end if he stays not nor turns back. If he constantly renews his mind with glimpses of the heavenly vision, he will reach the heavenly state.

That which can be conceived can be achieved.

Thought for the Evening

Have a thorough understanding of your work, and let it be your own; and as you proceed, ever following the inward guide, the infallible voice, you will pass on from victory to victory, and will rise step by step to higher resting-places, and your ever broadening outlook will gradually reveal to you the essential beauty and purpose of life. Self-purified, health will be yours; self-governed, power will be yours, and all that you do will prosper.

And I may stand where health, success, and power await my coming, if, each fleeting hour, I cling to love and patience; and abide with stainlessness; and never step aside from high integrity; so shall I see at last the land of immortality.

January Fourth

Thought for the Morning

When the tongue is well controlled and wisely subdued; when selfish impulses and unworthy thoughts no longer rush to the tongue demanding utterance; when the speech has become harmless, pure, gracious, gentle, and purposeful, and no word is uttered but in sincerity and truth—then are the five steps in virtuous speech accomplished, then is the second great lesson in Truth learned and mastered. Make pure thy heart, and thou wilt make thy life rich, sweet and beautiful.

Meditation for the Day

Our life is what we make it by our own thoughts and deeds.

MAN attains in the measure that he aspires. His longing to be is the gauge of what he can be. To fix the mind is to fore-ordain the achievement. As man can experience and know all low things, so he can experience and know all high things. As he has become human, so he can become divine. The turning of the mind in high and divine directions is the sole and needful task. What is impurity but the impure thoughts of the thinker?

What is purity but the pure thoughts of the thinker? One man does not do the thinking of another. Each man is pure or impure of himself alone. The man of aspiration sees before him the pathway up the heavenly heights, and his heart already experiences a foretaste of the final peace.

There is a life of victory over sin, and triumph over evil.

Thought for the Evening

Having clothed himself with humility, the first questions a man asks himself are:—

"How am I acting towards others?"
"What am I doing to others?"
"How am I thinking of others?"
"Are my thoughts of, and acts towards others prompted by unselfish love?"

As a man, in the silence of his soul, asks himself these searching questions, he will unerringly see where he has hitherto failed.

January Fifth

Thought for the Morning

To dwell in love always and towards all is to live the true life, is to have Life itself. Knowing this, the good man gives up himself unreservedly to the Spirit of Love, and dwells in Love towards all, contending with none, condemning none, but loving all.

The Christ Spirit of Love puts an end, not only to all sin, but to all division and contention.

Meditation for the Day

When a man wishes and wills he can find the good and the true.

THE Gates of Heaven are forever open, I and no one is prevented from entering! by any will or power but his own; but no one can enter the Kingdom of Heaven so long as he is enamoured of, and chooses, the seductions of hell, so long as he resigns himself to sin and sorrow.

There is a larger, higher, nobler, diviner life than that of sinning and suffering, which is so common in which, indeed, nearly all are immersed a life of victory over sin, and triumph over evil; a life wise and happy, benign and tranquil, virtuous and peaceful. This life can be found and lived now, and he who lives it is steadfast in the midst of change; restful among the restless; peaceful, though surrounded by strife.

Every moment is the time of choice; every hour is destiny.

Thought for the Evening

When sin and self are abandoned, the heart is restored to its imperishable Joy. Joy comes and fills the self-emptied heart; it abides with the peaceful; its reign is with the pure. Joy flees from the selfish, it deserts the quarrelsome; it is hidden from the impure. Joy cannot remain with the selfish; it is wedded to Love.

January Sixth

Thought for the Morning

In the pure heart there is no room left where personal judgments and hatreds can find lodgement, for it is filled to overflowing with tenderness and love; it sees no evil, and only as men succeed in seeing no evil in others will they become free from sin, and sorrow, and suffering. If men only understood that the heart that sins must sorrow, that the hateful mind tomorrow reaps its barren harvest, weeping, starving, resting not, nor sleeping; tenderness would fill their being, they would see with pity's seeing, if they only understood.

Meditation for the Day

The lover of the pure life renews his mind daily.

AS the energetic man of business is not daunted by difficulties, but studies how to overcome them, so the man of ceaseless aspiration is not crushed into submission by temptations, but meditates how he may fortify his mind; for the tempter is like a coward, he only creeps in at weak and unguarded points. The tempted one should study thoughtfully the nature and meaning of temptation, for until it is known it cannot be overcome. He who is to overcome temptation must understand how it arises in his own darkness and error, and must study, by introspection and meditation, how to disperse the darkness and supplant error by truth.

A man must know himself if he is to know truth. Self-knowledge is the handmaid of self-conquest.

Engage daily in holy meditation on Truth and its attainment.

Thought for the Evening

To stand face to face with truth; to arrive, after innumerable wanderings and pains, at wisdom and bliss; not to be finally defeated and cast out, but to ultimately triumph over every inward foe—such is man's divine destiny, such his glorious goal; and this, every saint, sage, and saviour has declared. A man only begins to be a man when he ceases to whine and revile, and commences to search for the hidden justice which regulates his life. And as he adapts his mind to that regulating factor, he ceases to accuse others as the cause of his condition, and builds himself up in strong and noble thoughts; ceases to kick against circumstances, but begins to use them as aids to his more rapid progress, and as a means of discovering the hidden power and possibilities within himself.

January Seventh

Thought for the Morning

The will to evil and the will to good are both within thee, which wilt thou employ? Thou knowest what is right and what is wrong, which wilt though love and foster, which destroy?

Thou art the chooser of thy thoughts and deeds; thou art the maker of thine inward state; the power is thine to be what thou wilt be; thou buildest Truth and Love, or lies and hate.

Meditation for the Day

As errors and impunities are revealed, purge them away.

EVERY step upward means the leaving of something behind and below. The high is reached only at the sacrifice of the low. The good is secured only by abandoning the evil. Knowledge is acquired only by the destruction of ignorance. Every acquisition has its price, which must be paid "to the uttermost farthing". Every animal, every creeping thing, possesses some gift, some power, which man, in his upward march, has laid down, which he has exchanged for some higher gift, or power. What great good men forfeit by clinging to old selfish habits! Behind every humble sacrifice a winged angel waits to bear us up the heights of knowledge and wisdom.

Let him who has attained guard against falling back. Let him be careful in little things, and be well fortified against the entrance of sin.

Aim, with ardor, for the attainment of a perfect life.

Thought for the Evening

The teaching of Jesus brings men back to the simple truth that righteousness, or *right-doing*, is entirely a matter of individual conduct, and not a mystical something apart from a man's thoughts and deeds.

Calmness and patience can become habitual by first grasping, through effort, a calm and patient thought, and then continuously thinking it, and living in it, until "use becomes second nature," and anger and impatience pass away for ever.

January Eighth

Thought for the Morning

Man is made or unmade by himself; in the armoury of thought he forges the weapons by which he destroys himself; he also fashions the tools with which he builds for himself heavenly mansions of joy and strength and peace. By the right choice and true application of thought man ascends to the Divine Perfection; by the abuse and wrong application of thought he descends below the level of the beast. Between these two extremes are all the grades of character and man is their maker and master.

As a being of Power, Intelligence, and Love, and the lord of his own thoughts, man holds the key to every situation.

Meditation for the Day

The strife of the world in all its forms has its origin in one common cause, namely, individual selfishness.

ALL the varied activities of human life are rooted in, and draw their vitality from, one common source the human heart. The cause of all suffering and all happiness resides, not in the outer activities of human life, but in the inner activities of the heart and mind; and every external agency is sustained by the life which it derives from human conduct.

The man who cannot endure to have his errors and shortcomings brought to the surface and made known, but tries to hide them, is unfit to walk the highway of Truth. He is not properly equipped to battle with and overcome temptation. He who cannot fearlessly face his lower nature cannot climb the rugged heights of renunciation.

Each man comes under the laws of his own being, never under the laws of another.

Thought for the Evening

Whatsoever you harbour in the inmost chambers of your heart will, sooner or later, by the inevitable law of reaction, shape itself in your outward life.

Every soul attracts its own, and nothing can possibly come to it that does not belong to it. To realize this is to recognize the universality of Divine Law.

If thou would'st right the world, and banish all its evils and its woes, make its wild places bloom, and its drear deserts blossom as the rose—then right thyself.

January Ninth

Thought for the Morning

Whatever conditions are rendering your life burdensome, you may pass out of and beyond them by developing and utilizing within you the transforming power of self-purification and self-conquest.

Before the divine radiance of a pure heart all darkness vanishes and all clouds melt away, and he who has conquered self has conquered the universe.

He who sets his foot firmly upon the path of self-conquest, who walks, aided by the staff of faith, the highway of self-sacrifice, will assuredly achieve the highest prosperity, and will reap abounding and enduring joy and bliss.

Meditation for the Day

When the soul is most tried, its need is greatest.

Do not despair because of failure. From your particular failure there is a special greatness, a peculiar wisdom, to be gained; and no teacher can lead you to that greatness, that wisdom, more surely and swiftly than your experience of failure. In every mistake you make, in every fall you encounter, there is a lesson of vital import if you will but search it out; and he who will stoop to discover the good in that which appears to be disastrous will rise superior to every event, and will utilize his failures as winged steeds to bear him to a final and supreme success.

Foolish men blame others for their lapses and sins, but let the truth-lover blame only himself. Let him acknowledge his complete responsibility for his own conduct.

*Where temptation is powerful, the greater and more
enduring will be the victory.*

Thought for the Evening

It is the silent and conquering thought forces which bring all things into manifestation. The universe grew out of thought.

To adjust all your thoughts to a perfect and unswerving faith in the omnipotence and supremacy of Good is to co-operate with that Good, and to realize within yourself the solution and destruction of all evil.

To mentally deny evil is not sufficient; it must, by daily practice, be risen above and understood. To affirm the Good mentally is inadequate; it must, by unswerving endeavour, be entered into and comprehended.

January Tenth

Thought for the Morning

Every thought you think is a force sent out. Whatever your position in life may be, before you can hope to enter into any measure of success, usefulness, and power, you must learn how to focus your thought forces by cultivating calmness and repose.

There is no difficulty, however great, but will yield before a calm and purposeful concentration of thought, and no legitimate object but may be speedily actualized by the intelligent use and direction of one's soul forces.

Think good thoughts, and they will quickly become actualized in your outward life in the form of good conditions.

Meditation for the Day

The great need of the soul is the need of that permanent Principle called Righteousness.

THE old must pass away before the new can appear. The old cottage must be demolished before the new mansion can appear upon its site. The old error must be destroyed before the new truth can come.... The old self must be renounced before the new man can be born. When the old self of temper, impatience, envy, pride, and impurity has perished, then in its place will appear the new man of gentleness, patience, goodwill, humility, and purity. Let the old life of sin and sorrow pass; let the new life of Righteousness and Joy come in.... Then all that was old and ugly will be made new and beautiful. It is in the realization of this Principle where the Kingdom of Heaven, the abiding home of the soul, resides, and which is the source and storehouse of every permanent blessing.

A life of virtue is noble and excellent.

Thought for the Evening

That which you would be and hope to be, you may be now. Non-accomplishment resides in your perpetual postponement, and, having the power to postpone, you also have the power to accomplish—to perpetually accomplish: realize this truth, and you shall be today, and every day, the ideal being of whom you dreamed.

Say to yourself, "I will live in my Ideal now; I will manifest my ideal now; I will be my Ideal now; and all that tempts me away from my Ideal I will not listen to; I will listen only to the voice of my Ideal."

January Eleventh

Thought for the Morning

Be as a flower; content to be, to grow in sweetness day by day. If thou would'st perfect thyself in knowledge, perfect thyself in Love. If thou would'st reach the Highest, ceaselessly cultivate a loving and compassionate heart.

To him who chooses Goodness, sacrificing all, is given that which is more than, and includes, all.

Meditation for the Day

*It matters little what is without, for it is all a reflection
of your own consciousness.*

THE deplorable failure of many outward and isolated reforms is traceable to the fact that their devotees pursue them as an end in themselves, failing to see that they are merely steps towards ultimate, individual perfection.

All true reform *must come from within*, in a changed heart and mind. The giving up of certain foods and drinks, and the breaking away from certain outward habits, are good and necessary beginnings; but they are only beginnings, and to end there is to fall far short of a true spiritual life. It is good, therefore, to cleanse the heart, to correct the mind, and to develop the understanding, for we know that the one thing needed is a regenerate heart.

*It matters everything what you are within, for everything
without will be mirrored and colored accordingly.*

Thought for the Evening

The Great Law never cheats any man of his just due.

Human life, when rightly lived, is simple with a beautiful simplicity.

He who comprehends the utter simplicity of life, who obeys its laws, and does not step aside into the dark paths and complex mazes of selfish desire, stands where no harm can reach him.

Then there is fullness of joy, abounding plenty, and rich and complete blessedness.

January Twelfth

Thought for the Morning

Every man reaps the results of his own thoughts and deeds, and suffers for his own wrong.

He who begins right, and continues right, does not need to desire, and search for felicitous results; they are already at hand; they follow as consequences; they are the certainties, the realities, of life.

Sweet is the rest and deep is the bliss of him who has freed his heart from its lusts and hatreds and dark desires.

Meditation for the Day

Renew your resolution daily, and in the hour of
temptation do not depart from the right path.

THE days are lengthening. Each day now the sun rises a little higher, and the light lingers a little longer. So each day we can strengthen our character; each day we can open our heart a little more to the light of Truth, and allow the Sun of Righteousness to shine more highly in our mind. The sun does not increase in volume or intensity, but the earth turns towards it, and receives more as it turns. All that there is of Truth and Good is now. It does not increase or diminish, but as we turn towards it we receive of its radiance and beneficence in ever-increasing abundance and power.

As the artisan acquires skill in fashioning the articles of his craft by daily and diligent practice with his tools, so do you acquire skill in fashioning good deeds by daily and diligent practice of the Truth.

You can acquire Truth only by practice.

Thought for the Evening

You are the creator of your own shadows; you desire, and then you grieve; renounce, and then you shall rejoice.

Of all the beautiful truths pertaining to the soul. . . none is more gladdening or fruitful of divine promise and confidence than this—that man is the master of thought, the moulder of character, and the maker and shaper of character, environment, and destiny.

January Thirteenth

Thought for the Morning

As darkness is a passing shadow, and light is a substance that remains, so sorrow is fleeting, but joy abides for ever. No true thing can pass away and become lost; no false thing can remain and be preserved. Sorrow is false, and it cannot live; joy is true, and it cannot die. Joy may become hidden for a time, but it can always be recovered; sorrow may remain for a period, but it can be transcended and dispersed.

Do not think your sorrow will remain; it will pass away like a cloud. Do not believe that the torments of sin are ever your portion; they will vanish like a hideous nightmare. Awake! Arise! Be holy and joyful.

Meditation for the Day

The wise purify their thoughts.

EVERY day is a new birth in time, holding out new beginnings, new possibilities, new achievements. The ages have witnessed the stars in their orbits, but this day hath no age witnessed. It is a new appearance, a new reality. It heralds a new life yea, a new order, a new society, a new age. It holds out new hopes, new opportunities, to all men. In it you can become a new man, a new woman. For you it can be the day of regeneration, renewal, rebirth. From the old past with its mistakes, failures, and sorrows, you can rise a new being, endued with power and purpose, and radiant with the inspiration of a new ideal.

Be chaste in mind and body. Abandon sensual pleasures. Purge the mind of selfishness, and live a life of exalted purity.

Be upright, gentle, and pure-hearted.

Thought for the Evening

Tribulation lasts only so long as there remains some chaff of self which needs to be removed. The *tribulum*, or threshing machine, ceases to work when all the grain is separated from the chaff; and when the last impurities are blown away from the soul, tribulation has completed its work, and there is no more need for it; then abiding joy is realized.

The sole and supreme use of suffering is to purify, to burn out all that is useless and impure. Suffering ceases for him who is pure. There could be no object in burning gold after the dross had been removed.

January Fourteenth

Thought for the Morning

In speaking of self-control, one is easily misunderstood. It should not be associated with a destructive repression, but with a constructive expression.

A man is happy, wise and great in the measure that he controls himself; he is wretched, foolish, and mean in the measure that he allows his animal nature to dominate his thoughts and actions.

He who controls himself, controls his life, his circumstances, his destiny; and wherever he goes he carries his happiness with him as an abiding possession.

Renunciation precedes regeneration. The permanent happiness which men seek in dissipation, excitement, and abandonment to unworthy pleasures, is found only in the life which reverses all this—the life of self-control.

Meditation for the Day

Exert yourself ceaselessly in decreasing evil and accumulating good.

VICTORY of all kinds is preceded by a season of preparation. It can no more appear spontaneously and erratically than can a flower or a mountain. Like them, it is the culminating point in a process of growth, in a series of causes and effects. No mere wishing, no magic word, will produce worldly success; it must be achieved by an orderly succession of well-directed efforts. No spiritual victory will be achieved by him who imagines that it does not begin until the hour of temptation arrives. All spiritual triumphs are gained in the silent hour of meditation, and through a series of successes in lesser trials. The time of great temptation is the climax of a conquest that long preparation has made certain and complete.

*Fix your minds on the practice of virtue, and the
comprehension and application of fixed and noble principles.*

Thought for the Evening

Law, not confusion, is the dominating principle in the universe; justice, not injustice is the soul and substance of life; and righteousness, not corruption, is the moulding and moving force in the spiritual government of the world. This being so, man has but the right himself to find that the universe is right.

When I am pure, I shall have solved the mystery of life; I shall be sure, when I am free from hatred, lust and strife, I am in Truth, and Truth abides in me; I shall be safe, and sane, and wholly free, when I am pure.

January Fifteenth

Thought for the Morning

If men only understood that their hatred and resentment slays their peace and sweet contentment, hurts themselves, helps not another, does not cheer one lonely brother, they would seek the better doing of good deeds which leaves no ruing—

If they only understood.

If men only understood how Love conquers; how prevailing is its might, grim hate assailing; how compassion endeth sorrow, maketh wise, and doth not borrow pain of passion, they would ever live in Love, in hatred never—

If they only understood.

Meditation for the Day

The Never-Ending Gladness awaits your Homecoming.

THE falling rain prepares the earth for the future crops of grain and fruit, so the rains of many sorrows showering upon the heart prepare and mellow it for the coming of that wisdom that perfects the mind and gladdens the heart. As the clouds darken the earth but to cool and fructify it, so the clouds of grief cast a shadow over the heart to prepare it for nobler things. The hour of sorrow is the hour of reverence. It puts an end to the shallow sneer, the ribald jest, the cruel calumny; it softens the heart with sympathy, and enriches the mind with thoughtfulness. Wisdom is mainly recollection of all that was learned by sorrow.

Do not think that your sorrow will remain; it will pass away like a cloud.

Where self ends, grief passes away.

Thought for the Evening

The grace and beauty that were in Jesus can be of no value to you—cannot be understood by you—unless they are also *in you*, and they can never be in you, until you practice them, for, apart from *doing*, the qualities which constitute goodness do not, as far as you are concerned, exist.

To adore Jesus for his good qualities is a long step towards Truth, but to practice those qualities is Truth itself; and he who fully adores the perfection of another will not rest content in his own imperfection, but will fashion his soul after the likeness of that other.

Therefore thou who adorest Jesus for his divine qualities, practice those qualities thyself, and thou too shalt be divine.

January Sixteenth

Thought for the Morning

Let a man realize that life in its totality proceeds from the mind, and lo, the way of blessedness is opened up to him! For he will then discover that he possesses the power to rule his mind and to fashion it in accordance with his Ideal.

So will he elect to strongly and steadfastly walk those pathways of thought and action which are altogether excellent; to him life will become beautiful and sacred; and, sooner or later, he will put to flight all evil, confusion, and suffering; for it is impossible for a man to fall short of liberation, enlightenment, and peace, who guards with unwearying diligence the gateway of his heart.

Meditation for the Day

*Live sweetly and happily, as becomes the dignity of
a true manhood and womanhood.*

THERE is no greater happiness than to be occupied with good, whether it be good thoughts, good actions, or good employment; for every good thing is fraught with bliss, and evil cannot enter the heart or house that is tenanted by all that is good. The mind whose doors are guarded by good shuts out unhappiness as the well-sentried garrison shuts out the foe. Unhappiness can only enter through unguarded doors, and even then its power over the tenant is not complete unless it find him occupied with evil. Not to entertain evil thoughts; not to do bad actions; not to engage in worthless or questionable employment, but to resort to good in all things this is the source of supreme happiness.

Pure happiness is the rightful and happy condition of the soul.

Thought for the Evening

By constantly overcoming self, a man gains a knowledge of the subtle intricacies of his mind; and it is this divine knowledge which enables him to become established in calmness.

Without self-knowledge there can be no abiding peace of mind, and those who are carried away by tempestuous passions, cannot approach the holy place where calmness reigns.

The weak man is like one who, having mounted a fiery steed, allows it to run away with him, and carry him withersoever it wills; the strong man is like one who, having mounted the steed, governs it with a masterly hand and makes it go in whatever direction and at whatever speed he commands.

January Seventeenth

Thought for the Morning

There is no strife, no selfishness, in the Kingdom; there is perfect harmony, equipoise, and rest.

Those who live in the Kingdom of Love, have all their needs supplied by the Law of Love.

As self is the root cause of all strife and suffering, so Love is the root cause of all peace and bliss. Those who are at rest in the Kingdom do not look for happiness in any outward possessions. They are freed from all anxiety and trouble and, resting in Love, they are the embodiment of happiness.

Meditation for the Day

*All things are orderly and sequential,
being governed by the law of causation.*

DO not trouble about results, or be anxious as to the future; but be troubled about personal shortcomings, and be anxious to remove them; for know this simple truth wrong does not result from right, and a good present cannot give birth to a bad future. You are the custodian of your deeds, but not of the results which flow from them. The deeds of today bring the happiness or sorrow of tomorrow. Be therefore concerned about what you think and do, rather than about what may or may not come to you; for he whose deeds are good does not concern himself about results, and is freed from fear of future ill.

*Verily the Law reigneth, and reigneth for ever, and
Justice and Love are its eternal ministers.*

Thought for the Evening

Let it not be supposed that the children of the Kingdom live in ease and indolence (these two sins are the first that have to be eradicated when the search for the Kingdom is entered upon); they live in a peaceful activity; in fact, they only truly live, for the life of self, with its train of worries, griefs, and fears, is not *real life*.

The children of the Kingdom are *known by their life*, they manifest the fruits of the Spirit—"Love, joy, peace, long-suffering, kindness, goodness, faithfulness, meekness, temperance, and self-control"—under all circumstances and vicissitudes.

January Eighteenth

Thought for the Morning

The gospel of Jesus is a gospel of *living and doing*. If it were not this it would not voice the Eternal Truth. Its Temple is *Purified Conduct*, the entrance-door to which is *Self-Surrender*. It invites men to shake off sin, and promises, as a result, joy and blessedness and perfect peace.

The Kingdom of Heaven is perfect trust, perfect knowledge, perfect peace. . . no sin can enter therein, no self-born thought or deed can pass its golden gates; no impure desire can defile its radiant robes. . . all may enter it who will, but all must pay the price—*the unconditional abandonment of self.*

Meditation for the Day

Speak only words which are truthful and sincere.

THE storm may rage without, but it cannot affect us if there is peace within. As by the fireside there is security from the fiercest storm, so the heart that is steadfast in the knowledge of Truth abides in peace, though all around be strife and perturbation. The bitter opposition of men and the unrest of the world cannot make us bitter and restless unless we enter into and co-operate with it. Rather, if we have peace in our heart, will the outer turmoil cause our peace to deepen, to take firmer root, and to show forth more abundantly in works of peace for the softening of human hearts and the enlightening of human minds.

Blessed is he who has no wrongs to remember, no injuries to forget, in whose pure heart no hateful thought about another can take root and flourish.

He who speaks evil of another cannot find the way of peace.

Thought for the Evening

I say this—and know it to be truth—*that circumstances can only affect you in so far as you allow them to do so.* You are swayed by circumstances because you have not a right understanding of the nature, use, and power of thought. You believe (and upon this little word *belief* hang all our joys and sorrows) that outward things have the power to make or mar your life; by so doing you submit to those outward things, confess that you are their slave, and they your unconditional master. By so doing you invest them with a power which they do not of themselves possess, and you succumb, in reality not to the circumstances, but to the gloom or gladness, the fear or hope, the strength of weakness, which your thought-sphere has thrown around them.

January Nineteenth

Thought for the Morning

If you are one of those who are praying for, and looking forward to a happier world beyond the grave, here is a message of gladness for you—you may enter into and realize that happy world now; it fills the whole universe, and it is within you, waiting for you to find, acknowledge, and possess.

Said one who understood the inner laws of Being—"When men shall say, lo here, or lo there, go not after them. The Kingdom of God is within you."

Meditation for the Day

Purification is necessarily severe. All becoming is painful.

WHEN a storm has subsided, and all is calm again, observe how all nature seems to pause in a restorative silence. A restful quiet pervades all things, so that even inanimate objects seem to participate in the recuperative repose. So when a too violent eagerness or a sudden burst of passion has spent itself, there comes a period of reflective thought, a time of calm, in which the mind is restored, and things are seen in their true outlines and right proportions. It is wise to take advantage of this quiet time by gaining a truer knowledge of one's self, and forming a more kindly judgment of others. The hour of calm is the hour of restoration.

Joy comes and fills the self-emptied heart; it abides with the peaceful; its reign is with the pure.

Make your every thought, word, and deed sweet and pure.

Thought for the Evening

Heaven and hell are inward states. Sink into self and all its gratifications, and you sink into hell; rise above self into that state of consciousness which is the utter denial and forgetfulness of self, and you enter heaven.

So long as you persist in selfishly seeking for your own personal happiness, so long will happiness elude you, and you will be sowing the seeds of wretchedness. In so far as you succeed in losing yourself in the service of others, in that measure will happiness come to you, and you will reap a harvest of bliss.

January Twentieth

Thought for the Morning

Sympathy given can never be wasted.

One aspect of sympathy is that of pity—pity for the distressed or pain stricken, with a desire to alleviate or help them in their sufferings. The world needs more of this divine quality.

"For pity makes the world soft to the weak, and noble for the strong."

Another form of sympathy is that of rejoicing with others who are more successful than ourselves, and though their success were our own.

Meditation for the Day

In the dark times of sorrow, men approach very near to Truth.

WHEN the tears flow, and the heart aches, remember then the sorrow of the world. When sorrow has overtaken you, remember then that it overtakes all; that none escape it; that it is the great fact in human life that makes religion a necessity. Think not that your pain is isolated and unjustly inflicted. It is but a fragment of the great pain of the world. It is the common experience of all. Perceiving this, let sorrow gently lead you into a deeper religion, a wider compassion, a tenderer regard for all men and all creatures. Let it bring you into greater love and deeper peace.

Bear well in mind that nothing can overtake you that does not belong to you, and that is not for your eternal good.

The end of sorrow is joy and peace.

Thought for the Evening

Sweet are companionships, pleasures, and material comforts, but they change and fade away. Sweeter still are Purity, Wisdom, and the knowledge of Truth, and these never change nor fade away.

He who has attained to the possession of spiritual things can never be deprived of his source of happiness; he will never have to part company with it, and wherever he goes in the whole universe, he will carry his possessions with him. His spiritual end will be the fullness of joy.

January Twenty-first

Thought for the Morning

Let your heart grow and expand with ever broadening love, until, freed from all hatred, and passion, and condemnation, it embraces the whole universe with thoughtful tenderness.

As the flower opens its petals to receive the morning light, so open your soul more and more to the glorious light of Truth.

Soar upward on the wings of aspiration; be fearless and believe in the loftiest possibilities.

Meditation for the Day

The sorrowless state is reached through sorrow.

AS light displaces darkness, and quiet follows storm, so gladness displaces sorrow, and peace comes after pain. The deeper wisdom which flows from acquaintance with sorrow brings with it a holier and more abiding joy than that shallow excitement that preceded sorrow. Between the lesser joys of the senses and the greater joy of the spirit lies the dark vale of sorrow through which all earthly pilgrims pass, and having passed through it, the Heavenly Joy, the Abiding Gladness, is henceforth our companion. They who have passed from the earthly to the heavenly pilgrimage have lifted the dark veil of sorrow from the radiant face of Truth.

He whose treasure is Truth, who fashions his life in
accordance with Wisdom, will find the Joy which
does not pass away; crossing the wide ocean of
illusion, he will come to the sorrowless Shore.

Thought for the Evening

Mind clothes itself in garments of its own making. Mind is the arbiter of life; it is the creator and shaper of conditions, and the recipient of its own results. It contains within itself both the power to create illusion and to perceive reality.

Mind is the infallible weaver of destiny; thought is the thread, good and evil deeds are the warp and woof, and the web, woven upon the loom of life, is character. Make pure thy heart, and thou wilt make thy life, rich, sweet, and beautiful, unmarred by strife.

January Twenty-second

Thought for the Morning

Cherish your visions; cherish your ideals; cherish the music that stirs in your heart, the beauty that forms in your mind, the loveliness that drapes your purest thoughts, for out of them will grow all delightful conditions, all heavenly environment; of these, if you will remain true to them, your world will at last be built.

Guard well thy mind, and, noble, strong, and free, nothing shall harm, disturb or conquer thee; for all thy foes are in thy heart and mind, there also thy salvation thou shalt find.

Meditation for the Day

*All outward oppression is but the shadow and effect
of the real oppression within.*

IN happiness and unhappiness, in joy and sorrow, in success and failure, in victory and defeat; in religion, business, circumstances; in all the issues of life, the determining factor is character. In the mentality of individuals lie the hidden causes of all that pertains to their outward life. Character is both cause and effect. It is the doer of deeds and the recipient of results. Heaven, hell, purgatory, are contained within it. The character that is impure and vicious will experience a life from which the elements of happiness and beauty are lacking, wheresoever they may be placed; but a pure and virtuous character will show forth a life that is happy and beautiful. As you make your character, so will you shape your life.

*To put away self and passion, and establish one's
self in right doing, this is the highest wisdom.*

Thought for the Evening

Dream lofty dreams, and as you dream so shall you become. Your vision is the promise of what you shall one day be; your Ideal is the prophecy of what you shall at last unveil.

The greatest achievement was at first and for a time a dream. The oak sleeps in the acorn; the bird waits in the egg; and in the highest vision of the soul a waking angel stirs.

Your circumstances may be uncongenial, but they shall not long remain so when you perceive an Ideal and strive to reach it.

January Twenty-third

Thought for the Morning

He who has conquered doubt and fear has conquered failure. His every thought is allied with power, and all difficulties are bravely met and wisely overcome. His purposes are seasonably planted, and they bloom and bring forth fruit which does not fall prematurely to the ground.

Thought allied fearlessly to purpose becomes creative force: he who knows this is ready to become something higher and stronger than a mere bundle of wavering thoughts and fluctuating sensations; he who does this has become the conscious and intelligent wielder of his mental powers.

Meditation for the Day

*Not departing from the path of holiness, but surmounting
all difficulties and continuing to the end—
whosoever does this will comprehend Truth.*

WHEN great difficulties arise, and troubles beset, regard your perplexity as a call to deeper thought and more vigorous action. Nothing will attack you that you are not capable of overcoming; no problem will vex you that you cannot solve. The greater your trial, the greater your test of strength, and the more complete and triumphant your victory. However complicated your maze of confusion may be, there is a way out of it, and the finding of that way will exercise your powers to the utmost, and will bring out all your latent skill, energy, and resource. When you have mastered that which threatens to master you, you will rejoice in a new-found strength.

*Knowing the Truth by practice, and being at one with
Truth, you will be invincible, for Truth cannot be
confounded or overthrown.*

Thought for the Evening

Man's true place in the Cosmos is that of a king, not a slave, a commander under the Law of Good, and not a helpless tool in the region of evil.

I write for men, not for babes; for those who are eager to learn, and earnest to achieve; for those who will put away (for the world's good) a petty personal indulgence, a selfish desire, a mean thought, and live on as though it were not, sans craving and regret.

Man is a master. If he were not, he could not act contrary to law.

Evil and weakness are self destructive. The universe is girt with goodness and strength, and it protects the good and the strong.

The angry man is the weak man.

January Twenty-fourth

Thought for the Morning

Not by learning will a man triumph over evil; not by much study will he overcome sin and sorrow. Only by conquering himself will he conquer evil; only by practicing righteousness will he put an end to sorrow.

Not for the clever, nor the learned, nor the self-confident is the Life Triumphant, but for the pure, the virtuous and wise. The former achieve their particular success in life, but the latter alone achieve the great success so invincible and complete that even in apparent defeat it shines with added victory.

Meditation for the Day

*Look not outside thee nor behind thee for the light
and blessedness of Truth, but look within.*

WE advance by a series of efforts. We gather strength, whether mental or physical, by a succession of strivings in given directions. Exertion, oft repeated, leads to power. It is by obeying this law that the athlete trains himself to accomplish wonderful feats of speed or endurance.

When the exertion is along intellectual lines, it leads to unusual talent, or genius; and when in spiritual channels, it leads to wisdom, or transcendent greatness. We should not mourn when circumstances are driving us to greater efforts and more protracted exertion. Events are only evil to the mind that makes them so. They are good to him that accepts their discipline as salutary.

*Thou wilt find Truth within the narrow sphere of
thy duty, even in the humble and hidden sacrifices
of thine own heart.*

Thought for the Evening

The true silence is not merely a silent tongue; it is a silent mind. To merely *hold one's tongue*, and yet to carry about a disturbed and rankling mind, is no remedy for weakness, and no source of power.

Silentness, to be powerful, must envelop the whole mind, must permeate every chamber of the heart; it must be the silence of peace.

To this broad, deep, abiding silentness a man attains only in the measure that he conquers himself.

January Twenty-fifth

Thought for the Morning

By curbing his tongue, a man gains possession of his mind.

The fool babbles, gossips, argues, and bandies words. He glories in the fact that he has had the last word, and has silenced his opponent. He exults in his own folly, is ever on the defensive, and wastes his energies in unprofitable channels. He is like a gardener who continues to dig and plant in unproductive soil.

The wise man avoids idle words, gossips, vain argument, and self-defence. He is content to appear defeated; rejoices when he is defeated; knowing that, having found and removed another error in himself, he has thereby become wiser.

Blessed is he who does not strive for the last word.

Meditation for the Day

There is no blessedness anywhere until impatience is sacrificed.

DESPONDENCY, anxiety, worry, and irritability cannot cure the ills against which they are directed. They only add more misery to the troubles that prompt them. The cultivation of a steadfast and serene spirit cannot be overlooked if life is to yield any measure of usefulness and happiness. The trifles, and even greater troubles, which annoy would soon dissolve and disappear if confronted with a temper that refuses to be ruffled and disturbed. Personal aims, wishes, schemes, and pleasures will meet with checks, rebuffs, and obstacles; and it is in learning to meet these reverses in a wise and calm spirit that we discover the true and abiding happiness within our heart.

When impatience and irritability are put away, then is realized and enjoyed the blessedness of a strong, quiet, and peaceful mind.

Thought for the Evening

Desire is the *craving for possession*; aspiration is the *hunger of the heart for peace*.

The craving for things leads ever farther and farther from peace, and not only ends in deprivation, but is in itself a state of perpetual want. Until it comes to an end, rest and satisfaction are impossible.

The hunger for things can never be satisfied, but the hunger for peace can, and the satisfaction of peace is found—is fully possessed, when all selfish desire is abandoned. Then there is fullness of joy, abounding plenty, and rich and complete blessedness.

January Twenty-sixth

Thought for the Morning

A man will reach the Kingdom by purifying himself, and he can only do this by pursuing a process of self-examination and self-analysis.

The selfishness must be discovered and understood before it can be removed. It is powerless to remove itself, neither will it pass away of itself. Darkness ceases only when light is introduced; so ignorance can only be dispersed by knowledge, selfishness by love.

A man must first of all be willing to lose himself (his self-seeking) before he can find himself (his Divine Self). He must realize that selfishness is not worth clinging to, that it is a master altogether unworthy of his service, and that divine goodness alone is worthy to be enthroned in his heart, as the supreme master of his life.

Meditation for the Day

The greatest blessedness comes to him who infuses into his mind the purest and noblest thoughts.

WE are becoming wise when we know and realize that happiness abides in certain habits of mind, or mental characteristics, rather than in material possessions, or in certain combinations of circumstances. It is a common delusion to imagine that if one only possessed this or that a little more money, a little more leisure, this man's talent, or that man's opportunities; or if one had better friends, or more favourable surroundings one would be happy with a perfect felicity. Alas! Discontent and misery lie in such vain wishes. If happiness is not already found within, it will never be found without. The happiness of a wise mind abides through all vicissitudes.

Your whole life is a series of effects, having their cause in thought—in your own thought.

Thought for the Evening

Be still, my soul, and know that peace is thine. Be steadfast, heart, and know that strength divine Belongs to thee; cease from thy turmoil, mind, and thou the Everlasting Rest shalt find.

If a man would have peace, let him exercise the spirit of peace; if he would find Love, let him dwell in the spirit of Love; if he would escape suffering, let him cease to inflict it; if he would do noble things for humanity, let him cease to do ignoble things for himself. If he will but quarry the mine of his own soul, he shall find there all the materials for building whatsoever he will, and he shall find there also the Central Rock on which to build in safety.

January Twenty-seventh

Thought for the Morning

Men go after much company, and seek out new excitements, but they are not acquainted with peace; in divers paths of pleasure they search for happiness, but they do not come to rest; through divers ways of laughter and feverish delirium they wander after gladness and life, but their tears are many and grievous, and they do not escape death.

Drifting upon the ocean of life in search of selfish indulgences, men are caught in its storms, and only after many tempests and much privation do they fly to the Rock of Refuge which rests in the deep silence of their own being.

Meditation for the Day

A sweet and happy soul is the ripened fruit of experience and wisdom.

THERE is an infinite patience in nature which it is profitable to contemplate. A comet may take a thousand years to complete its orbit; the sea may occupy ten thousand years in wearing away the land; the complete evolution of the human race may occupy millions of years. This should make us ashamed of our hurry, fussiness, discontent, disappointments, and ridiculous self-importance over trifling things of an hour or a day. Patience is conducive to the highest greatness, the most far-reaching usefulness, and the profoundest peace. Without it, life will lose much of its power and influence, and its joy will be largely destroyed.

"So with well-ordered strenuousness
Raise thou thy structure of Success."

He who fills with useful pursuits the minutes as they come and go grows old in honor and wisdom, and prosperity abides with him.

Thought for the Evening

Meditation centred upon divine realities is the very essence and soul of prayer. It is the silent reaching upward of the soul toward the Eternal.

Meditation is the intense dwelling, in thought, upon an idea or theme with the object of thoroughly comprehending it; and whatsoever you constantly meditate upon, you will not only come to understand, but will grow more and more into its likeness, for it will become incorporated with your very being, will become, in fact, your very self.

If, therefore, you constantly dwell upon that which is selfish and debasing, you will ultimately become selfish and debased; if you ceaselessly think upon that which is pure and unselfish, you will surely become pure and unselfish.

January Twenty-eighth

Thought for the Morning

There is no difficulty, however great, but will yield before a calm and powerful concentration of thought and no legitimate object but may be speedily actualized by the intelligent use and direction of one's soul forces.

Whatever your task may be, concentrate your whole mind upon it; throw into it all the energy of which you are capable. The faultless completion of small tasks, leads inevitably to larger tasks.

See to it that you rise by steady climbing, and you will never fall.

Meditation for the Day

No pure thought, no unselfish deed, can fall short of its
felicitous results, and every such result is a happy consummation.

IF today is cold and gloomy, is that a cause for despair? Do we not know that there are warm, bright days ahead? Already the birds are beginning to sing, and the tremulous trill in their little throats is prophetic of the approaching love of a new spring, and of the bounty of a summer that as yet is but a sleeping germ in the womb of this gloomy day, but whose birth is sure, and its full growth certain. No effort is vain. The spring of all your aspirations is near—very near; and the summer of your unselfish deeds will surely come to pass.

> Self shall depart, and Truth shall take its place;
> The Changeless One, the Indivisible,
> Shall take up His abode in me, and cleanse
> The White Robe of the Heart Invisible.

Go to your task with love in your heart, and you will
go to it light-hearted and cheerful.

Thought for the Evening

He who knows that Love is at the heart of all things, and has realized the all-sufficing power of that Love, has no room in his heart for condemnation.

If you love people and speak of them with praise, until they in some way thwart you, or do something of which you disapprove, and then you dislike them and speak of them with dispraise, you are not governed by the Love which is of God. If, in your heart, you are continually arraigning and condemning others, selfless love is hidden from you.

Train your mind in strong, impartial, and gentle thought; train your heart in purity and compassion; train your tongue to silence, and to true and stainless speech; so shall you enter the way of holiness and peace, and shall ultimately realize the immortal Love.

January Twenty-ninth

Thought for the Morning

If you would realize true prosperity, do not settle down, as many have done, into the belief that if you do right everything will go wrong. Do not allow the word "competition" to shake your faith in the supremacy of righteousness. I care not what men say about the "laws of competition," for do not I know the Unchangeable Law which shall one day put them all to rout, and which puts them to rout even now in the heart and life of the righteous man? And knowing this law I can contemplate all dishonesty with undisturbed repose, for I know where certain destruction awaits it.

Under all circumstances *do that which you believe to be right*, and trust the Law; trust the Divine Power which is immanent in the universe, and it will never desert you, and you will always be protected.

Meditation for the Day

*All evil is corrective and remedial, and is therefore
not permanent.*

BY earnest self-examination strive to realize, and not merely hold as a theory, that evil is a passing phase, a self-created shadow; that all your pains, sorrows, and misfortunes have come to you by a process of undeviating and absolutely perfect law; have come to you because you deserve and require them, and that by first enduring, and then understanding them, you may be made stronger, wiser, nobler. When you have fully entered into this realization, you will be in a position to mould your own circumstances, to transmute all evil into good, and to weave, with a master hand, the fabric of your destiny.

*Cease to be a disobedient child in the school of experience,
and begin to learn, with humility and patience,
the lessons that are set for your ultimate perfection.*

Thought for the Evening

Forget yourself entirely in the sorrows of others, and in ministering to others, and divine happiness will emancipate you from all sorrow and suffering. "Taking the first step with a good thought, the second with a good word, and the third with a good deed, I entered Paradise." And you also enter Paradise by pursuing the same course.

Lose yourself in the welfare of others; forget yourself in all that you do—this is the secret of abounding happiness. Ever be on the watch to guard against selfishness and learn faithfully the divine lessons of inward sacrifice; so shall you climb the highest heights of happiness, and shall remain in the never-clouded sunshine of universal joy, clothed in the shining garment of immortality.

January Thirtieth

Thought for the Morning

When the farmer has tilled and dressed his land and put in the seed, he knows that he has done all that he can possibly do, and that now he must trust to the elements, and wait patiently for the course of time to bring about the harvest, and that no amount of expectancy on his part will affect the result.

Even so, he who has realized Truth, goes forth as a sower of the seeds of goodness, purity, love, and peace, without expectancy and never looking for results, knowing that there is the Great Over-ruling Law which brings about its own harvest in due time, and which is alike the source of preservation and destruction.

Meditation for the Day

Meditation centered upon divine realities is the very essence and soul of prayer.

TELL me what that is upon which you most frequently and intensely think, that to which, in your silent hours, your soul most naturally turns, and I will tell you to what place of pain or peace you are travelling, and whether you are growing into the likeness of the divine or the bestial. There is an unavoidable tendency to become literally the embodiment of that quality upon which one most constantly thinks. Let, therefore, the object of your meditation be above and not below, so that every time that you revert to it in thought you will be lifted up; let it be pure and unmixed with any selfish element; so shall your heart become purified and drawn nearer to Truth, and not defiled and dragged more hopelessly into error.

Meditation is the secret of all growth in spiritual life and knowledge.

Thought for the Evening

The virtuous put a check upon themselves, and set a watch upon their passions and emotions; in this way they gain possession of the mind, and gradually acquire calmness; and as they acquire influence, power, greatness, abiding joy, and fullness and completeness of life.

He only finds peace who conquers himself, who strives, day by day, after greater self-possession, greater self-control, and greater calmness of mind.

Where the calm mind is there is strength and rest, there is love and wisdom; there is one who has fought successfully innumerable battles against self, who, after long toil in secret against his own failings, has triumphed at last.

January Thirty-first

Thought for the Morning

Sympathy bestowed increases its store in our own heart and enriches and fructifies our own life. Sympathy given is blessedness received; sympathy withheld is blessedness forfeited.

In the measure that a man increases and enlarges his sympathy so much nearer does he approach the ideal life, the perfect blessedness; and when his heart has become so mellowed that no hard, bitter, or cruel thought can enter, and detract from its permanent sweetness, then indeed is he richly and divinely blessed.

Meditation for the Day

*If you ceaselessly think upon that which is pure and unselfish, you will
surely become pure and unselfish.*

IF you are daily praying for wisdom, for peace, for loftier purity, and a fuller realization of Truth, and that for which you pray is still far from you, it means that you are praying for one thing, whilst living out in thought and act another. If you will cease from such waywardness, taking your mind off those things, the selfish clinging to which debars you from the possession of the stainless realities for which you pray; if you will no longer ask God to grant you that which you do not deserve, or to bestow upon you that love and compassion which you refuse to bestow upon others, but will commence to think and act in the spirit of Truth, you will day by day be growing into those realities, so that ultimately you will become one with them.

*Enter the path of Meditation, and let the supreme
object of your meditation be Truth.*

Thought for the Evening

Sweet is the rest and deep the bliss of him who has freed his heart from its lusts and hatreds and dark desires; and he who, without any shadow of bitterness resting upon him, and looking out upon the world with boundless compassion and love, can breathe, in his inmost heart, the blessing: Peace unto all living things, making no exceptions or distinctions—such a man has reached that happy ending which can never be taken away, for this is the perfection of life, the fullness of peace, the consummation of perfect blessedness.

February First

Thought for the Morning

In aiming at the life of blessedness, one of the simplest beginnings to be considered, and rightly made, is that which we all make every day—namely, the beginning of each day's life. There is a sense in which every day may be regarded as the beginning of a new life, in which one can think, act, and live newly, and in a wiser and better spirit. The right beginning of the day will be followed by a cheerfulness permeating the household with a sunny influence, and the tasks and duties of the day will be undertaken in a strong and confident spirit, and the whole day will be well lived.

Meditation for the Day

Unrest and pain and sorrow are the shadows of life.

IS there no way of escape from pain and sorrow? Are there no means by which the bonds of evil may be broken? Is permanent happiness and abiding peace a foolish dream? No, there is a way and I speak it with gladness by which evil may be slain for ever; there is a process by which every adverse condition or circumstance can be put on one side for ever, never to return; and there is a practice by which unbroken and unending peace and bliss can be partaken of and realized. And the beginning of the way which leads to this glorious realization is *the acquirement of a right understanding of the nature of evil*. It is not sufficient to deny or ignore evil; it must be understood.

*Men remain in evil because they are not willing or
prepared to learn the lesson which it came to teach them.*

Thought for the Evening

There can be no progress, no achievement, without sacrifice, and a man's worldly success will be in the measure that he sacrifices his confused animal thoughts, and fixes his mind on the development of his plans, and the strengthening of his resolution and self-reliance. And the higher he lifts his thoughts, the more manly, upright, and righteous he becomes, the greater will be his success, the more blessed and enduring will be his achievements.

February Second

Thought for the Morning

None but right acts can follow right thoughts; none but a right life can follow right acts; and by living a right life all blessedness is achieved. Mind is the Master-power that moulds and makes. And Man is Mind, and evermore he takes the tool of thought, and, shaping what he wills, brings forth a thousand joys, a thousand ills;—He thinks in secret, and it comes to pass: environment is but his looking-glass.

Meditation for the Day

*You must get outside yourself, and must begin to examine
and understand yourself.*

EVIL, when rightly understood, is found to be, not an unlimited power or principle in the universe, but a passing phase of human experience, and it therefore becomes a teacher to those who are willing to learn. Evil is not an abstract something outside yourself; it is an experience in your own heart, and by patiently examining and rectifying your heart you will be gradually led into the discovery of the origin and nature of evil, which will necessarily be followed by its complete eradication. . . . There is no evil in the universe which is not the result of ignorance, and which would not, if we were ready and willing to learn its lesson, lead us to higher wisdom, and then vanish away.

*Every soul attracts its own, and nothing can possibly
come to it that does not belong to it.*

Thought for the Evening

Calmness of mind is one of the beautiful jewels of wisdom. A man becomes calm in the measure that he understands himself as a thought-evolved being. . . and he as he develops a right understanding, and sees more and more clearly the internal relations of things by the action of cause and effect, he ceases to fret and fume, and worry and grieve, and remains poised, steadfast, serene.

February Third

Thought for the Morning

To follow, under all circumstances, the highest promptings within you; to be always true to the divine self; to reply upon the inward voice, the inward light, and to pursue your purpose with a fearless and restful heart, believing that the future will yield unto you the need of every thought and effort; knowing that the laws of the universe can never fail, and that your own will come back to you with mathematical exactitude—this is faith and the living of faith.

Meditation for the Day

What you are, so is your world.

ALL that you positively know is contained in your own experience; all that you ever will know must pass through the gateway of experience, and so become part of yourself. Your own thoughts, desires, and aspirations comprise your world, and, to you, all that there is in the universe of beauty, and joy, and bliss, or of ugliness, and sorrow, and pain, is contained within yourself. By your own thoughts you make or mar your life, your world, your universe. As you build within by the power of thought, so will your outward life and circumstances shape themselves accordingly. Whatsoever you harbour in the inmost chambers of your heart will, sooner or later, by the inevitable law of reaction, shape itself in your outward life.

Every soul is a complex combination of gathered experiences and thoughts, and the body is but an improvised vehicle for its manifestation.

Thought for the Evening

Have a thorough understanding of your work, and let it be your own; and as you proceed, ever following the inward guide, the infallible voice, you will pass on from victory to victory, and will rise step by step to higher resting-places, and your ever broadening outlook will gradually reveal to you the essential beauty and purpose of life. Self-purified, health will be yours; self-governed, power will be yours, and all that you do will prosper.

And I may stand where health, success, and power await my coming, if, each fleeting hour, I cling to love and patience; and abide with stainlessness; and never step aside from high integrity; so shall I see at last the land of immortality.

February Fourth

Thought for the Morning

When the tongue is well controlled and wisely subdued; when selfish impulses and unworthy thoughts no longer rush to the tongue demanding utterance; when the speech has become harmless, pure, gracious, gentle, and purposeful, and no word is uttered but in sincerity and truth—then are the five steps in virtuous speech accomplished, then is the second great lesson in Truth learned and mastered. Make pure thy heart, and thou wilt make thy life rich, sweet and beautiful.

Meditation for the Day

To them that seek the highest Good
All things subserve the wisest ends.

HE who clings to self is his own enemy, and is surrounded by enemies. He who relinquishes self is his own saviour, and is surrounded by friends like a protecting belt. Before the divine radiance of a pure heart all darkness vanishes and all clouds melt away, and he who has conquered self has conquered the universe. Come, then, out of your poverty; come out of your pain; come out of your troubles, and sighings, and complainings, and heartaches, and loneliness *by coming out of yourself*. Let the old tattered garment of your petty selfishness fall from you, and put on the new garment of universal Love. You will then realize the inward heaven, and it will be reflected in all your outward life.

All glory and all good await
The coming of Obedient feet.

Thought for the Evening

Having clothed himself with humility, the first questions a man asks himself are:—

"How am I acting towards others?"
"What am I doing to others?"
"How am I thinking of others?"
"Are my thoughts of, and acts towards others prompted by unselfish love?"

As a man, in the silence of his soul, asks himself these searching questions, he will unerringly see where he has hitherto failed.

February Fifth

Thought for the Morning

To dwell in love always and towards all is to live the true life, is to have Life itself. Knowing this, the good man gives up himself unreservedly to the Spirit of Love, and dwells in Love towards all, contending with none, condemning none, but loving all.

The Christ Spirit of Love puts an end, not only to all sin, but to all division and contention.

Meditation for the Day

All men's accomplishments were first wrought out
In thought, and then objectivised.

WHEN the thought-forces are directed in harmony with the over-ruling Law, they are up-building and preservative, but when subverted they become disintegrating and self-destructive. To adjust all your thoughts to a perfect and unswerving faith in the omnipotence and supremacy of Good is to co-operate with that Good, and to realize within yourself the solution and destruction of all evil. *Believe and ye shall live*. And here we have the true meaning of salvation; salvation from the darkness and negation of evil, by entering into and realizing the living light of the Eternal Good.

It is the silent and conquering thought-forces which
bring all things into manifestation.

Thought for the Evening

When sin and self are abandoned, the heart is restored to its imperishable Joy. Joy comes and fills the self-emptied heart; it abides with the peaceful; its reign is with the pure. Joy flees from the selfish, it deserts the quarrelsome; it is hidden from the impure. Joy cannot remain with the selfish; it is wedded to Love.

February Sixth

Thought for the Morning

In the pure heart there is no room left where personal judgments and hatreds can find lodgement, for it is filled to overflowing with tenderness and love; it sees no evil, and only as men succeed in seeing no evil in others will they become free from sin, and sorrow, and suffering. If men only understood that the heart that sins must sorrow, that the hateful mind tomorrow reaps its barren harvest, weeping, starving, resting not, nor sleeping; tenderness would fill their being, they would see with pity's seeing, if they only understood.

Meditation for the Day

*There is nothing that a strong faith and an unflinching
purpose may not accomplish.*

THERE is no difficulty, however great, but will yield before a calm and powerful concentration of thought, and no legitimate object but may be speedily actualized by the intelligent use and direction of one's soul-forces. Not until you have gone deeply and searchingly into your inner nature, and have overcome many enemies that lurk there, can you have any approximate conception of the subtle power of thought, of its inseparable relation to outward and material things, or of its magical potency, when rightly poised and directed, in re-adjusting and transforming the life-conditions. Every thought you think is a force sent out, and in accordance with its nature and intensity will it go out to seek a lodgement in minds receptive to it, and will react upon yourself for good or evil.

*Think good thoughts, and they will quickly become
actualized in your outward life in the form of good conditions.*

Thought for the Evening

To stand face to face with truth; to arrive, after innumerable wanderings and pains, at wisdom and bliss; not to be finally defeated and cast out, but to ultimately triumph over every inward foe—such is man's divine destiny, such his glorious goal; and this, every saint, sage, and saviour has declared. A man only begins to be a man when he ceases to whine and revile, and commences to search for the hidden justice which regulates his life. And as he adapts his mind to that regulating factor, he ceases to accuse others as the cause of his condition, and builds himself up in strong and noble thoughts; ceases to kick against circumstances, but begins to use them as aids to his more rapid progress, and as a means of discovering the hidden power and possibilities within himself.

February Seventh

Thought for the Morning

The will to evil and the will to good are both within thee, which wilt thou employ? Thou knowest what is right and what is wrong, which wilt though love and foster, which destroy?

Thou art the chooser of thy thoughts and deeds; thou art the maker of thine inward state; the power is thine to be what thou wilt be; thou buildest Truth and Love, or lies and hate.

Meditation for the Day

*He only is fitted to command and control who has
succeeded in commanding and controlling himself.*

IF you would acquire overcoming power, you must cultivate poise and passivity. You must be able to stand alone. All power is associated with immovability. The mountain, the massive rock, the storm-tried oak, all speak to us of power, because of their combined solitary grandeur and defiant fixity; while the shifting sand, the yielding twig, and the waving reed speak to us of weakness, because they are movable and non-resistant, and are utterly useless when detached from their fellows. He is the man of power who, when all his fellows are swayed by some emotion or passion, remains calm and unmoved. The hysterical, the fearful, the thoughtless and frivolous, let such seek company, or they will fall for lack of support; but the calm, the fearless, the thoughtful and grave, let such seek solitude, and to their power more power will be added.

*Be of single aim. Have a legitimate and useful
purpose, and devote yourself unreservedly to it.*

Thought for the Evening

The teaching of Jesus brings men back to the simple truth that righteousness, or *right-doing*, is entirely a matter of individual conduct, and not a mystical something apart from a man's thoughts and deeds.

Calmness and patience can become habitual by first grasping, through effort, a calm and patient thought, and then continuously thinking it, and living in it, until "use becomes second nature," and anger and impatience pass away for ever.

February Eighth

Thought for the Morning

Man is made or unmade by himself; in the armoury of thought he forges the weapons by which he destroys himself; he also fashions the tools with which he builds for himself heavenly mansions of joy and strength and peace. By the right choice and true application of thought man ascends to the Divine Perfection; by the abuse and wrong application of thought he descends below the level of the beast. Between these two extremes are all the grades of character and man is their maker and master.

As a being of Power, Intelligence, and Love, and the lord of his own thoughts, man holds the key to every situation.

Meditation for the Day

Self-seeking is self-destruction.

IF you would realize true prosperity, do not settle down, as many have done, into the belief that if you do right everything will go wrong. Do not allow the word competition to shake your faith in the supremacy of righteousness. I care not what man may say about the laws of competition, for do I not know the Unchangeable Law, which shall one day put them all to rout, and which puts them to rout even now in the heart and life of the righteous man? And knowing this Law I can contemplate all dishonesty with undisturbed repose, for I know where certain destruction awaits it. Those who have wandered from the highway of righteousness guard themselves against competition; those who always pursue the right need not to trouble about such defence.

Under all circumstances do that which you believe
to be right, and trust the Law; trust the Divine Power,
and you will always be protected.

Thought for the Evening

Whatsoever you harbour in the inmost chambers of your heart will, sooner or later, by the inevitable law of reaction, shape itself in your outward life.

Every soul attracts its own, and nothing can possibly come to it that does not belong to it. To realize this is to recognize the universality of Divine Law.

If thou would'st right the world, and banish all its evils and its woes, make its wild places bloom, and its drear deserts blossom as the rose—then right thyself.

February Ninth

Thought for the Morning

Whatever conditions are rendering your life burdensome, you may pass out of and beyond them by developing and utilizing within you the transforming power of self-purification and self-conquest.

Before the divine radiance of a pure heart all darkness vanishes and all clouds melt away, and he who has conquered self has conquered the universe.

He who sets his foot firmly upon the path of self-conquest, who walks, aided by the staff of faith, the highway of self-sacrifice, will assuredly achieve the highest prosperity, and will reap abounding and enduring joy and bliss.

Meditation for the Day

Perfect Love is Perfect Power.

THE wisely loving heart commands without exercising any authority. All things and all men obey him who obeys the Highest. He thinks, and lo! he has already accomplished! He speaks, and behold! a world hangs upon his simple utterances! He has harmonized his thoughts with the Imperishable and Unconquerable Forces, and for him weakness and uncertainty are no more. His every thought is a purpose; his every act an accomplishment; he moves with the Great Law, not setting his puny personal will against it, and he thus becomes a channel through which the Divine Power can flow in unimpeded and beneficent expression. He has thus become Power itself.

Perfect Love is Perfect Wisdom.

Thought for the Evening

It is the silent and conquering thought forces which bring all things into manifestation. The universe grew out of thought.

To adjust all your thoughts to a perfect and unswerving faith in the omnipotence and supremacy of Good is to co-operate with that Good, and to realize within yourself the solution and destruction of all evil.

To mentally deny evil is not sufficient; it must, by daily practice, be risen above and understood. To affirm the Good mentally is inadequate; it must, by unswerving endeavour, be entered into and comprehended.

February Tenth

Thought for the Morning

Every thought you think is a force sent out. Whatever your position in life may be, before you can hope to enter into any measure of success, usefulness, and power, you must learn how to focus your thought forces by cultivating calmness and repose.

There is no difficulty, however great, but will yield before a calm and purposeful concentration of thought, and no legitimate object but may be speedily actualized by the intelligent use and direction of one's soul forces.

Think good thoughts, and they will quickly become actualized in your outward life in the form of good conditions.

Meditation for the Day

*If you really seek Truth, you will be willing to make
the effort necessary for its achievement.*

AT the outset, meditation must be distinguished from *idle reverie*. There is nothing dreamy and unpractical about it. It is *a process of searching and uncompromising thought which allows nothing to remain but the simple and naked truth*. Thus meditating you will no longer strive to build yourself up in your prejudices, but, forgetting self, you will remember only that you are seeking the Truth. And so you will remove, one by one, the errors which you have built around yourself in the past, and will patiently wait for the revelation of Truth which will come when your errors have been sufficiently removed.

Let the supreme object of your meditation be Truth.

Thought for the Evening

That which you would be and hope to be, you may be now. Non-accomplishment resides in your perpetual postponement, and, having the power to postpone, you also have the power to accomplish—to perpetually accomplish: realize this truth, and you shall be today, and every day, the ideal being of whom you dreamed.

Say to yourself, "I will live in my Ideal now; I will manifest my ideal now; I will be my Ideal now; and all that tempts me away from my Ideal I will not listen to; I will listen only to the voice of my Ideal."

February Eleventh

Thought for the Morning

Be as a flower; content to be, to grow in sweetness day by day. If thou would'st perfect thyself in knowledge, perfect thyself in Love. If thou would'st reach the Highest, ceaselessly cultivate a loving and compassionate heart.

To him who chooses Goodness, sacrificing all, is given that which is more than, and includes, all.

Meditation for the Day

*As the flower opens its petals to receive the morning
light, so open your soul more and more to the glorious
light of Truth.*

SPIRITUAL meditation and self-discipline are inseparable; you will, therefore, commence to meditate upon yourself so as to try and understand yourself, for, remember, the great object you will have in view will be the complete removal of all your errors in order that you may realize Truth. You will begin to question your motives, thoughts, and acts, comparing them with your ideal, and endeavouring to look upon them with a calm and impartial eye. In this manner you will be continually gaining more of that mental and spiritual equilibrium without which men are but helpless straws upon the ocean of life.

*Soar upward on the wings of aspiration; be fearless,
and believe in the loftiest possibilities.*

Thought for the Evening

The Great Law never cheats any man of his just due.

Human life, when rightly lived, is simple with a beautiful simplicity.

He who comprehends the utter simplicity of life, who obeys its laws, and does not step aside into the dark paths and complex mazes of selfish desire, stands where no harm can reach him.

Then there is fullness of joy, abounding plenty, and rich and complete blessedness.

February Twelfth

Thought for the Morning

Every man reaps the results of his own thoughts and deeds, and suffers for his own wrong.

He who begins right, and continues right, does not need to desire, and search for felicitous results; they are already at hand; they follow as consequences; they are the certainties, the realities, of life.

Sweet is the rest and deep is the bliss of him who has freed his heart from its lusts and hatreds and dark desires.

Meditation for the Day

A beginning is a cause, and as such it must be followed by an effect.

THE nature of an initial impulse will always determine the body of its results. A beginning also presupposes an ending, a consummation, achievement, or goal. A gate leads to a path, and the path leads to some particular destination; so a beginning leads to results, and results lead to a completion.

There are right beginnings and wrong beginnings, which are followed by effects of a like nature. You can, by careful thought, avoid wrong beginnings and make right beginnings, and so escape evil results and enjoy good results. In aiming at the life of Blessedness, one of the simplest beginnings to be considered and rightly made is that which we all make every day namely, the beginning of each day's life.

The effect will always be of the same nature as the cause.

Thought for the Evening

You are the creator of your own shadows; you desire, and then you grieve; renounce, and then you shall rejoice.

Of all the beautiful truths pertaining to the soul. . . none is more gladdening or fruitful of divine promise and confidence than this—that man is the master of thought, the moulder of character, and the maker and shaper of character, environment, and destiny.

February Thirteenth

Thought for the Morning

As darkness is a passing shadow, and light is a substance that remains, so sorrow is fleeting, but joy abides for ever. No true thing can pass away and become lost; no false thing can remain and be preserved. Sorrow is false, and it cannot live; joy is true, and it cannot die. Joy may become hidden for a time, but it can always be recovered; sorrow may remain for a period, but it can be transcended and dispersed.

Do not think your sorrow will remain; it will pass away like a cloud. Do not believe that the torments of sin are ever your portion; they will vanish like a hideous nightmare. Awake! Arise! Be holy and joyful.

Meditation for the Day

Wisdom inheres in the common details of everyday existence.

EVERYTHING in the universe is made of little things, and the perfection of the great is based upon the perfection up of the small. If any detail of the universe were imperfect, the whole would be imperfect. If any particle were omitted, the aggregate would cease to be. Without a grain of dust there would be no world, and the whole is perfect because the grain of dust is perfect. Neglect of the small is confusion of the great. The snowdrop is as perfect as the star; the dewdrop is as symmetrical as the planet; the microbe is not less mathematically proportioned than the man. By laying stone upon stone, plumbing and fitting each with perfect adjustment, the temple at last stands forth in all its architectural beauty.

When the parts are made perfect, the Whole will be without blemish.

Thought for the Evening

Tribulation lasts only so long as there remains some chaff of self which needs to be removed. The *tribulum*, or threshing machine, ceases to work when all the grain is separated from the chaff; and when the last impurities are blown away from the soul, tribulation has completed its work, and there is no more need for it; then abiding joy is realized.

The sole and supreme use of suffering is to purify, to burn out all that is useless and impure. Suffering ceases for him who is pure. There could be no object in burning gold after the dross had been removed.

February Fourteenth

Thought for the Morning

In speaking of self-control, one is easily misunderstood. It should not be associated with a destructive repression, but with a constructive expression.

A man is happy, wise and great in the measure that he controls himself; he is wretched, foolish, and mean in the measure that he allows his animal nature to dominate his thoughts and actions.

He who controls himself, controls his life, his circumstances, his destiny; and wherever he goes he carries his happiness with him as an abiding possession.

Renunciation precedes regeneration. The permanent happiness which men seek in dissipation, excitement, and abandonment to unworthy pleasures, is found only in the life which reverses all this—the life of self-control.

Meditation for the Day

To neglect small tasks, or to execute them in a perfunctory manner, is a mark of weakness and folly.

THE great man knows the vast value that inheres in moments, words, greetings, meals, apparel, correspondence, rest, work, detached efforts, fleeting obligations, in the thousand-and-one little things which press upon him for attention—briefly, in the common details of life. He sees everything as divinely apportioned, needing only the application of dispassionate thought and action on his part to render life blessed and perfect. He neglects nothing, does not hurry, seeks to escape nothing but error and folly; attends to every duty as it is presented to him, and does not postpone and regret. By giving himself unreservedly to his nearest duty, he attains to that combined childlike simplicity and unconscious power which is greatness.

There is no way to strength and wisdom but by acting strongly and wisely in the present moment.

Thought for the Evening

Law, not confusion, is the dominating principle in the universe; justice, not injustice is the soul and substance of life; and righteousness, not corruption, is the moulding and moving force in the spiritual government of the world. This being so, man has but the right himself to find that the universe is right.

When I am pure, I shall have solved the mystery of life; I shall be sure, when I am free from hatred, lust and strife, I am in Truth, and Truth abides in me; I shall be safe, and sane, and wholly free, when I am pure.

February Fifteenth

Thought for the Morning

If men only understood that their hatred and resentment slays their peace and sweet contentment, hurts themselves, helps not another, does not cheer one lonely brother, they would seek the better doing of good deeds which leaves no ruing:—

If they only understood.

If men only understood how Love conquers; how prevailing is its might, grim hate assailing; how compassion endeth sorrow, maketh wise, and doth not borrow pain of passion, they would ever live in Love, in hatred never:—

If they only understood.

Meditation for the Day

*He who masters the small becomes the rightful
possessor of the great.*

THE foolish man thinks that little faults, little indulgences, little sins, are of no consequence; he persuades himself that so long as he does not commit flagrant immoralities he is virtuous, and even holy; but he is thereby deprived of virtue and holiness, and the world knows him accordingly; it does not reverence, adore, and love him; it passes him by; he is reckoned of no account; his influence is destroyed. The efforts of such a man to make the world virtuous, his exhortations to his fellow men to abandon great vices, are empty of substance and barren of fruitage. The insignificance which he attaches to his small vices permeates his whole character, and is the measure of his manhood.

*He who regards his smallest delinquencies as of the gravest
nature becomes a saint.*

Thought for the Evening

The grace and beauty that were in Jesus can be of no value to you—cannot be understood by you—unless they are also *in you*, and they can never be in you, until you practice them, for, apart from *doing*, the qualities which constitute goodness do not, as far as you are concerned, exist.

To adore Jesus for his good qualities is a long step towards Truth, but to practice those qualities is Truth itself; and he who fully adores the perfection of another will not rest content in his own imperfection, but will fashion his soul after the likeness of that other.

Therefore thou who adorest Jesus for his divine qualities, practice those qualities thyself, and thou too shalt be divine.

February Sixteenth

Thought for the Morning

Let a man realize that life in its totality proceeds from the mind, and lo, the way of blessedness is opened up to him! For he will then discover that he possesses the power to rule his mind and to fashion it in accordance with his Ideal.

So will he elect to strongly and steadfastly walk those pathways of thought and action which are altogether excellent; to him life will become beautiful and sacred; and, sooner or later, he will put to flight all evil, confusion, and suffering; for it is impossible for a man to fall short of liberation, enlightenment, and peace, who guards with unwearying diligence the gateway of his heart.

Meditation for the Day

Truth is wrapped up in infinitesimal details.

AS the year consists of a given number of sequential moments, so a man's character and life consists of a given number of sequential thoughts and deeds, and the finished whole will bear the impress of the parts. Little kindnesses, generosities, and sacrifices make up a kind and generous character. The truly honest man is honest in the minutest details of his life. The noble man is noble in every little thing he says and does. You do not live your life in the mass; you live it in fragments, and from these the mass emerges. You can will to live each fragment nobly if you choose, and, this being done, there can be no particle of baseness in the finished whole.

Thoroughness is genius.

Thought for the Evening

By constantly overcoming self, a man gains a knowledge of the subtle intricacies of his mind; and it is this divine knowledge which enables him to become established in calmness.

Without self-knowledge there can be no abiding peace of mind, and those who are carried away by tempestuous passions, cannot approach the holy place where calmness reigns.

The weak man is like one who, having mounted a fiery steed, allows it to run away with him, and carry him withersoever it wills; the strong man is like one who, having mounted the steed, governs it with a masterly hand and makes it go in whatever direction and at whatever speed he commands.

February Seventeenth

Thought for the Morning

There is no strife, no selfishness, in the Kingdom; there is perfect harmony, equipoise, and rest.

Those who live in the Kingdom of Love, have all their needs supplied by the Law of Love.

As self is the root cause of all strife and suffering, so Love is the root cause of all peace and bliss. Those who are at rest in the Kingdom do not look for happiness in any outward possessions. They are freed from all anxiety and trouble and, resting in Love, they are the embodiment of happiness.

Meditation for the Day

Truth in its very nature is ineffable and can only be lived.

TRUTH is the one Reality in the universe, the inward Harmony, the perfect Justice, the eternal Love. Nothing can be added to it, nor taken from it. It does not depend upon any man, but all men depend upon it. You cannot perceive the beauty of Truth while you are looking out from the eyes of self. If you are vain, you will colour everything with your own vanities. If lustful, your heart and mind will be clouded with the smoke and flames of passion, and everything will appear distorted through them. If proud and opinionative, you will see nothing in the whole universe except the magnitude and importance of your own opinions. The humble Truth-lover has learned to distinguish between *opinion* and *Truth*.

He who has most of Charity has most of Truth.

Thought for the Evening

Let it not be supposed that the children of the Kingdom live in ease and indolence (these two sins are the first that have to be eradicated when the search for the Kingdom is entered upon); they live in a peaceful activity; in fact, they only truly live, for the life of self, with its train of worries, griefs, and fears, is not *real life*.

The children of the Kingdom are *known by their life*, they manifest the fruits of the Spirit—"Love, joy, peace, long-suffering, kindness, goodness, faithfulness, meekness, temperance, and self-control"—under all circumstances and vicissitudes.

February Eighteenth

Thought for the Morning

The gospel of Jesus is a gospel of *living and doing*. If it were not this it would not voice the Eternal Truth. Its Temple is *Purified Conduct*, the entrance-door to which is *Self-Surrender*. It invites men to shake off sin, and promises, as a result, joy and blessedness and perfect peace.

The Kingdom of Heaven is perfect trust, perfect knowledge, perfect peace. . . no sin can enter therein, no self-born thought or deed can pass its golden gates; no impure desire can defile its radiant robes. . . all may enter it who will, but all must pay the price—*the unconditional abandonment of self.*

Meditation for the Day

There is but one religion, the religion of Truth.

YOU may easily know whether you are a child of Truth or a worshipper of self, if you will silently examine your mind, heart, and conduct. Do you harbour thoughts of suspicion, enmity, envy, lust, pride; or do you strenuously fight against these? If the former, you are chained to self, no matter what religion you may profess; if the latter, you are a candidate for Truth, even though outwardly you may profess no religion. Are you passionate, self-willed, ever seeking to gain your own ends, self-indulgent, and self-centred; or are you gentle, mild, unselfish, quit of every form of self-indulgence, and are ever ready to give up your own? If the former, self is your master; if the latter, Truth is the object of your affection.

The signs by which the Truth-lover is known are unmistakable.

Thought for the Evening

I say this—and know it to be truth—*that circumstances can only affect you in so far as you allow them to do so*. You are swayed by circumstances because you have not a right understanding of the nature, use, and power of thought. You believe (and upon this little word *belief* hang all our joys and sorrows) that outward things have the power to make or mar your life; by so doing you submit to those outward things, confess that you are their slave, and they your unconditional master. By so doing you invest them with a power which they do not of themselves possess, and you succumb, in reality not to the circumstances, but to the gloom or gladness, the fear or hope, the strength of weakness, which your thought-sphere has thrown around them.

February Nineteenth

Thought for the Morning

If you are one of those who are praying for, and looking forward to a happier world beyond the grave, here is a message of gladness for you—you may enter into and realize that happy world now; it fills the whole universe, and it is within you, waiting for you to find, acknowledge, and possess.

Said one who understood the inner laws of Being—"When men shall say, lo here, or lo there, go not after them. The Kingdom of God is within you."

Meditation for the Day

That which temptation appeals to and arouses is unconquered desire.

TEMPTATION waylays the man of aspiration until he touches the region of the divine consciousness, and beyond that border temptation cannot follow him. It is when a man begins to aspire that he begins to be tempted. Aspiration rouses up all the latent good and evil, in order that the man may be fully revealed to himself, for a man cannot overcome himself unless he fully knows himself. It can scarcely be said of the merely animal man that he is tempted, for the very presence of temptation means that there is a striving for a purer state. Animal desire and gratification is the normal condition of the man who has not yet risen into aspiration; he wishes for nothing more, nothing better, than his sensual enjoyments, and is, for the present, satisfied. Such a man cannot be tempted to fall, for he has not yet risen.

Aspiration can carry a man to heaven.

Thought for the Evening

Heaven and hell are inward states. Sink into self and all its gratifications, and you sink into hell; rise above self into that state of consciousness which is the utter denial and forgetfulness of self, and you enter heaven.

So long as you persist in selfishly seeking for your own personal happiness, so long will happiness elude you, and you will be sowing the seeds of wretchedness. In so far as you succeed in losing yourself in the service of others, in that measure will happiness come to you, and you will reap a harvest of bliss.

February Twentieth

Thought for the Morning

Sympathy given can never be waste.

One aspect of sympathy is that of pity—pity for the distressed or pain stricken, with a desire to alleviate or help them in their sufferings. The world needs more of this divine quality.

"For pity makes the world soft to the weak, and noble for the strong."

Another form of sympathy is that of rejoicing with others who are more successful than ourselves, and though their success were our own.

Meditation for the Day

A man must know himself, if he is to know Truth.

LET the tempted one know this: that he himself is both tempter and tempted; that all his enemies are within; that the flatterers which seduce, the taunts which stab, and the flames which burn, all spring from that inner region of ignorance and error in which he has hitherto lived; and knowing this, let him be assured of complete victory over evil. When he is sorely tempted, let him not mourn, therefore, but let him rejoice in that his strength is tried and his weakness exposed. For he who truly knows and humbly acknowledges his weakness will not be slow in setting about the acquisition of strength.

He who cannot fearlessly face his lower nature cannot climb the rugged heights of renunciation.

Thought for the Evening

Sweet are companionships, pleasures, and material comforts, but they change and fade away. Sweeter still are Purity, Wisdom, and the knowledge of Truth, and these never change nor fade away.

He who attained to the possession of spiritual things can never be deprived of his source of happiness; he will never have to part company with it, and wherever he goes in the whole universe, he will carry his possessions with him. His spiritual end will be the fullness of joy.

February Twenty-first

Thought for the Morning

Let your heart grow and expand with ever broadening love, until, freed from all hatred, and passion, and condemnation, it embraces the whole universe with thoughtful tenderness.

As the flower opens its petals to receive the morning light, so open your soul more and more to the glorious light of Truth.

Soar upward on the wings of aspiration; be fearless and believe in the loftiest possibilities.

Meditation for the Day

Seek diligently the path of holiness.

THE giving up of self is not merely the renunciation of outward things. It consists of the renunciation of the inward sin, the inward error. Not by giving up vain clothing; not by relinquishing riches; not by abstaining from certain foods; not by speaking smooth words; not by merely doing these things is the Truth found. But by giving up the spirit of vanity; by relinquishing the desire for riches; by abstaining from the lust of self-indulgence; by giving up all hatred, strife, condemnation, and self-seeking, and becoming gentle and pure at heart, by doing these things is the Truth found.

The renunciation of self is the way of Truth.

Thought for the Evening

Mind clothes itself in garments of its own making. Mind is the arbiter of life; it is the creator and shaper of conditions, and the recipient of its own results. It contains within itself both the power to create illusion and to perceive reality.

Mind is the infallible weaver of destiny; thought is the thread, good and evil deeds are the warp and woof, and the web, woven upon the loom of life, is character. Make pure thy heart, and thou wilt make thy life, rich, sweet, and beautiful, unmarred by strife.

February Twenty-second

Thought for the Morning

Cherish your visions; cherish your ideals; cherish the music that stirs in your heart, the beauty that forms in your mind, the loveliness that drapes your purest thoughts, for out of them will grow all delightful conditions, all heavenly environment; of these, if you will remain true to them, your world will at last be built.

Guard well thy mind, and, noble, strong, and free, nothing shall harm, disturb or conquer thee; for all thy foes are in thy heart and mind, there also thy salvation thou shalt find.

Meditation for the Day

He who ceases to be passion's slave becomes a master-builder in the Temple of Destiny.

MAN commences to develop power when, checking his impulses and selfish inclinations, he falls back upon the higher and calmer consciousness within him, and begins to steady himself upon a principle.

The realization of unchanging principles in consciousness is at once the source and secret of the highest power.

When, after much searching, and suffering, and sacrificing, the light of an eternal principle dawns upon the soul, a divine calm ensues and joy unspeakable gladdens the heart.

He who has realized such a principle ceases to wander, and remains poised and self-possessed.

Only that work endures that is built upon an indestructible principle.

Thought for the Evening

Dream lofty dreams, and as you dream so shall you become. Your vision is the promise of what you shall one day be; your Ideal is the prophecy of what you shall at last unveil.

The greatest achievement was at first and for a time a dream. The oak sleeps in the acorn; the bird waits in the egg; and in the highest vision of the soul a waking angel stirs.

Your circumstances may be uncongenial, but they shall not long remain so when you perceive an Ideal and strive to reach it.

February Twenty-third

Thought for the Morning

He who has conquered doubt and fear has conquered failure. His every thought is allied with power, and all difficulties are bravely met and wisely overcome. His purposes are seasonably planted, and they bloom and bring forth fruit which does not fall prematurely to the ground.

Thought allied fearlessly to purpose becomes creative force: he who knows this is ready to become something higher and stronger than a mere bundle of wavering thoughts and fluctuating sensations; he who does this has become the conscious and intelligent wielder of his mental powers.

Meditation for the Day

Men and women of real power and influence are few.

It is easy for a man, so long as he is left in the enjoyments of his possessions, to persuade himself that he believes in and adheres to the principles of Peace, Brotherhood, and Universal Love; but if, when his enjoyments are threatened, or he imagines they are threatened, he begins to clamour loudly for war, he shows that he believes in and stands upon, not Peace, Brotherhood, and Love, but strife, selfishness, and hatred.

He who does not desert his principles when threatened with the loss of every earthly thing, even to the loss of reputation and life, is the man of power, is the man whose every word endures, is the man whom the after-world honours, reveres, and worships.

There is no way to the acquirement of spiritual power
except by that inward illumination and enlightenment.

Thought for the Evening

Man's true place in the Cosmos is that of a king, not a slave, a commander under the Law of Good, and not a helpless tool in the region of evil.

I write for men, not for babes; for those who are eager to learn, and earnest to achieve; for those who will put away (for the world's good) a petty personal indulgence, a selfish desire, a mean thought, and live on as though it were not, sans craving and regret.

Man is a master. If he were not, he could not act contrary to law.

Evil and weakness are self destructive. The universe is girt with goodness and strength, and it protects the good and the strong.

The angry man is the weak man.

February Twenty-fourth

Thought for the Morning

Not by learning will a man triumph over evil; not by much study will he overcome sin and sorrow. Only by conquering himself will he conquer evil; only by practicing righteousness will he put an end to sorrow.

Not for the clever, nor the learned, nor the self-confident is the Life Triumphant, but for the pure, the virtuous and wise. The former achieve their particular success in life, but the latter alone achieve the great success so invincible and complete that even in apparent defeat it shines with added victory.

Meditation for the Day

All pain and sorrow is spiritual starvation, and aspiration is the cry for food.

MAN'S essential being is inward, invisible, spiritual, and as such it derives its life, its strength, from within not from without. Outward things are channels through which its energies are expended, but for renewal it must fall back on the inward silence. In so far as man seeks to drown this silence in the noisy pleasures of the senses, and endeavours to live in the conflicts of outward things, just so much does he reap the experiences of pain and sorrow, which, becoming at last intolerable, drive him back to the feet of the inward Comforter, to the shrine of the peaceful solitude within.

It is in solitude only that a man can be truly revealed to himself.

Thought for the Evening

The true silence is not merely a silent tongue; it is a silent mind. To merely *hold one's tongue*, and yet to carry about a disturbed and rankling mind, is no remedy for weakness, and no source of power.

Silentness, to be powerful, must envelop the whole mind, must permeate every chamber of the heart; it must be the silence of peace.

To this broad, deep, abiding silentness a man attains only in the measure that he conquers himself.

February Twenty-Fifth

Thought for the Morning

By curbing his tongue, a man gains possession of his mind.

The fool babbles, gossips, argues, and bandies words. He glories in the fact that he has had the last word, and has silenced his opponent. He exults in his own folly, is ever on the defensive, and wastes his energies in unprofitable channels. He is like a gardener who continues to dig and plant in unproductive soil.

The wise man avoids idle words, gossips, vain argument, and self-defence. He is content to appear defeated; rejoices when he is defeated; knowing that, having found and removed another error in himself, he has thereby become wiser.

Blessed is he who does not strive for the last word.

Meditation for the Day

Inward harmony is spiritual power.

TAKE the principle of Divine Love, and quietly and diligently meditate upon it with the object of arriving at a thorough understanding of it. Bring its searching light to bear upon all your habits, your actions, your speech and intercourse with others, your every secret thought and desire.

As you persevere in this course, the Divine Love will become more and more perfectly revealed to you, and your own shortcomings will stand out in more and more vivid contrast, spurring you on to renewed endeavour; and having once caught a glimpse of the incomparable majesty of that imperishable principle, you will never again rest in your weakness, your selfishness, your imperfection, but will pursue that Love until you have relinquished every discordant element, and have brought yourself into perfect harmony with it.

*Make no stay, no resting-place, until the inmost
garment of your soul is bereft of every stain.*

Thought for the Evening

Desire is the *craving for possession*; aspiration is the *hunger of the heart for peace*.

The craving for things leads ever farther and farther from peace, and not only ends in deprivation, but is in itself a state of perpetual want. Until it comes to an end, rest and satisfaction are impossible.

The hunger for things can never be satisfied, but the hunger for peace can, and the satisfaction of peace is found—is fully possessed, when all selfish desire is abandoned. Then there is fullness of joy, abounding plenty, and rich and complete blessedness.

February Twenty-sixth

Thought for the Morning

A man will reach the Kingdom by purifying himself, and he can only do this by pursuing a process of self-examination and self-analysis.

The selfishness must be discovered and understood before it can be removed. It is powerless to remove itself, neither will it pass away of itself. Darkness ceases only when light is introduced; so ignorance can only be dispersed by knowledge, selfishness by love.

A man must first of all be willing to lose himself (his self-seeking) before he can find himself (his Divine Self). He must realize that selfishness is not worth clinging to, that it is a master altogether unworthy of his service, and that divine goodness alone is worthy to be enthroned in his heart, as the supreme master of his life.

Meditation for the Day

*In solitude a man gathers strength to meet the
difficulties and temptations of life.*

JUST as the body requires rest for the recuperation of its forces, so the spirit requires solitude for the renewal of its energies. Solitude is as indispensable to man's spiritual welfare as sleep is to his bodily well-being; and pure thought, or meditation, which is evoked in solitude, is to the spirit what activity is to the body. As the body breaks down when deprived of the needful rest and sleep, so do the spirits of men break down when deprived of the necessary silence and solitude. Man, as a spiritual being, cannot be maintained in strength, uprightness, and peace except he periodically withdraw himself from the outer world of perishable things, and reach inwardly towards the abiding and imperishable realities.

*He who loves Truth, who desires and seeks wisdom,
will be much alone.*

Thought for the Evening

Be still, my soul, and know that peace is thine. Be steadfast, heart, and know that strength divine Belongs to thee; cease from thy turmoil, mind, and thou the Everlasting Rest shalt find.

If a man would have peace, let him exercise the spirit of peace; if he would find Love, let him dwell in the spirit of Love; if he would escape suffering, let him cease to inflict it; if he would do noble things for humanity, let him cease to do ignoble things for himself. If he will but quarry the mine of his own soul, he shall find there all the materials for building whatsoever he will, and he shall find there also the Central Rock on which to build in safety.

February Twenty-seventh

Thought for the Morning

Men go after much company, and seek out new excitements, but they are not acquainted with peace; in divers paths of pleasure they search for happiness, but they do not come to rest; through divers ways of laughter and feverish delirium they wander after gladness and life, but their tears are many and grievous, and they do not escape death.

Drifting upon the ocean of life in search of selfish indulgences, men are caught in its storms, and only after many tempests and much privation do they fly to the Rock of Refuge which rests in the deep silence of their own being.

Meditation for the Day

Human loves are reflections of the Divine Love.

MEN, clinging to self, and to the comfortless shadows of evil, are in the habit of thinking of Divine Love as something belonging to a God who is out of reach; as something outside themselves, and that must for ever remain outside. Truly, the Love of God is ever beyond the reach of self, but when the heart and mind are emptied of self then the selfless Love, the supreme Love, the Love that is of God, or Good, becomes an inward and abiding reality.

And this inward realization of holy Love is none other than the Love of Christ, that is so much talked about, and so little comprehended; the Love that not only saves the soul from sin, but lifts it also above the power of temptation.

Divine Love knows neither sorrow nor change.

Thought for the Evening

Meditation centred upon divine realities is the very essence and soul of prayer. It is the silent reaching upward of the soul toward the Eternal.

Meditation is the intense dwelling, in thought, upon an idea or theme with the object of thoroughly comprehending it; and whatsoever you constantly meditate upon, you will not only come to understand, but will grow more and more into its likeness, for it will become incorporated with your very being, will become, in fact, your very self.

If, therefore, you constantly dwell upon that which is selfish and debasing, you will ultimately become selfish and debased; if you ceaselessly think upon that which is pure and unselfish, you will surely become pure and unselfish.

February Twenty-eighth

Thought for the Morning

There is no difficulty, however great, but will yield before a calm and powerful concentration of thought and no legitimate object but may be speedily actualized by the intelligent use and direction of one's soul forces.

Whatever your task may be, concentrate your whole mind upon it; throw into it all the energy of which you are capable. The faultless completion of small tasks, leads inevitably to larger tasks.

See to it that you rise by steady climbing, and you will never fall.

Meditation for the Day

Let a man learn to stand alone.

IF a man can find no peace within himself, where shall he find it? If he dreads to be alone with himself, what steadfastness shall he find in company? If he can find no joy in communion with his own thoughts, how shall he escape misery in his contact with others? The man who has yet found nothing within himself upon which to stand will nowhere find a place of constant rest. Without is change, and decay, and insecurity; within is all surety and blessedness. The soul is sufficient of itself. Where the need is, there is the abundant supply. Your eternal dwelling-place is within.

Be rich in yourself, be complete in yourself.

Thought for the Evening

He who knows that Love is at the heart of all things, and has realized the all-sufficing power of that Love, has no room in his heart for condemnation.

If you love people and speak of them with praise, until they in some way thwart you, or do something of which you disapprove, and then you dislike them and speak of them with dispraise, you are not governed by the Love which is of God. If, in your heart, you are continually arraigning and condemning others, selfless love is hidden from you.

Train your mind in strong, impartial, and gentle thought; train your heart in purity and compassion; train your tongue to silence, and to true and stainless speech; so shall you enter the way of holiness and peace, and shall ultimately realize the immortal Love.

February Twenty-ninth

Thought for the Morning

If you would realize true prosperity, do not settle down, as many have done, into the belief that if you do right everything will go wrong. Do not allow the word "competition" to shake your faith in the supremacy of righteousness. I care not what men say about the "laws of competition," for do not I know the Unchangeable Law which shall one day put them all to rout, and which puts them to rout even now in the heart and life of the righteous man? And knowing this law I can contemplate all dishonesty with undisturbed repose, for I know where certain destruction awaits it.

Under all circumstances *do that which you believe to be right*, and trust the Law; trust the Divine Power which is immanent in the universe, and it will never desert you, and you will always be protected.

Meditation for the Day

Find your center of balance and succeed in standing alone.

UNTIL you can stand alone, looking for guidance neither to spirits nor mortals, gods nor men, but guiding yourself by the light of the truth within you, you are not unfettered and free, not altogether blessed. But do not mistake pride for self-reliance. To attempt to stand upon the crumbling foundation of pride is to be already fallen. No man depends upon others more than the proud man. His happiness is entirely in the hands of others. But the self-reliant man stands, not upon personal pride, but on an abiding law, principle, ideal, reality, within himself. Upon this he poises himself, refusing to be swept from his strong foothold either by the waves of passion within or the storms of opinion without.

Find the joy that results from well-earned freedom,
the peace that flows from wise self-possession,
the blessedness that inheres in native strength.

Thought for the Evening

Forget yourself entirely in the sorrows of others, and in ministering to others, and divine happiness will emancipate you from all sorrow and suffering. "Taking the first step with a good thought, the second with a good word, and the third with a good deed, I entered Paradise." And you also enter Paradise by pursuing the same course.

Lose yourself in the welfare of others; forget yourself in all that you do—this is the secret of abounding happiness. Ever be on the watch to guard against selfishness and learn faithfully the divine lessons of inward sacrifice; so shall you climb the highest heights of happiness, and shall remain in the never-clouded sunshine of universal joy, clothed in the shining garment of immortality.

March First

Thought for the Morning

In aiming at the life of blessedness, one of the simplest beginnings to be considered, and rightly made, is that which we all make every day—namely, the beginning of each day's life. There is a sense in which every day may be regarded as the beginning of a new life, in which one can think, act, and live newly, and in a wiser and better spirit. The right beginning of the day will be followed by a cheerfulness permeating the household with a sunny influence, and the tasks and duties of the day will be undertaken in a strong and confident spirit, and the whole day will be well lived.

Meditation for the Day

As the fountain from the hidden spring, so issues man's life from the secret recesses of his heart.

AS the heart, so is the life. The within is ceaselessly becoming the without. Nothing remains unrevealed. That which is hidden is but for a time; it ripens and comes forth at last. Seed, tree, blossom, and fruit is the fourfold order of the universe. From the state of a man's heart proceed the conditions of his life; his thoughts blossom into deeds, and his deeds bear the fruitage of character and destiny.

Life is ever unfolding from within, and revealing itself to the light, and thoughts engendered in the heart at last reveal themselves in words, actions, and things accomplished.

Mind clothes itself in garments of its own making.

Thought for the Evening

There can be no progress, no achievement, without sacrifice, and a man's worldly success will be in the measure that he sacrifices his confused animal thoughts, and fixes his mind on the development of his plans, and the strengthening of his resolution and self-reliance. And the higher he lifts his thoughts, the more manly, upright, and righteous he becomes, the greater will be his success, the more blessed and enduring will be his achievements.

March Second

Thought for the Morning

None but right acts can follow right thoughts; none but a right life can follow right acts; and by living a right life all blessedness is achieved. Mind is the Master-power that moulds and makes. And Man is Mind, and evermore he takes the tool of thought, and, shaping what he wills, brings forth a thousand joys, a thousand ills;—He thinks in secret, and it comes to pass: environment is but his looking-glass.

Meditation for the Day

There is no nobler work or higher science than that of self-perfection.

LET man realize that life in its totality proceeds from the mind, and lo, the way of blessedness is opened to him. For he will then discover that he possesses the power to rule his mind, and to fashion it in accordance with his ideal. So will he elect to strongly and steadfastly walk those pathways of thought and action which are altogether excellent; to him life will become beautiful and sacred; and, sooner or later, he will put to flight all evil, confusion, and suffering; for it is impossible for a man to fall short of liberation, enlightenment, and peace who guards with unwearying diligence the gateway of his heart.

He who aims at the possession of a calm, wise, and seeing mind engages in the most sublime task that man can undertake.

Thought for the Evening

Calmness of mind is one of the beautiful jewels of wisdom. A man becomes calm in the measure that he understands himself as a thought-evolved being... and he as he develops a right understanding, and sees more and more clearly the internal relations of things by the action of cause and effect, he ceases to fret and fume, and worry and grieve, and remains poised, steadfast, serene.

March Third

Thought for the Morning

To follow, under all circumstances, the highest promptings within you; to be always true to the divine self; to reply upon the inward voice, the inward light, and to pursue your purpose with a fearless and restful heart, believing that the future will yield unto you the need of every thought and effort; knowing that the laws of the universe can never fail, and that your own will come back to you with mathematical exactitude—this is faith and the living of faith.

Meditation for the Day

A thought constantly repeated at last becomes a fixed habit.

IT is in the nature of the mind to acquire knowledge by the repetition of its experiences. A thought which it is very difficult, at first, to hold and to dwell upon, at last becomes, by constantly being held in the mind, a natural and habitual condition. Just as a boy, when commencing to learn a trade, cannot even handle his tools aright, much less use them correctly, but after long repetition and practice plies them with perfect ease and consummate skill, so a state of mind at first apparently impossible of realization is, by perseverance and practice, at last acquired and built into the character as a natural and spontaneous condition.

In this power of the mind to form and reform its habits, its conditions, is contained the basis of man's salvation, and the open door to perfect liberty by the mastery of self.

When the heart is pure all outward things are pure.

Thought for the Evening

Have a thorough understanding of your work, and let it be your own; and as you proceed, ever following the inward guide, the infallible voice, you will pass on from victory to victory, and will rise step by step to higher resting-places, and your ever broadening outlook will gradually reveal to you the essential beauty and purpose of life. Self-purified, health will be yours; self-governed, power will be yours, and all that you do will prosper.

And I may stand where health, success, and power await my coming, if, each fleeting hour, I cling to love and patience; and abide with stainlessness; and never step aside from high integrity; so shall I see at last the land of immortality.

March Fourth

Thought for the Morning

When the tongue is well controlled and wisely subdued; when selfish impulses and unworthy thoughts no longer rush to the tongue demanding utterance; when the speech has become harmless, pure, gracious, gentle, and purposeful, and no word is uttered but in sincerity and truth—then are the five steps in virtuous speech accomplished, then is the second great lesson in Truth learned and mastered. Make pure thy heart, and thou wilt make thy life rich, sweet and beautiful.

Meditation for the Day

Every sin may be overcome.

A MAN'S life, in its totality, proceeds from his mind, and his mind is a combination of habits, which he can, by patient effort, modify to any extent, and over which he can gain complete ascendancy and control. Let a man realize this, and he has at once obtained possession of the key which shall open the door to his complete emancipation.

But emancipation from the ills of life (which are the ills of one's mind) is a matter of steady growth from within, and not a sudden acquisition from without. Hourly and daily must the mind be trained to think stainless thoughts, and to adopt right and dispassionate attitudes, until he has wrought out of it the Ideal of his holiest dreams.

The Higher Life is a higher living in thought, word, and deed.

Thought for the Evening

Having clothed himself with humility, the first questions a man asks himself are:—

"How am I acting towards others?"
"What am I doing to others?"
"How am I thinking of others?"
"Are my thoughts of, and acts towards others prompted by unselfish love?"

As a man, in the silence of his soul, asks himself these searching questions, he will unerringly see where he has hitherto failed.

March Fifth

Thought for the Morning

To dwell in love always and towards all is to live the true life, is to have Life itself. Knowing this, the good man gives up himself unreservedly to the Spirit of Love, and dwells in Love towards all, contending with none, condemning none, but loving all.

The Christ Spirit of Love puts an end, not only to all sin, but to all division and contention.

Meditation for the Day

*Without the right performance of Duty,
the higher virtues cannot be known.*

ALL duty should be regarded as sacred, and its faithful and unselfish performance one of the leading rules of conduct. All personal and selfish considerations should be extracted and cast away from the doing of one's duty; and when this is done, Duty ceases to be irksome, and becomes joyful. Duty is only irksome to him who craves some selfish enjoyment or benefit for himself. Let the man who is chafing under the irksomeness of his duty look to himself, and he will find that his wearisomeness proceeds, not from the duty itself, but from his selfish desire to escape it. He who neglects duty, be it great or small, or of a public or private nature, neglects Virtue; and he who in his heart rebels against Duty rebels against Virtue.

*The virtuous man concentrates his mind on the
perfect doing of his own duty.*

Thought for the Evening

When sin and self are abandoned, the heart is restored to its imperishable Joy. Joy comes and fills the self-emptied heart; it abides with the peaceful; its reign is with the pure. Joy flees from the selfish, it deserts the quarrelsome; it is hidden from the impure. Joy cannot remain with the selfish; it is wedded to Love.

March Sixth

Thought for the Morning

In the pure heart there is no room left where personal judgments and hatreds can find lodgement, for it is filled to overflowing with tenderness and love; it sees no evil, and only as men succeed in seeing no evil in others will they become free from sin, and sorrow, and suffering. If men only understood that the heart that sins must sorrow, that the hateful mind tomorrow reaps its barren harvest, weeping, starving, resting not, nor sleeping; tenderness would fill their being, they would see with pity's seeing, if they only understood.

Meditation for the Day

Man is the doer of his own deeds;
as such he is the maker of his own character.

THOSE things which befall a man are the reflections of himself; that destiny which pursued him, which he was powerless to escape by effort, or avert by prayer, was the relentless ghoul of his own wrong deeds demanding and enforcing restitution; those blessings and curses which come to him unbidden are the reverberating echoes of the sounds which he himself sent forth.

Man finds himself involved in the train of causation. His life is made up of causes and effects. It is both a sowing and a reaping. Each act of his is a cause which must be balanced by its effects. He chooses the cause (this is Free-will), he cannot choose, alter, or avert the effect (this is Fate); thus Free-will stands for the power to initiate causes, and destiny is involvement in effects.

Character is destiny.

Thought for the Evening

To stand face to face with truth; to arrive, after innumerable wanderings and pains, at wisdom and bliss; not to be finally defeated and cast out, but to ultimately triumph over every inward foe—such is man's divine destiny, such his glorious goal; and this, every saint, sage, and saviour has declared. A man only begins to be a man when he ceases to whine and revile, and commences to search for the hidden justice which regulates his life. And as he adapts his mind to that regulating factor, he ceases to accuse others as the cause of his condition, and builds himself up in strong and noble thoughts; ceases to kick against circumstances, but begins to use them as aids to his more rapid progress, and as a means of discovering the hidden power and possibilities within himself.

March Seventh

Thought for the Morning

The will to evil and the will to good are both within thee, which wilt thou employ? Thou knowest what is right and what is wrong, which wilt though love and foster, which destroy?

Thou art the chooser of thy thoughts and deeds; thou art the maker of thine inward state; the power is thine to be what thou wilt be; thou buildest Truth and Love, or lies and hate.

Meditation for the Day

*Every form of unhappiness springs from
a wrong condition of mind.*

ALL sin is ignorance. It is a condition of darkness and undevelopment. The wrong-thinker and the wrong -doer is in the same position in the school of life as is the ignorant pupil in the school of learning. He has yet to learn how to think and act correctly, that is, in accordance with Law. The pupil in learning is not happy so long as he does his lessons wrongly, and unhappiness cannot be escaped while sin remains unconquered. Life is a series of lessons. Some are diligent in learning them, and they become pure, wise, and altogether happy. Others are negligent, and do not apply themselves, and they remain impure, foolish, and unhappy.

Happiness is mental harmony.

Thought for the Evening

The teaching of Jesus brings men back to the simple truth that righteousness, or *right-doing*, is entirely a matter of individual conduct, and not a mystical something apart from a man's thoughts and deeds.

Calmness and patience can become habitual by first grasping, through effort, a calm and patient thought, and then continuously thinking it, and living in it, until "use becomes second nature," and anger and impatience pass away for ever.

March Eighth

Thought for the Morning

Man is made or unmade by himself; in the armoury of thought he forges the weapons by which he destroys himself; he also fashions the tools with which he builds for himself heavenly mansions of joy and strength and peace. By the right choice and true application of thought man ascends to the Divine Perfection; by the abuse and wrong application of thought he descends below the level of the beast. Between these two extremes are all the grades of character and man is their maker and master.

As a being of Power, Intelligence, and Love, and the lord of his own thoughts, man holds the key to every situation.

Meditation for the Day

If one would find peace, he must come out of passion.

SELFISHNESS, or passion, not only subsists in the gross forms of greed and glaringly ungoverned conditions of mind; it informs also every hidden thought which is subtly connected with the assumption and glorification of one's self; and it is most deceiving and subtle when it prompts one to dwell upon the selfishness of others, to accuse them of it and to talk about it. The man who continually dwells upon the selfishness in others will not thus overcome his own selfishness. Not by accusing others do we come out of selfishness, but by purifying ourselves. The way from passion to peace is not by hurling painful charges against others, but by overcoming one's self. By eagerly striving to subdue the selfishness of others, we remain passion-bound; by patiently overcoming our own selfishness we ascend into freedom.

The ascending pathway is always at hand.
It is the way of self-conquest.

Thought for the Evening

Whatsoever you harbour in the inmost chambers of your heart will, sooner or later, by the inevitable law of reaction, shape itself in your outward life.

Every soul attracts its own, and nothing can possibly come to it that does not belong to it. To realize this is to recognize the universality of Divine Law.

If thou would'st right the world, and banish all its evils and its woes, make its wild places bloom, and its drear deserts blossom as the rose—then right thyself.

March Ninth

Thought for the Morning

Whatever conditions are rendering your life burdensome, you may pass out of and beyond them by developing and utilizing within you the transforming power of self-purification and self-conquest.

Before the divine radiance of a pure heart all darkness vanishes and all clouds melt away, and he who has conquered self has conquered the universe.

He who sets his foot firmly upon the path of self-conquest, who walks, aided by the staff of faith, the highway of self-sacrifice, will assuredly achieve the highest prosperity, and will reap abounding and enduring joy and bliss.

Meditation for the Day

Aspiration—the rapture of the saints.

ON the wings of aspiration man rises from earth to heaven, from ignorance to knowledge, from the under darkness to the upper light. Without it he remains a grovelling animal, earthly, sensual, unenlightened, and uninspired. Aspiration is the longing for heavenly things—for righteousness, compassion, purity, love as distinguished from desire, which is the longing for earthly things—for selfish possessions, personal dominance, low pleasures, and sensual gratifications. For one to begin to aspire means that he is dissatisfied with his low estate, and is aiming at a higher condition. It is a sure sign that he is roused out of his lethargic sleep of animality, and has become conscious of nobler attainments and a fuller life.

Aspiration makes all things possible.

Thought for the Evening

It is the silent and conquering thought forces which bring all things into manifestation. The universe grew out of thought.

To adjust all your thoughts to a perfect and unswerving faith in the omnipotence and supremacy of Good is to co-operate with that Good, and to realize within yourself the solution and destruction of all evil.

To mentally deny evil is not sufficient; it must, by daily practice, be risen above and understood. To affirm the Good mentally is inadequate; it must, by unswerving endeavour, be entered into and comprehended.

March Tenth

Thought for the Morning

Every thought you think is a force sent out. Whatever your position in life may be, before you can hope to enter into any measure of success, usefulness, and power, you must learn how to focus your thought forces by cultivating calmness and repose.

There is no difficulty, however great, but will yield before a calm and purposeful concentration of thought, and no legitimate object but may be speedily actualized by the intelligent use and direction of one's soul forces.

Think good thoughts, and they will quickly become actualized in your outward life in the form of good conditions.

Meditation for the Day

The man of aspiration sees before him
the pathway up to the heavenly heights.

WHEN the rapture of aspiration touches the mind it at once refines it, and the dross of its impurities begins to fall away; yea, while aspiration holds the mind, no impurities can enter it, for the impure and the pure cannot at the same moment occupy the thought. But the effort of aspiration is at first spasmodic and short-lived. The mind falls back into its habitual error and must be constantly renewed.

To thirst for righteousness; to hunger for the pure life; to rise in holy rapture on the wings of angelic aspiration this is the right road to wisdom; this is the right striving for peace; this is the right beginning of the way divine.

The lover of the pure life renews his mind daily with
the invigorating glow of aspiration.

Thought for the Evening

That which you would be and hope to be, you may be now. Non-accomplishment resides in your perpetual postponement, and, having the power to postpone, you also have the power to accomplish—to perpetually accomplish: realize this truth, and you shall be today, and every day, the ideal being of whom you dreamed.

Say to yourself, "I will live in my Ideal now; I will manifest my ideal now; I will be my Ideal now; and all that tempts me away from my Ideal I will not listen to; I will listen only to the voice of my Ideal."

March Eleventh

Thought for the Morning

Be as a flower; content to be, to grow in sweetness day by day. If thou would'st perfect thyself in knowledge, perfect thyself in Love. If thou would'st reach the Highest, ceaselessly cultivate a loving and compassionate heart.

To him who chooses Goodness, sacrificing all, is given that which is more than, and includes, all.

Meditation for the Day

Error is sifted away. The Gold of Truth remains.

SPIRITUAL transmutation consists in an entire reversal of the ordinary self-seeking attitude of mind towards men and things, and this reversal brings about an entirely new set of experiences. Thus the desire for a certain pleasure is abandoned, cut off at its source, and not allowed to have any place in the consciousness; but the mental force which that desire represented is not annihilated, it is transferred to a higher region of thought, transmuted into a purer form of energy. The law of conservation of energy obtains universally in mind as in matter, and the force shut off in lower directions is liberated in higher realms of spiritual activity.

The clear and cloudless heights of spiritual enlightenment.

Thought for the Evening

The Great Law never cheats any man of his just due.

Human life, when rightly lived, is simple with a beautiful simplicity.

He who comprehends the utter simplicity of life, who obeys its laws, and does not step aside into the dark paths and complex mazes of selfish desire, stands where no harm can reach him.

Then there is fullness of joy, abounding plenty, and rich and complete blessedness.

March Twelfth

Thought for the Morning

Every man reaps the results of his own thoughts and deeds, and suffers for his own wrong.

He who begins right, and continues right, does not need to desire, and search for felicitous results; they are already at hand; they follow as consequences; they are the certainties, the realities, of life.

Sweet is the rest and deep is the bliss of him who has freed his heart from its lusts and hatreds and dark desires.

Meditation for the Day

*The early stage of transmutation is painful but brief, for the pain is
soon transformed into pure spiritual joy.*

ALONG the Saintly Way towards the divine life, the midway region of Transmutation is the Country of Sacrifice, it is the Plain of Renunciation. Old passions, old desires, old ambitions and thoughts, are cast away and abandoned, but only to reappear in some more beautiful, more permanent, more eternally satisfying form. As valuable jewels, long guarded and cherished, are thrown tearfully into the melting-pot, yet are remoulded into new and perfect adornments, so the spiritual alchemist, at first loath to part company with long-cherished thoughts and habits, at last gives them up, to discover, a little later, to his joy, that they have come back to him in the form of new faculties, rarer powers, and purer joys, spiritual jewels newly burnished, beautiful, and resplendent.

*The wise man meets passion with peace,
hatred with love,
and returns good for evil.*

Thought for the Evening

You are the creator of your own shadows; you desire, and then you grieve; renounce, and then you shall rejoice.

Of all the beautiful truths pertaining to the soul. . . none is more gladdening or fruitful of divine promise and confidence than this—that man is the master of thought, the moulder of character, and the maker and shaper of character, environment, and destiny.

March Thirteenth

Thought for the Morning

As darkness is a passing shadow, and light is a substance that remains, so sorrow is fleeting, but joy abides for ever. No true thing can pass away and become lost; no false thing can remain and be preserved. Sorrow is false, and it cannot live; joy is true, and it cannot die. Joy may become hidden for a time, but it can always be recovered; sorrow may remain for a period, but it can be transcended and dispersed.

Do not think your sorrow will remain; it will pass away like a cloud. Do not believe that the torments of sin are ever your portion; they will vanish like a hideous nightmare. Awake! Arise! Be holy and joyful.

Meditation for the Day

The present is the synthesis of the entire past; the net result of all that a man has ever thought and done is contained within him.

It is this knowledge of the Perfect Law working through and above all things; of the Perfect Justice operating in and adjusting all human affairs, that enables the good man to love his enemies, and to rise above all hatred, resentment, and complaining; for he knows that only his own can come to him, and that, though he be surrounded by persecutors, his enemies are but the blind instruments of a faultless retribution; and so he blames them not, but calmly receives his accounts, and patiently pays his moral debts. But this is not all; he does not merely pay his debts; he takes care not to contract any further debts. He watches himself and makes his deeds faultless.

Characteristics are fixed habits of mind, the results of deeds.

Thought for the Evening

Tribulation lasts only so long as there remains some chaff of self which needs to be removed. The *tribulum*, or threshing machine, ceases to work when all the grain is separated from the chaff; and when the last impurities are blown away from the soul, tribulation has completed its work, and there is no more need for it; then abiding joy is realized.

The sole and supreme use of suffering is to purify, to burn out all that is useless and impure. Suffering ceases for him who is pure. There could be no object in burning gold after the dross had been removed.

March Fourteenth

Thought for the Morning

In speaking of self-control, one is easily misunderstood. It should not be associated with a destructive repression, but with a constructive expression.

A man is happy, wise and great in the measure that he controls himself; he is wretched, foolish, and mean in the measure that he allows his animal nature to dominate his thoughts and actions.

He who controls himself, controls his life, his circumstances, his destiny; and wherever he goes he carries his happiness with him as an abiding possession.

Renunciation precedes regeneration. The permanent happiness which men seek in dissipation, excitement, and abandonment to unworthy pleasures, is found only in the life which reverses all this—the life of self-control.

Meditation for the Day

Heaven and hell are in this world.

NOTHING comes unbidden; where the shadow is, there also is the substance. That which comes to the individual is the product of his own deeds. As cheerful industry leads to greater industry and increasing prosperity, and labour shirked or undertaken discontentedly leads to a lesser degree of labour and decreasing prosperity, so with all the varied conditions of life as we see them they are *the effects of deeds*, destinies wrought by the thoughts and deeds of each particular individual. So also with the vast variety of characters they are the ripening and ripened growth of the sowing of deeds, a sowing not confined solely to this visible life, but going backward through that infinite life which traverses the portals of innumerable births and deaths, and which also will extend into the illimitable future, reaping its own harvests, eating the sweet and bitter fruits of its own deeds.

Life is a great school for the development of character.

Thought for the Evening

Law, not confusion, is the dominating principle in the universe; justice, not injustice is the soul and substance of life; and righteousness, not corruption, is the moulding and moving force in the spiritual government of the world. This being so, man has but the right himself to find that the universe is right.

When I am pure, I shall have solved the mystery of life; I shall be sure, when I am free from hatred, lust and strife, I am in Truth, and Truth abides in me; I shall be safe, and sane, and wholly free, when I am pure.

March Fifteenth

Thought for the Morning

If men only understood that their hatred and resentment slays their peace and sweet contentment, hurts themselves, helps not another, does not cheer one lonely brother, they would seek the better doing of good deeds which leaves no ruing:—

If they only understood.

If men only understood how Love conquers; how prevailing is its might, grim hate assailing; how compassion endeth sorrow, maketh wise, and doth not borrow pain of passion, they would ever live in Love, in hatred never:—

If they only understood.

Meditation for the Day

Purification of the heart by repetitive thought on pure things.

MAN is a *thought-being*, and his life and character are determined by the thoughts in which he habitually dwells. By practice, association, and habit, thoughts tend to repeat themselves with greater and greater ease and frequency, and so fix the character in a given direction by producing that automatic action which is called habit. By daily dwelling upon pure thoughts, the man of meditation forms the habit of pure and enlightened thinking which leads to pure and enlightened actions, and well-performed actions. By the ceaseless repetition of pure thoughts, he at last becomes one with those thoughts, and is a purified being, manifesting his attainment in pure actions.

Attainment of divine knowledge by embodying such purity in practical life.

Thought for the Evening

The grace and beauty that were in Jesus can be of no value to you—cannot be understood by you—unless they are also *in you*, and they can never be in you, until you practice them, for, apart from *doing*, the qualities which constitute goodness do not, as far as you are concerned, exist.

To adore Jesus for his good qualities is a long step towards Truth, but to practice those qualities is Truth itself; and he who fully adores the perfection of another will not rest content in his own imperfection, but will fashion his soul after the likeness of that other.

Therefore thou who adorest Jesus for his divine qualities, practice those qualities thyself, and thou too shalt be divine.

March Sixteenth

Thought for the Morning

Let a man realize that life in its totality proceeds from the mind, and lo, the way of blessedness is opened up to him! For he will then discover that he possesses the power to rule his mind and to fashion it in accordance with his Ideal.

So will he elect to strongly and steadfastly walk those pathways of thought and action which are altogether excellent; to him life will become beautiful and sacred; and, sooner or later, he will put to flight all evil, confusion, and suffering; for it is impossible for a man to fall short of liberation, enlightenment, and peace, who guards with unwearying diligence the gateway of his heart.

Meditation for the Day

*He who will control himself will put an end to all
his sufferings.*

BLESSED is that day, and not to be forgotten, when a man discovers that he himself is his own undoer and his own saviour. That within himself is the cause of all his suffering and lack of knowledge, and that also within is the source of all peace, enlightenment, and Godliness. Selfish thoughts, impure desires, and acts not shaped by Truth are the baneful seeds from which all suffering springs; while selfless thoughts, pure aspirations, and the sweet acts of Truth are the seeds from which all blessedness grows.

*He who will deny himself will find the holy place
where calmness lives.*

Thought for the Evening

By constantly overcoming self, a man gains a knowledge of the subtle intricacies of his mind; and it is this divine knowledge which enables him to become established in calmness.

Without self-knowledge there can be no abiding peace of mind, and those who are carried away by tempestuous passions, cannot approach the holy place where calmness reigns.

The weak man is like one who, having mounted a fiery steed, allows it to run away with him, and carry him withersoever it wills; the strong man is like one who, having mounted the steed, governs it with a masterly hand and makes it go in whatever direction and at whatever speed he commands.

March Seventeenth

Thought for the Morning

There is no strife, no selfishness, in the Kingdom; there is perfect harmony, equipoise, and rest.

Those who live in the Kingdom of Love, have all their needs supplied by the Law of Love.

As self is the root cause of all strife and suffering, so Love is the root cause of all peace and bliss. Those who are at rest in the Kingdom do not look for happiness in any outward possessions. They are freed from all anxiety and trouble and, resting in Love, they are the embodiment of happiness.

Meditation for the Day

He who will purify himself will destroy all his ignorance.

HE who governs his tongue is greater than a successful disputant in the arena of intellectualism; he who controls well his mind is more powerful than the king of many nations; and he who holds himself in entire subjection is more than gods and angels. When a man who is enslaved by self realizes that he must work out his own salvation, in that moment he will rise up in the dignity of his divine manhood and say, "Henceforward I will be a master in Israel, and not a slave in the House of Bondage."

Not until a man realizes this, and commences to patiently purify his inner life, can he find the way which leads to lasting peace.

A life of perfect peace and blessedness by means of self-government and self-enlightenment.

Thought for the Evening

Let it not be supposed that the children of the Kingdom live in ease and indolence (these two sins are the first that have to be eradicated when the search for the Kingdom is entered upon); they live in a peaceful activity; in fact, they only truly live, for the life of self, with its train of worries, griefs, and fears, is not *real life*.

The children of the Kingdom are *known by their life*, they manifest the fruits of the Spirit—"Love, joy, peace, long-suffering, kindness, goodness, faithfulness, meekness, temperance, and self-control"—under all circumstances and vicissitudes.

March Eighteenth

Thought for the Morning

The gospel of Jesus is a gospel of *living and doing*. If it were not this it would not voice the Eternal Truth. Its Temple is Purified Conduct, the entrance-door to which is *Self-Surrender*. It invites men to shake off sin, and promises, as a result, joy and blessedness and perfect peace.

The Kingdom of Heaven is perfect trust, perfect knowledge, perfect peace. . . no sin can enter therein, no self-born thought or deed can pass its golden gates; no impure desire can defile its radiant robes. . . all may enter it who will, but all must pay the price—*the unconditional abandonment of self.*

Meditation for the Day

Impatience is a handmaid of impulse, and never
helped any man.

YOU will be greatly helped if you devote at least *one hour* every day to quiet meditation on lofty moral subjects and their application to everyday life. In this way you will cultivate a calm, quiet strength, and will develop right perception and correct judgment. Do not be anxious to hurry matters. Do your duty to the very uttermost; live a disciplined and self-denying life; conquer impulse, and guide your actions by moral and spiritual Principles, as distinguished from your *feelings*, firmly believing that your object will be, in its own time, completely accomplished.

Still go on becoming, and as you grow more perfect
you will make fewer mistakes and will suffer less.

Thought for the Evening

I say this—and know it to be truth—*that circumstances can only affect you in so far as you allow them to do so*. You are swayed by circumstances because you have not a right understanding of the nature, use, and power of thought. You believe (and upon this little word *belief* hang all our joys and sorrows) that outward things have the power to make or mar your life; by so doing you submit to those outward things, confess that you are their slave, and they your unconditional master. By so doing you invest them with a power which they do not of themselves possess, and you succumb, in reality not to the circumstances, but to the gloom or gladness, the fear or hope, the strength of weakness, which your thought-sphere has thrown around them.

March Nineteenth

Thought for the Morning

If you are one of those who are praying for, and looking forward to a happier world beyond the grave, here is a message of gladness for you—you may enter into and realize that happy world now; it fills the whole universe, and it is within you, waiting for you to find, acknowledge, and possess.

Said one who understood the inner laws of Being—"When men shall say, lo here, or lo there, go not after them. The Kingdom of God is within you."

Meditation for the Day

The diadem of the King of Truth is a righteous life,
his scepter is the scepter of peace,
and his throne is in the hearts of mankind.

IN every heart there are two kings, but one is a usurper and tyrant; he is named self, and his thoughts and deeds are those of lust, hatred, passion, and strife; the other, the rightful monarch, is named Truth, and his thoughts and deeds are those of purity and love, meekness and peace. Brother, sister, to what monarch dost thou bow? What king hast thou crowned in thy heart? Well is it with thy soul if Thou canst say: "I bow down to the Monarch of Truth; in my inmost heart I have crowned the King of Peace." Blessed indeed and immortal shall he be who shall find in the inward and heavenly places the King of Righteousness, and shall bow his heart to Him.

Power resides in blamelessness of heart.
All earthly things are symbols.

Thought for the Evening

Heaven and hell are inward states. Sink into self and all its gratifications, and you sink into hell; rise above self into that state of consciousness which is the utter denial and forgetfulness of self, and you enter heaven.

So long as you persist in selfishly seeking for your own personal happiness, so long will happiness elude you, and you will be sowing the seeds of wretchedness. In so far as you succeed in losing yourself in the service of others, in that measure will happiness come to you, and you will reap a harvest of bliss.

March Twentieth

Thought for the Morning

Sympathy given can never be waste.

One aspect of sympathy is that of pity—pity for the distressed or pain stricken, with a desire to alleviate or help them in their sufferings. The world needs more of this divine quality.

"For pity makes the world soft to the weak, and noble for the strong."

Another form of sympathy is that of rejoicing with others who are more successful than ourselves, and though their success were our own.

Meditation for the Day

*It is by the eradication of the inward errors and impurities
alone that a knowledge of Truth can be gained.
There is no other way to wisdom and peace.*

THE peace which passeth understanding is a peace which no event or circumstance can shake or mar, because it is not merely a passing calm between two storms, but is an abiding peace that is born of knowledge. Men have not this peace, because they do not understand, because they do not *know*, and they do not understand and know because they are blinded and rendered ignorant by their own errors and impurities; and whilst they are unwilling to give these up, they cannot but remain entirely ignorant of impersonal Principles.

Whilst a man loves his lusts he cannot love wisdom.

Thought for the Evening

Sweet are companionships, pleasures, and material comforts, but they change and fade away. Sweeter still are Purity, Wisdom, and the knowledge of Truth, and these never change nor fade away.

He who attained to the possession of spiritual things can never be deprived of his source of happiness; he will never have to part company with it, and wherever he goes in the whole universe, he will carry his possessions with him. His spiritual end will be the fullness of joy.

March Twenty-first

Thought for the Morning

Let your heart grow and expand with ever broadening love, until, freed from all hatred, and passion, and condemnation, it embraces the whole universe with thoughtful tenderness.

As the flower opens its petals to receive the morning light, so open your soul more and more to the glorious light of Truth.

Soar upward on the wings of aspiration; be fearless and believe in the loftiest possibilities.

Meditation for the Day

*If we could suffer, even partly, through others,
our sufferings would be unjust.*

ARE our sufferings and troubles entirely the result of our own ignorance and wrongdoing, or are they partly or wholly brought about by others, and by outward conditions?

Our sufferings *are* just, and are entirely the result of our own ignorance, error, and wrongdoing.

"Ye suffer from yourselves, none else compels." If this were not so, if a man could commit an evil deed and escape, the consequences of that deed being visited upon an innocent person, then there would be no Law of Justice, and without such a Law the universe could not, even for a single moment, exist. All would be chaos. Upon the surface, men *appear* to suffer through others, but it is only an appearance—an appearance which a deeper knowledge dispels.

*Man is not the result of outward conditions;
outward conditions are the result of man.*

Thought for the Evening

Mind clothes itself in garments of its own making. Mind is the arbiter of life; it is the creator and shaper of conditions, and the recipient of its own results. It contains within itself both the power to create illusion and to perceive reality.

Mind is the infallible weaver of destiny; thought is the thread, good and evil deeds are the warp and woof, and the web, woven upon the loom of life, is character. Make pure thy heart, and thou wilt make thy life, rich, sweet, and beautiful, unmarred by strife.

March Twenty-second

Thought for the Morning

Cherish your visions; cherish your ideals; cherish the music that stirs in your heart, the beauty that forms in your mind, the loveliness that drapes your purest thoughts, for out of them will grow all delightful conditions, all heavenly environment; of these, if you will remain true to them, your world will at last be built.

Guard well thy mind, and, noble, strong, and free, nothing shall harm, disturb or conquer thee; for all thy foes are in thy heart and mind, there also thy salvation thou shalt find.

Meditation for the Day

In the knowledge of truth there is freedom.

MEN suffer because they love self, and do not love righteousness, and loving self they love their delusions, and it is by these that they are bound. There is one supreme liberty of which no man can be deprived by any but himself—*the liberty to love and to practise righteousness*. This includes all other liberties. It belongs to the whipped and chained slave equally as to the king, and he who will enter into this liberty will cast from him every chain. By this the slave will walk out from the presence of his oppressor, who will be powerless to stay him. By this the king will cease to be defiled by his surrounding luxuries, and will be a king indeed.

No outward oppressor can burden the righteous heart.

Thought for the Evening

Dream lofty dreams, and as you dream so shall you become. Your vision is the promise of what you shall one day be; your Ideal is the prophecy of what you shall at last unveil.

The greatest achievement was at first and for a time a dream. The oak sleeps in the acorn; the bird waits in the egg; and in the highest vision of the soul a waking angel stirs.

Your circumstances may be uncongenial, but they shall not long remain so when you perceive an Ideal and strive to reach it.

March Twenty-third

Thought for the Morning

He who has conquered doubt and fear has conquered failure. His every thought is allied with power, and all difficulties are bravely met and wisely overcome. His purposes are seasonably planted, and they bloom and bring forth fruit which does not fall prematurely to the ground.

Thought allied fearlessly to purpose becomes creative force: he who knows this is ready to become something higher and stronger than a mere bundle of wavering thoughts and fluctuating sensations; he who does this has become the conscious and intelligent wielder of his mental powers.

Meditation for the Day

Joy is to the sinless!

THE wise man knows. For him anxiety, fear, disappointment, and unrest have ceased, and under whatever condition or circumstance he may be placed his calmness will not be broken, and he will bend and adjust everything with capacity and wisdom. Nothing will cause him grief. When friends yield up the body of flesh, he knows that they still *are*, and does not sorrow over the shell they have discarded. None can injure him, for he has identified himself with that which is unaffected by change.

The knowledge which brings peace, then, is the knowledge of unchangeable Principles arrived at by the practice of pure goodness, righteousness, becoming one with which a man becomes immortal, unchangeable, indestructible.

Peace is to the pure.

Thought for the Evening

Man's true place in the Cosmos is that of a king, not a slave, a commander under the Law of Good, and not a helpless tool in the region of evil.

I write for men, not for babes; for those who are eager to learn, and earnest to achieve; for those who will put away (for the world's good) a petty personal indulgence, a selfish desire, a mean thought, and live on as though it were not, sans craving and regret.

Man is a master. If he were not, he could not act contrary to law.

Evil and weakness are self destructive. The universe is girt with goodness and strength, and it protects the good and the strong.

The angry man is the weak man.

March Twenty-fourth

Thought for the Morning

Not by learning will a man triumph over evil; not by much study will he overcome sin and sorrow. Only by conquering himself will he conquer evil; only by practicing righteousness will he put an end to sorrow.

Not for the clever, nor the learned, nor the self-confident is the Life Triumphant, but for the pure, the virtuous and wise. The former achieve their particular success in life, but the latter alone achieve the great success so invincible and complete that even in apparent defeat it shines with added victory.

Meditation for the Day

Love, meekness, gentleness, self-accusation, forgiveness, patience, compassion, reproof—these are the works of the Spirit.

THE flesh flatters; the Spirit reproves.

The flesh blindly gratifies; the Spirit wisely disciplines.

The flesh loves secrecy; the Spirit is open and clear.

The flesh remembers the injury of a friend; the Spirit forgives the bitterest enemy.

The flesh is noisy and rude; the Spirit is silent and gracious.

The flesh is subject to moods; the Spirit is always calm.

The flesh incites to impatience and anger; the Spirit controls with patience and serenity.

The flesh is thoughtless; the Spirit is thoughtful.

Hatred, pride, harshness, accusing others, revenge, anger, cruelty, and flattery—these are the works of the flesh.

Thought for the Evening

The true silence is not merely a silent tongue; it is a silent mind. To merely *hold one's tongue*, and yet to carry about a disturbed and rankling mind, is no remedy for weakness, and no source of power.

Silentness, to be powerful, must envelop the whole mind, must permeate every chamber of the heart; it must be the silence of peace.

To this broad, deep, abiding silentness a man attains only in the measure that he conquers himself.

March Twenty-fifth

Thought for the Morning

By curbing his tongue, a man gains possession of his mind.

The fool babbles, gossips, argues, and bandies words. He glories in the fact that he has had the last word, and has silenced his opponent. He exults in his own folly, is ever on the defensive, and wastes his energies in unprofitable channels. He is like a gardener who continues to dig and plant in unproductive soil.

The wise man avoids idle words, gossips, vain argument, and self-defence. He is content to appear defeated; rejoices when he is defeated; knowing that, having found and removed another error in himself, he has thereby become wiser.

Blessed is he who does not strive for the last word.

Meditation for the Day

*You can only help others in so far as you have
uplifted and purified yourself.*

A TRUTH is first perceived, and afterwards realized. The perception may be instantaneous, the realization is almost invariably a process of gradual unfoldment. You will have to *learn* to love, regarding yourself as a child; and as you make progress in learning, the Divine will unfold within you. You can only learn to love by constantly meditating upon Love as a divine principle, and by adjusting, day by day, all your thought, and words, and acts to it. Watch yourself closely, and when you think, or say, or do anything which is not born of pure unselfish love, resolve that you will henceforth guard yourself in that direction. By so doing you will every day grow purer, tenderer, holier, and soon you will find it easy to love, and will realize the Divine within you.

*When love is perfected and revealed in the heart,
Christ is known.*

Thought for the Evening

Desire is the *craving for possession*; aspiration is the *hunger of the heart for peace*.

The craving for things leads ever farther and farther from peace, and not only ends in deprivation, but is in itself a state of perpetual want. Until it comes to an end, rest and satisfaction are impossible.

The hunger for things can never be satisfied, but the hunger for peace can, and the satisfaction of peace is found—is fully possessed, when all selfish desire is abandoned. Then there is fullness of joy, abounding plenty, and rich and complete blessedness.

March Twenty-sixth

Thought for the Morning

A man will reach the Kingdom by purifying himself, and he can only do this by pursuing a process of self-examination and self-analysis.

The selfishness must be discovered and understood before it can be removed. It is powerless to remove itself, neither will it pass away of itself. Darkness ceases only when light is introduced; so ignorance can only be dispersed by knowledge, selfishness by love.

A man must first of all be willing to lose himself (his self-seeking) before he can find himself (his Divine Self). He must realize that selfishness is not worth clinging to, that it is a master altogether unworthy of his service, and that divine goodness alone is worthy to be enthroned in his heart, as the supreme master of his life.

Meditation for the Day

Follow faithfully where the inward light leads you.

It is well to become conscious of your shortcomings, for, having realized them, and feeling the necessity of overcoming them, you will, sooner or later, rise above them into the pure atmosphere of duty and unselfish love. You should not picture dark things in the future, but if you think of the future at all, think of it as bright. Above all, do your duty each day, and do it cheerfully and unselfishly, and then each day will bring its own measure of joy and peace, and the future will hold much happiness for you. The best way to overcome your faults is to perform all your duties faithfully, without thinking of any gain to yourself, and to do all you can to make others happy; speaking kindly to all, doing kind things when you can, and not retaliating when others do or say unkind things.

*Put your whole heart into the present, living it,
minute by minute, hour by hour, and day by day,
self-governed and pure.*

Thought for the Evening

Be still, my soul, and know that peace is thine. Be steadfast, heart, and know that strength divine Belongs to thee; cease from thy turmoil, mind, and thou the Everlasting Rest shalt find.

If a man would have peace, let him exercise the spirit of peace; if he would find Love, let him dwell in the spirit of Love; if he would escape suffering, let him cease to inflict it; if he would do noble things for humanity, let him cease to do ignoble things for himself. If he will but quarry the mine of his own soul, he shall find there all the materials for building whatsoever he will, and he shall find there also the Central Rock on which to build in safety.

March Twenty-seventh

Thought for the Morning

Men go after much company, and seek out new excitements, but they are not acquainted with peace; in divers paths of pleasure they search for happiness, but they do not come to rest; through divers ways of laughter and feverish delirium they wander after gladness and life, but their tears are many and grievous, and they do not escape death.

Drifting upon the ocean of life in search of selfish indulgences, men are caught in its storms, and only after many tempests and much privation do they fly to the Rock of Refuge which rests in the deep silence of their own being.

Meditation for the Day

The righteous man is invincible. No enemy can possibly overcome him.

THE righteous man, having nothing to hide, committing no acts which require stealth, and harbouring no thoughts and desires which he would not like others to know, is fearless and unashamed. His step is firm, his body upright, and his speech direct, and without ambiguity. He looks everybody in the face. How can he fear any, who wrongs none ? How can he be ashamed before any, who deceives none? And ceasing from all wrong, he can never be wronged; ceasing from all deceit, he can never be deceived. It is impossible for evil to overcome good, so the righteous man can never be brought low by the unrighteous.

He cannot be afflicted by weariness and unrest
whose heart is at peace with all.

Thought for the Evening

Meditation centred upon divine realities is the very essence and soul of prayer. It is the silent reaching upward of the soul toward the Eternal.

Meditation is the intense dwelling, in thought, upon an idea or theme with the object of thoroughly comprehending it; and whatsoever you constantly meditate upon, you will not only come to understand, but will grow more and more into its likeness, for it will become incorporated with your very being, will become, in fact, your very self.

If, therefore, you constantly dwell upon that which is selfish and debasing, you will ultimately become selfish and debased; if you ceaselessly think upon that which is pure and unselfish, you will surely become pure and unselfish.

March Twenty-eighth

Thought for the Morning

There is no difficulty, however great, but will yield before a calm and powerful concentration of thought and no legitimate object but may be speedily actualized by the intelligent use and direction of one's soul forces.

Whatever your task may be, concentrate your whole mind upon it; throw into it all the energy of which you are capable. The faultless completion of small tasks, leads inevitably to larger tasks.

See to it that you rise by steady climbing, and you will never fall.

Meditation for the Day

It is better to love than to accuse and denounce.

THERE is that outburst of passion which is called "righteous indignation" and it appears to be righteous, but looked at from a higher conception of conduct it is seen to be *not* righteous. There is a certain stamp of nobility about indignation at wrong or injustice, and it is certainly far higher and nobler than *indifference*, but there is a loftier nobility still, by which it is seen that indignation is never necessary, and where love and gentleness take its place, they overcome the wrong much more effectually. A person that is apparently wronged requires our pity, but the one who wrongs requires still more our compassion, for he is ignorantly laying up for himself a store of suffering: *he must reap the wrong he is sowing.*

When divine compassion is perceived in its fullness
and beauty, indignation and all forms of passion
cease to exercise any influence over us.

Thought for the Evening

He who knows that Love is at the heart of all things, and has realized the all-sufficing power of that Love, has no room in his heart for condemnation.

If you love people and speak of them with praise, until they in some way thwart you, or do something of which you disapprove, and then you dislike them and speak of them with dispraise, you are not governed by the Love which is of God. If, in your heart, you are continually arraigning and condemning others, selfless love is hidden from you.

Train your mind in strong, impartial, and gentle thought; train your heart in purity and compassion; train your tongue to silence, and to true and stainless speech; so shall you enter the way of holiness and peace, and shall ultimately realize the immortal Love.

March Twenty-ninth

Thought for the Morning

If you would realize true prosperity, do not settle down, as many have done, into the belief that if you do right everything will go wrong. Do not allow the word "competition" to shake your faith in the supremacy of righteousness. I care not what men say about the "laws of competition," for do not I know the Unchangeable Law which shall one day put them all to rout, and which puts them to rout even now in the heart and life of the righteous man? And knowing this law I can contemplate all dishonesty with undisturbed repose, for I know where certain destruction awaits it.

Under all circumstances *do that which you believe to be right*, and trust the Law; trust the Divine Power which is immanent in the universe, and it will never desert you, and you will always be protected.

Meditation for the Day

If a man would do a noble thing, and does not do it,
he is not exalted thereby, but debased.

THE term *Goodness* does not mean sickly sentiment, but *inward virtue*, the direct result of which is strength and power; therefore, the good man is not weak, the weak man is not good. We should not judge the souls of others in the spirit of condemnation; but we can judge of our own life and conduct by *results*. There is nothing more certain than this, the evil doer speedily *proves* that his evil produces misery; the good man *demonstrates* that his goodness results in happiness.

It is a fact that one may "flourish like a green bay tree" and yet be unrighteous, but we should also remember that the bay tree at last perishes, or is cut down, and such is the fate of the unrighteous.

An exalted being apart from an exalted life
is inconceivable and cannot be.

Thought for the Evening

Forget yourself entirely in the sorrows of others, and in ministering to others, and divine happiness will emancipate you from all sorrow and suffering. "Taking the first step with a good thought, the second with a good word, and the third with a good deed, I entered Paradise." And you also enter Paradise by pursuing the same course.

Lose yourself in the welfare of others; forget yourself in all that you do—this is the secret of abounding happiness. Ever be on the watch to guard against selfishness and learn faithfully the divine lessons of inward sacrifice; so shall you climb the highest heights of happiness, and shall remain in the never-clouded sunshine of universal joy, clothed in the shining garment of immortality.

March Thirtieth

Thought for the Morning

When the farmer has tilled and dressed his land and put in the seed, he knows that he has done all that he can possibly do, and that now he must trust to the elements, and wait patiently for the course of time to bring about the harvest, and that no amount of expectancy on his part will affect the result.

Even so, he who has realized Truth, goes forth as a sower of the seeds of goodness, purity, love, and peace, without expectancy and never looking for results, knowing that there is the Great Over-ruling Law which brings about its own harvest in due time, and which is alike the source of preservation and destruction.

Meditation for the Day

We know nothing higher than Goodness.

THE Teachers of mankind are few. A thousand years may pass by without the advent of such a one; but when the true Teacher does appear, the distinguishing feature by which he is known is *his life*. His *conduct* is different from other men, and his teaching is never derived from any man or book, *but from his own life*. The Teacher *first lives*, and then teaches others how they may likewise live. The proof and witness of his teaching is in himself, his life. Out of millions of preachers, one only is ultimately accepted by mankind as the true Teacher, and the one who is thus accepted and exalted is *he who lives*.

The supreme aim of all religions is to teach men how to live.

Thought for the Evening

The virtuous put a check upon themselves, and set a watch upon their passions and emotions; in this way they gain possession of the mind, and gradually acquire calmness; and as they acquire influence, power, greatness, abiding joy, and fullness and completeness of life.

He only finds peace who conquers himself, who strives, day by day, after greater self-possession, greater self-control, and greater calmness of mind.

Where the calm mind is there is strength and rest, there is love and wisdom; there is one who has fought successfully innumerable battles against self, who, after long toil in secret against his own failings, has triumphed at last.

March Thirty-first

Thought for the Morning

Sympathy bestowed increases its store in our own heart and enriches and fructifies our own life. Sympathy given is blessedness received; sympathy withheld is blessedness forfeited.

In the measure that a man increases and enlarges his sympathy so much nearer does he approach the ideal life, the perfect blessedness; and when his heart has become so mellowed that no hard, bitter, or cruel thought can enter, and detract from its permanent sweetness, then indeed is he richly and divinely blessed.

Meditation for the Day

Love is far beyond the reach of all selfish argument and can only be lived.

JESUS gave to the world a code of rules, by the observance of which all men could become sons of God, could live the Perfect Life. These rules or precepts are so simple, direct, and unmistakable that it is impossible to misunderstand them. So plain and unequivocal are they that even an unlettered child could grasp their meaning without difficulty. All of them are directly related to human conduct, and can be applied only by the individual in his own life. To carry out the spirit of these rules in one's daily conduct constitutes the whole duty of life, and lifts the individual into the full consciousness of his divine origin and nature, of his oneness with God, the Supreme Good.

*Men everywhere, in their inmost hearts,
know that Goodness is divine.*

Thought for the Evening

Sweet is the rest and deep the bliss of him who has freed his heart from its lusts and hatreds and dark desires; and he who, without any shadow of bitterness resting upon him, and looking out upon the world with boundless compassion and love, can breathe, in his inmost heart, the blessing: Peace unto all living things, making no exceptions or distinctions—such a man has reached that happy ending which can never be taken away, for this is the perfection of life, the fullness of peace, the consummation of perfect blessedness.

April First

Thought for the Morning

In aiming at the life of blessedness, one of the simplest beginnings to be considered, and rightly made, is that which we all make every day—namely, the beginning of each day's life. There is a sense in which every day may be regarded as the beginning of a new life, in which one can think, act, and live newly, and in a wiser and better spirit. The right beginning of the day will be followed by a cheerfulness permeating the household with a sunny influence, and the tasks and duties of the day will be undertaken in a strong and confident spirit, and the whole day will be well lived.

Meditation for the Day

A man has no character, no soul, no life,
apart from his thoughts and deeds.

EACH man is responsible for the thoughts which he thinks and the acts which he does, for his state of mind, and the life which he lives. No power, no event, no circumstance, can compel a man to evil and unhappiness. He himself is his own compeller. He thinks and acts by his own volition. No being, however wise and great—not even the Supreme—can make him good and happy. He himself must choose the good, and thereby find the happy. This life of triumph is not for those who are satisfied with any lower conditions; it is for those who thirst for it and are willing to achieve it; who are as eager for righteousness as the miser is for gold. It is always at hand, and is offered to all, and blessed are they who accept and embrace it; they will enter the world of Truth; they will find the Perfect Peace.

There is a larger, higher, nobler, diviner life
than that of sinning and suffering.

Thought for the Evening

There can be no progress, no achievement, without sacrifice, and a man's worldly success will be in the measure that he sacrifices his confused animal thoughts, and fixes his mind on the development of his plans, and the strengthening of his resolution and self-reliance. And the higher he lifts his thoughts, the more manly, upright, and righteous he becomes, the greater will be his success, the more blessed and enduring will be his achievements.

April Second

Thought for the Morning

None but right acts can follow right thoughts; none but a right life can follow right acts; and by living a right life all blessedness is achieved. Mind is the Master-power that moulds and makes. And Man is Mind, and evermore he takes the tool of thought, and, shaping what he wills, brings forth a thousand joys, a thousand ills;—He thinks in secret, and it comes to pass: environment is but his looking-glass.

Meditation for the Day

Man is; and as he thinks, so he is.

MAN'S life is actual; his thoughts are actual; his deeds are actual. To occupy ourselves with the investigation of things that are, is the way of wisdom. Man, considered as above, beyond, and separate from, mind and thought, is speculative and not actual, and to occupy ourselves with the study of things that are not, is the way of folly.

Man cannot be separated from his mind; his life cannot be separated from his thoughts. Mind, thought, and life are as inseparable as light, radiance, and colour. The facts are all-sufficient, and contain within themselves the ground-work of all knowledge concerning them.

To live is to think and act, and to think and act is to change.

Thought for the Evening

Calmness of mind is one of the beautiful jewels of wisdom. A man becomes calm in the measure that he understands himself as a thought-evolved being... and he as he develops a right understanding, and sees more and more clearly the internal relations of things by the action of cause and effect, he ceases to fret and fume, and worry and grieve, and remains poised, steadfast, serene.

April Third

Thought for the Morning

To follow, under all circumstances, the highest promptings within you; to be always true to the divine self; to reply upon the inward voice, the inward light, and to pursue your purpose with a fearless and restful heart, believing that the future will yield unto you the need of every thought and effort; knowing that the laws of the universe can never fail, and that your own will come back to you with mathematical exactitude—this is faith and the living of faith.

Meditation for the Day

Man as mind is subject to change. He is not something "made" and finally completed, but has within him the capacity for progress.

THE purification of the heart, the thinking of right thoughts, and the doing of good deeds what are they but calls to a higher, nobler mode of thought energizing forces urging men to effort in the choosing of thoughts which shall lift them into realms of greater power, greater good, greater bliss?

Aspiration, meditation, devotion these are the chief means which men in all ages employ to reach up to higher modes of thought, wider airs of peace, vaster realms of knowledge, for "as he thinketh in his heart, so is he"; he is saved from himself from his own folly and suffering—by creating within, new habits of thought; by becoming a new thinker, a new man.

Man's being is modified by every thought he thinks. Every experience affects his character.

Thought for the Evening

Have a thorough understanding of your work, and let it be your own; and as you proceed, ever following the inward guide, the infallible voice, you will pass on from victory to victory, and will rise step by step to higher resting-places, and your ever broadening outlook will gradually reveal to you the essential beauty and purpose of life. Self-purified, health will be yours; self-governed, power will be yours, and all that you do will prosper.

And I may stand where health, success, and power await my coming, if, each fleeting hour, I cling to love and patience; and abide with stainlessness; and never step aside from high integrity; so shall I see at last the land of immortality.

April Fourth

Thought for the Morning

When the tongue is well controlled and wisely subdued; when selfish impulses and unworthy thoughts no longer rush to the tongue demanding utterance; when the speech has become harmless, pure, gracious, gentle, and purposeful, and no word is uttered but in sincerity and truth—then are the five steps in virtuous speech accomplished, then is the second great lesson in Truth learned and mastered. Make pure thy heart, and thou wilt make thy life rich, sweet and beautiful.

Meditation for the Day

Only the choosing of wise thoughts, and, necessarily the doing of wise deeds, leads to wisdom.

THE multitudes, unenlightened concerning their spiritual nature, are the slaves of thought, but the sage is the master of thought. They follow blindly; he chooses intelligently. They obey the impulse of the moment, thinking of their immediate pleasure and happiness; he commands and subdues impulse, resting upon that which is permanently right. They, obeying blind impulse, violate the law of righteousness; he, conquering impulse, obeys the law of righteousness. The sage stands face to face with the facts of life. He knows the nature of thought. He understands and obeys the law of his being.

Thought determines character, condition, knowledge.

Thought for the Evening

Having clothed himself with humility, the first questions a man asks himself are:—

"How am I acting towards others?"
"What am I doing to others?"
"How am I thinking of others?"
"Are my thoughts of, and acts towards others prompted by unselfish love?"

As a man, in the silence of his soul, asks himself these searching questions, he will unerringly see where he has hitherto failed.

April Fifth

Thought for the Morning

To dwell in love always and towards all is to live the true life, is to have Life itself. Knowing this, the good man gives up himself unreservedly to the Spirit of Love, and dwells in Love towards all, contending with none, condemning none, but loving all.

The Christ Spirit of Love puts an end, not only to all sin, but to all division and contention.

Meditation for the Day

*Law cannot be partial. It is an unvarying mode of action,
disobeying which, we are hurt; obeying,
we are made happy.*

IT is not less kind that we should suffer the penalty of our wrong-doing than that we should enjoy the blessedness of our right-doing. If we could escape the effects of our ignorance and sin, all security would be gone, and there would be no refuge, for we could then be equally deprived of the result of our wisdom and goodness. Such a scheme would be one of caprice and cruelty, whereas law is a method of justice and kindness.

Indeed, the supreme law is the principle of eternal kindness, faultless in working, and infinite in application. It is none other than that

"Eternal Love, forever full,
 For ever flowing free,"

of which the Christian sings; and the "Boundless Compassion" of Buddhistic precept and poetry.

*Every pain we suffer brings us nearer to the knowledge
of the Divine Wisdom.*

Thought for the Evening

When sin and self are abandoned, the heart is restored to its imperishable Joy. Joy comes and fills the self-emptied heart; it abides with the peaceful; its reign is with the pure. Joy flees from the selfish, it deserts the quarrelsome; it is hidden from the impure. Joy cannot remain with the selfish; it is wedded to Love.

April Sixth

Thought for the Morning

In the pure heart there is no room left where personal judgments and hatreds can find lodgement, for it is filled to overflowing with tenderness and love; it sees no evil, and only as men succeed in seeing no evil in others will they become free from sin, and sorrow, and suffering. If men only understood that the heart that sins must sorrow, that the hateful mind tomorrow reaps its barren harvest, weeping, starving, resting not, nor sleeping; tenderness would fill their being, they would see with pity's seeing, if they only understood.

Meditation for the Day

Seers of the Cosmos do not mourn over the scheme of things.

BUDDHA always referred to the moral law of the universe as the Good Law, and indeed it is not rightly perceived if it is thought of as anything but good, for in it there can be no grain of evil, no element of unkindness. It is no iron-hearted monster crushing the weak and destroying the ignorant, but a soothing love and brooding compassion shielding the tenderest from harm, and protecting the strongest from a too destructive use of their strength. It destroys all evil, it preserves all good. It enfolds the tiniest seedling in its care, and it destroys the most colossal wrong with a breath. To perceive it, is the beatific vision; to know it, is the beatific bliss; and they who perceive and know it are at peace; they are glad for ever more.

The wise man bends his will and subjects his desire to the Divine Order.

Thought for the Evening

To stand face to face with truth; to arrive, after innumerable wanderings and pains, at wisdom and bliss; not to be finally defeated and cast out, but to ultimately triumph over every inward foe—such is man's divine destiny, such his glorious goal; and this, every saint, sage, and saviour has declared. A man only begins to be a man when he ceases to whine and revile, and commences to search for the hidden justice which regulates his life. And as he adapts his mind to that regulating factor, he ceases to accuse others as the cause of his condition, and builds himself up in strong and noble thoughts; ceases to kick against circumstances, but begins to use them as aids to his more rapid progress, and as a means of discovering the hidden power and possibilities within himself.

April Seventh

Thought for the Morning

The will to evil and the will to good are both within thee, which wilt thou employ? Thou knowest what is right and what is wrong, which wilt though love and foster, which destroy?

Thou art the chooser of thy thoughts and deeds; thou art the maker of thine inward state; the power is thine to be what thou wilt be; thou buildest Truth and Love, or lies and hate.

Meditation for the Day

Rise above the allurements of sin, and enter the Divine Consciousness, the Transcendent Life.

THERE comes a time in the process of transmutation when, with the decrease of evil and the accumulation of good, there dawns in the mind a new vision, a new consciousness, a new man. And when this is reached, the saint has become a sage; he has passed from the human life to the divine life. He is "born again" and there begins for him a new round of experiences; he wields a new power; a new universe opens out before his spiritual gaze. This is the stage of Transcendence; this I call the Transcendent Life.

When Transcendence is attained, then the limited personality is outgrown, and the divine life is known; evil is transcended, and Good is all-in-all.

As passion is the keynote of the self-life, so serenity is the keynote of the transcendent life.

Thought for the Evening

The teaching of Jesus brings men back to the simple truth that righteousness, or *right-doing*, is entirely a matter of individual conduct, and not a mystical something apart from a man's thoughts and deeds.

Calmness and patience can become habitual by first grasping, through effort, a calm and patient thought, and then continuously thinking it, and living in it, until "use becomes second nature," and anger and impatience pass away for ever.

April Eighth

Thought for the Morning

Man is made or unmade by himself; in the armoury of thought he forges the weapons by which he destroys himself; he also fashions the tools with which he builds for himself heavenly mansions of joy and strength and peace. By the right choice and true application of thought man ascends to the Divine Perfection; by the abuse and wrong application of thought he descends below the level of the beast. Between these two extremes are all the grades of character and man is their maker and master.

As a being of Power, Intelligence, and Love, and the lord of his own thoughts, man holds the key to every situation.

Meditation for the Day

When Perfect Good is realized and known, then calm vision is acquired.

THE transcendent life is ruled, not by passions, but by principles. It is founded, not upon fleeting impulses, but upon abiding laws. In its clear atmosphere, the orderly sequence of all things is revealed, so that there is seen to be no more room for sorrow, anxiety, or regret. While men are involved in the passions of self, they load themselves with cares, and trouble over many things; and more than all else do they trouble over their own little, burdened, pain-stricken personality, being anxious for its fleeting pleasures, for its protection and preservation, and for its eternal safety and continuance. Now in the life that is wise and good all this is transcended. Personal interests are replaced by universal purposes, and all cares, troubles, and anxieties concerning the pleasure and fate of the personality are dispelled like the feverish dreams of a night.

Universal Good is seen.

Thought for the Evening

Whatsoever you harbour in the inmost chambers of your heart will, sooner or later, by the inevitable law of reaction, shape itself in your outward life.

Every soul attracts its own, and nothing can possibly come to it that does not belong to it. To realize this is to recognize the universality of Divine Law.

If thou would'st right the world, and banish all its evils and its woes, make its wild places bloom, and its drear deserts blossom as the rose—then right thyself.

April Ninth

Thought for the Morning

Whatever conditions are rendering your life burdensome, you may pass out of and beyond them by developing and utilizing within you the transforming power of self-purification and self-conquest.

Before the divine radiance of a pure heart all darkness vanishes and all clouds melt away, and he who has conquered self has conquered the universe.

He who sets his foot firmly upon the path of self-conquest, who walks, aided by the staff of faith, the highway of self-sacrifice, will assuredly achieve the highest prosperity, and will reap abounding and enduring joy and bliss.

Meditation for the Day

Evil is an experience, and not a power.

IF it (evil) were an independent power in the universe, it could not be transcended by any being. But though not real as a power, it is real as a condition, an experience, for all experience is of the nature of reality. It is a state of ignorance, of undevelopment, and as such it recedes and disappears before the light of knowledge, as the intellectual ignorance of the child vanishes before the gradually accumulating learning, or as darkness dissolves before the rising light.

The painful experiences of evil pass away as the new experiences of good enter into and possess the field of consciousness.

*The transcendent man is he who is above and beyond
the dominion of self; he has transcended evil.*

Thought for the Evening

It is the silent and conquering thought forces which bring all things into manifestation. The universe grew out of thought.

To adjust all your thoughts to a perfect and unswerving faith in the omnipotence and supremacy of Good is to co-operate with that Good, and to realize within yourself the solution and destruction of all evil.

To mentally deny evil is not sufficient; it must, by daily practice, be risen above and understood. To affirm the Good mentally is inadequate; it must, by unswerving endeavour, be entered into and comprehended.

April Tenth

Thought for the Morning

Every thought you think is a force sent out. Whatever your position in life may be, before you can hope to enter into any measure of success, usefulness, and power, you must learn how to focus your thought forces by cultivating calmness and repose.

There is no difficulty, however great, but will yield before a calm and purposeful concentration of thought, and no legitimate object but may be speedily actualized by the intelligent use and direction of one's soul forces.

Think good thoughts, and they will quickly become actualized in your outward life in the form of good conditions.

Meditation for the Day

Whatsoever happens to the good man cannot cause him
perplexity or sorrow, for he knows its cause and issue.

IN looking back on the self-life which he has transcended, the divinely enlightened man sees that all the afflictions of that life were his schoolmasters teaching him, and leading him upward, and that in the measure that he penetrated their meaning, and lifted himself above them, they departed from him. Their mission to teach him having ended, they left him triumphant master of the field; for the lower cannot teach the higher; ignorance cannot instruct wisdom; evil cannot enlighten good; nor can the pupil set lessons for the master. That which is transcended cannot reach up to that which transcends. Evil can only teach in its own sphere, where it is regarded as a master; in the sphere of good it has no place, no authority.

The strong traveler on the highroad of truth
knows no such thing as resignation to evil;
he knows only obedience to good.

Thought for the Evening

That which you would be and hope to be, you may be now. Non-accomplishment resides in your perpetual postponement, and, having the power to postpone, you also have the power to accomplish—to perpetually accomplish: realize this truth, and you shall be today, and every day, the ideal being of whom you dreamed.

Say to yourself, "I will live in my Ideal now; I will manifest my ideal now; I will be my Ideal now; and all that tempts me away from my Ideal I will not listen to; I will listen only to the voice of my Ideal."

April Eleventh

Thought for the Morning

Be as a flower; content to be, to grow in sweetness day by day. If thou would'st perfect thyself in knowledge, perfect thyself in Love. If thou would'st reach the Highest, ceaselessly cultivate a loving and compassionate heart.

To him who chooses Goodness, sacrificing all, is given that which is more than, and includes, all.

Meditation for the Day

*He is brave who conquers another: but he
who conquers himself is supremely noble.*

BY the way of self-conquest is the Perfect Peace achieved. Man cannot understand it, cannot approach it, until he sees the supreme necessity of turning away from the fierce fighting of things without, and entering upon the noble warfare against evils within. He is already on the Saintly Way who has realized that the enemy of the world is within, and not without; that his own ungoverned thoughts are the source of confusion and strife; that his own unchastened desires are the violators of his peace, and of the peace of the world.

If a man has conquered lust and anger, hatred and pride, selfishness and greed, he has conquered the world.

*He who is victorious over another may in turn be defeated;
but he who overcomes himself will never be subdued.*

Thought for the Evening

The Great Law never cheats any man of his just due.

Human life, when rightly lived, is simple with a beautiful simplicity.

He who comprehends the utter simplicity of life, who obeys its laws, and does not step aside into the dark paths and complex mazes of selfish desire, stands where no harm can reach him.

Then there is fullness of joy, abounding plenty, and rich and complete blessedness.

April Twelfth

Thought for the Morning

Every man reaps the results of his own thoughts and deeds, and suffers for his own wrong.

He who begins right, and continues right, does not need to desire, and search for felicitous results; they are already at hand; they follow as consequences; they are the certainties, the realities, of life.

Sweet is the rest and deep is the bliss of him who has freed his heart from its lusts and hatreds and dark desires.

Meditation for the Day

*Force and strife work upon the passions and fears,
but love and peace reach and reform the heart.*

HE who is overcome by force is not thereby overcome in his heart: he may be a greater enemy than before; but he who is overcome by the spirit of peace is thereby changed at heart. He that was an enemy has become a friend.

The pure-hearted and wise have peace in their hearts; it enters into their actions; they apply it in their lives. It is more powerful than strife; it conquers where force would fail. Its wings shield the righteous. Under its protection, the harmless are not harmed. It affords a secure shelter from the heat of selfish struggle. It is a refuge for the defeated, a tent for the lost, and a temple for the pure.

*When divine good is practised, life is bliss.
Bliss is the normal condition of the good man.*

Thought for the Evening

You are the creator of your own shadows; you desire, and then you grieve; renounce, and then you shall rejoice.

Of all the beautiful truths pertaining to the soul. . . none is more gladdening or fruitful of divine promise and confidence than this—that man is the master of thought, the moulder of character, and the maker and shaper of character, environment, and destiny.

April Thirteenth

Thought for the Morning

As darkness is a passing shadow, and light is a substance that remains, so sorrow is fleeting, but joy abides for ever. No true thing can pass away and become lost; no false thing can remain and be preserved. Sorrow is false, and it cannot live; joy is true, and it cannot die. Joy may become hidden for a time, but it can always be recovered; sorrow may remain for a period, but it can be transcended and dispersed.

Do not think your sorrow will remain; it will pass away like a cloud. Do not believe that the torments of sin are ever your portion; they will vanish like a hideous nightmare. Awake! Arise! Be holy and joyful.

Meditation for the Day

He who has realized the Love that is divine has become a new man.

THIS Love, this Wisdom, this Peace, this tranquil state of mind and heart, may be attained to, may be realized, by all who are willing and ready to yield up self, and who are prepared to humbly enter into a comprehension of all that the giving up of self involves. There is no arbitrary power in the universe, and the strongest chains of fate by which men are bound are self-forged. Men are chained to that which causes suffering because they desire to be so, because they love their chains, because they think their little dark prison of self is sweet and beautiful, and they are afraid that if they desert that prison they will lose all that is real and worth having.

"Ye suffer from yourselves, none else compels,
None other holds ye that ye live and die."

To the divinely wise, knowledge and Love are one and inseparable.

Thought for the Evening

Tribulation lasts only so long as there remains some chaff of self which needs to be removed. The *tribulum*, or threshing machine, ceases to work when all the grain is separated from the chaff; and when the last impurities are blown away from the soul, tribulation has completed its work, and there is no more need for it; then abiding joy is realized.

The sole and supreme use of suffering is to purify, to burn out all that is useless and impure. Suffering ceases for him who is pure. There could be no object in burning gold after the dross had been removed.

April Fourteenth

Thought for the Morning

In speaking of self-control, one is easily misunderstood. It should not be associated with a destructive repression, but with a constructive expression.

A man is happy, wise and great in the measure that he controls himself; he is wretched, foolish, and mean in the measure that he allows his animal nature to dominate his thoughts and actions.

He who controls himself, controls his life, his circumstances, his destiny; and wherever he goes he carries his happiness with him as an abiding possession.

Renunciation precedes regeneration. The permanent happiness which men seek in dissipation, excitement, and abandonment to unworthy pleasures, is found only in the life which reverses all this—the life of self-control.

Meditation for the Day

*The world does not understand the Love that is selfless
because it is engrossed in the pursuit of its own pleasures.*

AS the shadow follows the form, and as smoke comes after fire, so effect follows cause, and suffering and bliss follow the thoughts and deeds of men. There is no effect in the world around us but has its hidden or revealed cause, and that cause is in accordance with absolute justice. Men reap a harvest of suffering because in the near or distant past they have sown the seeds of evil; they reap a harvest of bliss also as a result of their own sowing of the seeds of good. Let a man meditate upon this, let him strive to understand it, and he will then begin to sow only seeds of good, and will burn up the tares and weeds which he has formerly grown in the garden of his heart.

*It is toward the complete realization of this
divine Love that the whole world is moving.*

Thought for the Evening

Law, not confusion, is the dominating principle in the universe; justice, not injustice is the soul and substance of life; and righteousness, not corruption, is the moulding and moving force in the spiritual government of the world. This being so, man has but the right himself to find that the universe is right.

When I am pure, I shall have solved the mystery of life; I shall be sure, when I am free from hatred, lust and strife, I am in Truth, and Truth abides in me; I shall be safe, and sane, and wholly free, when I am pure.

April Fifteenth

Thought for the Morning

If men only understood that their hatred and resentment slays their peace and sweet contentment, hurts themselves, helps not another, does not cheer one lonely brother, they would seek the better doing of good deeds which leaves no ruing:—

If they only understood.

If men only understood how Love conquers; how prevailing is its might, grim hate assailing; how compassion endeth sorrow, maketh wise, and doth not borrow pain of passion, they would ever live in Love, in hatred never:—

If they only understood.

Meditation for the Day

He who purifies his own heart is the world's greatest benefactor.

THE world is, and will be for many years to come, shut out from that Golden Age which is the realization of selfless Love. You, if you are willing, may enter it now, by rising above your selfish self; if you will pass from prejudice, hatred, and condemnation to gentle and forgiving love.

Where hatred, dislike, and condemnation are, selfless Love does not abide. It resides only in the heart that has ceased from all condemnation.

He who knows that Love is at the heart of all things, and has realized the all-sufficing power of that Love, has no room in his heart for condemnation.

Let men and women take this course, and lo!
the Golden Age is at hand.

Thought for the Evening

The grace and beauty that were in Jesus can be of no value to you—cannot be understood by you—unless they are also *in you*, and they can never be in you, until you practice them, for, apart from *doing*, the qualities which constitute goodness do not, as far as you are concerned, exist.

To adore Jesus for his good qualities is a long step towards Truth, but to practice those qualities is Truth itself; and he who fully adores the perfection of another will not rest content in his own imperfection, but will fashion his soul after the likeness of that other.

Therefore thou who adorest Jesus for his divine qualities, practice those qualities thyself, and thou too shalt be divine.

April Sixteenth

Thought for the Morning

Let a man realize that life in its totality proceeds from the mind, and lo, the way of blessedness is opened up to him! For he will then discover that he possesses the power to rule his mind and to fashion it in accordance with his Ideal.

So will he elect to strongly and steadfastly walk those pathways of thought and action which are altogether excellent; to him life will become beautiful and sacred; and, sooner or later, he will put to flight all evil, confusion, and suffering; for it is impossible for a man to fall short of liberation, enlightenment, and peace, who guards with unwearying diligence the gateway of his heart.

Meditation for the Day

Only the pure in heart see God.

HE whose heart is centred in the supreme Love does not brand and classify men; does not seek to convert men to his own views, nor to convince them of the superiority of his methods. Knowing the Law of Love, he lives it, and maintains the same calm attitude of mind and sweetness of heart towards all. The debased and the virtuous, the foolish and the wise, the learned and the unlearned, the selfish and the unselfish, receive alike the benediction of his tranquil thought.

You can only attain to this supreme knowledge, this divine Love, by unremitting endeavour in self-discipline, and by gaining victory after victory over yourself.

*Enter into the New Birth, and the Love that does not die
will be awakened within you, and you will be at peace.*

Thought for the Evening

By constantly overcoming self, a man gains a knowledge of the subtle intricacies of his mind; and it is this divine knowledge which enables him to become established in calmness.

Without self-knowledge there can be no abiding peace of mind, and those who are carried away by tempestuous passions, cannot approach the holy place where calmness reigns.

The weak man is like one who, having mounted a fiery steed, allows it to run away with him, and carry him withersoever it wills; the strong man is like one who, having mounted the steed, governs it with a masterly hand and makes it go in whatever direction and at whatever speed he commands.

April Seventeenth

Thought for the Morning

There is no strife, no selfishness, in the Kingdom; there is perfect harmony, equipoise, and rest.

Those who live in the Kingdom of Love, have all their needs supplied by the Law of Love.

As self is the root cause of all strife and suffering, so Love is the root cause of all peace and bliss. Those who are at rest in the Kingdom do not look for happiness in any outward possessions. They are freed from all anxiety and trouble and, resting in Love, they are the embodiment of happiness.

Meditation for the Day

Where there is pure spiritual knowledge, Love is perfected and fully realized.

TRAIN your mind in strong, impartial, and gentle thought; train your heart in purity and compassion; train your tongue to silence and to true and stainless speech; so shall you enter the way of holiness and peace, and shall ultimately realize the immortal Love. So living, without seeking to convert, you will convince; without arguing, you will teach; not cherishing ambition, the wise will find you out; and without striving to gain men's opinions, you will subdue their hearts. For Love is all-conquering, all-powerful; and the thoughts, and deeds, and words of Love can never perish.

This is the realization of selfless Love.

Thought for the Evening

Let it not be supposed that the children of the Kingdom live in ease and indolence (these two sins are the first that have to be eradicated when the search for the Kingdom is entered upon); they live in a peaceful activity; in fact, they only truly live, for the life of self, with its train of worries, griefs, and fears, is not *real life*.

The children of the Kingdom are *known by their life*, they manifest the fruits of the Spirit—"Love, joy, peace, long-suffering, kindness, goodness, faithfulness, meekness, temperance, and self-control"—under all circumstances and vicissitudes.

April Eighteenth

Thought for the Morning

The gospel of Jesus is a gospel of *living and doing*. If it were not this it would not voice the Eternal Truth. Its Temple is *Purified Conduct*, the entrance-door to which is *Self-Surrender*. It invites men to shake off sin, and promises, as a result, joy and blessedness and perfect peace.

The Kingdom of Heaven is perfect trust, perfect knowledge, perfect peace. . . no sin can enter therein, no self-born thought or deed can pass its golden gates; no impure desire can defile its radiant robes. . . all may enter it who will, but all must pay the price—*the unconditional abandonment of self.*

Meditation for the Day

Rejoice! for the morning has dawned: the Truth has awakened us.

WE have opened our eyes, and the dark night of terror is no more. Long have we slept in matter and sensation; long did we struggle in the painful nightmare of evil; but now we are awake in Spirit and Truth: We have found the Good, and the struggle with evil is ended.

We slept, yet knew not that we slept. We suffered, yet knew not that we suffered. We were troubled in our dreaming, yet none could awake us, for all were dreaming like ourselves. Yet there came a pause in our dreaming; our sleep was stayed. Truth spoke to us, and we heard; and lo! we opened our eyes, and saw. We slumbered, and saw not; we slept, and knew not; but now we are awake and see. Yea, we know we are awake because we have seen Holiness, and we love sin no more.

How beautiful is Truth!
How glorious is the realm of reality!
How ineffable is the bliss of Holiness!

Thought for the Evening

I say this—and know it to be truth—*that circumstances can only affect you in so far as you allow them to do so.* You are swayed by circumstances because you have not a right understanding of the nature, use, and power of thought. You believe (and upon this little word *belief* hang all our joys and sorrows) that outward things have the power to make or mar your life; by so doing you submit to those outward things, confess that you are their slave, and they your unconditional master. By so doing you invest them with a power which they do not of themselves possess, and you succumb, in reality not to the circumstances, but to the gloom or gladness, the fear or hope, the strength of weakness, which your thought-sphere has thrown around them.

April Nineteenth

Thought for the Morning

If you are one of those who are praying for, and looking forward to a happier world beyond the grave, here is a message of gladness for you—you may enter into and realize that happy world now; it fills the whole universe, and it is within you, waiting for you to find, acknowledge, and possess.

Said one who understood the inner laws of Being—"When men shall say, lo here, or lo there, go not after them. The Kingdom of God is within you."

Meditation for the Day

Abandon error for Truth, and illusion for Reality.

To sin is to dream, and to love sin is to love darkness. They who love darkness are involved in the darkness; they have not yet seen the light. He who has seen the light does not choose to walk in darkness. To see the Truth is to love it, and, in comparison, error has no beauty. The dreamer is now in pleasure, now in pain; this hour in confidence, the next in fear. He is without stability, and has no abiding refuge.

When the monsters of remorse and retribution pursue him, whither can he fly? There is no place of safety unless he awake. Let the dreamer struggle with his dream; let him strive to realize the illusory nature of all self-seeking desire, and lo! he will open his spiritual eyes upon the world of Light and Truth. He will be happy, sane, and peaceful, seeing things as they are.

Truth is the Light of the universe, the day of the mind.

Thought for the Evening

Heaven and hell are inward states. Sink into self and all its gratifications, and you sink into hell; rise above self into that state of consciousness which is the utter denial and forgetfulness of self, and you enter heaven.

So long as you persist in selfishly seeking for your own personal happiness, so long will happiness elude you, and you will be sowing the seeds of wretchedness. In so far as you succeed in losing yourself in the service of others, in that measure will happiness come to you, and you will reap a harvest of bliss.

April Twentieth

Thought for the Morning

Sympathy given can never be waste.

One aspect of sympathy is that of pity—pity for the distressed or pain stricken, with a desire to alleviate or help them in their sufferings. The world needs more of this divine quality.

"For pity makes the world soft to the weak, and noble for the strong."

Another form of sympathy is that of rejoicing with others who are more successful than ourselves, and though their success were our own.

Meditation for the Day

The Knowledge of Truth is an abiding consolation.

WHEN all else fails, Truth does not fail. When the heart is desolate and the world affords no shelter, Truth provides a peaceful refuge and a quiet rest. The cares of life are many, and its path is beset with difficulties; but Truth is greater than care, and is superior to all difficulties. Truth lightens our burdens; it lights up our pathway with the radiance of joy. Loved ones pass away, friends fail, and possessions disappear. Where then is the voice of comfort? Where is the whisper of consolation? Truth is the comforter of the comfortless, and the consoler of them that are deserted. Truth does not pass away, nor fail, nor disappear. Truth bestows the consolation of abiding peace. Be alert, and listen, that ye may hear the call of Truth, even the voice of the Great Awakener.

Truth removes the sting from affliction,
and disperses the clouds of trouble.

Thought for the Evening

Sweet are companionships, pleasures, and material comforts, but they change and fade away. Sweeter still are Purity, Wisdom, and the knowledge of Truth, and these never change nor fade away.

He who attained to the possession of spiritual things can never be deprived of his source of happiness; he will never have to part company with it, and wherever he goes in the whole universe, he will carry his possessions with him. His spiritual end will be the fullness of joy.

April Twenty-First

Thought for the Morning

Let your heart grow and expand with ever broadening love, until, freed from all hatred, and passion, and condemnation, it embraces the whole universe with thoughtful tenderness.

As the flower opens its petals to receive the morning light, so open your soul more and more to the glorious light of Truth.

Soar upward on the wings of aspiration; be fearless and believe in the loftiest possibilities.

Meditation for the Day

He who clings to his delusions, loving self and sin, cannot find the Truth.

TRUTH brings joy out of sorrow, and I peace out of perturbation; it points the selfish to the Way of Good, and sinners to the Path of Holiness. Its spirit is the doing of Righteousness. To the earnest and faithful it brings consolation; upon the obedient it bestows the crown of peace. I take refuge in Truth: Yea, in the Spirit of Good, in the knowledge of Good, and in the doing of Good I abide. And I am reassured and comforted. It is to me as though malice were not, and hatred had vanished away. Lust is confined to the nethermost darkness, it hath no way in Truth's transcendent Light. Pride is broken up and dissolved, and vanity is melted away as a mist. I have set my face towards the Perfect Good, and my feet in the Blameless Way; and because of this I am consoled.

I am strengthened and comforted, having found refuge in Truth.

Thought for the Evening

Mind clothes itself in garments of its own making. Mind is the arbiter of life; it is the creator and shaper of conditions, and the recipient of its own results. It contains within itself both the power to create illusion and to perceive reality.

Mind is the infallible weaver of destiny; thought is the thread, good and evil deeds are the warp and woof, and the web, woven upon the loom of life, is character. Make pure thy heart, and thou wilt make thy life, rich, sweet, and beautiful, unmarred by strife.

April Twenty-second

Thought for the Morning

Cherish your visions; cherish your ideals; cherish the music that stirs in your heart, the beauty that forms in your mind, the loveliness that drapes your purest thoughts, for out of them will grow all delightful conditions, all heavenly environment; of these, if you will remain true to them, your world will at last be built.

Guard well thy mind, and, noble, strong, and free, nothing shall harm, disturb or conquer thee; for all thy foes are in thy heart and mind, there also thy salvation thou shalt find.

Meditation for the Day

A pure heart and a blameless life avail.
They are filled with joy and peace.

OUR good deeds remain with us, they save and protect us. Evil deeds are error. Our evil deeds follow us, they overthrow us in the hour of temptation. The evil doer is not protected from sorrow; but the good doer is shielded from all harm. The fool says unto his evil deed, "Remain thou hidden, be thou unexposed"—but his evil is already published, and his sorrow is sure. If we are in evil, what shall protect us? What keep us from misery and confusion? Nor man nor woman, nor wealth nor power, nor heaven nor earth, shall keep us from confusion. From the results of evil there is no escape; no refuge and no protection. If we are in Good, what shall overtake us? What bring us to misery and confusion? Nor man nor woman, nor poverty nor sickness, nor heaven nor earth, shall bring us to confusion.

There is a straight way and a quiet rest.

Thought for the Evening

Dream lofty dreams, and as you dream so shall you become. Your vision is the promise of what you shall one day be; your Ideal is the prophecy of what you shall at last unveil.

The greatest achievement was at first and for a time a dream. The oak sleeps in the acorn; the bird waits in the egg; and in the highest vision of the soul a waking angel stirs.

Your circumstances may be uncongenial, but they shall not long remain so when you perceive an Ideal and strive to reach it.

April Twenty-third

Thought for the Morning

He who has conquered doubt and fear has conquered failure. His every thought is allied with power, and all difficulties are bravely met and wisely overcome. His purposes are seasonably planted, and they bloom and bring forth fruit which does not fall prematurely to the ground.

Thought allied fearlessly to purpose becomes creative force: he who knows this is ready to become something higher and stronger than a mere bundle of wavering thoughts and fluctuating sensations; he who does this has become the conscious and intelligent wielder of his mental powers.

Meditation for the Day

Be glad and not sorrowful, all ye who love Truth!
For your sorrows shall pass away, like the mists of the morning.

DISCIPLE: Teacher of teachers, instruct Thou me.

Master: Ask, and I will answer.

Disciple: I have read much, but am ignorant still; I have studied the doctrines of the schools, but have not become wise thereby; I know the scriptures by heart, but peace is hidden from me. Point out to me, O Master! the way of knowledge. Reveal to me the highway of divine wisdom; lead Thou Thy child into the path of peace.

Master: The way of knowledge, O Disciple! is by searching the heart; the highway of wisdom is by the practice of righteousness; and by a sinless life is found the way of peace.

Behold where Love Eternal rests concealed!
(The deathless Love that seemed so far away!)
E'en in the lowly heart; it stands revealed
To him who lives the sinless life today.

Thought for the Evening

Man's true place in the Cosmos is that of a king, not a slave, a commander under the Law of Good, and not a helpless tool in the region of evil.

I write for men, not for babes; for those who are eager to learn, and earnest to achieve; for those who will put away (for the world's good) a petty personal indulgence, a selfish desire, a mean thought, and live on as though it were not, sans craving and regret.

Man is a master. If he were not, he could not act contrary to law.

Evil and weakness are self destructive. The universe is girt with goodness and strength, and it protects the good and the strong.

The angry man is the weak man.

April Twenty-fourth

Thought for the Morning

Not by learning will a man triumph over evil; not by much study will he overcome sin and sorrow. Only by conquering himself will he conquer evil; only by practicing righteousness will he put an end to sorrow.

Not for the clever, nor the learned, nor the self-confident is the Life Triumphant, but for the pure, the virtuous and wise. The former achieve their particular success in life, but the latter alone achieve the great success so invincible and complete that even in apparent defeat it shines with added victory.

Meditation for the Day

Great is the conquest which thou hast entered upon,
even the mighty conquest of thyself;
be faithful and thou shalt overcome.

DISCIPLE: Lead me, O Master! For my darkness is very great! Will the darkness lift, O Master? Will trial end in victory, and will there be an end to my many sorrows?

Master: When thy heart is pure the darkness will disappear. When thy mind is freed from passion, thou wilt reach the end of trial, and when the thought of self-preservation is yielded up, there will be no more cause for sorrow. Thou art now upon the way of discipline and purification; all my disciples must walk that way. Before thou canst enter the white light of knowledge, before thou canst behold the full glory of Truth, all thy impurities must be purged away, thy delusions all dispelled, and thy mind fortified with endurance. Relax not thy faith in Truth; forget not that Truth is eternally supreme; remember that I, the Lord of Truth, am watching over thee.

Be faithful, and endure, and I will teach thee all things.

Thought for the Evening

The true silence is not merely a silent tongue; it is a silent mind. To merely *hold one's tongue*, and yet to carry about a disturbed and rankling mind, is no remedy for weakness, and no source of power.

Silentness, to be powerful, must envelop the whole mind, must permeate every chamber of the heart; it must be the silence of peace.

To this broad, deep, abiding silentness a man attains only in the measure that he conquers himself.

April Twenty-fifth

Thought for the Morning

By curbing his tongue, a man gains possession of his mind.

The fool babbles, gossips, argues, and bandies words. He glories in the fact that he has had the last word, and has silenced his opponent. He exults in his own folly, is ever on the defensive, and wastes his energies in unprofitable channels. He is like a gardener who continues to dig and plant in unproductive soil.

The wise man avoids idle words, gossips, vain argument, and self-defence. He is content to appear defeated; rejoices when he is defeated; knowing that, having found and removed another error in himself, he has thereby become wiser.

Blessed is he who does not strive for the last word.

Meditation for the Day

Blessed is he who obeys the Truth, he shall not remain comfortless.

DISCIPLE: What are the greater and the lesser powers?

Master: Hear me again, O Disciple! Walking faithfully the path of discipline and purification, not abandoning it, but submitting to its austerities, thou wilt acquire the three lesser powers of discipleship; thou wilt also receive the three greater powers. And the greater and the lesser powers will render thee invincible. *Self-control*, *Self-reliance*, and *Watchfulness*—these are the three lesser powers. *Steadfastness*, *Patience*, *Gentleness*—these are the three greater powers. When thy mind is well-controlled, and in thy keeping; when thou reliest upon no external aid, but upon Truth alone; and when thou art ceaselessly watchful over thy thoughts and actions then thou wilt approach the Supreme Light.

Thy darkness will pass away forever,
and joy and light will wait upon thy footsteps.

Thought for the Evening

Desire is the *craving for possession*; aspiration is the *hunger of the heart for peace*.

The craving for things leads ever farther and farther from peace, and not only ends in deprivation, but is in itself a state of perpetual want. Until it comes to an end, rest and satisfaction are impossible.

The hunger for things can never be satisfied, but the hunger for peace can, and the satisfaction of peace is found—is fully possessed, when all selfish desire is abandoned. Then there is fullness of joy, abounding plenty, and rich and complete blessedness.

April Twenty-sixth

Thought for the Morning

A man will reach the Kingdom by purifying himself, and he can only do this by pursuing a process of self-examination and self-analysis.

The selfishness must be discovered and understood before it can be removed. It is powerless to remove itself, neither will it pass away of itself. Darkness ceases only when light is introduced; so ignorance can only be dispersed by knowledge, selfishness by love.

A man must first of all be willing to lose himself (his self-seeking) before he can find himself (his Divine Self). He must realize that selfishness is not worth clinging to, that it is a master altogether unworthy of his service, and that divine goodness alone is worthy to be enthroned in his heart, as the supreme master of his life.

Meditation for the Day

Be strenuous in effort, patient in endurance, strong in resolution.

BY these four things is the heart defiled—the craving for pleasure, the clinging to temporal things, the love of self, the lust for personal continuance; from these four defilements spring all sins and sorrows. Wash thou thy heart; put away sensual cravings; detach thy mind from the wish for possessions; abandon self-defence and self-importance. Thus putting away all cravings, thou wilt attain to satisfaction; detaching thy mind from the love of perishable things, thou wilt acquire wisdom; abandoning the thought of self, thou wilt come to peace. He who is pure is free from desire; he does not crave for sensual excitements; he sets no value on perishable things; he is the same in riches and poverty, in success or failure, in victory or defeat, in life or death. His happiness remains, his rest is sure.

Hold fast to love, and let it shape thy doing.

Thought for the Evening

Be still, my soul, and know that peace is thine. Be steadfast, heart, and know that strength divine Belongs to thee; cease from thy turmoil, mind, and thou the Everlasting Rest shalt find.

If a man would have peace, let him exercise the spirit of peace; if he would find Love, let him dwell in the spirit of Love; if he would escape suffering, let him cease to inflict it; if he would do noble things for humanity, let him cease to do ignoble things for himself. If he will but quarry the mine of his own soul, he shall find there all the materials for building whatsoever he will, and he shall find there also the Central Rock on which to build in safety.

April Twenty-seventh

Thought for the Morning

Men go after much company, and seek out new excitements, but they are not acquainted with peace; in divers paths of pleasure they search for happiness, but they do not come to rest; through divers ways of laughter and feverish delirium they wander after gladness and life, but their tears are many and grievous, and they do not escape death.

Drifting upon the ocean of life in search of selfish indulgences, men are caught in its storms, and only after many tempests and much privation do they fly to the Rock of Refuge which rests in the deep silence of their own being.

Meditation for the Day

*Instruct me in the doing which is according to the Eternal,
so that I may be watchful, and fail not.*

THE unrighteous man is swayed by his feelings; likes and dislikes are his masters; prejudices and partialities blind him; desiring and suffering, craving and sorrowing, self-control he knows not, and great is his unrest. The righteous man is master of his moods; likes and dislikes he has abandoned as childish things; prejudice and partiality he has put away. Desiring nothing, he does not suffer; not craving enjoyment, sorrow does not overtake him; perfect in self-control, great peace abides with him.

Do not condemn, resent, or retaliate; do not argue, or become a partisan. Maintain thy calmness with all sides; be just, and speak the truth. Act in gentleness, compassion, and charity. Be infinitely patient. Hold fast to love, and let it shape thy doing. Have goodwill to all without distinction. Think equally of all, and be disturbed by none.

Be thoughtful and wise, strong and kindhearted.

Thought for the Evening

Meditation centred upon divine realities is the very essence and soul of prayer. It is the silent reaching upward of the soul toward the Eternal.

Meditation is the intense dwelling, in thought, upon an idea or theme with the object of thoroughly comprehending it; and whatsoever you constantly meditate upon, you will not only come to understand, but will grow more and more into its likeness, for it will become incorporated with your very being, will become, in fact, your very self.

If, therefore, you constantly dwell upon that which is selfish and debasing, you will ultimately become selfish and debased; if you ceaselessly think upon that which is pure and unselfish, you will surely become pure and unselfish.

April Twenty-eighth

Thought for the Morning

There is no difficulty, however great, but will yield before a calm and powerful concentration of thought and no legitimate object but may be speedily actualized by the intelligent use and direction of one's soul forces.

Whatever your task may be, concentrate your whole mind upon it; throw into it all the energy of which you are capable. The faultless completion of small tasks, leads inevitably to larger tasks.

See to it that you rise by steady climbing, and you will never fall.

Meditation for the Day

Be watchful, that no thought of self creep in again and stain thee.

THINK of thyself as abolished. In all thy doing think of the good of others and of the world, and not of pleasure or reward to thyself. Thou art no longer separate and divided from men, thou art one with all. No longer strive against others for thyself, but sympathize with all. Regard no man as thine enemy, for thou art the friend of all men. Be at peace with all. Pour out compassion on all living things, and let boundless charity adorn thy words and deeds. Such is the glad way of Truth; such is the doing which is according to the Eternal. Filled with joy is the right-doer; he acts from principles which do not change and pass away. He is one with the Eternal, and has passed beyond unrest. The peace of the righteous man is perfect; it is not disturbed by change and impermanence. Freed from passion, he is equal-minded, calm, and does not sorrow; he sees things as they are, and is no more confused.

Open thine eyes to the Eternal Light.

Thought for the Evening

He who knows that Love is at the heart of all things, and has realized the all-sufficing power of that Love, has no room in his heart for condemnation.

If you love people and speak of them with praise, until they in some way thwart you, or do something of which you disapprove, and then you dislike them and speak of them with dispraise, you are not governed by the Love which is of God. If, in your heart, you are continually arraigning and condemning others, selfless love is hidden from you.

Train your mind in strong, impartial, and gentle thought; train your heart in purity and compassion; train your tongue to silence, and to true and stainless speech; so shall you enter the way of holiness and peace, and shall ultimately realize the immortal Love.

April Twenty-ninth

Thought for the Morning

If you would realize true prosperity, do not settle down, as many have done, into the belief that if you do right everything will go wrong. Do not allow the word "competition" to shake your faith in the supremacy of righteousness. I care not what men say about the "laws of competition," for do not I know the Unchangeable Law which shall one day put them all to rout, and which puts them to rout even now in the heart and life of the righteous man? And knowing this law I can contemplate all dishonesty with undisturbed repose, for I know where certain destruction awaits it.

Under all circumstances *do that which you believe to be right*, and trust the Law; trust the Divine Power which is immanent in the universe, and it will never desert you, and you will always be protected.

Meditation for the Day

Knowledge is for him who seeks;
Wisdom crowneth him who strives;
Peace in sinless silence speaks:
All things perish, Truth survives.

INCREASE thy strength and self-reliance; make
The specters of thy mind obey thy will;
See thou command thyself, nor let no mood,
No subtle passion nor no swift desire
Hurl thee to baseness; but, shouldst thou be hurled,
Rise, and regain thy manhood, taking gain
Of lowliness and wisdom from thy fall.
Strive ever for the mastery of thy mind,
And glean some good from every circumstance
That shall confront thee; make thy store of strength
Richer for ills encountered and overcome.
Submit to naught but nobleness; rejoice
Like a strong athlete straining for the prize,
When thy full strength is tried.

Follow where Virtue leads High and still higher;
Listen where Pureness pleads,
Quench not her fire.
Lo! he shall see Reality,
Who cometh upward, Cleansed from all desire.

Thought for the Evening

Forget yourself entirely in the sorrows of others, and in ministering to others, and divine happiness will emancipate you from all sorrow and suffering. "Taking the first step with a good thought, the second with a good word, and the third with a good deed, I entered Paradise." And you also enter Paradise by pursuing the same course.

Lose yourself in the welfare of others; forget yourself in all that you do—this is the secret of abounding happiness. Ever be on the watch to guard against selfishness and learn faithfully the divine lessons of inward sacrifice; so shall you climb the highest heights of happiness, and shall remain in the never-clouded sunshine of universal joy, clothed in the shining garment of immortality.

April Thirtieth

Thought for the Morning

When the farmer has tilled and dressed his land and put in the seed, he knows that he has done all that he can possibly do, and that now he must trust to the elements, and wait patiently for the course of time to bring about the harvest, and that no amount of expectancy on his part will affect the result.

Even so, he who has realized Truth, goes forth as a sower of the seeds of goodness, purity, love, and peace, without expectancy and never looking for results, knowing that there is the Great Over-ruling Law which brings about its own harvest in due time, and which is alike the source of preservation and destruction.

Meditation for the Day

Deliverance shall him entrance who strives
with sins and sorrows, tears and pains,
Till he attains.

BE not the slave
Of lusts and cravings and indulgences,
Of disappointments, miseries, and griefs,
Fears, doubts, and lamentations, but control
Thyself with calmness: master that in thee
Which masters others, and which heretofore
Has mastered thee: let not thy passions rule,
But rule thy passions; subjugate thyself
Till passion is transmuted into peace,
And wisdom crown thee; so shalt thou attain
And, by attaining, know.

Look thou within. Lo! In the midst of change
Abides the Changeless; at the heart of strife
The Perfect Peace reposes. At the root
Of all the restless striving of the world
Is passion. Whoso follows passion findeth pain,
But whoso conquers passion findeth peace.

I am ignorant, yet strive to know; nor will I cease to strive till I attain.

Thought for the Evening

The virtuous put a check upon themselves, and set a watch upon their passions and emotions; in this way they gain possession of the mind, and gradually acquire calmness;

and as they acquire influence, power, greatness, abiding joy, and fullness and completeness of life.

He only finds peace who conquers himself, who strives, day by day, after greater self-possession, greater self-control, and greater calmness of mind.

Where the calm mind is there is strength and rest, there is love and wisdom; there is one who has fought successfully innumerable battles against self, who, after long toil in secret against his own failings, has triumphed at last.

May First

Thought for the Morning

In aiming at the life of blessedness, one of the simplest beginnings to be considered, and rightly made, is that which we all make every day—namely, the beginning of each day's life. There is a sense in which every day may be regarded as the beginning of a new life, in which one can think, act, and live newly, and in a wiser and better spirit. The right beginning of the day will be followed by a cheerfulness permeating the household with a sunny influence, and the tasks and duties of the day will be undertaken in a strong and confident spirit, and the whole day will be well lived.

Meditation for the Day

Comfort ye! The heights of Blessed Vision ye shall reach.

EOLAUS: I know that sorrow follows passion; know
That grief and emptiness, and heartaches wait
Upon all earthly joys; so am I sad;
Yet Truth must be, and being, can be found;
And though I am in sorrow, this I know
I shall be glad when I have found the Truth.

Prophet: There is no gladness like the joy of Truth.
The pure in heart swim in a sea of bliss
That evermore nor sorrow knows, nor pain;
For who can see the Cosmos and be sad?
To know is to be happy; they rejoice
Who have attained Perfection; these are they
Who live, and know, and realize the Truth.

He findeth Truth who findeth self-control.

Thought for the Evening

There can be no progress, no achievement, without sacrifice, and a man's worldly success will be in the measure that he sacrifices his confused animal thoughts, and fixes his mind on the development of his plans, and the strengthening of his resolution and self-reliance. And the higher he lifts his thoughts, the more manly, upright, and righteous he becomes, the greater will be his success, the more blessed and enduring will be his achievements.

May Second

Thought for the Morning

None but right acts can follow right thoughts; none but a right life can follow right acts; and by living a right life all blessedness is achieved. Mind is the Master-power that moulds and makes. And Man is Mind, and evermore he takes the tool of thought, and, shaping what he wills, brings forth a thousand joys, a thousand ills;—He thinks in secret, and it comes to pass: environment is but his looking-glass.

Meditation for the Day

Not in any of the three worlds can the soul find lasting satisfaction,
apart from the realization of righteousness.

EVERY soul, consciously or unconsciously, hungers for righteousness, and every soul seeks to gratify that hunger in its own particular way, and in accordance with its own particular state of knowledge. The hunger is one, and the righteousness is one, but the pathways by which righteousness is sought are many. They who seek consciously are blessed, and shall shortly find that final and permanent satisfaction of soul which righteousness alone can give, for they have come into a knowledge of the true path. They who seek unconsciously, although for a time they may bathe in a sea of pleasure, are not blessed, for they are carving out for themselves pathways of suffering, over which they must walk with torn and wounded feet, and the soul will cry out for its lost heritage—the eternal heritage of the righteous.

Blessed are they who earnestly and intelligently seek.

Thought for the Evening

Calmness of mind is one of the beautiful jewels of wisdom. A man becomes calm in the measure that he understands himself as a thought-evolved being. . . and he as he develops a right understanding, and sees more and more clearly the internal relations of things by the action of cause and effect, he ceases to fret and fume, and worry and grieve, and remains poised, steadfast, serene.

May Third

Thought for the Morning

To follow, under all circumstances, the highest promptings within you; to be always true to the divine self; to reply upon the inward voice, the inward light, and to pursue your purpose with a fearless and restful heart, believing that the future will yield unto you the need of every thought and effort; knowing that the laws of the universe can never fail, and that your own will come back to you with mathematical exactitude—this is faith and the living of faith.

Meditation for the Day

Glorious, radiant, free, detached from the tyranny of self!

THE journey to the Kingdom may be a long and tedious one, or it may be short and rapid. It may occupy a minute, or it may take a thousand ages. Everything depends on the faith and belief of the searcher. The majority cannot "enter in because of their unbelief"; for how can men realize righteousness when they do not believe in it, nor in the possibility of its accomplishment? Neither is it necessary to leave the outer world, and one's duties therein. Nay, it can only be found through the unselfish performance of one's duty. But all who believe, and aspire to achieve, will sooner or later arrive at victory, if, amid all their worldly duties, they faint not, nor lose sight of the Ideal Goodness, and continue, with unshaken resolve, to "press on to Perfection".

The outward life harmonizes itself with the inward music.

Thought for the Evening

Have a thorough understanding of your work, and let it be your own; and as you proceed, ever following the inward guide, the infallible voice, you will pass on from victory to victory, and will rise step by step to higher resting-places, and your ever broadening outlook will gradually reveal to you the essential beauty and purpose of life. Self-purified, health will be yours; self-governed, power will be yours, and all that you do will prosper.

And I may stand where health, success, and power await my coming, if, each fleeting hour, I cling to love and patience; and abide with stainlessness; and never step aside from high integrity; so shall I see at last the land of immortality.

May Fourth

Thought for the Morning

When the tongue is well controlled and wisely subdued; when selfish impulses and unworthy thoughts no longer rush to the tongue demanding utterance; when the speech has become harmless, pure, gracious, gentle, and purposeful, and no word is uttered but in sincerity and truth—then are the five steps in virtuous speech accomplished, then is the second great lesson in Truth learned and mastered. Make pure thy heart, and thou wilt make thy life rich, sweet and beautiful.

Meditation for the Day

The regulation and purification of conduct.

THE whole journey from the Kingdom of Strife to the Kingdom of Love resolves itself into a process which may be summed up in the following words:—the regulation and purification of conduct. Such a process must, if assiduously pursued, necessarily lead to perfection. It will also be seen that as the man obtains the mastery over certain forces within himself, he arrives at a knowledge of all the laws which operate in the realm of all these forces, and by watching the ceaseless working of cause and effect within himself, until he understands it, he then understands it in its universal adjustments in the body of humanity.

The process is also one of simplification of the mind, a sifting away of all but the essential gold in character.

He lives no longer for himself, he lives for others:
and so living, he enjoys the highest bliss, the deepest peace.

Thought for the Evening

Having clothed himself with humility, the first questions a man asks himself are:—

"How am I acting towards others?"
"What am I doing to others?"
"How am I thinking of others?"
"Are my thoughts of, and acts towards others prompted by unselfish love?"

As a man, in the silence of his soul, asks himself these searching questions, he will unerringly see where he has hitherto failed.

May Fifth

Thought for the Morning

To dwell in love always and towards all is to live the true life, is to have Life itself. Knowing this, the good man gives up himself unreservedly to the Spirit of Love, and dwells in Love towards all, contending with none, condemning none, but loving all.

The Christ Spirit of Love puts an end, not only to all sin, but to all division and contention.

Meditation for the Day

*Apart from the earnest striving to live out
the teachings of Jesus, there can be no true life.*

A GOOD man is the flower of humanity, and to daily grow purer, nobler, more Godlike, by overcoming some selfish tendency, is to be continually drawing nearer to the Divine Heart. "He that would be My disciple, let him deny himself daily" is a statement which none can misunderstand or misapply, howsoever he may ignore it. Nowhere in the universe is there any substitute for Goodness; and until a man has this, he has nothing worthy or enduring. To the possession of Goodness there is only one way, and that is, *to give up all and everything that is opposed to Goodness*. Every selfish desire must be eradicated; every impure thought must be yielded up; every clinging to opinion must be sacrificed; and it is in the doing of this that constitutes the following of Christ.

*That which is above all creeds, beliefs, and opinions
is a loving and self-sacrificing heart.*

Thought for the Evening

When sin and self are abandoned, the heart is restored to its imperishable Joy. Joy comes and fills the self-emptied heart; it abides with the peaceful; its reign is with the pure. Joy flees from the selfish, it deserts the quarrelsome; it is hidden from the impure. Joy cannot remain with the selfish; it is wedded to Love.

May Sixth

Thought for the Morning

In the pure heart there is no room left where personal judgments and hatreds can find lodgement, for it is filled to overflowing with tenderness and love; it sees no evil, and only as men succeed in seeing no evil in others will they become free from sin, and sorrow, and suffering. If men only understood that the heart that sins must sorrow, that the hateful mind tomorrow reaps its barren harvest, weeping, starving, resting not, nor sleeping; tenderness would fill their being, they would see with pity's seeing, if they only understood.

Meditation for the Day

To dwell in love always and towards all
is to live the true life, is to have Life itself.

JESUS so lived, and all men may so live, if they will humbly and faithfully carry out His precepts. So long as they refuse to do this, clinging to their desires, passions, and opinions, they cannot be ranked as His disciples; they are the disciples of self. "Verily, verily, I say unto you: whosoever committeth sin is the servant of sin," is the searching declaration of Jesus. Let men cease to delude themselves with the belief that they can retain their bad tempers, their lusts, their harsh words and judgments, their personal hatreds, their petty contentions and darling opinions, and yet have Christ. All that divides man from man, and man from Goodness, is not of Christ, for Christ is Love.

Sin and Christ cannot dwell together, and he who
accepts the Christ-life of pure Goodness ceases from sin.

Thought for the Evening

To stand face to face with truth; to arrive, after innumerable wanderings and pains, at wisdom and bliss; not to be finally defeated and cast out, but to ultimately triumph over every inward foe—such is man's divine destiny, such his glorious goal; and this, every saint, sage, and saviour has declared. A man only begins to be a man when he ceases to whine and revile, and commences to search for the hidden justice which regulates his life. And as he adapts his mind to that regulating factor, he ceases to accuse others as the cause of his condition, and builds himself up in strong and noble thoughts; ceases to kick against circumstances, but begins to use them as aids to his more rapid progress, and as a means of discovering the hidden power and possibilities within himself.

May Seventh

Thought for the Morning

The will to evil and the will to good are both within thee, which wilt thou employ? Thou knowest what is right and what is wrong, which wilt though love and foster, which destroy?

Thou art the chooser of thy thoughts and deeds; thou art the maker of thine inward state; the power is thine to be what thou wilt be; thou buildest Truth and Love, or lies and hate.

Meditation for the Day

When Christ is disputed about, Christ is lost.

IT is no less selfish and sinful to cling to opinion than to cling to impure desire. Knowing this, the good man gives up himself unreservedly to the Spirit of Love, and dwells in Love towards all, contending with none, condemning none, hating none, but loving all, seeing behind their opinions, their creeds, and their sins, into their striving, suffering, and sorrowing hearts. "He that loveth his life shall lose it." Eternal life belongs to him who will obediently relinquish his petty, narrowing, sin-loving, strife-producing personal self, for only by so doing can he enter into the large, beautiful, free, and glorious life of abounding Love. Herein is the Path of Life; for the Straight Gate is the Gate of Goodness.

The narrow way is the Way of Renunciation, or self-sacrifice.

Thought for the Evening

The teaching of Jesus brings men back to the simple truth that righteousness, or *right-doing*, is entirely a matter of individual conduct, and not a mystical something apart from a man's thoughts and deeds.

Calmness and patience can become habitual by first grasping, through effort, a calm and patient thought, and then continuously thinking it, and living in it, until "use becomes second nature," and anger and impatience pass away for ever.

May Eighth

Thought for the Morning

Man is made or unmade by himself; in the armoury of thought he forges the weapons by which he destroys himself; he also fashions the tools with which he builds for himself heavenly mansions of joy and strength and peace. By the right choice and true application of thought man ascends to the Divine Perfection; by the abuse and wrong application of thought he descends below the level of the beast. Between these two extremes are all the grades of character and man is their maker and master.

As a being of Power, Intelligence, and Love, and the lord of his own thoughts, man holds the key to every situation.

Meditation for the Day

A man can learn nothing unless he regards himself as a learner.

"How am I acting towards others?"
"What am I doing for others?"
"How am I thinking of others?"

"Are my thoughts of, and acts towards others, prompted by unselfish love, as I would theirs should be to me; or are they the outcome of personal dislike, of petty revenge, or of narrow bigotry and condemnation?"

As a man, in the sacred silence of his soul, asks himself these searching questions, applying all his thoughts and acts to the spirit of the primary precept of the Christ, his understanding will become illuminated, so that he will unerringly see where he has hitherto failed; and he will see what he has got to do in rectifying his heart and conduct, and the way in which it is to be done.

Evil is not worth resisting.
The practice of the good is supremely excellent.

Thought for the Evening

Whatsoever you harbour in the inmost chambers of your heart will, sooner or later, by the inevitable law of reaction, shape itself in your outward life.

Every soul attracts its own, and nothing can possibly come to it that does not belong to it. To realize this is to recognize the universality of Divine Law.

If thou would'st right the world, and banish all its evils and its woes, make its wild places bloom, and its drear deserts blossom as the rose—then right thyself.

May Ninth

Thought for the Morning

Whatever conditions are rendering your life burdensome, you may pass out of and beyond them by developing and utilizing within you the transforming power of self-purification and self-conquest.

Before the divine radiance of a pure heart all darkness vanishes and all clouds melt away, and he who has conquered self has conquered the universe.

He who sets his foot firmly upon the path of self-conquest, who walks, aided by the staff of faith, the highway of self-sacrifice, will assuredly achieve the highest prosperity, and will reap abounding and enduring joy and bliss.

Meditation for the Day

Personal antipathies, however natural they may be
to the animal man, can have no place in the divine life.

WHILST a man is engaged in resisting evil, he is not only not practising the good, he is actually involved in the like passion and prejudice which he condemns in another; and as a direct result of his attitude of mind, he himself is resisted by others as evil. Resist a man, a party, a religion, a government, as evil, and you yourself will be resisted as evil. He who considers it as a great evil that he should be persecuted and condemned, let him cease to persecute and condemn. Let him turn away from all that he has hitherto regarded as evil, and begin to look for the good. So deep and far-reaching is this precept that the practice of it will fake a man far up the heights of spiritual knowledge and attainment.

He who will keep the precepts of Jesus will conquer
himself, and will become divinely illuminated.

Thought for the Evening

It is the silent and conquering thought forces which bring all things into manifestation. The universe grew out of thought.

To adjust all your thoughts to a perfect and unswerving faith in the omnipotence and supremacy of Good is to co-operate with that Good, and to realize within yourself the solution and destruction of all evil.

To mentally deny evil is not sufficient; it must, by daily practice, be risen above and understood. To affirm the Good mentally is inadequate; it must, by unswerving endeavour, be entered into and comprehended.

May Tenth

Thought for the Morning

Every thought you think is a force sent out. Whatever your position in life may be, before you can hope to enter into any measure of success, usefulness, and power, you must learn how to focus your thought forces by cultivating calmness and repose.

There is no difficulty, however great, but will yield before a calm and purposeful concentration of thought, and no legitimate object but may be speedily actualized by the intelligent use and direction of one's soul forces.

Think good thoughts, and they will quickly become actualized in your outward life in the form of good conditions.

Meditation for the Day

Humanity is essentially divine.

SO long as man dwelt in the habitations of sin that he has at last come to regard himself as native to it, and as being cut off from the Divine Source, which he believes to be outside and away from him. Man is primarily a spiritual being, and as such, is of the nature and substance of the Eternal Spirit, the Unchangeable Reality, which men call God. Goodness, not sin, is his rightful condition; perfection, not imperfection, is his heritage, and this a man may enter into and realize *now* if he will grant the condition, which is the denial or abandonment of self, that is, of his feverish desires, his proud will, his egotism and self-seeking all that which St. Paul calls the "natural man".

Jesus, in His divine goodness, knew the human heart,
and He knew that it was good.

Thought for the Evening

That which you would be and hope to be, you may be now. Non-accomplishment resides in your perpetual postponement, and, having the power to postpone, you also have the power to accomplish—to perpetually accomplish: realize this truth, and you shall be today, and every day, the ideal being of whom you dreamed.

Say to yourself, "I will live in my Ideal now; I will manifest my ideal now; I will be my Ideal now; and all that tempts me away from my Ideal I will not listen to; I will listen only to the voice of my Ideal."

May Eleventh

Thought for the Morning

Be as a flower; content to be, to grow in sweetness day by day. If thou would'st perfect thyself in knowledge, perfect thyself in Love. If thou would'st reach the Highest, ceaselessly cultivate a loving and compassionate heart.

To him who chooses Goodness, sacrificing all, is given that which is more than, and includes, all.

Meditation for the Day

He who would find how good at heart men are, let him
throw away all his ideas and suspicions about the "evil" in others,
and find and practise the good within himself.

MAN has within him the divine power by which he can rise to the highest heights of spiritual achievement; by which he can shake off sin and shame and sorrow, and do the will of the Father, the Supreme Good; by which he can conquer all the powers of darkness within, and stand radiant and free; by which he can subdue the world, and scale the lofty pinnacles of God. This can man, by choice, by resolve, and by his divine strength, accomplish; but he can only accomplish it in and by *obedience*; he must choose meekness and lowliness of heart; he must abandon strife for peace; passion for purity; hatred for love; self-seeking for self-sacrifice, and must overcome evil with good.

This is the holy way of Truth;
this is the safe and abiding salvation;
this is the yoke and burden of the Christ.

Thought for the Evening

The Great Law never cheats any man of his just due.

Human life, when rightly lived, is simple with a beautiful simplicity.

He who comprehends the utter simplicity of life, who obeys its laws, and does not step aside into the dark paths and complex mazes of selfish desire, stands where no harm can reach him.

Then there is fullness of joy, abounding plenty, and rich and complete blessedness.

May Twelfth

Thought for the Morning

Every man reaps the results of his own thoughts and deeds, and suffers for his own wrong.

He who begins right, and continues right, does not need to desire, and search for felicitous results; they are already at hand; they follow as consequences; they are the certainties, the realities, of life.

Sweet is the rest and deep is the bliss of him who has freed his heart from its lusts and hatreds and dark desires.

Meditation for the Day

The Gospel of Jesus is a Gospel of living and doing.

THAT Jesus was meek, and lowly, and loving, and compassionate, and pure is very beautiful, but it is not sufficient; it is necessary that you also should be meek, and lowly, and loving, and compassionate, and pure. That Jesus subordinated His own will to the will of the Father, it is inspiring to know, but it is not sufficient; it is necessary that you, too, should likewise subordinate your will to that of the overruling Good. The grace and beauty and goodness that were in Jesus can be of no value to you, cannot be understood by you, unless they are also *in you*, and they can never be in you until you *practice* them, for, apart from *doing*, the qualities which constitute Goodness do not, as far as you are concerned, exist.

Pure Goodness is religion, and outside it there is no religion.

Thought for the Evening

You are the creator of your own shadows; you desire, and then you grieve; renounce, and then you shall rejoice.

Of all the beautiful truths pertaining to the soul. . . none is more gladdening or fruitful of divine promise and confidence than this—that man is the master of thought, the moulder of character, and the maker and shaper of character, environment, and destiny.

May Thirteenth

Thought for the Morning

As darkness is a passing shadow, and light is a substance that remains, so sorrow is fleeting, but joy abides for ever. No true thing can pass away and become lost; no false thing can remain and be preserved. Sorrow is false, and it cannot live; joy is true, and it cannot die. Joy may become hidden for a time, but it can always be recovered; sorrow may remain for a period, but it can be transcended and dispersed.

Do not think your sorrow will remain; it will pass away like a cloud. Do not believe that the torments of sin are ever your portion; they will vanish like a hideous nightmare. Awake! Arise! Be holy and joyful.

Meditation for the Day

*They are the doers of the Father's will
who shape their conduct to the Divine precepts.*

TO us and to all there is no sufficiency, I no blessedness, no peace to be derived I from the goodness of another, not even the goodness of God; not until the goodness is *done* by us, not until it is, by constant effort, incorporated into our being, can we know and possess its blessedness and peace. Therefore, thou who adorest Jesus for His divine qualities, practise those qualities thyself, and thou too shalt be divine.

The teaching of Jesus brings men back to the simple truth that righteousness, or *right-doing*, is entirely a matter of individual conduct, and not a mystical something apart from a man's thoughts and actions, and that each must be righteous for himself; each must be a *doer* of the word, and it is a man's *own* doing that brings him peace and gladness of heart, not the doing of another.

It is only the doer of forgiveness who tastes the sweets of forgiveness.

Thought for the Evening

Tribulation lasts only so long as there remains some chaff of self which needs to be removed. The *tribulum*, or threshing machine, ceases to work when all the grain is separated from the chaff; and when the last impurities are blown away from the soul, tribulation has completed its work, and there is no more need for it; then abiding joy is realized.

The sole and supreme use of suffering is to purify, to burn out all that is useless and impure. Suffering ceases for him who is pure. There could be no object in burning gold after the dross had been removed.

May Fourteenth

Thought for the Morning

In speaking of self-control, one is easily misunderstood. It should not be associated with a destructive repression, but with a constructive expression.

A man is happy, wise and great in the measure that he controls himself; he is wretched, foolish, and mean in the measure that he allows his animal nature to dominate his thoughts and actions.

He who controls himself, controls his life, his circumstances, his destiny; and wherever he goes he carries his happiness with him as an abiding possession.

Renunciation precedes regeneration. The permanent happiness which men seek in dissipation, excitement, and abandonment to unworthy pleasures, is found only in the life which reverses all this—the life of self-control.

Meditation for the Day

The Christ is the Spirit of Love.

WHEN Jesus said, "Without Me ye can do nothing," He spoke not of His perishable form, but of the Universal Spirit of Love, of which His conduct was a perfect manifestation; and this utterance of His is the statement of a simple truth; for the works of men are vain and worthless when they are done for personal ends, and he himself remains a perishable being, immersed in darkness and fearing death, so long as he lives in his personal gratifications. The animal in man can never respond to and know the divine; only the divine can respond to the divine. The spirit of hatred in man can never vibrate in unison with the Spirit of Love; Love only can apprehend Love, and become linked with it. Man is divine; man is of the substance of Love; this he may realize if he will relinquish the impure, personal elements which he has hitherto been blindly following, and will fly to the impersonal Realities of the Christ Spirit.

In this Principle of Love,
all Knowledge, Intelligence, and Wisdom
are contained.

Thought for the Evening

Law, not confusion, is the dominating principle in the universe; justice, not injustice is the soul and substance of life; and righteousness, not corruption, is the moulding and moving force in the spiritual government of the world. This being so, man has but the right himself to find that the universe is right.

When I am pure, I shall have solved the mystery of life; I shall be sure, when I am free from hatred, lust and strife, I am in Truth, and Truth abides in me; I shall be safe, and sane, and wholly free, when I am pure.

May Fifteenth

Thought for the Morning

If men only understood that their hatred and resentment slays their peace and sweet contentment, hurts themselves, helps not another, does not cheer one lonely brother, they would seek the better doing of good deeds which leaves no ruing:—

If they only understood.

If men only understood how Love conquers; how prevailing is its might, grim hate assailing; how compassion endeth sorrow, maketh wise, and doth not borrow pain of passion, they would ever live in Love, in hatred never:—

If they only understood.

Meditation for the Day

Love is not complete until it is lived by man.

EVERY precept of Jesus demands the unconditional sacrifice of some selfish, personal element, before it can be carried out. Man cannot know the Real whilst he clings to the unreal; he cannot do the work of Truth whilst he clings to error. Whilst a man cherishes lust, hatred, pride, vanity, self-indulgence, covetousness, he can do nothing, for the works of all these sinful elements are unreal and perishable. Only when he takes refuge in the Spirit of Love within, and becomes patient, gentle, pure, pitiful, and forgiving, does he the works of Righteousness, and bears the fruits of Life. The vine is not a vine without its branches, and even then it is not complete until those branches *bear fruit.*

Daily practising love towards all in heart and mind and deed, harbouring no injurious or impure thoughts, he discovers the imperishable Principles of his being.

Man's only refuge from sin is sinless Love.

Thought for the Evening

The grace and beauty that were in Jesus can be of no value to you—cannot be understood by you—unless they are also *in you*, and they can never be in you, until you practice them, for, apart from *doing*, the qualities which constitute goodness do not, as far as you are concerned, exist.

To adore Jesus for his good qualities is a long step towards Truth, but to practice those qualities is Truth itself; and he who fully adores the perfection of another will not rest content in his own imperfection, but will fashion his soul after the likeness of that other.

Therefore thou who adorest Jesus for his divine qualities, practice those qualities thyself, and thou too shalt be divine.

May Sixteenth

Thought for the Morning

Let a man realize that life in its totality proceeds from the mind, and lo, the way of blessedness is opened up to him! For he will then discover that he possesses the power to rule his mind and to fashion it in accordance with his Ideal.

So will he elect to strongly and steadfastly walk those pathways of thought and action which are altogether excellent; to him life will become beautiful and sacred; and, sooner or later, he will put to flight all evil, confusion, and suffering; for it is impossible for a man to fall short of liberation, enlightenment, and peace, who guards with unwearying diligence the gateway of his heart.

Meditation for the Day

Before a man can know Love as the abiding Reality within him, he must utterly abandon all those human tendencies which frustrate its perfect manifestation.

MAN can only consciously ally himself, to the Vine of Love by deserting all strife, and hatred, and condemnation, and impurity, and pride, and self-seeking, and by thinking and doing loving deeds. By so doing he awakens within him the divine nature which he has heretofore been crucifying and denying. Every time a man gives way to anger, impatience, greed, pride, vanity, or any form of personal selfishness, he denies the Christ, he shuts himself out from Love. And thus only is Christ denied, and not by refusing to adopt a formulated creed. Christ is only known to him who by constant striving has converted himself from a sinful to a pure being, who by noble, moral effort has succeeded in relinquishing that perishable self, which is the source of all suffering and sorrow and unrest, and has become rational, gentle, peaceful, loving, and pure.

Such glorious realization is the crown of evolution, the supreme aim of existence.

Thought for the Evening

By constantly overcoming self, a man gains a knowledge of the subtle intricacies of his mind; and it is this divine knowledge which enables him to become established in calmness.

Without self-knowledge there can be no abiding peace of mind, and those who are carried away by tempestuous passions, cannot approach the holy place where calmness reigns.

The weak man is like one who, having mounted a fiery steed, allows it to run away with him, and carry him withersoever it wills; the strong man is like one who, having mounted the steed, governs it with a masterly hand and makes it go in whatever direction and at whatever speed he commands.

May Seventeenth

Thought for the Morning

There is no strife, no selfishness, in the Kingdom; there is perfect harmony, equipoise, and rest.

Those who live in the Kingdom of Love, have all their needs supplied by the Law of Love.

As self is the root cause of all strife and suffering, so Love is the root cause of all peace and bliss. Those who are at rest in the Kingdom do not look for happiness in any outward possessions. They are freed from all anxiety and trouble and, resting in Love, they are the embodiment of happiness.

Meditation for the Day

As self is the root cause of all strife and suffering, so Love
is the root cause of all peace and bliss.

THOSE who are at rest in the Kingdom do not look for happiness in any outward possession. They see that all l such possessions are mere transient effects that come when they are required, and, after their purpose is served, pass away. They never think of these things (money, clothing, food, etc.) except as mere accessories and *effects* of the true Life. They are, therefore, freed from all anxiety and trouble, and, resting in Love, they are the embodiment of Happiness. Standing upon the imperishable Principles of Purity, Compassion, Wisdom, and Love, they are immortal, and know they are immortal; they are one with God, the Supreme Good, and know they are one with God. Seeing the realities of things, they can find no room anywhere for condemnation.

All men are essentially divine, though unaware of their divine nature.

Thought for the Evening

Let it not be supposed that the children of the Kingdom live in ease and indolence (these two sins are the first that have to be eradicated when the search for the Kingdom is entered upon); they live in a peaceful activity; in fact, they only truly live, for the life of self, with its train of worries, griefs, and fears, is not *real life*.

The children of the Kingdom are *known by their life*, they manifest the fruits of the Spirit—"Love, joy, peace, long-suffering, kindness, goodness, faithfulness, meekness, temperance, and self-control"—under all circumstances and vicissitudes.

May Eighteenth

Thought for the Morning

The gospel of Jesus is a gospel of *living and doing*. If it were not this it would not voice the Eternal Truth. Its Temple is *Purified Conduct*, the entrance-door to which is *Self-Surrender*. It invites men to shake off sin, and promises, as a result, joy and blessedness and perfect peace.

The Kingdom of Heaven is perfect trust, perfect knowledge, perfect peace. . . no sin can enter therein, no self-born thought or deed can pass its golden gates; no impure desire can defile its radiant robes. . . all may enter it who will, but all must pay the price—*the unconditional abandonment of self.*

Meditation for the Day

All so-called evil is seen to be rooted in ignorance.

LET it not be supposed that the children of the Kingdom live in ease and indolence (these two sins are the first that have to be eradicated when the search for the Kingdom is entered upon); they live in a peaceful activity; in fact, *they only* truly live, for the life of self, with its train of worries, griefs, and fears, is not *real* life. They perform all their duties with the most scrupulous diligence, apart from thoughts of self, and employ all their means, as well as powers and faculties, which are greatly intensified, in building up the Kingdom of Righteousness in the hearts of others, and in the world around them. This is their work, first by example, then by precept. They sorrow no more, but live in perpetual gladness, for, though they see the suffering in the world, they also see the final Bliss and the Eternal Refuge.

Whosoever is ready may come now.

Thought for the Evening

I say this—and know it to be truth—*that circumstances can only affect you in so far as you allow them to do so.* You are swayed by circumstances because you have not a right understanding of the nature, use, and power of thought. You believe (and upon this little word *belief* hang all our joys and sorrows) that outward things have the power to make or mar your life; by so doing you submit to those outward things, confess that you are their slave, and they your unconditional master. By so doing you invest them with a power which they do not of themselves possess, and you succumb, in reality not to the circumstances, but to the gloom or gladness, the fear or hope, the strength of weakness, which your thought-sphere has thrown around them.

May Nineteenth

Thought for the Morning

If you are one of those who are praying for, and looking forward to a happier world beyond the grave, here is a message of gladness for you—you may enter into and realize that happy world now; it fills the whole universe, and it is within you, waiting for you to find, acknowledge, and possess.

Said one who understood the inner laws of Being—"When men shall say, lo here, or lo there, go not after them. The Kingdom of God is within you."

Meditation for the Day

Heaven is not a speculative thing beyond the tomb
but a real, ever-present Heaven in the heart.

THE only salvation recognized and taught by Jesus is salvation from sin, and the effects of sin, *here and now*; and this must be effected by utterly abandoning sin, which, having done, the Kingdom of God is realized in the heart as a state of perfect knowledge, perfect blessedness, perfect peace.

"Except a man be born again, he cannot see the Kingdom of God." A man must become a new creature, and how can he become new except by utterly abandoning the old? That man's last state is worse than his first who imagines that, though still continuing to cling to his old temper, his old opinionativeness, his old vanity, his old selfishness, he is constituted a "new creature" in some mysterious and unexplainable way by the adoption of some particular theology or religious formula.

Heaven is where Love rules, and where peace is never absent.

Thought for the Evening

Heaven and hell are inward states. Sink into self and all its gratifications, and you sink into hell; rise above self into that state of consciousness which is the utter denial and forgetfulness of self, and you enter heaven.

So long as you persist in selfishly seeking for your own personal happiness, so long will happiness elude you, and you will be sowing the seeds of wretchedness. In so far as you succeed in losing yourself in the service of others, in that measure will happiness come to you, and you will reap a harvest of bliss.

May Twentieth

Thought for the Morning

Sympathy given can never be waste.

One aspect of sympathy is that of pity—pity for the distressed or pain stricken, with a desire to alleviate or help them in their sufferings. The world needs more of this divine quality.

"For pity makes the world soft to the weak, and noble for the strong."

Another form of sympathy is that of rejoicing with others who are more successful than ourselves, and though their success were our own.

Meditation for the Day

*To the faithful, humble, and true will be revealed the sublime
Vision of the Perfect One.*

GOOD NEWS indeed is that message of Jesus which reveals to man His divine possibilities; which says in substance to sin-stricken humanity, "Take up thy bed and walk"; which tells man that he need no longer remain the creature of darkness and ignorance and sin, if he will but believe in *Goodness*, and will watch and strive and conquer until he has actualized in his life the Goodness that is sinless. And in thus believing and overcoming, man has not only the guide of that Perfect Rule which Jesus has embodied in His precepts, he has also the inward Guide, the Spirit of Truth in his own heart, "The Light that lighteth every man that cometh into the world," which, as he follows it, will infallibly witness to the divine origin of those precepts.

Realize the perfect Goodness of the Eternal Christ.

Thought for the Evening

Sweet are companionships, pleasures, and material comforts, but they change and fade away. Sweeter still are Purity, Wisdom, and the knowledge of Truth, and these never change nor fade away.

He who attained to the possession of spiritual things can never be deprived of his source of happiness; he will never have to part company with it, and wherever he goes in the whole universe, he will carry his possessions with him. His spiritual end will be the fullness of joy.

May Twenty-first

Thought for the Morning

Let your heart grow and expand with ever broadening love, until, freed from all hatred, and passion, and condemnation, it embraces the whole universe with thoughtful tenderness.

As the flower opens its petals to receive the morning light, so open your soul more and more to the glorious light of Truth.

Soar upward on the wings of aspiration; be fearless and believe in the loftiest possibilities.

Meditation for the Day

The Kingdom of Heaven is perfect trust, perfect knowledge, perfect peace.

THE children of the Kingdom are *known by their life*. They manifest the fruits of the Spirit—"love, joy, peace, long-suffering, kindness, goodness, faithfulness, meekness, temperance, self-control" under all circumstances and vicissitudes. They are entirely free from anger, fear, suspicion, jealousy, caprice, anxiety, and grief. Living in the Righteousness of God, they manifest qualities which are the very reverse of those which obtain in the world, and which are regarded by the world as foolish. They demand no *rights*; they do not defend themselves; do not retaliate; do good to those who attempt to injure them; manifest the same gentle spirit towards those who oppose and attack them, as towards those who agree with them; do not pass judgment on others; condemn no man and no system, and live at peace with all.

That Kingdom is in the heart of every man and woman.

Thought for the Evening

Mind clothes itself in garments of its own making. Mind is the arbiter of life; it is the creator and shaper of conditions, and the recipient of its own results. It contains within itself both the power to create illusion and to perceive reality.

Mind is the infallible weaver of destiny; thought is the thread, good and evil deeds are the warp and woof, and the web, woven upon the loom of life, is character. Make pure thy heart, and thou wilt make thy life, rich, sweet, and beautiful, unmarred by strife.

May Twenty-second

Thought for the Morning

Cherish your visions; cherish your ideals; cherish the music that stirs in your heart, the beauty that forms in your mind, the loveliness that drapes your purest thoughts, for out of them will grow all delightful conditions, all heavenly environment; of these, if you will remain true to them, your world will at last be built.

Guard well thy mind, and, noble, strong, and free, nothing shall harm, disturb or conquer thee; for all thy foes are in thy heart and mind, there also thy salvation thou shalt find.

Meditation for the Day

Find the Kingdom by daily effort and patient work.

TEMPLE of Righteousness is built, and its four walls are the four Principles—Purity, Wisdom, Compassion, Love. Peace is its roof, its floor is Steadfastness, its entrance door is Selfless Duty, its atmosphere is Inspiration, and its music is the Joy of the perfect. It cannot be shaken, and, being eternal and indestructible, there is no more need to seek protection in taking thought for the things of the morrow. And the Kingdom of Heaven being established in the heart, the obtaining of the material necessities of life is no more considered, for, having found the Highest, all these things are added as effect to cause, the struggle for existence has ceased, and the spiritual, mental, and material needs are daily supplied from the Universal Abundance.

Pay the price . . . the unconditional abandonment of self.

Thought for the Evening

Dream lofty dreams, and as you dream so shall you become. Your vision is the promise of what you shall one day be; your Ideal is the prophecy of what you shall at last unveil.

The greatest achievement was at first and for a time a dream. The oak sleeps in the acorn; the bird waits in the egg; and in the highest vision of the soul a waking angel stirs.

Your circumstances may be uncongenial, but they shall not long remain so when you perceive an Ideal and strive to reach it.

May Twenty-third

Thought for the Morning

He who has conquered doubt and fear has conquered failure. His every thought is allied with power, and all difficulties are bravely met and wisely overcome. His purposes are seasonably planted, and they bloom and bring forth fruit which does not fall prematurely to the ground.

Thought allied fearlessly to purpose becomes creative force: he who knows this is ready to become something higher and stronger than a mere bundle of wavering thoughts and fluctuating sensations; he who does this has become the conscious and intelligent wielder of his mental powers.

Meditation for the Day

All things are possible now, and only now.

NOW is the reality in which time is; contained. It is more and greater than time; it is an ever-present reality. It knows neither past nor future, and is eternally potent and substantial. Every minute, every day, every year is a dream as soon as it has passed, and exists only as an imperfect and unsubstantial picture in the memory, if it be not entirely obliterated.

Past and future are dreams; *now* is a reality. All things are now; all power, all possibility, all action is now. Not to act and accomplish now is not to act and accomplish at all. To live in thoughts of what you might have done, or in dreams of what you mean to do, this is folly; but to put away regret, to anchor anticipation, and to do and to work *now*, this is wisdom.

Man has all power now.

Thought for the Evening

Man's true place in the Cosmos is that of a king, not a slave, a commander under the Law of Good, and not a helpless tool in the region of evil.

I write for men, not for babes; for those who are eager to learn, and earnest to achieve; for those who will put away (for the world's good) a petty personal indulgence, a selfish desire, a mean thought, and live on as though it were not, sans craving and regret.

Man is a master. If he were not, he could not act contrary to law.

Evil and weakness are self destructive. The universe is girt with goodness and strength, and it protects the good and the strong.

The angry man is the weak man.

May Twenty-fourth

Thought for the Morning

Not by learning will a man triumph over evil; not by much study will he overcome sin and sorrow. Only by conquering himself will he conquer evil; only by practicing righteousness will he put an end to sorrow.

Not for the clever, nor the learned, nor the self-confident is the Life Triumphant, but for the pure, the virtuous and wise. The former achieve their particular success in life, but the latter alone achieve the great success so invincible and complete that even in apparent defeat it shines with added victory.

Meditation for the Day

Cease to tread every byway that tempts thy soul into the shadow-land.

MAN has all power now; but not knowing this, he says, "I will be perfect next year, or, in so many years, or in so many lives." The dwellers in the Kingdom of God, who live only in the now, say, "I am perfect now," and refraining from all sin now, and ceaselessly guarding all the portals of the mind, not looking to the past nor to the future, nor turning to the left or right, they remain eternally holy and blessed. "Now is the accepted time, now is the day of salvation." Say to yourself, "I will live in my Ideal now; I will be my Ideal now; and all that tempts me away from my Ideal I will not listen to; I will listen only to the voice of my Ideal." Thus resolving, and thus doing, you shall not depart from the Highest, and shall eternally manifest the Truth.

Manifest thy native and divine strength now.

Thought for the Evening

The true silence is not merely a silent tongue; it is a silent mind. To merely *hold one's tongue*, and yet to carry about a disturbed and rankling mind, is no remedy for weakness, and no source of power.

Silentness, to be powerful, must envelop the whole mind, must permeate every chamber of the heart; it must be the silence of peace.

To this broad, deep, abiding silentness a man attains only in the measure that he conquers himself.

May Twenty-fifth

Thought for the Morning

By curbing his tongue, a man gains possession of his mind.

The fool babbles, gossips, argues, and bandies words. He glories in the fact that he has had the last word, and has silenced his opponent. He exults in his own folly, is ever on the defensive, and wastes his energies in unprofitable channels. He is like a gardener who continues to dig and plant in unproductive soil.

The wise man avoids idle words, gossips, vain argument, and self-defence. He is content to appear defeated; rejoices when he is defeated; knowing that, having found and removed another error in himself, he has thereby become wiser.

Blessed is he who does not strive for the last word.

Meditation for the Day

Be resolute. Be of single purpose. Renew your resolution daily.

IN the hour of temptation do not depart from the right path. Avoid excitement. When passions are aroused, restrain and subdue them. When the mind would wander, bring it back to rest on higher things. Do not think—"I can get Truth from the Teacher, or from the books." You can acquire Truth only by practice. The teacher and the books can do no more than give instructions; and you must apply them. Those only who practise faithfully the rules and lessons given, and rely entirely upon their own efforts, will become enlightened. The Truth must be earned. Do not be led away by phenomenal appearances, or seek communications with spirits, or the dead; but attain to virtue, wisdom, and knowledge of the Supreme Law by the practice of Truth. Trust the Teacher; trust the Law; trust the path of Righteousness.

Put away all wavering and doubt,
and practise the lessons of wisdom with unlimited faith.

Thought for the Evening

Desire is the *craving for possession*; aspiration is the *hunger of the heart for peace*.

The craving for things leads ever farther and farther from peace, and not only ends in deprivation, but is in itself a state of perpetual want. Until it comes to an end, rest and satisfaction are impossible.

The hunger for things can never be satisfied, but the hunger for peace can, and the satisfaction of peace is found—is fully possessed, when all selfish desire is abandoned. Then there is fullness of joy, abounding plenty, and rich and complete blessedness.

May Twenty-sixth

Thought for the Morning

A man will reach the Kingdom by purifying himself, and he can only do this by pursuing a process of self-examination and self-analysis.

The selfishness must be discovered and understood before it can be removed. It is powerless to remove itself, neither will it pass away of itself. Darkness ceases only when light is introduced; so ignorance can only be dispersed by knowledge, selfishness by love.

A man must first of all be willing to lose himself (his self-seeking) before he can find himself (his Divine Self). He must realize that selfishness is not worth clinging to, that it is a master altogether unworthy of his service, and that divine goodness alone is worthy to be enthroned in his heart, as the supreme master of his life.

Meditation for the Day

Avoid exaggerations. The Truth is sufficient.

SPEAK only words which are truthful and sincere. Do not deceive either by word, look, or gesture. Avoid slander as you would a deadly snake, lest you be caught in its toils. He who speaks evil of another cannot find the way of peace. Put away all dissipations of idle gossip. Do not talk about the private affairs of others, or discuss the ways of Society, or criticize the eminent. Do not recriminate, or accuse others of offences, but meet all offences with blameless conduct. Do not condemn those who are not walking in the righteous path, but protect them with compassion, walking the path yourself. Quench the flame of anger with the pure water of Truth. Be modest in your words, and do not utter, or participate in, coarse, frivolous, or unseemly jests. Gravity and reverence are marks of purity and wisdom.

Do not dispute about Truth, but live it.

Thought for the Evening

Be still, my soul, and know that peace is thine. Be steadfast, heart, and know that strength divine Belongs to thee; cease from thy turmoil, mind, and thou the Everlasting Rest shalt find.

If a man would have peace, let him exercise the spirit of peace; if he would find Love, let him dwell in the spirit of Love; if he would escape suffering, let him cease to inflict it; if he would do noble things for humanity, let him cease to do ignoble things for himself. If he will but quarry the mine of his own soul, he shall find there all the materials for building whatsoever he will, and he shall find there also the Central Rock on which to build in safety.

May Twenty-seventh

Thought for the Morning

Men go after much company, and seek out new excitements, but they are not acquainted with peace; in divers paths of pleasure they search for happiness, but they do not come to rest; through divers ways of laughter and feverish delirium they wander after gladness and life, but their tears are many and grievous, and they do not escape death.

Drifting upon the ocean of life in search of selfish indulgences, men are caught in its storms, and only after many tempests and much privation do they fly to the Rock of Refuge which rests in the deep silence of their own being.

Meditation for the Day

Abstinence, sobriety, and self-control are good.

Do your duty with the utmost faithfulness, putting away all thought of reward. Let no thought of pleasure I or self entice you from your duty. Do not interfere with the duties of others. Be upright in all things. Under the most severe trial, though your happiness and life should seem to be at stake, do not swerve from the right. The man of unconquerable integrity is invincible; he cannot be confounded, and he escapes from the painful mazes of doubt and bewilderment. If one should abuse or accuse, or speak ill of you, remain silent and self-controlled, striving to understand that the wrong-doer cannot injure you unless you retaliate, and allow yourself to be carried away by the same wrong condition of mind. Strive, also, to meet the evil-doer with compassion, seeing how he is injuring himself.

The pure-minded cannot think, "I have been injured by another."
They know no enemy but self.

Thought for the Evening

Meditation centred upon divine realities is the very essence and soul of prayer. It is the silent reaching upward of the soul toward the Eternal.

Meditation is the intense dwelling, in thought, upon an idea or theme with the object of thoroughly comprehending it; and whatsoever you constantly meditate upon, you will not only come to understand, but will grow more and more into its likeness, for it will become incorporated with your very being, will become, in fact, your very self.

If, therefore, you constantly dwell upon that which is selfish and debasing, you will ultimately become selfish and debased; if you ceaselessly think upon that which is pure and unselfish, you will surely become pure and unselfish.

May Twenty-eighth

Thought for the Morning

There is no difficulty, however great, but will yield before a calm and powerful concentration of thought and no legitimate object but may be speedily actualized by the intelligent use and direction of one's soul forces.

Whatever your task may be, concentrate your whole mind upon it; throw into it all the energy of which you are capable. The faultless completion of small tasks, leads inevitably to larger tasks.

See to it that you rise by steady climbing, and you will never fall.

Meditation for the Day

Let your charity increase and extend till self is swallowed up in kindness.

BEAR no ill-will. Subdue anger and overcome hatred. Think of all, and act towards all, with the same unalterable kindness and compassion. Do not, under the severest trial, give way to bitterness, or words of resentment; but meet anger with calmness, mockery with patience, and hatred with love. Do not be a partisan, but be a peacemaker. Do not increase division between man and man, or promote strife by taking sides with one party against another, but give equal justice, equal love, equal goodwill to all. Do not disparage other teachers, other religions, or other schools of thought. Do not set up barriers between rich and poor, employer and employed, governor and governed, master and servant, but be equal-minded towards all, perceiving their several duties. By constantly controlling the mind, subduing bitterness and resentment, and striving to acquire a steadfast kindness, the spirit of goodwill will at last be born.

Be strong, energetic, steadfast.

Thought for the Evening

He who knows that Love is at the heart of all things, and has realized the all-sufficing power of that Love, has no room in his heart for condemnation.

If you love people and speak of them with praise, until they in some way thwart you, or do something of which you disapprove, and then you dislike them and speak of them with dispraise, you are not governed by the Love which is of God. If, in your heart, you are continually arraigning and condemning others, selfless love is hidden from you.

Train your mind in strong, impartial, and gentle thought; train your heart in purity and compassion; train your tongue to silence, and to true and stainless speech; so shall you enter the way of holiness and peace, and shall ultimately realize the immortal Love.

May Twenty-Ninth

Thought for the Morning

If you would realize true prosperity, do not settle down, as many have done, into the belief that if you do right everything will go wrong. Do not allow the word "competition" to shake your faith in the supremacy of righteousness. I care not what men say about the "laws of competition," for do not I know the Unchangeable Law which shall one day put them all to rout, and which puts them to rout even now in the heart and life of the righteous man? And knowing this law I can contemplate all dishonesty with undisturbed repose, for I know where certain destruction awaits it.

Under all circumstances *do that which you believe to be right*, and trust the Law; trust the Divine Power which is immanent in the universe, and it will never desert you, and you will always be protected.

Meditation for the Day

Be right-minded, intelligent, and clear-seeing.

BRING reason to bear on all things. Test all things. Be eager to know and understand. Be logical in thought. Be consistent in word and action. Bring the searchlight of knowledge to bear on your condition of mind, in order to simplify it and remove its errors. Question yourself with searching scrutiny. Let go of belief, hearsay, and speculation, and lay hold on knowledge. He who stands upon knowledge acquired by practice is filled with a sublime yet lowly confidence, and is able to speak the word of Truth with power. Master the task of discrimination. Learn to distinguish between good and evil; to perceive the facts of life, and understand them in their relation one to another. Awake the mind to see the orderly sequence of cause and effect in all things, both mental and material. Thus will be revealed the worthlessness of pleasure-seeking and sin, and the glory and gladness of a life of sublime virtue and spotless purity.

Truth is. There is no chaos.

Thought for the Evening

Forget yourself entirely in the sorrows of others, and in ministering to others, and divine happiness will emancipate you from all sorrow and suffering. "Taking the first step with a good thought, the second with a good word, and the third with a good deed, I entered Paradise." And you also enter Paradise by pursuing the same course.

Lose yourself in the welfare of others; forget yourself in all that you do—this is the secret of abounding happiness. Ever be on the watch to guard against selfishness and learn faithfully the divine lessons of inward sacrifice; so shall you climb the highest heights of happiness, and shall remain in the never-clouded sunshine of universal joy, clothed in the shining garment of immortality.

May Thirtieth

Thought for the Morning

When the farmer has tilled and dressed his land and put in the seed, he knows that he has done all that he can possibly do, and that now he must trust to the elements, and wait patiently for the course of time to bring about the harvest, and that no amount of expectancy on his part will affect the result.

Even so, he who has realized Truth, goes forth as a sower of the seeds of goodness, purity, love, and peace, without expectancy and never looking for results, knowing that there is the Great Over-ruling Law which brings about its own harvest in due time, and which is alike the source of preservation and destruction.

Meditation for the Day

Train your mind to grasp the Great Law
of Causation which is unfailing justice.

THEN you will see, not with fleshly eyes, but with the pure and single eye of; Truth. You will then understand your nature—perceiving how, as a mental being, you have evolved through countless ages of experience, how you have risen, through an unbroken line of lives, from low to high, and from high to higher still—how the ever-changing tendencies of the mind have been built up by thought and action—how your deeds have made you what you are. Thus, understanding your own nature, you will understand the nature of all beings, and will dwell always in compassion. You will understand the Great Law, not only universally and in the abstract, but also in its particular application to individuals. Then self will be ended. It will be dispersed like a cloud, and Truth will be all in all.

Find no room for hatred,
no room for self,
no room for sorrow.

Thought for the Evening

The virtuous put a check upon themselves, and set a watch upon their passions and emotions; in this way they gain possession of the mind, and gradually acquire calmness; and as they acquire influence, power, greatness, abiding joy, and fullness and completeness of life.

He only finds peace who conquers himself, who strives, day by day, after greater self-possession, greater self-control, and greater calmness of mind.

Where the calm mind is there is strength and rest, there is love and wisdom; there is one who has fought successfully innumerable battles against self, who, after long toil in secret against his own failings, has triumphed at last.

May Thirty-first

Thought for the Morning

Sympathy bestowed increases its store in our own heart and enriches and fructifies our own life. Sympathy given is blessedness received; sympathy withheld is blessedness forfeited.

In the measure that a man increases and enlarges his sympathy so much nearer does he approach the ideal life, the perfect blessedness; and when his heart has become so mellowed that no hard, bitter, or cruel thought can enter, and detract from its permanent sweetness, then indeed is he richly and divinely blessed.

Meditation for the Day

Be self-reliant, but let thy self-reliance be saintly and not selfish.

FOLLY and wisdom, weakness and strength, are within a man, and not in any external thing, neither do they spring from any external cause. A man cannot be strong for another, he can only be strong for himself; he cannot overcome for another, he can only overcome for himself. You may learn of another, but you must accomplish for yourself. Put away all external props, and rely upon the Truth within you. A creed will not bear a man up in the hour of temptation; he must possess the inward Knowledge which slays temptation. A speculative philosophy will prove a shadowy thing in the time of calamity; a man must have the inward Wisdom which puts an end to grief. The Unfailing Wisdom is found only by constant practice in pure thinking and well-doing; by harmonizing one's mind and heart to those things which are beautiful, lovable, and true.

Goodness is the aim of all religions.

Thought for the Evening

Sweet is the rest and deep the bliss of him who has freed his heart from its lusts and hatreds and dark desires; and he who, without any shadow of bitterness resting upon him, and looking out upon the world with boundless compassion and love, can breathe, in his inmost heart, the blessing: Peace unto all living things, making no exceptions or distinctions—such a man has reached that happy ending which can never be taken away, for this is the perfection of life, the fullness of peace, the consummation of perfect blessedness.

June First

Thought for the Morning

In aiming at the life of blessedness, one of the simplest beginnings to be considered, and rightly made, is that which we all make every day—namely, the beginning of each day's life. There is a sense in which every day may be regarded as the beginning of a new life, in which one can think, act, and live newly, and in a wiser and better spirit. The right beginning of the day will be followed by a cheerfulness permeating the household with a sunny influence, and the tasks and duties of the day will be undertaken in a strong and confident spirit, and the whole day will be well lived.

Meditation for the Day

*The incentive to self-sacrificing labor
does not reside in any theory about the universe,
but in the spirit of love and compassion.*

THE spirit of love does not decrease when a man realizes that perfect justice obtains in the spiritual government of the world; on the other hand, it is increased and intensified, for he knows that men suffer *because they do not understand*, because they err in ignorance. "The comfortably conditioned" are frequently involved in greater suffering than the poor, and, like others, are garnering their own mixed harvest of happiness and suffering. This teaching of Absolute Justice is not more encouraging for the rich than for the poor, for while it tells the rich, who are selfish and oppressive, or who misuse their wealth, that they must reap the results of all their actions, it also tells the suffering and oppressed that, as they are now reaping what they have formerly sown, they may, and surely will, by sowing the good seeds of purity, love, and peace, shortly also reap a harvest of good, and so rise above their present woes.

*The painful consequences of all self-seeking
must be met and passed through.*

Thought for the Evening

There can be no progress, no achievement, without sacrifice, and a man's worldly success will be in the measure that he sacrifices his confused animal thoughts, and fixes his mind on the development of his plans, and the strengthening of his resolution and self-reliance. And the higher he lifts his thoughts, the more manly, upright, and righteous he becomes, the greater will be his success, the more blessed and enduring will be his achievements.

June Second

Thought for the Morning

None but right acts can follow right thoughts; none but a right life can follow right acts; and by living a right life all blessedness is achieved. Mind is the Master-power that moulds and makes. And Man is Mind, and evermore he takes the tool of thought, and, shaping what he wills, brings forth a thousand joys, a thousand ills;—He thinks in secret, and it comes to pass: environment is but his looking-glass.

Meditation for the Day

Man is the maker of happiness and misery.

FIXED attitudes of mind determine courses of conduct, and from courses of conduct come those reactions called happinesses and unhappinesses. This being so, it follows that, to alter the reactive condition, one must alter the active thought. To exchange misery for happiness it is necessary to reverse the fixed attitude of mind and habitual course of conduct which is the cause of misery, and the reverse effect will appear in the mind and life. A man has no power to be happy while thinking and acting selfishly; he cannot be unhappy while thinking and acting unselfishly. Wheresoever the cause is, there the effect will appear. Man cannot abrogate effects, but he can alter causes. He can purify his nature; he can remould his character. There is great power in self-conquest; there is great joy in transforming oneself.

Each man is circumscribed by his own thoughts.

Thought for the Evening

Calmness of mind is one of the beautiful jewels of wisdom. A man becomes calm in the measure that he understands himself as a thought-evolved being. . . and he as he develops a right understanding, and sees more and more clearly the internal relations of things by the action of cause and effect, he ceases to fret and fume, and worry and grieve, and remains poised, steadfast, serene.

June Third

Thought for the Morning

To follow, under all circumstances, the highest promptings within you; to be always true to the divine self; to reply upon the inward voice, the inward light, and to pursue your purpose with a fearless and restful heart, believing that the future will yield unto you the need of every thought and effort; knowing that the laws of the universe can never fail, and that your own will come back to you with mathematical exactitude—this is faith and the living of faith.

Meditation for the Day

Men live in spheres low or high according to the nature of their thoughts.

CONSIDER the man whose mind is suspicious, covetous, envious. How small and mean and drear everything appears to him. Having no grandeur in himself, he sees no grandeur anywhere, being ignoble himself, he is incapable of seeing nobility in any being; selfish as he himself is, he sees in the most exalted acts of unselfishness only motives that are mean and base.

Consider again the man whose mind is unsuspecting, generous, magnanimous. How wondrous and beautiful is his world. He sees men as true, and to him they are true. In his presence the meanest forget their nature, and for the moment become like himself, getting a glimpse, albeit confused, in that temporary upliftment of a higher order of things, of an immeasurably nobler and happier life.

Refrain from harboring thoughts that are dark and hateful,
and cherish thoughts that are bright and beautiful.

Thought for the Evening

Have a thorough understanding of your work, and let it be your own; and as you proceed, ever following the inward guide, the infallible voice, you will pass on from victory to victory, and will rise step by step to higher resting-places, and your ever broadening outlook will gradually reveal to you the essential beauty and purpose of life. Self-purified, health will be yours; self-governed, power will be yours, and all that you do will prosper.

And I may stand where health, success, and power await my coming, if, each fleeting hour, I cling to love and patience; and abide with stainlessness; and never step aside from high integrity; so shall I see at last the land of immortality.

June Fourth

Thought for the Morning

When the tongue is well controlled and wisely subdued; when selfish impulses and unworthy thoughts no longer rush to the tongue demanding utterance; when the speech has become harmless, pure, gracious, gentle, and purposeful, and no word is uttered but in sincerity and truth—then are the five steps in virtuous speech accomplished, then is the second great lesson in Truth learned and mastered. Make pure thy heart, and thou wilt make thy life rich, sweet and beautiful.

Meditation for the Day

*The small-minded man and the large-hearted man
live in two different worlds though they be neighbors.*

THE kingdom of heaven is not taken by violence, but he who conforms to its principles receives the password. The ruffian moves in a society of ruffians; the saint is one of an elect brotherhood whose communion is divine music. All men are mirrors reflecting according to their own surface. All men, looking at the world of men and things, are looking into a mirror which gives back their own reflection.

Each man moves in the limited or expansive circle of his own thoughts, and all outside that circle is non-existent to him. He only knows that which he has *become*. The narrower the boundary, the more convinced is the man that there is no further limit, no other circle. The lesser cannot contain the greater, and he has no means of apprehending the larger minds; such knowledge comes only by growth.

*Men, like schoolboys, find themselves in standards or classes
to which their ignorance or knowledge entitles them.*

Thought for the Evening

Having clothed himself with humility, the first questions a man asks himself are:—

"How am I acting towards others?"
"What am I doing to others?"
"How am I thinking of others?"
"Are my thoughts of, and acts towards others prompted by unselfish love?"

As a man, in the silence of his soul, asks himself these searching questions, he will unerringly see where he has hitherto failed.

June Fifth

Thought for the Morning

To dwell in love always and towards all is to live the true life, is to have Life itself. Knowing this, the good man gives up himself unreservedly to the Spirit of Love, and dwells in Love towards all, contending with none, condemning none, but loving all.

The Christ Spirit of Love puts an end, not only to all sin, but to all division and contention.

Meditation for the Day

The world of things is the other half of the world of thoughts.

THE inner informs the outer. The greater embraces the lesser. Matter is the counterpart of mind. Events are streams of thoughts. Circumstances are combinations of thought, and the outer conditions and actions of others in which each man is involved, are intimately related to his own mental needs and development. Man is a part of his surroundings. He is not separate from his fellows, but is bound closely to them by the peculiar intimacy and interaction of deeds, and by those fundamental laws of thought which are the roots of human society. One cannot alter external things to suit his passing whims and wishes, but he can set aside his whims and wishes; he can so alter his attitude of mind towards externals, that they will assume a different aspect. He cannot mould the actions of others towards him, but he can rightly fashion his actions towards them.

Things follow thoughts.
Alter your thoughts,
and things will receive a new adjustment.

Thought for the Evening

When sin and self are abandoned, the heart is restored to its imperishable Joy. Joy comes and fills the self-emptied heart; it abides with the peaceful; its reign is with the pure. Joy flees from the selfish, it deserts the quarrelsome; it is hidden from the impure. Joy cannot remain with the selfish; it is wedded to Love.

June Sixth

Thought for the Morning

In the pure heart there is no room left where personal judgments and hatreds can find lodgement, for it is filled to overflowing with tenderness and love; it sees no evil, and only as men succeed in seeing no evil in others will they become free from sin, and sorrow, and suffering. If men only understood that the heart that sins must sorrow, that the hateful mind tomorrow reaps its barren harvest, weeping, starving, resting not, nor sleeping; tenderness would fill their being, they would see with pity's seeing, if they only understood.

Meditation for the Day

*The perfecting of one's own deeds is man's highest duty
and most sublime accomplishment.*

THE cause of your bondage as of your deliverance is within. The injury that comes to you through others is the rebound of your own deed, the reflex of your own mental attitude. *They* are the instruments, *you* are the cause. Destiny is ripened fruits. The fruit of life, both bitter and sweet, is received by each man in just measure. The righteous man is free. None can injure him; none can destroy him; none can rob him of his peace. His attitude towards men, born of understanding, disarms their power to wound him. Any injury which they may try to inflict rebounds upon themselves to their own hurt, leaving him unharmed and untouched. The good that goes from him is his perennial fount of happiness, his eternal source of strength. Its root is serenity, its flower is joy.

External things and deeds are powerless to injure you.

Thought for the Evening

To stand face to face with truth; to arrive, after innumerable wanderings and pains, at wisdom and bliss; not to be finally defeated and cast out, but to ultimately triumph over every inward foe—such is man's divine destiny, such his glorious goal; and this, every saint, sage, and saviour has declared. A man only begins to be a man when he ceases to whine and revile, and commences to search for the hidden justice which regulates his life. And as he adapts his mind to that regulating factor, he ceases to accuse others as the cause of his condition, and builds himself up in strong and noble thoughts; ceases to kick against circumstances, but begins to use them as aids to his more rapid progress, and as a means of discovering the hidden power and possibilities within himself.

June Seventh

Thought for the Morning

The will to evil and the will to good are both within thee, which wilt thou employ? Thou knowest what is right and what is wrong, which wilt though love and foster, which destroy?

Thou art the chooser of thy thoughts and deeds; thou art the maker of thine inward state; the power is thine to be what thou wilt be; thou buildest Truth and Love, or lies and hate.

Meditation for the Day

The man is the all-important factor.

MAN imagines he could do great things if he were not hampered by circumstances by want of money, want of time, want of influence, and want of freedom from family ties. In reality the man is not hindered by these things at all. He, in his mind, ascribes to them a power which they do not possess, and he submits, not to them, but to his opinions about them, that is, to a weak element in his nature. The real "want" that hampers him is *the want of the right attitude of mind*. When he regards his circumstances as spurs to his resources, when he sees that his so-called "drawbacks" are the very steps up which he is to mount successfully to his achievement, then his necessity gives birth to invention, and the "hindrances" are transformed into aids.

He who complains of his circumstances has not yet become a man.

Thought for the Evening

The teaching of Jesus brings men back to the simple truth that righteousness, or *right-doing*, is entirely a matter of individual conduct, and not a mystical something apart from a man's thoughts and deeds.

Calmness and patience can become habitual by first grasping, through effort, a calm and patient thought, and then continuously thinking it, and living in it, until "use becomes second nature," and anger and impatience pass away for ever.

June Eighth

Thought for the Morning

Man is made or unmade by himself; in the armoury of thought he forges the weapons by which he destroys himself; he also fashions the tools with which he builds for himself heavenly mansions of joy and strength and peace. By the right choice and true application of thought man ascends to the Divine Perfection; by the abuse and wrong application of thought he descends below the level of the beast. Between these two extremes are all the grades of character and man is their maker and master.

As a being of Power, Intelligence, and Love, and the lord of his own thoughts, man holds the key to every situation.

Meditation for the Day

Nothing can prevent us from accomplishing the aims of our life.

MAN'S power subsists in discrimination and choice. Man does not create one jot of the universal conditions or laws; they are the essential principles of things, and are neither made nor unmade. He discovers, not makes, them. Ignorance of them is at the root of the world's pain. To defy them is folly and bondage. Who is the freer man, the thief who defies the laws of his country, or the honest citizen who obeys them? Who, again, is the freer man, the fool who thinks he can live as he likes, or the wise man who chooses to do only that which is right?

Man is, in the nature of things, a being of habit, and this he cannot alter; but he can alter his habits. He cannot alter the law of his nature, but he can adapt his nature to the law.

He is the good man whose habits of thought and action are good.

Thought for the Evening

Whatsoever you harbour in the inmost chambers of your heart will, sooner or later, by the inevitable law of reaction, shape itself in your outward life.

Every soul attracts its own, and nothing can possibly come to it that does not belong to it. To realize this is to recognize the universality of Divine Law.

If thou would'st right the world, and banish all its evils and its woes, make its wild places bloom, and its drear deserts blossom as the rose—then right thyself.

June Ninth

Thought for the Morning

Whatever conditions are rendering your life burdensome, you may pass out of and beyond them by developing and utilizing within you the transforming power of self-purification and self-conquest.

Before the divine radiance of a pure heart all darkness vanishes and all clouds melt away, and he who has conquered self has conquered the universe.

He who sets his foot firmly upon the path of self-conquest, who walks, aided by the staff of faith, the highway of self-sacrifice, will assuredly achieve the highest prosperity, and will reap abounding and enduring joy and bliss.

Meditation for the Day

He becomes the master of the lower by enlisting in the service of the higher.

MAN repeats the same thoughts, the same actions, the same experiences over and over again, until they are incorporated with his being, until they are built into his character as part of himself. Evolution is mental accumulation. Man today is the result of millions of repetitious thoughts and acts. He is not ready-made, he becomes, and is still becoming. His character is pre-determined by his own choice. The thought, the act, which he chooses, that, by habit, he becomes.

Thus each man is an accumulation of thoughts and deeds. The characteristics which he manifests instinctively and without effort are lines of thought and action become, by long repetition, automatic; for it is the nature of habit to become, at last, unconscious, to repeat, as it were, itself without any apparent choice or effort on the part of its possessor; and in due time it takes such complete possession of the individual as to appear to render his will powerless to counteract it.

Habit is repetition. Faculty is fixed habit.

Thought for the Evening

It is the silent and conquering thought forces which bring all things into manifestation. The universe grew out of thought.

To adjust all your thoughts to a perfect and unswerving faith in the omnipotence and supremacy of Good is to co-operate with that Good, and to realize within yourself the solution and destruction of all evil.

To mentally deny evil is not sufficient; it must, by daily practice, be risen above and understood. To affirm the Good mentally is inadequate; it must, by unswerving endeavour, be entered into and comprehended.

June Tenth

Thought for the Morning

Every thought you think is a force sent out. Whatever your position in life may be, before you can hope to enter into any measure of success, usefulness, and power, you must learn how to focus your thought forces by cultivating calmness and repose.

There is no difficulty, however great, but will yield before a calm and purposeful concentration of thought, and no legitimate object but may be speedily actualized by the intelligent use and direction of one's soul forces.

Think good thoughts, and they will quickly become actualized in your outward life in the form of good conditions.

Meditation for the Day

By thoughts man binds himself.

IT is true that man is the instrument of mental forces—or to be more accurate, he is those forces—but they are not blind, and he can direct them into new channels. In a word, he can take himself in hand and reconstruct his habits; for though it is also true that he is born with a given character, that character is the product of numberless lives during which it has been slowly built up by choice and effort, and in this life it will be considerably modified by new experiences.

No matter how apparently helpless a man has become under the tyranny of a bad habit, or a bad characteristic and they are essentially the same he can, so long as sanity remains, break away from it and become free.

A changed attitude of mind changes the character, the habits, the life.

Thought for the Evening

That which you would be and hope to be, you may be now. Non-accomplishment resides in your perpetual postponement, and, having the power to postpone, you also have the power to accomplish—to perpetually accomplish: realize this truth, and you shall be today, and every day, the ideal being of whom you dreamed.

Say to yourself, "I will live in my Ideal now; I will manifest my ideal now; I will be my Ideal now; and all that tempts me away from my Ideal I will not listen to; I will listen only to the voice of my Ideal."

June Eleventh

Thought for the Morning

Be as a flower; content to be, to grow in sweetness day by day. If thou would'st perfect thyself in knowledge, perfect thyself in Love. If thou would'st reach the Highest, ceaselessly cultivate a loving and compassionate heart.

To him who chooses Goodness, sacrificing all, is given that which is more than, and includes, all.

Meditation for the Day

The body is the image of the mind.

ONE who suffers in body will not necessarily at once be cured when he begins to fashion his mind on moral and harmonious principles; indeed, for a time, while the body is bringing to a crisis, and throwing off the effects of former inharmonies, the morbid condition may appear to be intensified. As a man does not gain perfect peace immediately he enters upon the path of righteousness, but must, except in rare instances, pass through a painful period of adjustment, neither does he, with the same rare exception, at once acquire perfect health. Time is required for bodily as well as mental readjustment, and even if health is not reached, it will be approached. If the mind be made robust, the bodily condition will take a secondary and subordinate place, and will cease to have that primary importance which so many give to it.

Mental harmony, or moral wholeness, makes for bodily health.

Thought for the Evening

The Great Law never cheats any man of his just due.

Human life, when rightly lived, is simple with a beautiful simplicity.

He who comprehends the utter simplicity of life, who obeys its laws, and does not step aside into the dark paths and complex mazes of selfish desire, stands where no harm can reach him.

Then there is fullness of joy, abounding plenty, and rich and complete blessedness.

June Twelfth

Thought for the Morning

Every man reaps the results of his own thoughts and deeds, and suffers for his own wrong.

He who begins right, and continues right, does not need to desire, and search for felicitous results; they are already at hand; they follow as consequences; they are the certainties, the realities, of life.

Sweet is the rest and deep is the bliss of him who has freed his heart from its lusts and hatreds and dark desires.

Meditation for the Day

Reach out into a comprehension of the Infinite.

WHILST vainly imagining that the pleasures of earth are real and satisfying, pain and sorrow continually remind man of their unreal and unsatisfying nature. Ever striving to believe that complete satisfaction is to be found in material things, he is conscious of an inward and persistent revolt against this belief, which revolt is at once a refutation of his essential mortality, and an inherent and imperishable proof that only in the immortal, the eternal, the infinite, can he find abiding satisfaction and unbroken peace.

Man is essentially and spiritually divine and eternal, and, immersed in mortality and troubled unrest, he is striving to enter into a consciousness of his real nature.

The common ground of faith—the root and spring of all religion,
the heart of Love!

Thought for the Evening

You are the creator of your own shadows; you desire, and then you grieve; renounce, and then you shall rejoice.

Of all the beautiful truths pertaining to the soul. . . none is more gladdening or fruitful of divine promise and confidence than this—that man is the master of thought, the moulder of character, and the maker and shaper of character, environment, and destiny.

June Thirteenth

Thought for the Morning

As darkness is a passing shadow, and light is a substance that remains, so sorrow is fleeting, but joy abides for ever. No true thing can pass away and become lost; no false thing can remain and be preserved. Sorrow is false, and it cannot live; joy is true, and it cannot die. Joy may become hidden for a time, but it can always be recovered; sorrow may remain for a period, but it can be transcended and dispersed.

Do not think your sorrow will remain; it will pass away like a cloud. Do not believe that the torments of sin are ever your portion; they will vanish like a hideous nightmare. Awake! Arise! Be holy and joyful.

Meditation for the Day

The restful Reality of the Eternal Heart.

THE spirit of man is inseparable from the Infinite, and can be satisfied with nothing short of the Infinite, and the burden of pain will continue to weigh upon man's heart, and the shadows of sorrow to darken his pathway, until, ceasing from wanderings in the dream-world of matter, he comes back to his home in the reality of the Eternal.

As the smallest drop of water detached from the ocean contains all the qualities of the ocean, so man, detached in consciousness from the Infinite, contains within himself its likeness; and as the drop of water must, by the law of nature, ultimately find its way back to the ocean and lose itself in its silent depths, so must man, by the unfailing law of his nature, at last return to his source, and lose himself in the heart of the Infinite.

To become one with the Infinite is the goal of man.

Thought for the Evening

Tribulation lasts only so long as there remains some chaff of self which needs to be removed. The *tribulum*, or threshing machine, ceases to work when all the grain is separated from the chaff; and when the last impurities are blown away from the soul, tribulation has completed its work, and there is no more need for it; then abiding joy is realized.

The sole and supreme use of suffering is to purify, to burn out all that is useless and impure. Suffering ceases for him who is pure. There could be no object in burning gold after the dross had been removed.

June Fourteenth

Thought for the Morning

In speaking of self-control, one is easily misunderstood. It should not be associated with a destructive repression, but with a constructive expression.

A man is happy, wise and great in the measure that he controls himself; he is wretched, foolish, and mean in the measure that he allows his animal nature to dominate his thoughts and actions.

He who controls himself, controls his life, his circumstances, his destiny; and wherever he goes he carries his happiness with him as an abiding possession.

Renunciation precedes regeneration. The permanent happiness which men seek in dissipation, excitement, and abandonment to unworthy pleasures, is found only in the life which reverses all this—the life of self-control.

Meditation for the Day

Enter into perfect harmony with the Eternal Law,
which is Wisdom, Love, and Peace.

THIS divine state is, and must ever be, incomprehensible to the merely personal. Personality, separateness, selfishness, are one and the same, and are the antithesis of wisdom and divinity. By the unqualified surrender of the personality, separateness and selfishness cease, and man enters into the possession of his divine heritage of immortality and infinity.

Such surrender of the personality is regarded by the worldly and selfish mind as the most grievous of all calamities, the most irreparable loss, yet it is the one supreme and incomparable blessing, the only real and lasting gain. The mind unenlightened upon the inner laws of being and upon the nature and destiny of its own life clings to transient appearances, things which have in them no enduring substantiality, and so clinging, perishes, for the time being, amid the shattered wreckage of its own illusions.

Love is universal, supreme, all-sufficing.
This is the realization of selfless love.

Thought for the Evening

Law, not confusion, is the dominating principle in the universe; justice, not injustice is the soul and substance of life; and righteousness, not corruption, is the moulding and moving force in the spiritual government of the world. This being so, man has but the right himself to find that the universe is right.

When I am pure, I shall have solved the mystery of life; I shall be sure, when I am free from hatred, lust and strife, I am in Truth, and Truth abides in me; I shall be safe, and sane, and wholly free, when I am pure.

June Fifteenth

Thought for the Morning

If men only understood that their hatred and resentment slays their peace and sweet contentment, hurts themselves, helps not another, does not cheer one lonely brother, they would seek the better doing of good deeds which leaves no ruing:—

If they only understood.

If men only understood how Love conquers; how prevailing is its might, grim hate assailing; how compassion endeth sorrow, maketh wise, and doth not borrow pain of passion, they would ever live in Love, in hatred never:—

If they only understood.

Meditation for the Day

When a man's soul is clouded with selfishness
in any or every form,
he loses the power of spiritual discrimination,
and confuses the temporal with the eternal.

MEN cling to and gratify the flesh as though it were going to last forever, and though they try to forget the nearness and inevitably of its dissolution, the dread of death and of the loss of all that they cling to clouds their happiest ours, and the chilling shadow of their own selfishness follows them like a remorseless spectre.

And with the accumulation of temporal comforts and luxuries, the divinity within men is drugged, and they sink deeper and deeper into materiality, into the perishable life of the senses; and where there is sufficient intellect, theories concerning the immortality of the flesh come to be regarded as infallible truths.

The perishable in the universe can never become permanent;
the permanent can never pass away.

Thought for the Evening

The grace and beauty that were in Jesus can be of no value to you—cannot be understood by you—unless they are also *in you*, and they can never be in you, until you practice them, for, apart from *doing*, the qualities which constitute goodness do not, as far as you are concerned, exist.

To adore Jesus for his good qualities is a long step towards Truth, but to practice those qualities is Truth itself; and he who fully adores the perfection of another will not rest content in his own imperfection, but will fashion his soul after the likeness of that other.

Therefore thou who adorest Jesus for his divine qualities, practice those qualities thyself, and thou too shalt be divine.

June Sixteenth

Thought for the Morning

Let a man realize that life in its totality proceeds from the mind, and lo, the way of blessedness is opened up to him! For he will then discover that he possesses the power to rule his mind and to fashion it in accordance with his Ideal.

So will he elect to strongly and steadfastly walk those pathways of thought and action which are altogether excellent; to him life will become beautiful and sacred; and, sooner or later, he will put to flight all evil, confusion, and suffering; for it is impossible for a man to fall short of liberation, enlightenment, and peace, who guards with unwearying diligence the gateway of his heart.

Meditation for the Day

Man cannot immortalize the flesh.

ALL nature in its myriad forms of life, is changeable, impermanent, unenduring. Only the informing Principle of nature endures. Nature is many, and is marked by separation. The informing Principle is one, and is marked by unity. By overcoming the senses and the selfishness within, which is the overcoming of nature, man emerges from the chrysalis of the personal and illusory, and wings himself into the glorious light of the impersonal, the region of Truth, out of which all perishable forms come.

Let men, therefore, practise self-denial; let them conquer their animal inclinations; let them refuse to be enslaved by luxury and pleasure; let them practise virtue, and grow daily into higher and ever higher virtue, until at last they grow into the Divine.

Only by realizing the God state of consciousness does man enter into immortality.

Thought for the Evening

By constantly overcoming self, a man gains a knowledge of the subtle intricacies of his mind; and it is this divine knowledge which enables him to become established in calmness.

Without self-knowledge there can be no abiding peace of mind, and those who are carried away by tempestuous passions, cannot approach the holy place where calmness reigns.

The weak man is like one who, having mounted a fiery steed, allows it to run away with him, and carry him withersoever it wills; the strong man is like one who, having mounted the steed, governs it with a masterly hand and makes it go in whatever direction and at whatever speed he commands.

June Seventeenth

Thought for the Morning

There is no strife, no selfishness, in the Kingdom; there is perfect harmony, equipoise, and rest.

Those who live in the Kingdom of Love, have all their needs supplied by the Law of Love.

As self is the root cause of all strife and suffering, so Love is the root cause of all peace and bliss. Those who are at rest in the Kingdom do not look for happiness in any outward possessions. They are freed from all anxiety and trouble and, resting in Love, they are the embodiment of happiness.

Meditation for the Day

This only is true service to forget oneself in love towards all.

WHOEVER fights ceaselessly against his own selfishness, and strives to supplant it with all-embracing love, is a saint, whether he live in a cottage or in the midst of riches and influence; or whether he preaches or remains obscure.

To the worldling, who is beginning to aspire towards higher things, the saint, such as a sweet St. Francis of Assisi, or a conquering St. Anthony, is a glorious and inspiring spectacle; to the saint, an equally enrapturing sight is that of the sage, sitting serene and holy, the conqueror of sin and sorrow, no more tormented by regret and remorse, and whom even temptation can never reach; and yet even the sage is drawn on by a still more glorious vision, that of the Saviour actively manifesting His knowledge in selfless works, and rendering His divinity more potent for good by sinking Himself in the throbbing, sorrowing heart of mankind.

Only the work that is impersonal can live.

Thought for the Evening

Let it not be supposed that the children of the Kingdom live in ease and indolence (these two sins are the first that have to be eradicated when the search for the Kingdom is entered upon); they live in a peaceful activity; in fact, they only truly live, for the life of self, with its train of worries, griefs, and fears, is not *real life*.

The children of the Kingdom are *known by their life*, they manifest the fruits of the Spirit—"Love, joy, peace, long-suffering, kindness, goodness, faithfulness, meekness, temperance, and self-control"—under all circumstances and vicissitudes.

June Eighteenth

Thought for the Morning

The gospel of Jesus is a gospel of *living and doing*. If it were not this it would not voice the Eternal Truth. Its Temple is *Purified Conduct*, the entrance-door to which is *Self-Surrender*. It invites men to shake off sin, and promises, as a result, joy and blessedness and perfect peace.

The Kingdom of Heaven is perfect trust, perfect knowledge, perfect peace. . . no sin can enter therein, no self-born thought or deed can pass its golden gates; no impure desire can defile its radiant robes. . . all may enter it who will, but all must pay the price—*the unconditional abandonment of self.*

Meditation for the Day

Where duties, howsoever humble, are done without self-interest,
and with joyful sacrifice, there is true service and enduring work.

IT is given to the world to learn one great and divine lesson—the lesson of absolute unselfishness. The saints, sages, and saviours of all time are they who have submitted themselves to this task, and have learned and lived it. All the scriptures of the world are framed to teach this one lesson, all the great teachers reiterate it. It is too simple for the world which, scorning it, stumbles along in the complex ways of selfishness.

To search for this righteousness is to walk the Way of Truth and Peace, and he who enters this Way will soon perceive that Immortality which is independent of birth and death, and will realize that in the divine economy of the universe the humblest effort is not lost. The world will not have finished its long journey until every soul has entered into the blissful realization of its own divinity.

A pure heart is the end of all religion and the beginning of divinity.

Thought for the Evening

I say this—and know it to be truth—*that circumstances can only affect you in so far as you allow them to do so.* You are swayed by circumstances because you have not a right understanding of the nature, use, and power of thought. You believe (and upon this little word *belief* hang all our joys and sorrows) that outward things have the power to make or mar your life; by so doing you submit to those outward things, confess that you are their slave, and they your unconditional master. By so doing you invest them with a power which they do not of themselves possess, and you succumb, in reality not to the circumstances, but to the gloom or gladness, the fear or hope, the strength of weakness, which your thought-sphere has thrown around them.

June Nineteenth

Thought for the Morning

If you are one of those who are praying for, and looking forward to a happier world beyond the grave, here is a message of gladness for you—you may enter into and realize that happy world now; it fills the whole universe, and it is within you, waiting for you to find, acknowledge, and possess.

Said one who understood the inner laws of Being—"When men shall say, lo here, or lo there, go not after them. The Kingdom of God is within you."

Meditation for the Day

In the external universe there is ceaseless turmoil, change, and unrest;
at the heart of all things there is undisturbed repose;
in this deep silence dwelleth the Eternal.

AS there are depths in the ocean which the fiercest storm cannot reach, so there are silent, holy depths in the heart of man which the storms of sin and sorrow can never disturb. To reach this silence and to live consciously in it is peace.

Discord is rife in the outward world, but unbroken harmony holds sway at the heart of the universe. The human soul reaches blindly toward the harmony of the sinless state, and to reach this state and to live consciously in it is peace. Come away, for a while, from external things, from the pleasure of the senses, from the arguments of the intellect, from the noise and the excitements of the world, and withdraw yourself into the inmost chamber of your heart, and there, free from the sacrilegious intrusion of all selfish desires, you will find a holy calm, a blissful repose; the faultless eye of Truth will open within you, and you will see things as they really are.

Become as little children.

Thought for the Evening

Heaven and hell are inward states. Sink into self and all its gratifications, and you sink into hell; rise above self into that state of consciousness which is the utter denial and forgetfulness of self, and you enter heaven.

So long as you persist in selfishly seeking for your own personal happiness, so long will happiness elude you, and you will be sowing the seeds of wretchedness. In so far as you succeed in losing yourself in the service of others, in that measure will happiness come to you, and you will reap a harvest of bliss.

June Twentieth

Thought for the Morning

Sympathy given can never be waste.

One aspect of sympathy is that of pity—pity for the distressed or pain stricken, with a desire to alleviate or help them in their sufferings. The world needs more of this divine quality.

"For pity makes the world soft to the weak, and noble for the strong."

Another form of sympathy is that of rejoicing with others who are more successful than ourselves, and though their success were our own.

Meditation for the Day

*Hatred severs human lives, fosters persecution,
and hurls nations into ruthless war.*

MEN cry "Peace! Peace!" where there is no peace, but, on the contrary, discord, disquietude, and strife. Apart from that wisdom which is inseparable from self-renunciation, there can be no real and abiding peace.

The peace which results from social comfort, passing gratification, or worldly victory is transitory in its nature, and is burnt up in the heat of fiery trial. Only the Peace of Heaven endures through all trial, and only the selfless heart can know the Peace of Heaven.

Holiness alone is undying peace. Self-control leads to it, and the ever-increasing Light of Wisdom guides the pilgrim on his way. It is partaken of in a measure as soon as the path of virtue is entered upon, but it is only, realized in its fullness when self disappears in the consummation of a stainless life.

*This inward peace, this silence, this harmony,
this love is the Kingdom of Heaven.*

Thought for the Evening

Sweet are companionships, pleasures, and material comforts, but they change and fade away. Sweeter still are Purity, Wisdom, and the knowledge of Truth, and these never change nor fade away.

He who attained to the possession of spiritual things can never be deprived of his source of happiness; he will never have to part company with it, and wherever he goes in the whole universe, he will carry his possessions with him. His spiritual end will be the fullness of joy.

June Twenty-first

Thought for the Morning

Let your heart grow and expand with ever broadening love, until, freed from all hatred, and passion, and condemnation, it embraces the whole universe with thoughtful tenderness.

As the flower opens its petals to receive the morning light, so open your soul more and more to the glorious light of Truth.

Soar upward on the wings of aspiration; be fearless and believe in the loftiest possibilities.

Meditation for the Day

Realize the Light that never fades!

IF, O reader! you would realize the Joy that never ends, and the tranquillity that cannot be disturbed; if you would leave behind for ever your sins, your sorrows, your anxieties, and perplexities; if, I say, you would partake of this salvation, this supremely glorious Life, then conquer yourself. Bring every thought, every impulse, every desire into perfect obedience to the divine power resident within you. There is no other way to peace but this; and if you refuse to walk it, your much praying and your strict adherence to ritual will be fruitless and unavailing, and neither gods nor angels can help you. Only to him that overcometh is given the white stone of the regenerate life, on which is written the New and Ineffable Name.

The holy place within you is your real and eternal self:
it is the divine within you.

Thought for the Evening

Mind clothes itself in garments of its own making. Mind is the arbiter of life; it is the creator and shaper of conditions, and the recipient of its own results. It contains within itself both the power to create illusion and to perceive reality.

Mind is the infallible weaver of destiny; thought is the thread, good and evil deeds are the warp and woof, and the web, woven upon the loom of life, is character. Make pure thy heart, and thou wilt make thy life, rich, sweet, and beautiful, unmarred by strife.

June Twenty-second

Thought for the Morning

Cherish your visions; cherish your ideals; cherish the music that stirs in your heart, the beauty that forms in your mind, the loveliness that drapes your purest thoughts, for out of them will grow all delightful conditions, all heavenly environment; of these, if you will remain true to them, your world will at last be built.

Guard well thy mind, and, noble, strong, and free, nothing shall harm, disturb or conquer thee; for all thy foes are in thy heart and mind, there also thy salvation thou shalt find.

Meditation for the Day

Spiritual Principles can only be acquired after long discipline
in the pursuit and practice of Virtue.

THE schoolmaster never attempts to teach his pupils the abstract principles of mathematics at the commencement; he knows that by such a method teaching would be vain, and learning impossible. He first places before them a very simple sum, and, having explained it, leaves them to *do it*. When, after repeated failures and ever-renewed effort, they have succeeded in doing it correctly, a more difficult task is set them, and then another and another; and not until the pupils have, through many years of diligent application, mastered all the lessons in arithmetic does he attempt to unfold to them the underlying mathematical principles.

Thus practice ever precedes knowledge
Even in the ordinary things of the world,
and in spiritual things, in the living of the higher life,
this law is rigid in its exactions.

Thought for the Evening

Dream lofty dreams, and as you dream so shall you become. Your vision is the promise of what you shall one day be; your Ideal is the prophecy of what you shall at last unveil.

The greatest achievement was at first and for a time a dream. The oak sleeps in the acorn; the bird waits in the egg; and in the highest vision of the soul a waking angel stirs.

Your circumstances may be uncongenial, but they shall not long remain so when you perceive an Ideal and strive to reach it.

June Twenty-third

Thought for the Morning

He who has conquered doubt and fear has conquered failure. His every thought is allied with power, and all difficulties are bravely met and wisely overcome. His purposes are seasonably planted, and they bloom and bring forth fruit which does not fall prematurely to the ground.

Thought allied fearlessly to purpose becomes creative force: he who knows this is ready to become something higher and stronger than a mere bundle of wavering thoughts and fluctuating sensations; he who does this has become the conscious and intelligent wielder of his mental powers.

Meditation for the Day

Truth can only be arrived at by daily and hourly doing the lessons of Virtue.

IN a properly governed household the child is first taught to be obedient, and to conduct itself properly under all circumstances. The child is not even told why it must do this, but is commanded to do it, and only after it has so far succeeded in doing what is right and proper is it told *why* it should do it. No father would attempt to teach his child the principles of ethics before exacting from it the practice of filial duty and social virtue.

Virtue can only be known by *doing*, and the knowledge of Truth can only be arrived at by perfecting oneself in the practice of Virtue; and to be complete in the practice and acquisition of Virtue is to be complete in the knowledge of Truth.

Undaunted by failure, and made stronger by difficulties.

Thought for the Evening

Man's true place in the Cosmos is that of a king, not a slave, a commander under the Law of Good, and not a helpless tool in the region of evil.

I write for men, not for babes; for those who are eager to learn, and earnest to achieve; for those who will put away (for the world's good) a petty personal indulgence, a selfish desire, a mean thought, and live on as though it were not, sans craving and regret.

Man is a master. If he were not, he could not act contrary to law.

Evil and weakness are self destructive. The universe is girt with goodness and strength, and it protects the good and the strong.

The angry man is the weak man.

June Twenty-fourth

Thought for the Morning

Not by learning will a man triumph over evil; not by much study will he overcome sin and sorrow. Only by conquering himself will he conquer evil; only by practicing righteousness will he put an end to sorrow.

Not for the clever, nor the learned, nor the self-confident is the Life Triumphant, but for the pure, the virtuous and wise. The former achieve their particular success in life, but the latter alone achieve the great success so invincible and complete that even in apparent defeat it shines with added victory.

Meditation for the Day

*Learn the lessons of Virtue, and thus build up in the strength of knowledge,
destroying ignorance and the ills of life.*

WHERE Love is, God is, and where Goodness lives
There Christ abides; and he who daily strives
'Gainst self and selfishness, shaping his mind
For Truth and Purity, shall surely find
The Master's presence in his inmost heart.
God shall be one with him (and not apart)
Who overcomes himself, and makes his life
Godlike and holy; banishing all strife
Far from him; letting hate and anger die,
And greed and pride and fleshly lusts that lie
To God and Goodness: great shall be his peace,
Happy and everlasting his release
From pain and sorrow who doth conquer sin.
To the pure heart comes God and dwells therein:
He only who the Path of Good hath trod
Hath found the Life that's "hid with Christ in God."

"Make pure thy heart, and thou wilt make thy life
Rich, sweet, and beautiful, unmarred by strife."

Thought for the Evening

The true silence is not merely a silent tongue; it is a silent mind. To merely *hold one's tongue*, and yet to carry about a disturbed and rankling mind, is no remedy for weakness, and no source of power.

Silentness, to be powerful, must envelop the whole mind, must permeate every chamber of the heart; it must be the silence of peace.

To this broad, deep, abiding silentness a man attains only in the measure that he conquers himself.

June Twenty-fifth

Thought for the Morning

By curbing his tongue, a man gains possession of his mind.

The fool babbles, gossips, argues, and bandies words. He glories in the fact that he has had the last word, and has silenced his opponent. He exults in his own folly, is ever on the defensive, and wastes his energies in unprofitable channels. He is like a gardener who continues to dig and plant in unproductive soil.

The wise man avoids idle words, gossips, vain argument, and self-defence. He is content to appear defeated; rejoices when he is defeated; knowing that, having found and removed another error in himself, he has thereby become wiser.

Blessed is he who does not strive for the last word.

Meditation for the Day

Stimulate the mind to watchfulness and reflection.

IT will be seen that the first step in the discipline of the mind is the overcoming of indolence. This is the easiest step, and until it is perfectly accomplished the other steps cannot be taken. The clinging to indolence constitutes a complete barrier to the Path of Truth. Indolence consists in giving the body more ease and sleep than it requires, in procrastinating, and in shirking and neglecting those things which should receive immediate attention. This condition of laziness must be overcome by rousing up the body at an early hour, giving it just the amount of sleep it requires for complete recuperation, and by doing, promptly and vigorously, every task and duty, no matter how small, as it comes along.

The heart must be purified of sensual and gustatory lust.

Thought for the Evening

Desire is the *craving for possession*; aspiration is *the hunger of the heart for peace.*

The craving for things leads ever farther and farther from peace, and not only ends in deprivation, but is in itself a state of perpetual want. Until it comes to an end, rest and satisfaction are impossible.

The hunger for things can never be satisfied, but the hunger for peace can, and the satisfaction of peace is found—is fully possessed, when all selfish desire is abandoned. Then there is fullness of joy, abounding plenty, and rich and complete blessedness.

June Twenty-sixth

Thought for the Morning

A man will reach the Kingdom by purifying himself, and he can only do this by pursuing a process of self-examination and self-analysis.

The selfishness must be discovered and understood before it can be removed. It is powerless to remove itself, neither will it pass away of itself. Darkness ceases only when light is introduced; so ignorance can only be dispersed by knowledge, selfishness by love.

A man must first of all be willing to lose himself (his self-seeking) before he can find himself (his Divine Self). He must realize that selfishness is not worth clinging to, that it is a master altogether unworthy of his service, and that divine goodness alone is worthy to be enthroned in his heart, as the supreme master of his life.

Meditation for the Day

A listless mind could not achieve any kind of success.

SUCCESS is rooted in a subtle mental brooding along a given line. It subsists in an individual characteristic, or combination of characteristics, and not in a particular circumstance, or set of circumstances. The circumstances appear, it is true, and form part of the success, but these would be useless without the mind that can penetrate and utilize them.

At the root of every success there is some form of well-husbanded and well-directed energy. There has been some persistent brooding of the mind upon a project. Success is like a flower: it may appear more or less suddenly, but it is the finished product of a long series of efforts, of preparatory stages. Men see the success, but the preparation for it, the innumerable mental processes that led up to it, are hidden from them.

Without exertion nothing can be accomplished.

Thought for the Evening

Be still, my soul, and know that peace is thine. Be steadfast, heart, and know that strength divine Belongs to thee; cease from thy turmoil, mind, and thou the Everlasting Rest shalt find.

If a man would have peace, let him exercise the spirit of peace; if he would find Love, let him dwell in the spirit of Love; if he would escape suffering, let him cease to inflict it; if he would do noble things for humanity, let him cease to do ignoble things for himself. If he will but quarry the mine of his own soul, he shall find there all the materials for building whatsoever he will, and he shall find there also the Central Rock on which to build in safety.

June Twenty-seventh

Thought for the Morning

Men go after much company, and seek out new excitements, but they are not acquainted with peace; in divers paths of pleasure they search for happiness, but they do not come to rest; through divers ways of laughter and feverish delirium they wander after gladness and life, but their tears are many and grievous, and they do not escape death.

Drifting upon the ocean of life in search of selfish indulgences, men are caught in its storms, and only after many tempests and much privation do they fly to the Rock of Refuge which rests in the deep silence of their own being.

Meditation for the Day

In order to achieve the higher forms of success, a man must give up anxiety, hurry, and fussiness.

PRESSING forward persistently along a given way is sure to lead to a destination that is definitely associated with that way. Frequent going aside, or turning back, will render effort fruitless; no destination will be reached; success will remain afar off.

Effort, and the more effort, and then effort again, is the keynote of success. As the simple old saying has it:

"If at first you don't succeed, Try again."

All the precepts of successful business men are precepts of *doing*; all the precepts of the wise teachers are precepts of *doing*. To cease to do is to cease to be of any use in the economy of life. Doing means effort, exertion.

Transmute the energy that wears and breaks down into that deeper and less obtrusive kind that preserves and builds up.

Thought for the Evening

Meditation centred upon divine realities is the very essence and soul of prayer. It is the silent reaching upward of the soul toward the Eternal.

Meditation is the intense dwelling, in thought, upon an idea or theme with the object of thoroughly comprehending it; and whatsoever you constantly meditate upon, you will not only come to understand, but will grow more and more into its likeness, for it will become incorporated with your very being, will become, in fact, your very self.

If, therefore, you constantly dwell upon that which is selfish and debasing, you will ultimately become selfish and debased; if you ceaselessly think upon that which is pure and unselfish, you will surely become pure and unselfish.

June Twenty-eighth

Thought for the Morning

There is no difficulty, however great, but will yield before a calm and powerful concentration of thought and no legitimate object but may be speedily actualized by the intelligent use and direction of one's soul forces.

Whatever your task may be, concentrate your whole mind upon it; throw into it all the energy of which you are capable. The faultless completion of small tasks, leads inevitably to larger tasks.

See to it that you rise by steady climbing, and you will never fall.

Meditation for the Day

The silent, calm people will manifest
a more enduring form of success
than those who are noisy and restless.

WHEN a man exchanges coppers for silver, and silver for gold, he does not thereby give up the use of money; he exchanges a heavy mass for one that is lighter and smaller but more valuable. So when a man exchanges hurry for deliberation, and deliberation for calmness, he does not give up effort, he merely exchanges a diffusive and more or less ineffective energy for a more highly concentrated, effective, and valuable form.

Yet even the crudest forms of effort are necessary at first, for without them to begin with the higher forms could not be acquired. The child must crawl before it can walk; it must babble before it can talk; it must talk before it can compose. Man begins in weakness and ends in strength, but from beginning to end he advances by the efforts he makes, by the exertion he puts forth.

The root of success is in character.

Thought for the Evening

He who knows that Love is at the heart of all things, and has realized the all-sufficing power of that Love, has no room in his heart for condemnation.

If you love people and speak of them with praise, until they in some way thwart you, or do something of which you disapprove, and then you dislike them and speak of them with dispraise, you are not governed by the Love which is of God. If, in your heart, you are continually arraigning and condemning others, selfless love is hidden from you.

Train your mind in strong, impartial, and gentle thought; train your heart in purity and compassion; train your tongue to silence, and to true and stainless speech; so shall you enter the way of holiness and peace, and shall ultimately realize the immortal Love.

June Twenty-ninth

Thought for the Morning

If you would realize true prosperity, do not settle down, as many have done, into the belief that if you do right everything will go wrong. Do not allow the word "competition" to shake your faith in the supremacy of righteousness. I care not what men say about the "laws of competition," for do not I know the Unchangeable Law which shall one day put them all to rout, and which puts them to rout even now in the heart and life of the righteous man? And knowing this law I can contemplate all dishonesty with undisturbed repose, for I know where certain destruction awaits it.

Under all circumstances *do that which you believe to be right*, and trust the Law; trust the Divine Power which is immanent in the universe, and it will never desert you, and you will always be protected.

Meditation for the Day

The law which punishes us is the law which preserves us.

WHEN in their ignorance men would destroy themselves, its everlasting arms are thrown about them in loving, albeit sometimes painful, protection. Every pain we suffer brings us nearer to the knowledge of the Divine Wisdom. Every blessedness we enjoy speaks to us of the perfection of the Great Law, and of the fullness of bliss that shall be man's when he has come to his heritage of divine knowledge. We progress by learning, and we learn, up to a certain point, by suffering. When the heart is mellowed by love, the law of love is perceived in all its wonderful kindness; when wisdom is acquired, peace is assured. We cannot alter the law of things, which is of sublime perfection, but we can alter ourselves so as to comprehend more and more of that perfection, and make its grandeur ours.

To wish to bring down the perfect to the imperfect is the crown of folly,
but to strive to bring the imperfect up to the perfect is the height of wisdom.

Thought for the Evening

Forget yourself entirely in the sorrows of others, and in ministering to others, and divine happiness will emancipate you from all sorrow and suffering. "Taking the first step with a good thought, the second with a good word, and the third with a good deed, I entered Paradise." And you also enter Paradise by pursuing the same course.

Lose yourself in the welfare of others; forget yourself in all that you do—this is the secret of abounding happiness. Ever be on the watch to guard against selfishness and learn faithfully the divine lessons of inward sacrifice; so shall you climb the highest heights of happiness, and shall remain in the never-clouded sunshine of universal joy, clothed in the shining garment of immortality.

June Thirtieth

Thought for the Morning

When the farmer has tilled and dressed his land and put in the seed, he knows that he has done all that he can possibly do, and that now he must trust to the elements, and wait patiently for the course of time to bring about the harvest, and that no amount of expectancy on his part will affect the result.

Even so, he who has realized Truth, goes forth as a sower of the seeds of goodness, purity, love, and peace, without expectancy and never looking for results, knowing that there is the Great Over-ruling Law which brings about its own harvest in due time, and which is alike the source of preservation and destruction.

Meditation for the Day

Seers of the Cosmos do not mourn over the scheme of things.

SEERS of the Cosmos see the universe as a perfect whole, and not as an imperfect jumble of parts. The Great Teachers are men of abiding joy and heavenly peace.

The blind captive of unholy desire may cry:

> "Ah! Love, could you and I with Him conspire
> To grasp this sorry scheme of things entire,
> Would we not shatter it to bits, and then
> Remold it nearer to the heart's desire?"

This is the wish of the voluptuary, the wish to enjoy unlawful pleasures to any extent, and not reap any painful consequences. It is such men who regard the universe as a "sorry scheme of things". They want the universe to bend to their will and desire; want lawlessness, not law; but the wise man bends his will and subjects his desires to the Divine Order, and he sees the universe as the glorious perfection of an infinitude of parts.

To perceive it, is the beatific vision; to know it, is the beatific bliss.

Thought for the Evening

The virtuous put a check upon themselves, and set a watch upon their passions and emotions; in this way they gain possession of the mind, and gradually acquire calmness; and as they acquire influence, power, greatness, abiding joy, and fullness and completeness of life.

He only finds peace who conquers himself, who strives, day by day, after greater self-possession, greater self-control, and greater calmness of mind.

Where the calm mind is there is strength and rest, there is love and wisdom; there is one who has fought successfully innumerable battles against self, who, after long toil in secret against his own failings, has triumphed at last.

July First

Thought for the Morning

In aiming at the life of blessedness, one of the simplest beginnings to be considered, and rightly made, is that which we all make every day—namely, the beginning of each day's life. There is a sense in which every day may be regarded as the beginning of a new life, in which one can think, act, and live newly, and in a wiser and better spirit. The right beginning of the day will be followed by a cheerfulness permeating the household with a sunny influence, and the tasks and duties of the day will be undertaken in a strong and confident spirit, and the whole day will be well lived.

Meditation for the Day

Wisdom is the aim of every philosophy.

IN whatever condition a man finds himself, he can always find the True; and he can find it only by so utilizing his present condition as to become strong and wise. The effeminate hankering after rewards, and the craven fear of punishment, let them be put away forever, and let a man joyfully bend himself to the faithful performance of all his duties, forgetting himself and his worthless pleasures, and living strong and pure and self-contained; so shall he surely find the Unfailing Wisdom, the God-like Patience and Strength. "The situation that has not its Duty, its Ideal, was never yet occupied by man." All that is beautiful and blessed is in thyself, not in thy neighbour's wealth. Thou art poor? Thou art poor indeed if thou art not stronger than thy poverty! Thou hast suffered calamities? Tell me, wilt thou cure calamity by adding anxiety to it? There is no evil but will vanish if thou wilt wisely meet it.

Canst thou mend a broken vase by weeping over it?

Thought for the Evening

There can be no progress, no achievement, without sacrifice, and a man's worldly success will be in the measure that he sacrifices his confused animal thoughts, and fixes his mind on the development of his plans, and the strengthening of his resolution and self-reliance. And the higher he lifts his thoughts, the more manly, upright, and righteous he becomes, the greater will be his success, the more blessed and enduring will be his achievements.

July Second

Thought for the Morning

None but right acts can follow right thoughts; none but a right life can follow right acts; and by living a right life all blessedness is achieved. Mind is the Master-power that moulds and makes. And Man is Mind, and evermore he takes the tool of thought, and, shaping what he wills, brings forth a thousand joys, a thousand ills;—He thinks in secret, and it comes to pass: environment is but his looking-glass.

Meditation for the Day

The might of meekness!

THE man who conquers another by force is strong; the man who conquers himself by Meekness is mighty. He who conquers another by force will himself likewise be conquered; he who conquers himself by Meekness will never be overthrown, for the human cannot overcome the divine. The meek man is triumphant in defeat. Socrates lives the more by being put to death; in the crucified Jesus the risen Christ is revealed; and Stephen, in receiving his stoning, defies the hurting power of stones. That which is real cannot be destroyed, but only that which is unreal. When a man finds that within him which is real, which is constant, abiding, changeless, and eternal, he enters into that Reality, and becomes meek. All the powers of darkness will come against him, but they will do him no hurt, and will at last depart from him.

Meekness is a divine quality, and as such is all powerful.

Thought for the Evening

Calmness of mind is one of the beautiful jewels of wisdom. A man becomes calm in the measure that he understands himself as a thought-evolved being... and he as he develops a right understanding, and sees more and more clearly the internal relations of things by the action of cause and effect, he ceases to fret and fume, and worry and grieve, and remains poised, steadfast, serene.

July Third

Thought for the Morning

To follow, under all circumstances, the highest promptings within you; to be always true to the divine self; to reply upon the inward voice, the inward light, and to pursue your purpose with a fearless and restful heart, believing that the future will yield unto you the need of every thought and effort; knowing that the laws of the universe can never fail, and that your own will come back to you with mathematical exactitude—this is faith and the living of faith.

Meditation for the Day

Nothing is hidden from him who overcomes himself.

INTO the cause of causes shall thou penetrate, and lifting, one after another, every veil of illusion, shalt reach at last the inmost Heart of Being. Thus becoming one with Life, thou shalt know all life, and, seeing into causes, and knowing realities, thou shalt be no more anxious about thyself, and others, and the world, but shalt see that all things that are, are engines of the Great Law. Canopied with gentleness, thou shalt bless where others curse; love where others hate; forgive where others condemn; yield where others strive; give up where others grasp; lose where others gain. And in their strength they shall be weak; and in thy weakness thou shalt be strong; yea, thou shalt mightily prevail. "Therefore, when Heaven would save a man, it enfolds him with gentleness."

He that hath not unbroken gentleness hath not Truth.

Thought for the Evening

Have a thorough understanding of your work, and let it be your own; and as you proceed, ever following the inward guide, the infallible voice, you will pass on from victory to victory, and will rise step by step to higher resting-places, and your ever broadening outlook will gradually reveal to you the essential beauty and purpose of life. Self-purified, health will be yours; self-governed, power will be yours, and all that you do will prosper.

And I may stand where health, success, and power await my coming, if, each fleeting hour, I cling to love and patience; and abide with stainlessness; and never step aside from high integrity; so shall I see at last the land of immortality.

July Fourth

Thought for the Morning

When the tongue is well controlled and wisely subdued; when selfish impulses and unworthy thoughts no longer rush to the tongue demanding utterance; when the speech has become harmless, pure, gracious, gentle, and purposeful, and no word is uttered but in sincerity and truth—then are the five steps in virtuous speech accomplished, then is the second great lesson in Truth learned and mastered. Make pure thy heart, and thou wilt make thy life rich, sweet and beautiful.

Meditation for the Day

How can he fear any who wrongs none?

THE righteous man is invincible. No enemy can possibly overcome or confound him; and he needs no other protection than that of his own integrity and holiness. As it is impossible for evil to overcome Good, so the righteous man can never be brought low by the unrighteous. Slander, envy, hatred, malice can never reach him, nor cause him any suffering, and those who try to injure him only succeed ultimately in bringing ignominy upon themselves.

The righteous man having nothing to hide, committing no acts which require stealth, and harbouring no thoughts and desires which he would not like others to know, is fearless and unashamed. His step is firm, his body upright, and his speech direct and without ambiguity. He looks everybody in the face. How can he be ashamed before any who deceives none?

Ceasing from all wrong you can never be wronged;
ceasing from all deceit you can never be deceived.

Thought for the Evening

Having clothed himself with humility, the first questions a man asks himself are:—

"How am I acting towards others?"
"What am I doing to others?"
"How am I thinking of others?"
"Are my thoughts of, and acts towards others prompted by unselfish love?"

As a man, in the silence of his soul, asks himself these searching questions, he will unerringly see where he has hitherto failed.

July Fifth

Thought for the Morning

To dwell in love always and towards all is to live the true life, is to have Life itself. Knowing this, the good man gives up himself unreservedly to the Spirit of Love, and dwells in Love towards all, contending with none, condemning none, but loving all.

The Christ Spirit of Love puts an end, not only to all sin, but to all division and contention.

Meditation for the Day

The universe is preserved because Love is at the Heart of it.

THE Children of Light who abide in the Kingdom of Heaven see the universe, and all that it contains, as the manifestation of one Law—the Law of Love. They see Love as the moulding, sustaining, protecting, and perfecting Power immanent in all things animate and inanimate. To them Love is not merely and only a rule of life, it is the Law of life, it is Life itself. Knowing this, they order their whole life in accordance with Love, not regarding their own personality. By thus practising obedience to the Highest, to divine Love, they become conscious partakers of the power of Love, and so arrive at perfect Freedom as Masters of Destiny. Love is Perfect Harmony, pure bliss, and contains, therefore, no element of suffering. Let a man think no thought and do no act that is not in accordance with pure Love, and suffering shall no more trouble him.

Love is the only preserving power.

Thought for the Evening

When sin and self are abandoned, the heart is restored to its imperishable Joy. Joy comes and fills the self-emptied heart; it abides with the peaceful; its reign is with the pure. Joy flees from the selfish, it deserts the quarrelsome; it is hidden from the impure. Joy cannot remain with the selfish; it is wedded to Love.

July Sixth

Thought for the Morning

In the pure heart there is no room left where personal judgments and hatreds can find lodgement, for it is filled to overflowing with tenderness and love; it sees no evil, and only as men succeed in seeing no evil in others will they become free from sin, and sorrow, and suffering. If men only understood that the heart that sins must sorrow, that the hateful mind tomorrow reaps its barren harvest, weeping, starving, resting not, nor sleeping; tenderness would fill their being, they would see with pity's seeing, if they only understood.

Meditation for the Day

To know Love is to know that there is
no harmful power in the whole universe.

IF a man would know Love, and partake of its undying bliss, he must practise it in his heart; he must become Love. He who always acts from the spirit of Love is never deserted, is never left in a dilemma or difficulty, for Love (impersonal Love) is both Knowledge and Power. He who has learned how to Love has learned how to master every difficulty, how to transmute every failure into success, how to clothe every event and condition in garments of blessedness and beauty.

The way to Love is by self-mastery, and, travelling that way, a man builds himself up in Knowledge as he proceeds. Arriving at Love, he enters into full possession of body and mind, by right of the divine Power which he has earned. "Perfect Love casteth out fear."

Perfect Love is perfect Harmlessness.
And he who has destroyed in himself
all thoughts of harm, and all desire to harm,
receives the universal protection.

Thought for the Evening

To stand face to face with truth; to arrive, after innumerable wanderings and pains, at wisdom and bliss; not to be finally defeated and cast out, but to ultimately triumph over every inward foe—such is man's divine destiny, such his glorious goal; and this, every saint, sage, and saviour has declared. A man only begins to be a man when he ceases to whine and revile, and commences to search for the hidden justice which regulates his life. And as he adapts his mind to that regulating factor, he ceases to accuse others as the cause of his condition, and builds himself up in strong and noble thoughts; ceases to kick against circumstances, but begins to use them as aids to his more rapid progress, and as a means of discovering the hidden power and possibilities within himself.

July Seventh

Thought for the Morning

The will to evil and the will to good are both within thee, which wilt thou employ? Thou knowest what is right and what is wrong, which wilt though love and foster, which destroy?

Thou art the chooser of thy thoughts and deeds; thou art the maker of thine inward state; the power is thine to be what thou wilt be; thou buildest Truth and Love, or lies and hate.

Meditation for the Day

By self-enlightenment is Perfect Freedom found.

THERE is no bondage in the Heavenly Life. There is Perfect Freedom. This is its great glory. This Supreme Freedom is gained only by obedience. He who obeys the Highest co-operates with the Highest, and so masters every force within himself and every condition without. A man may choose the lower and neglect the Higher, but the Higher is never overcome by the lower: herein lies the revelation of Freedom. Let a man choose the Higher and abandon the lower; he shall then establish himself as an overcomer, and shall realize Perfect Freedom.

To give the reins to inclination is the only slavery; to conquer oneself is the only freedom. The slave to self loves his chains, and will not have one of them broken for fear he would be depriving himself of some cherished delight. He thus defeats and enslaves himself.

The Land of Perfect Freedom lies through the Gate of Knowledge.

Thought for the Evening

The teaching of Jesus brings men back to the simple truth that righteousness, or *right-doing*, is entirely a matter of individual conduct, and not a mystical something apart from a man's thoughts and deeds.

Calmness and patience can become habitual by first grasping, through effort, a calm and patient thought, and then continuously thinking it, and living in it, until "use becomes second nature," and anger and impatience pass away for ever.

July Eighth

Thought for the Morning

Man is made or unmade by himself; in the armoury of thought he forges the weapons by which he destroys himself; he also fashions the tools with which he builds for himself heavenly mansions of joy and strength and peace. By the right choice and true application of thought man ascends to the Divine Perfection; by the abuse and wrong application of thought he descends below the level of the beast. Between these two extremes are all the grades of character and man is their maker and master.

As a being of Power, Intelligence, and Love, and the lord of his own thoughts, man holds the key to every situation.

Meditation for the Day

Man will be free when he is freed from self.

ALL outward oppression is but the shadow and effect of the real oppression within. For ages the oppressed have cried for liberty, and a thousand man-made statutes have failed to give it to them. They can give it only to themselves; they shall find it only in obedience to the Divine Statutes which are inscribed upon their hearts. Let them resort to the inward Freedom, and the shadow of oppression shall no more darken the earth. Let men cease to oppress themselves, and no man shall oppress his brother. Men legislate for an *outward* freedom, yet continue to render such freedom impossible of achievement by fostering an inward condition of enslavement. They thus pursue a shadow without, and ignore the substance within. All outward forms of bondage and oppression will cease to be when man ceases to be the willing bond-slave of passion, error, and ignorance.

Freedom is to the free!

Thought for the Evening

Whatsoever you harbour in the inmost chambers of your heart will, sooner or later, by the inevitable law of reaction, shape itself in your outward life.

Every soul attracts its own, and nothing can possibly come to it that does not belong to it. To realize this is to recognize the universality of Divine Law.

If thou would'st right the world, and banish all its evils and its woes, make its wild places bloom, and its drear deserts blossom as the rose—then right thyself.

July Ninth

Thought for the Morning

Whatever conditions are rendering your life burdensome, you may pass out of and beyond them by developing and utilizing within you the transforming power of self-purification and self-conquest.

Before the divine radiance of a pure heart all darkness vanishes and all clouds melt away, and he who has conquered self has conquered the universe.

He who sets his foot firmly upon the path of self-conquest, who walks, aided by the staff of faith, the highway of self-sacrifice, will assuredly achieve the highest prosperity, and will reap abounding and enduring joy and bliss.

Meditation for the Day

The True, the Beautiful, the Great
is always childlike, and is perennially fresh and young.

THE great man is always the good man; he is always simple. He draws from, nay, lives in, the inexhaustible fountain of divine Goodness within; he inhabits the Heavenly Places; communes with the vanished great ones; lives with the Invisible: he is inspired, and breathes the airs of Heaven.

He who would be great, let him learn to be good. He will therefore become great by not seeking greatness. Aiming at greatness, a man arrives at nothingness; aiming at nothingness he arrives at greatness. The desire to be great is an indication of littleness, of personal vanity and obtrusiveness. The willingness to disappear from gaze, the titter absence of self-aggrandizement, is the witness of greatness. Littleness seeks and loves authority. Greatness is never authoritative, and it thereby becomes the authority to which the after ages appeal.

Be thy simple self, thy better self, the impersonal self,
and lo! thou art great!

Thought for the Evening

It is the silent and conquering thought forces which bring all things into manifestation. The universe grew out of thought.

To adjust all your thoughts to a perfect and unswerving faith in the omnipotence and supremacy of Good is to co-operate with that Good, and to realize within yourself the solution and destruction of all evil.

To mentally deny evil is not sufficient; it must, by daily practice, be risen above and understood. To affirm the Good mentally is inadequate; it must, by unswerving endeavour, be entered into and comprehended.

July Tenth

Thought for the Morning

Every thought you think is a force sent out. Whatever your position in life may be, before you can hope to enter into any measure of success, usefulness, and power, you must learn how to focus your thought forces by cultivating calmness and repose.

There is no difficulty, however great, but will yield before a calm and purposeful concentration of thought, and no legitimate object but may be speedily actualized by the intelligent use and direction of one's soul forces.

Think good thoughts, and they will quickly become actualized in your outward life in the form of good conditions.

Meditation for the Day

The greatness that is flawless, rounded, and complete
is above and beyond all art.

WOULDST thou preach the living Word? Thou shall forgo thyself, and become that Word. Thou shalt know one thing—*that the human heart is good, is divine*; thou shalt live one thing Love. Thou shalt love all, seeing no evil, believing no evil; then, though thou speak but little, thy every act shall be a power, thy every word a precept. By thy pure thought, thy selfless deed, though it appear hidden, thou shalt preach, down the ages, to untold multitudes of aspiring souls.

To him who chooses Goodness, sacrificing all, is given that which includes all. He becomes the possessor of the Best, communes with the Highest, and enters the company of the Great.

The greatness that is flawless, rounded, and complete
is above and beyond all art.
It is Perfect Goodness in manifestation:
therefore the greatest souls are always Teachers.

Thought for the Evening

That which you would be and hope to be, you may be now. Non-accomplishment resides in your perpetual postponement, and, having the power to postpone, you also have the power to accomplish—to perpetually accomplish: realize this truth, and you shall be today, and every day, the ideal being of whom you dreamed.

Say to yourself, "I will live in my Ideal now; I will manifest my ideal now; I will be my Ideal now; and all that tempts me away from my Ideal I will not listen to; I will listen only to the voice of my Ideal."

July Eleventh

Thought for the Morning

Be as a flower; content to be, to grow in sweetness day by day. If thou would'st perfect thyself in knowledge, perfect thyself in Love. If thou would'st reach the Highest, ceaselessly cultivate a loving and compassionate heart.

To him who chooses Goodness, sacrificing all, is given that which is more than, and includes, all.

Meditation for the Day

Every natural law has its spiritual counterpart.

THOUGHTS are seeds, which, falling in the soil of the mind, germinate and develop until they reach the completed stage, blossoming into deeds good or bad, brilliant or stupid, according to their nature, and ending as seeds of thought to be again sown in other minds. A teacher is a sower of seed, a spiritual agriculturist, while he who teaches himself is the wise farmer of his own mental plot. The growth of a thought is as the growth of a plant. The seed must be sown seasonably, and time is required for its full development into the plant of knowledge and the flower of wisdom.

The seen is the mirror of the unseen.

Thought for the Evening

The Great Law never cheats any man of his just due.

Human life, when rightly lived, is simple with a beautiful simplicity.

He who comprehends the utter simplicity of life, who obeys its laws, and does not step aside into the dark paths and complex mazes of selfish desire, stands where no harm can reach him.

Then there is fullness of joy, abounding plenty, and rich and complete blessedness.

July Twelfth

Thought for the Morning

Every man reaps the results of his own thoughts and deeds, and suffers for his own wrong.

He who begins right, and continues right, does not need to desire, and search for felicitous results; they are already at hand; they follow as consequences; they are the certainties, the realities, of life.

Sweet is the rest and deep is the bliss of him who has freed his heart from its lusts and hatreds and dark desires.

Meditation for the Day

Energy to be productive must not only be directed towards good ends,
it must be carefully controlled and conserved.

THE advice of one of the Great Teachers to his disciples, "Keep wide awake," tersely expresses the necessity for tireless energy if one's purpose is to be accomplished, and is equally good advice to the salesman as to the saint. "Eternal vigilance is the price of liberty," and liberty is the reaching of one's fixed ends. It was the same Teacher who said: "If anything is to be done, let a man do it at once; let him attack it vigorously! "The wisdom of this advice is seen when it is remembered that action is creative, that increase and development follow upon legitimate use. To get more energy we must use to the full that which we already possess. Only to him that puts his hand vigorously to some task do power and freedom come.

Noise and hurry are so much energy running to waste.

Thought for the Evening

You are the creator of your own shadows; you desire, and then you grieve; renounce, and then you shall rejoice.

Of all the beautiful truths pertaining to the soul. . . none is more gladdening or fruitful of divine promise and confidence than this—that man is the master of thought, the moulder of character, and the maker and shaper of character, environment, and destiny.

July Thirteenth

Thought for the Morning

As darkness is a passing shadow, and light is a substance that remains, so sorrow is fleeting, but joy abides for ever. No true thing can pass away and become lost; no false thing can remain and be preserved. Sorrow is false, and it cannot live; joy is true, and it cannot die. Joy may become hidden for a time, but it can always be recovered; sorrow may remain for a period, but it can be transcended and dispersed.

Do not think your sorrow will remain; it will pass away like a cloud. Do not believe that the torments of sin are ever your portion; they will vanish like a hideous nightmare. Awake! Arise! Be holy and joyful.

Meditation for the Day

It is a great delusion that noise means power.

WHERE calmness is, there is the greatest power. Calmness is the sure indication of a strong, well-trained, patiently disciplined mind. The calm man knows his business, be sure of it. His words are few, but they tell. His schemes are well planned, and they work true, like a well-balanced machine. He sees a long way ahead, and makes straight for his object. The enemy, Difficulty, he converts into a friend, and makes profitable use of him, for he has studied well how to "agree with his adversary while he is in the way with him." Like a wise general, he has anticipated all emergencies. Indeed, he is *the man who is prepared beforehand*. In his meditations, in the counsels of his judgment, he has conferred with causes, and has caught the bent of all contingencies. He is never taken by surprise; is never in a hurry; is safe in the keeping of his own steadfastness; and is sure of his ground.

Working steam is not heard.
It is the escaping steam which makes a great noise.

Thought for the Evening

Tribulation lasts only so long as there remains some chaff of self which needs to be removed. The *tribulum*, or threshing machine, ceases to work when all the grain is separated from the chaff; and when the last impurities are blown away from the soul, tribulation has completed its work, and there is no more need for it; then abiding joy is realized.

The sole and supreme use of suffering is to purify, to burn out all that is useless and impure. Suffering ceases for him who is pure. There could be no object in burning gold after the dross had been removed.

July Fourteenth

Thought for the Morning

In speaking of self-control, one is easily misunderstood. It should not be associated with a destructive repression, but with a constructive expression.

A man is happy, wise and great in the measure that he controls himself; he is wretched, foolish, and mean in the measure that he allows his animal nature to dominate his thoughts and actions.

He who controls himself, controls his life, his circumstances, his destiny; and wherever he goes he carries his happiness with him as an abiding possession.

Renunciation precedes regeneration. The permanent happiness which men seek in dissipation, excitement, and abandonment to unworthy pleasures, is found only in the life which reverses all this—the life of self-control.

Meditation for the Day

Energy is the first pillar in the temple of prosperity.

CALMNESS, as distinguished from the dead placidity of languor, is the acme of concentrated energy. There is a focused mentality behind it. In agitation and excitement the mentality is dispersed. It is irresponsible, and is without force or weight. The fussy, peevish, irritable man has no influence. He repels, not attracts. He wonders why his "easy-going" neighbour succeeds, and is sought after, while he, who is always hurrying, worrying, and troubling (he miscalls it *striving*), fails, and is avoided. His neighbour, being a calmer man, not more easygoing but more deliberate, gets through more work, does it more skilfully, and is more self-possessed and manly. This is the reason of his success and influence. His energy is controlled and used, while the other man's energy is dispersed and abused.

No energy means no capacity.

Thought for the Evening

Law, not confusion, is the dominating principle in the universe; justice, not injustice is the soul and substance of life; and righteousness, not corruption, is the moulding and moving force in the spiritual government of the world. This being so, man has but the right himself to find that the universe is right.

When I am pure, I shall have solved the mystery of life; I shall be sure, when I am free from hatred, lust and strife, I am in Truth, and Truth abides in me; I shall be safe, and sane, and wholly free, when I am pure.

July Fifteenth

Thought for the Morning

If men only understood that their hatred and resentment slays their peace and sweet contentment, hurts themselves, helps not another, does not cheer one lonely brother, they would seek the better doing of good deeds which leaves no ruing:—

If they only understood.

If men only understood how Love conquers; how prevailing is its might, grim hate assailing; how compassion endeth sorrow, maketh wise, and doth not borrow pain of passion, they would ever live in Love, in hatred never:—

If they only understood.

Meditation for the Day

*The spendthrift can never become rich, but, if he begin
with riches, must soon become poor.*

THE poor man who is to become rich must begin at the bottom, and must not wish, or try, to appear affluent by attempting something far beyond his means. There is always plenty of room and scope at the bottom, and it is a safe place from which to begin, as there is nothing below, and everything above. Many a young business man comes at once to grief by swagger and display, which he foolishly imagines are necessary to success, but which, deceiving no one but himself, lead quickly to ruin. A modest and true beginning, in any sphere, will better ensure success than an exaggerated advertisement of one's standing and importance.

The thrifty and prudent are on the way to riches.

Thought for the Evening

The grace and beauty that were in Jesus can be of no value to you—cannot be understood by you—unless they are also *in you*, and they can never be in you, until you practice them, for, apart from *doing*, the qualities which constitute goodness do not, as far as you are concerned, exist.

To adore Jesus for his good qualities is a long step towards Truth, but to practice those qualities is Truth itself; and he who fully adores the perfection of another will not rest content in his own imperfection, but will fashion his soul after the likeness of that other.

Therefore thou who adorest Jesus for his divine qualities, practice those qualities thyself, and thou too shalt be divine.

July Sixteenth

Thought for the Morning

Let a man realize that life in its totality proceeds from the mind, and lo, the way of blessedness is opened up to him! For he will then discover that he possesses the power to rule his mind and to fashion it in accordance with his Ideal.

So will he elect to strongly and steadfastly walk those pathways of thought and action which are altogether excellent; to him life will become beautiful and sacred; and, sooner or later, he will put to flight all evil, confusion, and suffering; for it is impossible for a man to fall short of liberation, enlightenment, and peace, who guards with unwearying diligence the gateway of his heart.

Meditation for the Day

Vanity leading to excessive luxury in clothing is a vice
which should be studiously avoided by virtuous people.

AN obtrusive display in clothing and jewellery bespeaks a vulgar and empty mind. Modest and cultured people are modest and becoming in their dress, and their spare money is wisely used in further enhancing their culture and virtue. Education and progress are of more importance to them than needless, vain apparel; and literature, art, and science are encouraged thereby. A true refinement is in the mind and behaviour, and a mind adorned with virtue and intelligence cannot add to its attractiveness (though it may detract from it) by an ostentatious display of the body.

Simplicity in dress, as in other things, is the best.

Thought for the Evening

By constantly overcoming self, a man gains a knowledge of the subtle intricacies of his mind; and it is this divine knowledge which enables him to become established in calmness.

Without self-knowledge there can be no abiding peace of mind, and those who are carried away by tempestuous passions, cannot approach the holy place where calmness reigns.

The weak man is like one who, having mounted a fiery steed, allows it to run away with him, and carry him withersoever it wills; the strong man is like one who, having mounted the steed, governs it with a masterly hand and makes it go in whatever direction and at whatever speed he commands.

July Seventeenth

Thought for the Morning

There is no strife, no selfishness, in the Kingdom; there is perfect harmony, equipoise, and rest.

Those who live in the Kingdom of Love, have all their needs supplied by the Law of Love.

As self is the root cause of all strife and suffering, so Love is the root cause of all peace and bliss. Those who are at rest in the Kingdom do not look for happiness in any outward possessions. They are freed from all anxiety and trouble and, resting in Love, they are the embodiment of happiness.

Meditation for the Day

*Money wasted can be restored; health wasted can be restored;
but time wasted can never be restored.*

THE man who gets up early in order to think and plan, that he may weigh and consider and forecast, will always manifest greater skill and success in his particular pursuit than the man who lies in bed till the last moment, and only gets up in time to begin breakfast. An hour spent in this way before breakfast will prove of the greatest value in making one's efforts fruitful. It is a means of calming and clarifying the mind, and of focusing one's energies so as to render them more powerful and effective. The best and most abiding success is that which is made before eight o'clock in the morning. He who is at his business at six o'clock will always—all other conditions being equal—be a long way ahead of the man who is in bed at eight.

The day is not lengthened for any man.

Thought for the Evening

Let it not be supposed that the children of the Kingdom live in ease and indolence (these two sins are the first that have to be eradicated when the search for the Kingdom is entered upon); they live in a peaceful activity; in fact, they only truly live, for the life of self, with its train of worries, griefs, and fears, is not *real life*.

The children of the Kingdom are *known by their life*, they manifest the fruits of the Spirit— "Love, joy, peace, long-suffering, kindness, goodness, faithfulness, meekness, temperance, and self-control"—under all circumstances and vicissitudes.

July Eighteenth

Thought for the Morning

The gospel of Jesus is a gospel of *living and doing*. If it were not this it would not voice the Eternal Truth. Its Temple is Purified Conduct, the entrance-door to which is *Self-Surrender*. It invites men to shake off sin, and promises, as a result, joy and blessedness and perfect peace.

The Kingdom of Heaven is perfect trust, perfect knowledge, perfect peace. . . no sin can enter therein, no self-born thought or deed can pass its golden gates; no impure desire can defile its radiant robes. . . all may enter it who will, but all must pay the price—*the unconditional abandonment of self.*

Meditation for the Day

Wisdom is the highest form of skill.

THERE is *one* right way of doing everything, even the smallest, and a thousand wrong ways. Skill consists in finding the one right way, and adhering to it. The inefficient bungle confusedly about among the thousand wrong ways, and do not adopt the right one when it is pointed out to them. They do this in some cases because they think, in their ignorance, that they know best, thereby placing themselves in a position where *it* becomes impossible to learn, even though it be only to learn how to clean a window or sweep a floor. Thoughtlessness and inefficiency are all too common. There is plenty of room in the world for thoughtful and efficient people. Employers of labour know how difficult it is to get the best workmanship. The good workman, whether with tools or brains, whether with speech or thought, will always find a place for the exercise of his skill.

Skill is gained by thoughtfulness and attention.

Thought for the Evening

I say this—and know it to be truth—*that circumstances can only affect you in so far as you allow them to do so.* You are swayed by circumstances because you have not a right understanding of the nature, use, and power of thought. You believe (and upon this little word *belief* hang all our joys and sorrows) that outward things have the power to make or mar your life; by so doing you submit to those outward things, confess that you are their slave, and they your unconditional master. By so doing you invest them with a power which they do not of themselves possess, and you succumb, in reality not to the circumstances, but to the gloom or gladness, the fear or hope, the strength of weakness, which your thought-sphere has thrown around them.

July Nineteenth

Thought for the Morning

If you are one of those who are praying for, and looking forward to a happier world beyond the grave, here is a message of gladness for you—you may enter into and realize that happy world now; it fills the whole universe, and it is within you, waiting for you to find, acknowledge, and possess.

Said one who understood the inner laws of Being—"When men shall say, lo here, or lo there, go not after them. The Kingdom of God is within you."

Meditation for the Day

There is no striking a cheap bargain with prosperity.

AS the bubble cannot endure, so the fraud cannot prosper. He makes a feverish spurt in the acquirement of money, and then collapses. Nothing is ever gained, ever can be gained, by fraud. It is but wrested for a time, to be again returned with heavy interest. But fraud is not confined to the unscrupulous swindler. All who are getting, or trying to get, money without giving an equivalent are practising fraud, whether they know it or not. Men who are anxiously scheming how to get money without working for it are frauds, and mentally they are closely allied to the thief and swindler under whose influence they come, sooner or later, and who deprives them of their capital.

Prosperity must be purchased,
not only with intelligent labor,
but with moral force.

Thought for the Evening

Heaven and hell are inward states. Sink into self and all its gratifications, and you sink into hell; rise above self into that state of consciousness which is the utter denial and forgetfulness of self, and you enter heaven.

So long as you persist in selfishly seeking for your own personal happiness, so long will happiness elude you, and you will be sowing the seeds of wretchedness. In so far as you succeed in losing yourself in the service of others, in that measure will happiness come to you, and you will reap a harvest of bliss.

July Twentieth

Thought for the Morning

Sympathy given can never be waste.

One aspect of sympathy is that of pity—pity for the distressed or pain stricken, with a desire to alleviate or help them in their sufferings. The world needs more of this divine quality.

"For pity makes the world soft to the weak, and noble for the strong."

Another form of sympathy is that of rejoicing with others who are more successful than ourselves, and though their success were our own.

Meditation for the Day

Sterling integrity tells wherever it is,
and stamps its hall-mark on all transactions.

To be complete and strong, integrity must embrace the whole man, and extend to all the details of his life; and it must be so thorough and permanent as to withstand all temptations to swerve into compromise. To fail in one point is to fail in all, and to admit, under stress, a compromise with falsehood, howsoever necessary and insignificant it may appear, is to throw down the shield of integrity, and to stand exposed to the onslaughts of evil.

The man who works as carefully and conscientiously when his employer is away as when his eye is on him, will not long remain in an inferior position. Such integrity in duty, in performing the details of his work, will quickly lead him into the fertile regions of prosperity.

The man of integrity is in line with the fixed law of things.
He is like a strong tree whose roots are fed by perennial springs,
and which no tempest can lay low.

Thought for the Evening

Sweet are companionships, pleasures, and material comforts, but they change and fade away. Sweeter still are Purity, Wisdom, and the knowledge of Truth, and these never change nor fade away.

He who attained to the possession of spiritual things can never be deprived of his source of happiness; he will never have to part company with it, and wherever he goes in the whole universe, he will carry his possessions with him. His spiritual end will be the fullness of joy.

July Twenty-first

Thought for the Morning

Let your heart grow and expand with ever broadening love, until, freed from all hatred, and passion, and condemnation, it embraces the whole universe with thoughtful tenderness.

As the flower opens its petals to receive the morning light, so open your soul more and more to the glorious light of Truth.

Soar upward on the wings of aspiration; be fearless and believe in the loftiest possibilities.

Meditation for the Day

Ignorant men imagine that dishonesty is a short cut to prosperity.

HONESTY is the surest way to success. The day at last comes when the dishonest man repents in sorrow and suffering; but no man ever needs to repent of having been honest. Even when the honest man fails—as he does sometimes through lacking other of those pillars, such as energy, economy, or system—his failure is not the grievous thing that it is to the dishonest man, for he can always rejoice in the fact that he has never defrauded a fellow-being. Even in his darkest hour he finds repose in a clear conscience.

The dishonest man is morally short-sighted.

Thought for the Evening

Mind clothes itself in garments of its own making. Mind is the arbiter of life; it is the creator and shaper of conditions, and the recipient of its own results. It contains within itself both the power to create illusion and to perceive reality.

Mind is the infallible weaver of destiny; thought is the thread, good and evil deeds are the warp and woof, and the web, woven upon the loom of life, is character. Make pure thy heart, and thou wilt make thy life, rich, sweet, and beautiful, unmarred by strife.

July Twenty-second

Thought for the Morning

Cherish your visions; cherish your ideals; cherish the music that stirs in your heart, the beauty that forms in your mind, the loveliness that drapes your purest thoughts, for out of them will grow all delightful conditions, all heavenly environment; of these, if you will remain true to them, your world will at last be built.

Guard well thy mind, and, noble, strong, and free, nothing shall harm, disturb or conquer thee; for all thy foes are in thy heart and mind, there also thy salvation thou shalt find.

Meditation for the Day

Strong men have strong purposes,
and strong purposes lead to strong achievements.

INVINCIBILITY is a glorious protector, but it only envelops the man whose integrity is perfectly pure and unassailable. Never to violate, even in the most insignificant particular, is to be invincible against all the assaults of innuendo, slander, and misrepresentation. The man who has failed in one point is vulnerable, and the shaft of evil, like the arrow in the heel of Achilles, will lay him low. Pure and perfect integrity is proof against all attack and injury, enabling its possessor to meet all opposition and persecution with dauntless courage and sublime equanimity. No amount of talent, intellect, or business acumen can give a man that power of mind and peace of heart which come from an enlightened acceptance and observance of lofty moral principles.

Moral force is the greatest power.

Thought for the Evening

Dream lofty dreams, and as you dream so shall you become. Your vision is the promise of what you shall one day be; your Ideal is the prophecy of what you shall at last unveil.

The greatest achievement was at first and for a time a dream. The oak sleeps in the acorn; the bird waits in the egg; and in the highest vision of the soul a waking angel stirs.

Your circumstances may be uncongenial, but they shall not long remain so when you perceive an Ideal and strive to reach it.

July Twenty-third

Thought for the Morning

He who has conquered doubt and fear has conquered failure. His every thought is allied with power, and all difficulties are bravely met and wisely overcome. His purposes are seasonably planted, and they bloom and bring forth fruit which does not fall prematurely to the ground.

Thought allied fearlessly to purpose becomes creative force: he who knows this is ready to become something higher and stronger than a mere bundle of wavering thoughts and fluctuating sensations; he who does this has become the conscious and intelligent wielder of his mental powers.

Meditation for the Day

The test of a man is in his immediate acts, and not in his ultra sentiments.

SYMPATHY should not be confounded with that maudlin and superficial sentiment which, like a pretty flower without root, presently perishes and leaves behind neither seed nor fruit. To fall into hysterical weeping when parting with a friend, or on hearing of some suffering abroad, is not sympathy. Neither are bursts of violent indignation against the cruelties and injustices of others any indication of a sympathetic mind. If one is cruel at home—if he badgers his wife, or beats his children, or abuses his servants, or stabs his neighbours with shafts of sarcasm—what hypocrisy is in his profession of love for suffering people who are outside the immediate range of his influence! What shallow sentiment informs his bursts of indignation against the injustices and hard-heartedness in the world around him!

Sympathy is a deep, inexpressible tenderness
which is shown in a consistently self-forgetful, gentle character.

Thought for the Evening

Man's true place in the Cosmos is that of a king, not a slave, a commander under the Law of Good, and not a helpless tool in the region of evil.

I write for men, not for babes; for those who are eager to learn, and earnest to achieve; for those who will put away (for the world's good) a petty personal indulgence, a selfish desire, a mean thought, and live on as though it were not, sans craving and regret.

Man is a master. If he were not, he could not act contrary to law.

Evil and weakness are self destructive. The universe is girt with goodness and strength, and it protects the good and the strong.

The angry man is the weak man.

July Twenty-fourth

Thought for the Morning

Not by learning will a man triumph over evil; not by much study will he overcome sin and sorrow. Only by conquering himself will he conquer evil; only by practicing righteousness will he put an end to sorrow.

Not for the clever, nor the learned, nor the self-confident is the Life Triumphant, but for the pure, the virtuous and wise. The former achieve their particular success in life, but the latter alone achieve the great success so invincible and complete that even in apparent defeat it shines with added victory.

Meditation for the Day

Lack of sympathy arises in egotism; sympathy arises in love.

SYMPATHY leads us to the hearts of all men, so that we become spiritually united to them, and when they suffer we feel the pain; when they are glad, we rejoice with them; when they are despised and persecuted, we spiritually descend with them into the depths, and take into our hearts their humiliation and distress; and he who has this binding, uniting spirit of sympathy can never be cynical and condemnatory, can never pass thoughtless and cruel judgments upon his fellows, because in his tenderness of heart he is ever with them in their pain.

But to have reached this ripened sympathy, it must needs be that he has loved much, suffered much, and sounded the dark depths of sorrow. It springs from acquaintance with the profoundest experiences, so that a man has had conceit, thoughtlessness, and selfishness burnt out of his heart.

Sympathy, in its real and profound sense,
is oneness with others in their strivings and sufferings.

Thought for the Evening

The true silence is not merely a silent tongue; it is a silent mind. To merely *hold one's tongue*, and yet to carry about a disturbed and rankling mind, is no remedy for weakness, and no source of power.

Silentness, to be powerful, must envelop the whole mind, must permeate every chamber of the heart; it must be the silence of peace.

To this broad, deep, abiding silentness a man attains only in the measure that he conquers himself.

July Twenty-fifth

Thought for the Morning

By curbing his tongue, a man gains possession of his mind.

The fool babbles, gossips, argues, and bandies words. He glories in the fact that he has had the last word, and has silenced his opponent. He exults in his own folly, is ever on the defensive, and wastes his energies in unprofitable channels. He is like a gardener who continues to dig and plant in unproductive soil.

The wise man avoids idle words, gossips, vain argument, and self-defence. He is content to appear defeated; rejoices when he is defeated; knowing that, having found and removed another error in himself, he has thereby become wiser.

Blessed is he who does not strive for the last word.

Meditation for the Day

Gentleness is the hall-mark of spiritual culture.

LET a man beware of greed, of meanness, of envy, of jealousy, of suspicion, for these things, if harboured, will rob him of all that is best in life, aye, even all that is best in material things, as well as all that is best in character and happiness. Let him be liberal of heart and generous of hand, magnanimous and trusting, not only giving cheerfully and often of his substance, but allowing his friends and fellow-men freedom of thought and action—let him be thus, and honour, plenty, and prosperity will come knocking at his door for admittance as his friends and guests.

Gentleness is akin to divinity.

Thought for the Evening

Desire is the *craving for possession*; aspiration is the *hunger of the heart for peace*.

The craving for things leads ever farther and farther from peace, and not only ends in deprivation, but is in itself a state of perpetual want. Until it comes to an end, rest and satisfaction are impossible.

The hunger for things can never be satisfied, but the hunger for peace can, and the satisfaction of peace is found—is fully possessed, when all selfish desire is abandoned. Then there is fullness of joy, abounding plenty, and rich and complete blessedness.

July Twenty-sixth

Thought for the Morning

A man will reach the Kingdom by purifying himself, and he can only do this by pursuing a process of self-examination and self-analysis.

The selfishness must be discovered and understood before it can be removed. It is powerless to remove itself, neither will it pass away of itself. Darkness ceases only when light is introduced; so ignorance can only be dispersed by knowledge, selfishness by love.

A man must first of all be willing to lose himself (his self-seeking) before he can find himself (his Divine Self). He must realize that selfishness is not worth clinging to, that it is a master altogether unworthy of his service, and that divine goodness alone is worthy to be enthroned in his heart, as the supreme master of his life.

Meditation for the Day

A gentle man, one whose good behavior is prompted
by thoughtfulness and kindliness, is always loved,
whatever may be his origin.

THE man who has perfected himself in gentleness never quarrels. He never returns the hard word; he leaves it alone, or meets it with a gentle word, which is far more powerful than wrath. Gentleness is wedded to wisdom, and the wise man has overcome all anger in himself, and so understands how to overcome it in others. The gentle man is saved from most of the disturbances and turmoils with which uncontrolled men afflict themselves. While they are wearing themselves out with wasteful and needless strain, he is quiet and composed, and such quietness and composure are strong to win in the battle of life.

Argument analyses the outer skin, but sympathy reaches to the heart.

Thought for the Evening

Be still, my soul, and know that peace is thine. Be steadfast, heart, and know that strength divine Belongs to thee; cease from thy turmoil, mind, and thou the Everlasting Rest shalt find.

If a man would have peace, let him exercise the spirit of peace; if he would find Love, let him dwell in the spirit of Love; if he would escape suffering, let him cease to inflict it; if he would do noble things for humanity, let him cease to do ignoble things for himself. If he will but quarry the mine of his own soul, he shall find there all the materials for building whatsoever he will, and he shall find there also the Central Rock on which to build in safety.

July Twenty-seventh

Thought for the Morning

Men go after much company, and seek out new excitements, but they are not acquainted with peace; in divers paths of pleasure they search for happiness, but they do not come to rest; through divers ways of laughter and feverish delirium they wander after gladness and life, but their tears are many and grievous, and they do not escape death.

Drifting upon the ocean of life in search of selfish indulgences, men are caught in its storms, and only after many tempests and much privation do they fly to the Rock of Refuge which rests in the deep silence of their own being.

Meditation for the Day

Spurious things have no value, whether they be bric-a-brac or men.

IT is all-important that we be real; that we harbour no wish to appear other than what we are; that we simulate no virtue, assume no excellency, adopt no disguise. The hypocrite thinks he can hoodwink the world and the eternal law of the world. There is but one person that he hoodwinks, and that is himself, and for that the law of the world inflicts its righteous penalty. There is an old theory that the excessively wicked are annihilated. I think to be a pretender is to come as near to annihilation as a man can get, for there is a sense in which a man is gone, and in his place there is but a mirage of shams.

The sound-hearted man becomes an exemplar:
he is more than a man;
he is a reality, a force, a molding principle.

Thought for the Evening

Meditation centred upon divine realities is the very essence and soul of prayer. It is the silent reaching upward of the soul toward the Eternal.

Meditation is the intense dwelling, in thought, upon an idea or theme with the object of thoroughly comprehending it; and whatsoever you constantly meditate upon, you will not only come to understand, but will grow more and more into its likeness, for it will become incorporated with your very being, will become, in fact, your very self.

If, therefore, you constantly dwell upon that which is selfish and debasing, you will ultimately become selfish and debased; if you ceaselessly think upon that which is pure and unselfish, you will surely become pure and unselfish.

July Twenty-eighth

Thought for the Morning

There is no difficulty, however great, but will yield before a calm and powerful concentration of thought and no legitimate object but may be speedily actualized by the intelligent use and direction of one's soul forces.

Whatever your task may be, concentrate your whole mind upon it; throw into it all the energy of which you are capable. The faultless completion of small tasks, leads inevitably to larger tasks.

See to it that you rise by steady climbing, and you will never fall.

Meditation for the Day

Evil is an experience, and not a power.

THE painful experiences of evil pass away as the new experiences of good enter into and possess the field of consciousness. And what are the new experiences of good? They are many and beautiful—such as the joyful knowledge of freedom from sin; the absence of remorse; deliverance from all the torments of temptation; ineffable joy in conditions and circumstances which formerly caused deep affliction; imperviousness to hurt by the actions of others; great patience and sweetness of character; serenity of mind under all circumstances; emancipation from doubt, fear, and anxiety; freedom from all dislike, envy, and enmity.

Evil is a state of ignorance, of undevelopment,
and as such it recedes and disappears before the light of knowledge.

Thought for the Evening

He who knows that Love is at the heart of all things, and has realized the all-sufficing power of that Love, has no room in his heart for condemnation.

If you love people and speak of them with praise, until they in some way thwart you, or do something of which you disapprove, and then you dislike them and speak of them with dispraise, you are not governed by the Love which is of God. If, in your heart, you are continually arraigning and condemning others, selfless love is hidden from you.

Train your mind in strong, impartial, and gentle thought; train your heart in purity and compassion; train your tongue to silence, and to true and stainless speech; so shall you enter the way of holiness and peace, and shall ultimately realize the immortal Love.

July Twenty-ninth

Thought for the Morning

If you would realize true prosperity, do not settle down, as many have done, into the belief that if you do right everything will go wrong. Do not allow the word "competition" to shake your faith in the supremacy of righteousness. I care not what men say about the "laws of competition," for do not I know the Unchangeable Law which shall one day put them all to rout, and which puts them to rout even now in the heart and life of the righteous man? And knowing this law I can contemplate all dishonesty with undisturbed repose, for I know where certain destruction awaits it.

Under all circumstances *do that which you believe to be right*, and trust the Law; trust the Divine Power which is immanent in the universe, and it will never desert you, and you will always be protected.

Meditation for the Day

When divine good is practised, life is bliss.

TO have transcendent virtue is to enjoy transcendent felicity. The beatific blessedness which Jesus holds out is promised to those having the beatific virtues—to the merciful, the pure in heart, the peacemakers, and so on. The higher virtue does not merely and only lead to happiness, it is happiness. It is impossible for a man of transcendent virtue to be unhappy. The cause of unhappiness must be sought and found in the self-loving elements, and not in the self-sacrificing qualities. A man may have virtue and be unhappy, but not so if he have divine virtue. Human virtue is mingled with self, and therefore with sorrow; but from divine virtue every taint of self has been purged away, and with it every vestige of misery.

Truth lies upward and beyond.

Thought for the Evening

Forget yourself entirely in the sorrows of others, and in ministering to others, and divine happiness will emancipate you from all sorrow and suffering. "Taking the first step with a good thought, the second with a good word, and the third with a good deed, I entered Paradise." And you also enter Paradise by pursuing the same course.

Lose yourself in the welfare of others; forget yourself in all that you do—this is the secret of abounding happiness. Ever be on the watch to guard against selfishness and learn faithfully the divine lessons of inward sacrifice; so shall you climb the highest heights of happiness, and shall remain in the never-clouded sunshine of universal joy, clothed in the shining garment of immortality.

July Thirtieth

Thought for the Morning

When the farmer has tilled and dressed his land and put in the seed, he knows that he has done all that he can possibly do, and that now he must trust to the elements, and wait patiently for the course of time to bring about the harvest, and that no amount of expectancy on his part will affect the result.

Even so, he who has realized Truth, goes forth as a sower of the seeds of goodness, purity, love, and peace, without expectancy and never looking for results, knowing that there is the Great Over-ruling Law which brings about its own harvest in due time, and which is alike the source of preservation and destruction.

Meditation for the Day

Where passion is, peace is not; where peace is, passion is not.

MEN pray for peace, yet cling to passion; they foster strife, yet pray for heavenly rest. This is ignorance, profound spiritual ignorance; it is not to know the first letter in the alphabet of things divine. Hatred and love, strife and peace, cannot dwell together in the same heart. Where one is admitted as a welcome guest, the other will be turned away as an unwelcome stranger. He who despises another will be despised by others; he who opposes his fellow-men will himself be resisted. He should not be surprised, and mourn, that men are divided. He should know that he is propagating strife. He should understand his lack of peace.

By the way of self-conquest is the Perfect Peace achieved.

Thought for the Evening

The virtuous put a check upon themselves, and set a watch upon their passions and emotions; in this way they gain possession of the mind, and gradually acquire calmness; and as they acquire influence, power, greatness, abiding joy, and fullness and completeness of life.

He only finds peace who conquers himself, who strives, day by day, after greater self-possession, greater self-control, and greater calmness of mind.

Where the calm mind is there is strength and rest, there is love and wisdom; there is one who has fought successfully innumerable battles against self, who, after long toil in secret against his own failings, has triumphed at last.

July Thirty-first

Thought for the Morning

Sympathy bestowed increases its store in our own heart and enriches and fructifies our own life. Sympathy given is blessedness received; sympathy withheld is blessedness forfeited.

In the measure that a man increases and enlarges his sympathy so much nearer does he approach the ideal life, the perfect blessedness; and when his heart has become so mellowed that no hard, bitter, or cruel thought can enter, and detract from its permanent sweetness, then indeed is he richly and divinely blessed.

Meditation for the Day

*If men only understood
That the wrong act of a brother
Should not call from them another.*

IF men only understood
That *their* wrong can never smother
The wrong doing of another;
That by hatred hate increases,
And by Good all evil ceases,
They would cleanse their hearts and actions,
Banish thence all vile detractions—
   If they only understood.

   If men only understood
That the heart that sins *must* sorrow,
That the hateful mind tomorrow
Reaps its barren harvest, weeping,
Starving, resting not, nor sleeping,
Tenderness would fill their being,
They would see with Pity's seeing—
   If they only understood.

*If men only understood
How Love conquers...
... They would ever
Live in Love, in hatred never—
If they only understood.*

Thought for the Evening

Sweet is the rest and deep the bliss of him who has freed his heart from its lusts and hatreds and dark desires; and he who, without any shadow of bitterness resting upon him, and looking out upon the world with boundless compassion and love, can breathe, in his inmost heart, the blessing: Peace unto all living things, making no exceptions or distinctions—such a man has reached that happy ending which can never be taken away, for this is the perfection of life, the fullness of peace, the consummation of perfect blessedness.

August First

Thought for the Morning

In aiming at the life of blessedness, one of the simplest beginnings to be considered, and rightly made, is that which we all make every day—namely, the beginning of each day's life. There is a sense in which every day may be regarded as the beginning of a new life, in which one can think, act, and live newly, and in a wiser and better spirit. The right beginning of the day will be followed by a cheerfulness permeating the household with a sunny influence, and the tasks and duties of the day will be undertaken in a strong and confident spirit, and the whole day will be well lived.

Meditation for the Day

Let a man abandon self, let him overcome the world, let him deny the personal; by this pathway only can he enter into the heart of the Infinite.

"GOODWILL gives insight", and only he who has so conquered his personality that he has but one attitude of mind, that of goodwill, is possessed of divine insight, and is capable of distinguishing the true from the false. The supremely good man is, therefore, the wise man, the divine man, the enlightened seer, the knower of the Eternal. Where you find unbroken gentleness, enduring patience, sublime lowliness, graciousness of speech, self-control, self-forgetfulness, and deep and abounding sympathy, look there for the highest wisdom, seek the company of such a one, for he has realized the Divine, he lives with the Eternal, he has become one with the Infinite. Those who are spiritually awakened have alone comprehended the Universal Reality where all appearances are dispersed and dreaming and delusion are destroyed.

To center one's life in the Great Law of Love is to enter into rest, harmony, peace.

Thought for the Evening

There can be no progress, no achievement, without sacrifice, and a man's worldly success will be in the measure that he sacrifices his confused animal thoughts, and fixes his mind on the development of his plans, and the strengthening of his resolution and self-reliance. And the higher he lifts his thoughts, the more manly, upright, and righteous he becomes, the greater will be his success, the more blessed and enduring will be his achievements.

August Second

Thought for the Morning

None but right acts can follow right thoughts; none but a right life can follow right acts; and by living a right life all blessedness is achieved. Mind is the Master-power that moulds and makes. And Man is Mind, and evermore he takes the tool of thought, and, shaping what he wills, brings forth a thousand joys, a thousand ills;—He thinks in secret, and it comes to pass: environment is but his looking-glass.

Meditation for the Day

*To enter into a realization of the Infinite and Eternal
is to rise superior to time.*

To refrain from all participation in evil and discord; to cease from all resistance to evil, and from the omission of that which is good, and to fall back upon unswerving obedience to the holy calm within, is to enter into the inmost heart of things, is to attain to a living, conscious experience of that eternal and infinite principle which must ever remain a hidden mystery to the merely perceptive intellect. Until this principle is realized, the soul is not established in peace, and he who so realizes is truly wise; not wise with the wisdom of the learned, but with the simplicity of a blameless heart and of a divine manhood. There is one Great Law which exacts unconditional obedience, one unifying principle which is the basis of all diversity, one eternal Truth wherein all the problems of earth pass away like shadows.

*To realize this Law, this Unity, this Truth,
is to enter into the Infinite, is to become one with the Eternal.*

Thought for the Evening

Calmness of mind is one of the beautiful jewels of wisdom. A man becomes calm in the measure that he understands himself as a thought-evolved being... and he as he develops a right understanding, and sees more and more clearly the internal relations of things by the action of cause and effect, he ceases to fret and fume, and worry and grieve, and remains poised, steadfast, serene.

August Third

Thought for the Morning

To follow, under all circumstances, the highest promptings within you; to be always true to the divine self; to reply upon the inward voice, the inward light, and to pursue your purpose with a fearless and restful heart, believing that the future will yield unto you the need of every thought and effort; knowing that the laws of the universe can never fail, and that your own will come back to you with mathematical exactitude—this is faith and the living of faith.

Meditation for the Day

*Become established in Immortality, Heaven, and the Spirit,
which make up the Empire of Light.*

ENTERING into the Infinite is not a mere theory or sentiment. It is a vital experience which is the result of assiduous practice in inward purification. When the body is no longer to be, even remotely, the real man; when all appetites and desires are thoroughly subdued and purified; when the emotions are rested and calm; and when the oscillation of the intellect ceases and perfect poise is secured, then, and not till then, does consciousness become one with the Infinite; not till then is childlike wisdom and profound peace secured.

Men grow weary and grey over the dark problems of life, and finally pass away and leave them unsolved because they cannot see their way out of the darkness of the personality, being too much engrossed in its limitations.

*Seeking to save his personal life, man forfeits the greater impersonal
Life of Truth; clinging to the perishable, he is shut out
from a knowledge of the Eternal.*

Thought for the Evening

Have a thorough understanding of your work, and let it be your own; and as you proceed, ever following the inward guide, the infallible voice, you will pass on from victory to victory, and will rise step by step to higher resting-places, and your ever broadening outlook will gradually reveal to you the essential beauty and purpose of life. Self-purified, health will be yours; self-governed, power will be yours, and all that you do will prosper.

And I may stand where health, success, and power await my coming, if, each fleeting hour, I cling to love and patience; and abide with stainlessness; and never step aside from high integrity; so shall I see at last the land of immortality.

August Fourth

Thought for the Morning

When the tongue is well controlled and wisely subdued; when selfish impulses and unworthy thoughts no longer rush to the tongue demanding utterance; when the speech has become harmless, pure, gracious, gentle, and purposeful, and no word is uttered but in sincerity and truth—then are the five steps in virtuous speech accomplished, then is the second great lesson in Truth learned and mastered. Make pure thy heart, and thou wilt make thy life rich, sweet and beautiful.

Meditation for the Day

Self and error are synonymous.

ERROR is involved in the darkness of unfathomable complexity, but eternal simplicity is the glory of Truth. Love of self shuts men out from Truth, and seeking their own personal happiness they lose the deeper, purer, and more abiding bliss. Says Carlyle, "There is in man a higher than happiness. He can do without happiness, and instead thereof find blessedness. . . Love not pleasure, love God. This is the Everlasting Yea, wherein all contradiction is solved; wherein whoso walks and works, it is well with him."

He who has yielded up that self, that personality that most men love, and to which they cling with such fierce tenacity has left behind him all perplexity, and has entered into a simplicity so profoundly simple as to be looked upon by the world, involved as it is in a network of error, as foolishness.

At rest in the Infinite.

Thought for the Evening

Having clothed himself with humility, the first questions a man asks himself are:—

"How am I acting towards others?"
"What am I doing to others?"
"How am I thinking of others?"
"Are my thoughts of, and acts towards others prompted by unselfish love?"

As a man, in the silence of his soul, asks himself these searching questions, he will unerringly see where he has hitherto failed.

August Fifth

Thought for the Morning

To dwell in love always and towards all is to live the true life, is to have Life itself. Knowing this, the good man gives up himself unreservedly to the Spirit of Love, and dwells in Love towards all, contending with none, condemning none, but loving all.

The Christ Spirit of Love puts an end, not only to all sin, but to all division and contention.

Meditation for the Day

The region of Reality. Unchanging principle.

WHEN a man has yielded up his lusts, his errors, his opinions and prejudices, he has entered into possession of the knowledge of God, having slain the selfish desire for heaven, and along with it the ignorant fear of hell; having relinquished even the love of life itself, he has gained supreme bliss and Life Eternal, the Life which bridges life and death, and knows its own immortality. Having yielded up all without reservation, he has gained all, and rests in peace on the bosom of the Infinite.

Only he who has become so free from self as to be equally content to be annihilated as to live, or to live as to be annihilated, is fit to enter into the Infinite. Only he who, ceasing to trust his perishable self, has learned to trust in boundless measure the Great Law, the Supreme Good, is prepared to partake of undying bliss.

By the surrender of self all difficulties are overcome.

Thought for the Evening

When sin and self are abandoned, the heart is restored to its imperishable Joy. Joy comes and fills the self-emptied heart; it abides with the peaceful; its reign is with the pure. Joy flees from the selfish, it deserts the quarrelsome; it is hidden from the impure. Joy cannot remain with the selfish; it is wedded to Love.

August Sixth

Thought for the Morning

In the pure heart there is no room left where personal judgments and hatreds can find lodgement, for it is filled to overflowing with tenderness and love; it sees no evil, and only as men succeed in seeing no evil in others will they become free from sin, and sorrow, and suffering. If men only understood that the heart that sins must sorrow, that the hateful mind tomorrow reaps its barren harvest, weeping, starving, resting not, nor sleeping; tenderness would fill their being, they would see with pity's seeing, if they only understood.

Meditation for the Day

There is no more regret, nor disappointment, nor remorse,
where all selfishness has ceased.

THE spirit of Love which is manifested as a perfect and rounded life is the crown of being and the supreme end of knowledge upon this earth.

How does a man act under trial and temptation? Many men boast of being in possession of Truth who are continually swayed by grief, disappointment, and passion, and who sink under the first little trial that comes along. Truth is nothing if not unchangeable, and in so far as a man takes his stand upon Truth does he become steadfast in virtue, does he rise superior to his passions and emotions and changeable personality.

Men formulate perishable dogmas, and call them Truth. Truth cannot be formulated; it is ineffable, and ever beyond the reach of intellect. It can only be experienced by practice; it can only be manifested in a stainless heart and a perfect life.

He who is patient, calm, and forgiving
under all circumstances manifests the Truth.

Thought for the Evening

To stand face to face with truth; to arrive, after innumerable wanderings and pains, at wisdom and bliss; not to be finally defeated and cast out, but to ultimately triumph over every inward foe—such is man's divine destiny, such his glorious goal; and this, every saint, sage, and saviour has declared. A man only begins to be a man when he ceases to whine and revile, and commences to search for the hidden justice which regulates his life. And as he adapts his mind to that regulating factor, he ceases to accuse others as the cause of his condition, and builds himself up in strong and noble thoughts; ceases to kick against circumstances, but begins to use them as aids to his more rapid progress, and as a means of discovering the hidden power and possibilities within himself.

August Seventh

Thought for the Morning

The will to evil and the will to good are both within thee, which wilt thou employ? Thou knowest what is right and what is wrong, which wilt though love and foster, which destroy?

Thou art the chooser of thy thoughts and deeds; thou art the maker of thine inward state; the power is thine to be what thou wilt be; thou buildest Truth and Love, or lies and hate.

Meditation for the Day

Practise heart-virtue, and search humbly
and diligently for the Truth.

TRUTH will never be proved by wordy arguments and learned treatises, for if men do not perceive the Truth in infinite patience, undying forgiveness, and all-embracing compassion, no words can ever prove it to them.

It is an easy matter for the passionate to be calm and patient when they are in the midst of calmness, or when they are alone. It is equally easy for the uncharitable to be gentle and kind when they are dealt kindly with, but he who retains his patience and calmness under all trial, who remains sublimely meek and gentle under the most trying circumstances, he, and he alone, is possessed of the spotless Truth. And this is so because such lofty virtues belong to the Divine, and can only be manifested by one who has attained to the highest wisdom, who has relinquished his passionate and self-seeking nature, who has realized the supreme and unchangeable Law, and has brought himself into harmony with it.

There is one great all-embracing Law
which is the foundation of the universe,
the Law of Love.

Thought for the Evening

The teaching of Jesus brings men back to the simple truth that righteousness, or *right-doing*, is entirely a matter of individual conduct, and not a mystical something apart from a man's thoughts and deeds.

Calmness and patience can become habitual by first grasping, through effort, a calm and patient thought, and then continuously thinking it, and living in it, until "use becomes second nature," and anger and impatience pass away for ever.

August Eighth

Thought for the Morning

Man is made or unmade by himself; in the armoury of thought he forges the weapons by which he destroys himself; he also fashions the tools with which he builds for himself heavenly mansions of joy and strength and peace. By the right choice and true application of thought man ascends to the Divine Perfection; by the abuse and wrong application of thought he descends below the level of the beast. Between these two extremes are all the grades of character and man is their maker and master.

As a being of Power, Intelligence, and Love, and the lord of his own thoughts, man holds the key to every situation.

Meditation for the Day

To become possessed of a knowledge of the Law of Love,
to enter into conscious harmony with it,
is to become immortal, invincible, indestructible.

IT is because of the effort of the soul to realize this Law that men come again and again to live, to suffer, and to die; and when realized, suffering ceases, personality is dispersed, and the fleshly life and death are destroyed, for consciousness becomes one with the Eternal.

The Law is absolutely impersonal, and its highest manifested expression is that of Service. When the purified heart has realized Truth, it is then called upon to make the last, the greatest, and holiest sacrifice, the sacrifice of the well-earned enjoyment of Truth. It is by virtue of this sacrifice that the divinely-emancipated soul comes to dwell amongst the lowliest and least, and to be esteemed the servant of all mankind.

The Spirit of Love is alone singled out as worthy
to receive the unstinted worship of posterity.

Thought for the Evening

Whatsoever you harbour in the inmost chambers of your heart will, sooner or later, by the inevitable law of reaction, shape itself in your outward life.

Every soul attracts its own, and nothing can possibly come to it that does not belong to it. To realize this is to recognize the universality of Divine Law.

If thou would'st right the world, and banish all its evils and its woes, make its wild places bloom, and its drear deserts blossom as the rose—then right thyself.

August Ninth

Thought for the Morning

Whatever conditions are rendering your life burdensome, you may pass out of and beyond them by developing and utilizing within you the transforming power of self-purification and self-conquest.

Before the divine radiance of a pure heart all darkness vanishes and all clouds melt away, and he who has conquered self has conquered the universe.

He who sets his foot firmly upon the path of self-conquest, who walks, aided by the staff of faith, the highway of self-sacrifice, will assuredly achieve the highest prosperity, and will reap abounding and enduring joy and bliss.

Meditation for the Day

Truth cannot be limited.

THE glory alike of the saint, the sage, and the saviour is this—that he has realized the most profound lowliness, the most sublime unselfishness; having given up all, even his own personality, all his works are holy and enduring, for they are freed from every taint of self. He gives, yet never thinks of receiving; he works, yet without regretting the past or anticipating the future, and never looks for reward.

When the farmer has tilled and dressed his land and put in the seed, he knows that he has done all that he can possibly do, and that now he must trust to the elements, and wait patiently for the course of time to bring about the harvest, and that no amount of expectancy on his part will affect the result, liven so, he who has realized the Truth goes forth as a sower of the seeds of goodness, purity, love, and peace, without expectancy, and never looking for results, knowing that there is the Great Over-ruling Law which brings about its own harvest in due time, and which is alike the source of preservation and destruction.

Every holy man became such
by unremitting perseverance in self-sacrifice.

Thought for the Evening

It is the silent and conquering thought forces which bring all things into manifestation. The universe grew out of thought.

To adjust all your thoughts to a perfect and unswerving faith in the omnipotence and supremacy of Good is to co-operate with that Good, and to realize within yourself the solution and destruction of all evil.

To mentally deny evil is not sufficient; it must, by daily practice, be risen above and understood. To affirm the Good mentally is inadequate; it must, by unswerving endeavour, be entered into and comprehended.

August Tenth

Thought for the Morning

Every thought you think is a force sent out. Whatever your position in life may be, before you can hope to enter into any measure of success, usefulness, and power, you must learn how to focus your thought forces by cultivating calmness and repose.

There is no difficulty, however great, but will yield before a calm and purposeful concentration of thought, and no legitimate object but may be speedily actualized by the intelligent use and direction of one's soul forces.

Think good thoughts, and they will quickly become actualized in your outward life in the form of good conditions.

Meditation for the Day

He who enters upon the holy way begins by
Restraining his passions.

WHAT the saints, sages, and saviours have accomplished, you likewise may accomplish if you will only tread the way which they trod and pointed out, the way of self-sacrifice, of self-denying service.

Truth is very simple. It says, "Give up self", "Come unto Me" (away from all that defiles) "and I will give you rest." All the mountains of commentary that have been piled upon it cannot hide it from the heart that is earnestly seeking for righteousness. It does not require learning; it can he known in spite of learning. Disguised under many forms by erring, self-seeking men, the beautiful simplicity and clear transparency of Truth remains unaltered and undimmed, and the unselfish heart enters into and partakes of its shining radiance. Not by weaving complex theories, not by building up speculative philosophies, is Truth realized; but by weaving the web of inward purity, by building up the Temple of a stainless life, is Truth realized.

Saintship is the beginning of holiness.

Thought for the Evening

That which you would be and hope to be, you may be now. Non-accomplishment resides in your perpetual postponement, and, having the power to postpone, you also have the power to accomplish—to perpetually accomplish: realize this truth, and you shall be today, and every day, the ideal being of whom you dreamed.

Say to yourself, "I will live in my Ideal now; I will manifest my ideal now; I will be my Ideal now; and all that tempts me away from my Ideal I will not listen to; I will listen only to the voice of my Ideal."

August Eleventh

Thought for the Morning

Be as a flower; content to be, to grow in sweetness day by day. If thou would'st perfect thyself in knowledge, perfect thyself in Love. If thou would'st reach the Highest, ceaselessly cultivate a loving and compassionate heart.

To him who chooses Goodness, sacrificing all, is given that which is more than, and includes, all.

Meditation for the Day

Only when you identify yourself with the Divine
Can you be said to be "clothed and in your right mind".

THE divine within is the abode of peace, the temple of wisdom, the dwelling place of immortality. Apart from this inward resting-place, this Mount of Vision, there can be no tine peace, no knowledge of the Divine, and if you can remain there for one minute, one hour, or one day, it is possible for you to remain there always. All your sins and sorrows, your fears and anxieties, are your own, and you can cling to them or you can give them up. Of your own accord you cling to your unrest; of your own accord you can come to abiding peace. No one else can give up sin for you; you must give it up yourself. The greatest Teacher can do no more than walk the way of Truth for himself, and point it out to you; you yourself must walk it for yourself. You can obtain freedom and peace alone by your own efforts, by yielding up that which binds the soul, and which is destructive of peace.

Give up all self-seeking; give up self, and lo!
The Peace of God is yours.

Thought for the Evening

The Great Law never cheats any man of his just due.

Human life, when rightly lived, is simple with a beautiful simplicity.

He who comprehends the utter simplicity of life, who obeys its laws, and does not step aside into the dark paths and complex mazes of selfish desire, stands where no harm can reach him.

Then there is fullness of joy, abounding plenty, and rich and complete blessedness.

August Twelfth

Thought for the Morning

Every man reaps the results of his own thoughts and deeds, and suffers for his own wrong.

He who begins right, and continues right, does not need to desire, and search for felicitous results; they are already at hand; they follow as consequences; they are the certainties, the realities, of life.

Sweet is the rest and deep is the bliss of him who has freed his heart from its lusts and hatreds and dark desires.

Meditation for the Day

Come out of the storms of sin and anguish.

O THOU who wouldst teach men of Truth!
    Hast thou passed through the desert of doubt?
    Art thou purged by the fires of sorrow?
      Hath truth
The fiends of opinion cast out
  Of thy human heart? Is thy soul so fair
That no false thought can ever harbor there?

O thou who wouldst teach men of Love!
   Hast thou passed through the place of despair?
Hast thou wept through the dark night of grief?
     does it move
  (Now freed from its sorrow and care)
Thy human heart to pitying gentleness,
Looking on wrong, and hate, and ceaseless stress?

O thou who wouldst teach men of Peace!
   Hast thou crossed the wide ocean of strife?
Hast thou found on the Shores of the Silence release

    From all the wild unrest of life?
From thy human heart hath all striving gone,
Leaving but Truth, and Love, and Peace alone?

Twelfth Enter the inward resting-place.

Thought for the Evening

You are the creator of your own shadows; you desire, and then you grieve; renounce, and then you shall rejoice.

Of all the beautiful truths pertaining to the soul. . . none is more gladdening or fruitful of divine promise and confidence than this—that man is the master of thought, the moulder of character, and the maker and shaper of character, environment, and destiny.

August Thirteenth

Thought for the Morning

As darkness is a passing shadow, and light is a substance that remains, so sorrow is fleeting, but joy abides for ever. No true thing can pass away and become lost; no false thing can remain and be preserved. Sorrow is false, and it cannot live; joy is true, and it cannot die. Joy may become hidden for a time, but it can always be recovered; sorrow may remain for a period, but it can be transcended and dispersed.

Do not think your sorrow will remain; it will pass away like a cloud. Do not believe that the torments of sin are ever your portion; they will vanish like a hideous nightmare. Awake! Arise! Be holy and joyful.

Meditation for the Day

Make yourself pure and lovable, and you will be loved by all.

THINK of your servants with kindness, consider their happiness and comfort, and never demand of them that extremity of service which you yourself would not care to perform were you in their place. Rare and beautiful is that humility of soul by which a servant entirely forgets himself in his master's good; but far rarer, and more beautiful with a divine beauty, is that nobility of soul by which a man, forgetting his own happiness, seeks the happiness of those who are under his authority, and who depend upon him for their bodily sustenance. And such a man's happiness is increased tenfold, nor does he need to complain of those whom he employs. Said a well-known and extensive employer of labour, who never needs to dismiss an employee: "I have always had the happiest relations with my workpeople. If you ask me how it is to be accounted for, I can only say that it has been my aim from the first to do to them as I would wish to be done by."

Be friendly towards others, and friends will soon flock round you.

Thought for the Evening

Tribulation lasts only so long as there remains some chaff of self which needs to be removed. The *tribulum*, or threshing machine, ceases to work when all the grain is separated from the chaff; and when the last impurities are blown away from the soul, tribulation has completed its work, and there is no more need for it; then abiding joy is realized.

The sole and supreme use of suffering is to purify, to burn out all that is useless and impure. Suffering ceases for him who is pure. There could be no object in burning gold after the dross had been removed.

August Fourteenth

Thought for the Morning

In speaking of self-control, one is easily misunderstood. It should not be associated with a destructive repression, but with a constructive expression.

A man is happy, wise and great in the measure that he controls himself; he is wretched, foolish, and mean in the measure that he allows his animal nature to dominate his thoughts and actions.

He who controls himself, controls his life, his circumstances, his destiny; and wherever he goes he carries his happiness with him as an abiding possession.

Renunciation precedes regeneration. The permanent happiness which men seek in dissipation, excitement, and abandonment to unworthy pleasures, is found only in the life which reverses all this—the life of self-control.

Meditation for the Day

To dwell continually in good thoughts is to throw around oneself a psychic atmosphere of sweetness and power which leaves its impress upon all who come in contact with it.

AS the rising sun puts to rout the helpless shadows, so are all the impotent forces of evil put to flight by the searching rays of positive thought which shine forth from a heart made strong in purity and faith.

Where there is sterling faith and uncompromising purity there is health, there is success, there is power. In such a one, disease, failure, and disaster can find no lodgement, for there is nothing on which they can feed.

Even physical conditions are largely determined by mental states, and to this truth the scientific world is rapidly being drawn. The old, materialistic belief that a man is what his body makes him is rapidly passing away, and is being replaced by the inspiring belief that man is superior to his body, and that his body is what he makes it by the power of thought.

There is no evil in the universe but has its root and origin in the mind.

Thought for the Evening

Law, not confusion, is the dominating principle in the universe; justice, not injustice is the soul and substance of life; and righteousness, not corruption, is the moulding and moving force in the spiritual government of the world. This being so, man has but the right himself to find that the universe is right.

When I am pure, I shall have solved the mystery of life; I shall be sure, when I am free from hatred, lust and strife, I am in Truth, and Truth abides in me; I shall be safe, and sane, and wholly free, when I am pure.

August Fifteenth

Thought for the Morning

If men only understood that their hatred and resentment slays their peace and sweet contentment, hurts themselves, helps not another, does not cheer one lonely brother, they would seek the better doing of good deeds which leaves no ruing:—

If they only understood.

If men only understood how Love conquers; how prevailing is its might, grim hate assailing; how compassion endeth sorrow, maketh wise, and doth not borrow pain of passion, they would ever live in Love, in hatred never:—

If they only understood.

Meditation for the Day

Renounce.

IF you are given to anger, worry, jealousy, greed, or any other inharmonious state of mind, and expect perfect physical health, you are expecting the impossible, for you are continually sowing the seeds of disease in your mind. Such conditions of mind are carefully shunned by the wise man, for he knows them to be far more dangerous than a bad drain or an infected house.

If you would be free from all physical aches and pains, and would enjoy perfect physical harmony, then put your mind in order, and harmonize your thoughts. Think joyful thoughts; think loving thoughts; let the elixir of goodwill course through your veins, and you will need no other medicine. Put away your jealousies, your suspicions, your worries, your hatreds, your selfish indulgences, and you will put away your dyspepsia, your biliousness, your nervousness and aching joints.

If you would secure health, you must learn to work without friction.

Thought for the Evening

The grace and beauty that were in Jesus can be of no value to you—cannot be understood by you—unless they are also *in you*, and they can never be in you, until you practice them, for, apart from *doing*, the qualities which constitute goodness do not, as far as you are concerned, exist.

To adore Jesus for his good qualities is a long step towards Truth, but to practice those qualities is Truth itself; and he who fully adores the perfection of another will not rest content in his own imperfection, but will fashion his soul after the likeness of that other.

Therefore thou who adorest Jesus for his divine qualities, practice those qualities thyself, and thou too shalt be divine.

August Sixteenth

Thought for the Morning

Let a man realize that life in its totality proceeds from the mind, and lo, the way of blessedness is opened up to him! For he will then discover that he possesses the power to rule his mind and to fashion it in accordance with his Ideal.

So will he elect to strongly and steadfastly walk those pathways of thought and action which are altogether excellent; to him life will become beautiful and sacred; and, sooner or later, he will put to flight all evil, confusion, and suffering; for it is impossible for a man to fall short of liberation, enlightenment, and peace, who guards with unwearying diligence the gateway of his heart.

Meditation for the Day

Order your thoughts and you will order your life.

POUR the oil of tranquillity upon the turbulent waters of the passions and prejudices, and the tempests of misfortune, however they may threaten, will be powerless to wreck the barque[1] of your soul, as it threads its way across the ocean of life. And if that barque be piloted by a cheerful and never-failing faith, its course will be doubly sure, and many perils will pass it by which would otherwise attack it. By the power of faith every enduring work is accomplished. Faith in the Supreme; faith in the over-ruling Law; faith in your work, and in your power to accomplish that work—here is the rock upon which you must build if you would achieve, if you would stand and not fall.

Follow, under all circumstances, the highest promptings within you.

Thought for the Evening

By constantly overcoming self, a man gains a knowledge of the subtle intricacies of his mind; and it is this divine knowledge which enables him to become established in calmness.

Without self-knowledge there can be no abiding peace of mind, and those who are carried away by tempestuous passions, cannot approach the holy place where calmness reigns.

The weak man is like one who, having mounted a fiery steed, allows it to run away with him, and carry him withersoever it wills; the strong man is like one who, having mounted the steed, governs it with a masterly hand and makes it go in whatever direction and at whatever speed he commands.

---

[1] Barque – A sailing ship with from three to five masts.

August Seventeenth

Thought for the Morning

There is no strife, no selfishness, in the Kingdom; there is perfect harmony, equipoise, and rest.

Those who live in the Kingdom of Love, have all their needs supplied by the Law of Love.

As self is the root cause of all strife and suffering, so Love is the root cause of all peace and bliss. Those who are at rest in the Kingdom do not look for happiness in any outward possessions. They are freed from all anxiety and trouble and, resting in Love, they are the embodiment of happiness.

Meditation for the Day

Let your heart grow large and loving and unselfish,
and great and lasting will be your influence and success.

CULTIVATE a pure and unselfish spirit, and combine with purity and faith singleness of purpose, and you are evolving from the elements enduring success of greatness and power.

If your present position is distasteful to you, and your heart is not in your work, nevertheless perform your duties with scrupulous diligence; and whilst resting your mind in the idea that the better position and greater opportunities are waiting for you, ever keep an active mental outlook for budding possibilities, so that when the critical moment arrives, and the new channel presents itself, you will step into it with your mind fully prepared for the undertaking, and with that intelligence and foresight which is born of mental discipline.

Whatever your task may be, concentrate your whole mind upon it, throw into it all the energy of which you are capable. The faultless completion of small tasks leads inevitably to larger tasks.

Learn by constant practice how to husband your resources,
and to concentrate them, at any moment, upon a given point.

Thought for the Evening

Let it not be supposed that the children of the Kingdom live in ease and indolence (these two sins are the first that have to be eradicated when the search for the Kingdom is entered upon); they live in a peaceful activity; in fact, they only truly live, for the life of self, with its train of worries, griefs, and fears, is not *real life*.

The children of the Kingdom are *known by their life*, they manifest the fruits of the Spirit—"Love, joy, peace, long-suffering, kindness, goodness, faithfulness, meekness, temperance, and self-control"—under all circumstances and vicissitudes.

August Eighteenth

Thought for the Morning

The gospel of Jesus is a gospel of *living and doing*. If it were not this it would not voice the Eternal Truth. Its Temple is *Purified Conduct*, the entrance-door to which is *Self-Surrender*. It invites men to shake off sin, and promises, as a result, joy and blessedness and perfect peace.

The Kingdom of Heaven is perfect trust, perfect knowledge, perfect peace. . . no sin can enter therein, no self-born thought or deed can pass its golden gates; no impure desire can defile its radiant robes. . . all may enter it who will, but all must pay the price—*the unconditional abandonment of self.*

Meditation for the Day

Passion is not power; it is the abuse of power, the dispersion of power.

WHEN that young man, whom I knew, passing through continual reverses and misfortunes, was mocked by his friends and told to desist from further effort, and he replied, "The time is not far distant when you will marvel at my good fortune and success," he showed that he was possessed of that silent and irresistible power which has taken him over innumerable difficulties, and crowned his life with success.

If you have not this power, you may acquire it by practice, and the beginning of power is likewise the beginning of wisdom. You must commence by overcoming those purposeless trivialities to which you have hitherto been a willing victim. Boisterous and uncontrolled laughter, slander and idle talk, and joking merely to raise a laugh all these things must be put on one side as so much waste of valuable energy.

*Be of single aim; have a legitimate and useful purpose,
and devote yourself unreservedly to it.*

Thought for the Evening

I say this—and know it to be truth—*that circumstances can only affect you in so far as you allow them to do so.* You are swayed by circumstances because you have not a right understanding of the nature, use, and power of thought. You believe (and upon this little word *belief* hang all our joys and sorrows) that outward things have the power to make or mar your life; by so doing you submit to those outward things, confess that you are their slave, and they your unconditional master. By so doing you invest them with a power which they do not of themselves possess, and you succumb, in reality not to the circumstances, but to the gloom or gladness, the fear or hope, the strength of weakness, which your thought-sphere has thrown around them.

August Nineteenth

Thought for the Morning

If you are one of those who are praying for, and looking forward to a happier world beyond the grave, here is a message of gladness for you—you may enter into and realize that happy world now; it fills the whole universe, and it is within you, waiting for you to find, acknowledge, and possess.

Said one who understood the inner laws of Being—"When men shall say, lo here, or lo there, go not after them. The Kingdom of God is within you."

Meditation for the Day

*Happiness is that inward state of perfect satisfaction
which is joy and peace.*

THE satisfaction which results from gratified desire is brief and illusionary, and is always followed by an increased demand for gratification. Desire is insatiable as the ocean, and clamours louder and louder as its demands are attended to. It claims ever-increasing service from its deluded devotees, until at last they are struck down with physical or mental anguish, and are hurled into the purifying fires of suffering. Desire is the region of hell, and all torments are centred there. The giving up of desire is the realization of heaven, and all delights await the pilgrim there.

> "I sent my soul through the invisible,
> Some letter of that after life to spell,
> And by and by my soul returned to me,
> And whispered,
> 'I myself am heaven and hell.'"

Heaven and hell are inward states.

Thought for the Evening

Heaven and hell are inward states. Sink into self and all its gratifications, and you sink into hell; rise above self into that state of consciousness which is the utter denial and forgetfulness of self, and you enter heaven.

So long as you persist in selfishly seeking for your own personal happiness, so long will happiness elude you, and you will be sowing the seeds of wretchedness. In so far as you succeed in losing yourself in the service of others, in that measure will happiness come to you, and you will reap a harvest of bliss.

August Twentieth

Thought for the Morning

Sympathy given can never be waste.

One aspect of sympathy is that of pity—pity for the distressed or pain stricken, with a desire to alleviate or help them in their sufferings. The world needs more of this divine quality.

"For pity makes the world soft to the weak, and noble for the strong."

Another form of sympathy is that of rejoicing with others who are more successful than ourselves, and though their success were our own.

Meditation for the Day

To seek selfishly is only to lose happiness

SINK into self and all its gratifications, and you sink into hell; rise above self into that state of consciousness which is the utter denial and forgetfulness of self, and you enter heaven. Self is blind, without judgment, not possessed of true knowledge, and always leads to suffering. Correct perception, unbiased judgment, and true knowledge belong only to the divine state, and only in so far as you realize this divine consciousness can you know what real happiness is. So long as you persist in selfishly seeking for your own happiness, so long will happiness elude you, and you will be sowing the seeds of wretchedness. In so far as you succeed in losing yourself in the service of others, in that measure will happiness come to you, and you will reap a harvest of bliss.

Abiding happiness will come to you
when, ceasing to selfishly cling,
you are willing to give up.

Thought for the Evening

Sweet are companionships, pleasures, and material comforts, but they change and fade away. Sweeter still are Purity, Wisdom, and the knowledge of Truth, and these never change nor fade away.

He who attained to the possession of spiritual things can never be deprived of his source of happiness; he will never have to part company with it, and wherever he goes in the whole universe, he will carry his possessions with him. His spiritual end will be the fullness of joy.

August Twenty-first

Thought for the Morning

Let your heart grow and expand with ever broadening love, until, freed from all hatred, and passion, and condemnation, it embraces the whole universe with thoughtful tenderness.

As the flower opens its petals to receive the morning light, so open your soul more and more to the glorious light of Truth.

Soar upward on the wings of aspiration; be fearless and believe in the loftiest possibilities.

Meditation for the Day

*Whatsoever you constantly meditate upon you
will not only come to understand,
but will grow more and more into its likeness.*

SPIRITUAL meditation is the pathway to Divinity. It is the mystic ladder which reaches from earth to heaven, from error to Truth, from pain to peace. Every saint has climbed it; every sinner must sooner or later come to it, and every weary pilgrim that turns his back upon self and the world, and sets his face resolutely towards the Father's Home, must plant his feet upon its golden rounds. Without its aid you cannot grow into the divine state, the divine likeness, the divine peace, and the fadeless glories and unpolluting joys of Truth will remain hidden from you.

*If you constantly dwell upon that which is selfish and debasing,
you will ultimately become selfish and debased.*

Thought for the Evening

Mind clothes itself in garments of its own making. Mind is the arbiter of life; it is the creator and shaper of conditions, and the recipient of its own results. It contains within itself both the power to create illusion and to perceive reality.

Mind is the infallible weaver of destiny; thought is the thread, good and evil deeds are the warp and woof, and the web, woven upon the loom of life, is character. Make pure thy heart, and thou wilt make thy life, rich, sweet, and beautiful, unmarred by strife.

August Twenty-second

Thought for the Morning

Cherish your visions; cherish your ideals; cherish the music that stirs in your heart, the beauty that forms in your mind, the loveliness that drapes your purest thoughts, for out of them will grow all delightful conditions, all heavenly environment; of these, if you will remain true to them, your world will at last be built.

Guard well thy mind, and, noble, strong, and free, nothing shall harm, disturb or conquer thee; for all thy foes are in thy heart and mind, there also thy salvation thou shalt find.

Meditation for the Day

*If you would enter into possession of profound and abiding peace,
come now and enter the path of meditation.*

SELECT some portion of the day in which to meditate, and keep that period sacred to your purpose. The best time is the very early morning when the spirit of repose is upon everything. All natural conditions will then be in your favour; the passions, after the long bodily fast of the night, will be subdued, the excitements and worries of the previous day will have died away, and the mind, strong and yet restful, will be receptive to spiritual instruction. Indeed, one of the first efforts you will be called upon to make will be to shake off lethargy and indulgence, and if you refuse you will be unable to advance, for the demands of the spirit are imperative.

The sluggard and the self-indulgent can have no knowledge of Truth.

Thought for the Evening

Dream lofty dreams, and as you dream so shall you become. Your vision is the promise of what you shall one day be; your Ideal is the prophecy of what you shall at last unveil.

The greatest achievement was at first and for a time a dream. The oak sleeps in the acorn; the bird waits in the egg; and in the highest vision of the soul a waking angel stirs.

Your circumstances may be uncongenial, but they shall not long remain so when you perceive an Ideal and strive to reach it.

August Twenty-third

Thought for the Morning

He who has conquered doubt and fear has conquered failure. His every thought is allied with power, and all difficulties are bravely met and wisely overcome. His purposes are seasonably planted, and they bloom and bring forth fruit which does not fall prematurely to the ground.

Thought allied fearlessly to purpose becomes creative force: he who knows this is ready to become something higher and stronger than a mere bundle of wavering thoughts and fluctuating sensations; he who does this has become the conscious and intelligent wielder of his mental powers.

Meditation for the Day

The direct outcome of your meditations will be a calm, spiritual strength.

IF you are given to hatred or anger, you will meditate upon gentleness and forgiveness, so as to become acutely alive to a sense of your harsh and foolish conduct. You will then begin to dwell in thoughts of love, of gentleness, of abounding forgiveness; and as you overcome the lower by the higher, there will gradually, silently steal into your heart a knowledge of the divine Law of Love with an understanding of its bearing upon all the intricacies of life and conduct. And in applying this knowledge to your every thought, word, and act, you will grow more and more gentle, more and more loving, more and more divine. Arid thus with every error, every selfish desire, every human weakness; by the power of meditation is it overcome; and as each sin, each error, is thrust out, a fuller and clearer measure of the Light of Truth illumines the pilgrim soul.

Great is the overcoming power of holy thought.

Thought for the Evening

Man's true place in the Cosmos is that of a king, not a slave, a commander under the Law of Good, and not a helpless tool in the region of evil.

I write for men, not for babes; for those who are eager to learn, and earnest to achieve; for those who will put away (for the world's good) a petty personal indulgence, a selfish desire, a mean thought, and live on as though it were not, sans craving and regret.

Man is a master. If he were not, he could not act contrary to law.

Evil and weakness are self destructive. The universe is girt with goodness and strength, and it protects the good and the strong.

The angry man is the weak man.

August Twenty-fourth

Thought for the Morning

Not by learning will a man triumph over evil; not by much study will he overcome sin and sorrow. Only by conquering himself will he conquer evil; only by practicing righteousness will he put an end to sorrow.

Not for the clever, nor the learned, nor the self-confident is the Life Triumphant, but for the pure, the virtuous and wise. The former achieve their particular success in life, but the latter alone achieve the great success so invincible and complete that even in apparent defeat it shines with added victory.

Meditation for the Day

*Meditation will enrich the soul with saving remembrance
in the hour of strife, of sorrow, or of temptation.*

AS, by the power of meditation, you grow in wisdom, you will relinquish, more and more, your selfish desires which are fickle, impermanent, and productive of sorrow and pain; and will take your stand, with increasing steadfastness and trust, upon unchangeable principles, and will realize heavenly rest.

The use of meditation is the requirement of a knowledge of eternal principles, and the power which results from meditation is the ability to rest upon and trust those principles, and so become one with the Eternal. The end of meditation is, therefore, direct knowledge of Truth, God, and the realization of divine and profound peace.

Strive to rise, by the power of meditation, above all selfish clinging to partial gods or party creeds; above dead formalities and lifeless ignorance.

Remember that you are to grow into Truth by steady perseverance.

Thought for the Evening

The true silence is not merely a silent tongue; it is a silent mind. To merely *hold one's tongue*, and yet to carry about a disturbed and rankling mind, is no remedy for weakness, and no source of power.

Silentness, to be powerful, must envelop the whole mind, must permeate every chamber of the heart; it must be the silence of peace.

To this broad, deep, abiding silentness a man attains only in the measure that he conquers himself.

August Twenty-fifth

Thought for the Morning

By curbing his tongue, a man gains possession of his mind.

The fool babbles, gossips, argues, and bandies words. He glories in the fact that he has had the last word, and has silenced his opponent. He exults in his own folly, is ever on the defensive, and wastes his energies in unprofitable channels. He is like a gardener who continues to dig and plant in unproductive soil.

The wise man avoids idle words, gossips, vain argument, and self-defence. He is content to appear defeated; rejoices when he is defeated; knowing that, having found and removed another error in himself, he has thereby become wiser.

Blessed is he who does not strive for the last word.

Meditation for the Day

Believe that a life of perfect holiness is possible.

So believing, so aspiring, so meditating, divinely sweet and beautiful will be your spiritual experiences, and glorious the revelations that will enrapture your inward vision. As you realize the divine Love, the divine Justice, the Perfect Law of Good, or God, great will be your bliss and deep your peace. Old things will pass away, and all things will become new. The veil of the material universe, so dense and impenetrable to the eye of error, so thin and gauzy to the eye of Truth, will be lifted and the spiritual universe will be revealed. Time will cease, and you will live only in Eternity. Change and mortality will no more cause you anxiety and sorrow, for you will become established in the unchangeable, and will dwell in the very heart of immortality.

He who believes climbs rapidly the heavenly hills.

Thought for the Evening

Desire is the *craving for possession*; aspiration is the *hunger of the heart for peace*.

The craving for things leads ever farther and farther from peace, and not only ends in deprivation, but is in itself a state of perpetual want. Until it comes to an end, rest and satisfaction are impossible.

The hunger for things can never be satisfied, but the hunger for peace can, and the satisfaction of peace is found—is fully possessed, when all selfish desire is abandoned. Then there is fullness of joy, abounding plenty, and rich and complete blessedness.

August Twenty-sixth

Thought for the Morning

A man will reach the Kingdom by purifying himself, and he can only do this by pursuing a process of self-examination and self-analysis.

The selfishness must be discovered and understood before it can be removed. It is powerless to remove itself, neither will it pass away of itself. Darkness ceases only when light is introduced; so ignorance can only be dispersed by knowledge, selfishness by love.

A man must first of all be willing to lose himself (his self-seeking) before he can find himself (his Divine Self). He must realize that selfishness is not worth clinging to, that it is a master altogether unworthy of his service, and that divine goodness alone is worthy to be enthroned in his heart, as the supreme master of his life.

Meditation for the Day

Where self is, Truth is not; where Truth is, self is not.

UPON the battlefield of the human soul two masters are ever contending for the crown of supremacy, for the kingship and dominion of the heart; the master of self, called also the "Prince of this world" and the master of Truth, called also the Father God. The master self is that rebellious one whose weapons are passion, pride, avarice, vanity, self-will, implements of darkness; the master Truth is that meek and lowly one whose weapons are gentleness, patience, purity, sacrifice, humility, love, instruments of Light.

In every soul the battle is waged, and as a soldier cannot engage at once in two opposing armies, so every heart is enlisted either in the ranks of self or of Truth. There is no half-and-half course. Jesus, the manifested Christ, declared that "No man can serve two masters; for either he will hate the one and love the other; or else he will hold to the one and despise the other. Ye cannot serve God and Mammon."

*You cannot perceive the beauty of Truth
while you are looking out through the eyes of self.*

Thought for the Evening

Be still, my soul, and know that peace is thine. Be steadfast, heart, and know that strength divine Belongs to thee; cease from thy turmoil, mind, and thou the Everlasting Rest shalt find.

If a man would have peace, let him exercise the spirit of peace; if he would find Love, let him dwell in the spirit of Love; if he would escape suffering, let him cease to inflict it; if he would do noble things for humanity, let him cease to do ignoble things for himself. If he will but quarry the mine of his own soul, he shall find there all the materials for building whatsoever he will, and he shall find there also the Central Rock on which to build in safety.

August Twenty-seventh

Thought for the Morning

Men go after much company, and seek out new excitements, but they are not acquainted with peace; in divers paths of pleasure they search for happiness, but they do not come to rest; through divers ways of laughter and feverish delirium they wander after gladness and life, but their tears are many and grievous, and they do not escape death.

Drifting upon the ocean of life in search of selfish indulgences, men are caught in its storms, and only after many tempests and much privation do they fly to the Rock of Refuge which rests in the deep silence of their own being.

Meditation for the Day

The lovers of Truth worship Truth with the sacrifice of self.

DO you seek to know and to realize Truth? Then you must be prepared to sacrifice, to renounce to the uttermost, for Truth in all its glory can only be perceived and known when the last vestige of self has disappeared.

The eternal Christ declared that he who would be His disciple must "deny himself daily." Are you willing to deny yourself, to give up your lusts, your prejudices, your opinions? If so, you may enter the narrow way of Truth, and find that peace from which the world is shut out. The absolute denial, the utter extinction of self is the perfect state of Truth, and all religions and philosophies are but so many aids to this supreme attainment.

As you let self die, you will be reborn in Truth.

Thought for the Evening

Meditation centred upon divine realities is the very essence and soul of prayer. It is the silent reaching upward of the soul toward the Eternal.

Meditation is the intense dwelling, in thought, upon an idea or theme with the object of thoroughly comprehending it; and whatsoever you constantly meditate upon, you will not only come to understand, but will grow more and more into its likeness, for it will become incorporated with your very being, will become, in fact, your very self.

If, therefore, you constantly dwell upon that which is selfish and debasing, you will ultimately become selfish and debased; if you ceaselessly think upon that which is pure and unselfish, you will surely become pure and unselfish.

August Twenty-eighth

Thought for the Morning

There is no difficulty, however great, but will yield before a calm and powerful concentration of thought and no legitimate object but may be speedily actualized by the intelligent use and direction of one's soul forces.

Whatever your task may be, concentrate your whole mind upon it; throw into it all the energy of which you are capable. The faultless completion of small tasks, leads inevitably to larger tasks.

See to it that you rise by steady climbing, and you will never fall.

Meditation for the Day

Every holy man is a savior of mankind.

WHEN men, lost in the devious ways of error and self, have forgotten the "heavenly birth", the state of holiness and Truth, they set up artificial standards by which to judge one another, and make acceptance of, and adherence to, their own particular theology the test of Truth; and so men are divided one against another, and there is ceaseless enmity and strife, and unending sorrow and suffering.

Reader, do you seek to realize the birth into Truth? There is only one way: *Let self die.* All those lusts, appetites, desires, opinions, limited conceptions, and prejudices to which you have hitherto so tenaciously clung, let them fall from you. Let them no longer hold you in bondage, and Truth will be yours. Cease to look upon your own religion as superior to all others, and strive humbly to learn the supreme lesson of charity.

To be in the world and yet not of the world is the highest perfection.

Thought for the Evening

He who knows that Love is at the heart of all things, and has realized the all-sufficing power of that Love, has no room in his heart for condemnation.

If you love people and speak of them with praise, until they in some way thwart you, or do something of which you disapprove, and then you dislike them and speak of them with dispraise, you are not governed by the Love which is of God. If, in your heart, you are continually arraigning and condemning others, selfless love is hidden from you.

Train your mind in strong, impartial, and gentle thought; train your heart in purity and compassion; train your tongue to silence, and to true and stainless speech; so shall you enter the way of holiness and peace, and shall ultimately realize the immortal Love.

August Twenty-ninth

Thought for the Morning

If you would realize true prosperity, do not settle down, as many have done, into the belief that if you do right everything will go wrong. Do not allow the word "competition" to shake your faith in the supremacy of righteousness. I care not what men say about the "laws of competition," for do not I know the Unchangeable Law which shall one day put them all to rout, and which puts them to rout even now in the heart and life of the righteous man? And knowing this law I can contemplate all dishonesty with undisturbed repose, for I know where certain destruction awaits it.

Under all circumstances *do that which you believe to be right*, and trust the Law; trust the Divine Power which is immanent in the universe, and it will never desert you, and you will always be protected.

Meditation for the Day

The cause of all power, as of all weakness, is within.

A THOROUGH understanding of this Great Law which permeates the universe leads to the acquirement of that state of mind known as *obedience*. To know that justice, harmony, and love are supreme in the universe is likewise to know that all adverse and painful conditions are the result of our own disobedience to that Law. Such knowledge leads to strength and power, and it is upon such knowledge alone that a true life and an enduring success and happiness can be built. To be patient under all circumstances, and to accept all circumstances as necessary factors in your training, is to rise superior to all painful conditions, and to overcome them with an overcoming which is sure, and which leaves no fear of their return, for by the power of obedience to law they are utterly slain.

There is no progress apart from unfoldment within.

Thought for the Evening

Forget yourself entirely in the sorrows of others, and in ministering to others, and divine happiness will emancipate you from all sorrow and suffering. "Taking the first step with a good thought, the second with a good word, and the third with a good deed, I entered Paradise." And you also enter Paradise by pursuing the same course.

Lose yourself in the welfare of others; forget yourself in all that you do—this is the secret of abounding happiness. Ever be on the watch to guard against selfishness and learn faithfully the divine lessons of inward sacrifice; so shall you climb the highest heights of happiness, and shall remain in the never-clouded sunshine of universal joy, clothed in the shining garment of immortality.

August Thirtieth

Thought for the Morning

When the farmer has tilled and dressed his land and put in the seed, he knows that he has done all that he can possibly do, and that now he must trust to the elements, and wait patiently for the course of time to bring about the harvest, and that no amount of expectancy on his part will affect the result.

Even so, he who has realized Truth, goes forth as a sower of the seeds of goodness, purity, love, and peace, without expectancy and never looking for results, knowing that there is the Great Over-ruling Law which brings about its own harvest in due time, and which is alike the source of preservation and destruction.

Meditation for the Day

There is no sure foothold in prosperity or peace
except by orderly advancement in knowledge.

PERHAPS the chains of poverty hang heavily upon you, and you are friendless and alone, and you long with an intense longing that your load may be lightened; but the load continues, and you seem to be enveloped in an ever-increasing darkness. Perhaps you complain, you bewail your lot, you blame your birth, your parents, your employer, or the unjust Powers who have bestowed upon you so undeservedly poverty and hardship, and upon another affluence and ease. Cease your complaining and fretting; none of these things which you blame are the cause of your poverty; the cause is within yourself, and where the cause is, there is the remedy.

There is no room for a complainer
in a universe of law, and worry is soul-suicide.

Thought for the Evening

The virtuous put a check upon themselves, and set a watch upon their passions and emotions; in this way they gain possession of the mind, and gradually acquire calmness; and as they acquire influence, power, greatness, abiding joy, and fullness and completeness of life.

He only finds peace who conquers himself, who strives, day by day, after greater self-possession, greater self-control, and greater calmness of mind.

Where the calm mind is there is strength and rest, there is love and wisdom; there is one who has fought successfully innumerable battles against self, who, after long toil in secret against his own failings, has triumphed at last.

August Thirty-first

Thought for the Morning

Sympathy bestowed increases its store in our own heart and enriches and fructifies our own life. Sympathy given is blessedness received; sympathy withheld is blessedness forfeited.

In the measure that a man increases and enlarges his sympathy so much nearer does he approach the ideal life, the perfect blessedness; and when his heart has become so mellowed that no hard, bitter, or cruel thought can enter, and detract from its permanent sweetness, then indeed is he richly and divinely blessed.

Meditation for the Day

What your thoughts are, that is your real self.

THE world around, both animate and inanimate, wears the aspect with which your thoughts clothe it. "All that we are is the result of what we have thought; it is founded on our thoughts; it is made up of our thoughts." Thus said Buddha, and it therefore follows that if a man is happy, it is because he dwells in happy thoughts; if miserable, because he dwells in despondent and debilitating thoughts. Whether one be fearful or fearless, foolish or wise, troubled or serene, within that soul lies the cause of its own state or states, and never without. And now I seem to hear a chorus of voices exclaim, "But do you really mean to say that outward circumstances do not affect our minds?" I do not say that, but I say this, and know it to be an infallible truth, *that circumstances can only affect you in so far as you allow them to do so.*

You are swayed by circumstances because you have not a right understanding of the nature, use, and power of thought.

Thought for the Evening

Sweet is the rest and deep the bliss of him who has freed his heart from its lusts and hatreds and dark desires; and he who, without any shadow of bitterness resting upon him, and looking out upon the world with boundless compassion and love, can breathe, in his inmost heart, the blessing: Peace unto all living things, making no exceptions or distinctions—such a man has reached that happy ending which can never be taken away, for this is the perfection of life, the fullness of peace, the consummation of perfect blessedness.

September First

Thought for the Morning

In aiming at the life of blessedness, one of the simplest beginnings to be considered, and rightly made, is that which we all make every day—namely, the beginning of each day's life. There is a sense in which every day may be regarded as the beginning of a new life, in which one can think, act, and live newly, and in a wiser and better spirit. The right beginning of the day will be followed by a cheerfulness permeating the household with a sunny influence, and the tasks and duties of the day will be undertaken in a strong and confident spirit, and the whole day will be well lived.

Meditation for the Day

To make a useful and happy life dependent upon health is to put matter before mind, is to subordinate spirit to body.

MEN of robust minds do not dwell upon their bodily condition if it be in any way disordered—*they ignore it*, and work on, live on, as though it were not. This ignoring of the body not only keeps the mind sane and strong, but it is the best resource for curing the body. If we cannot have a perfectly sound body, we can have a healthy mind, and a healthy mind is the best route to a sound body.

A sickly mind is more deplorable than a disordered body, and it leads to sickness of body. The mental invalid is in a far more pitiable condition than the bodily invalid. There are invalids (every physician knows them) who only need to lift themselves into a strong, unselfish, happy frame of mind to discover that their body is whole and capable.

Moral principles are the soundest foundations for health, as well as for happiness.

Thought for the Evening

There can be no progress, no achievement, without sacrifice, and a man's worldly success will be in the measure that he sacrifices his confused animal thoughts, and fixes his mind on the development of his plans, and the strengthening of his resolution and self-reliance. And the higher he lifts his thoughts, the more manly, upright, and righteous he becomes, the greater will be his success, the more blessed and enduring will be his achievements.

September Second

Thought for the Morning

None but right acts can follow right thoughts; none but a right life can follow right acts; and by living a right life all blessedness is achieved. Mind is the Master-power that moulds and makes. And Man is Mind, and evermore he takes the tool of thought, and, shaping what he wills, brings forth a thousand joys, a thousand ills;—He thinks in secret, and it comes to pass: environment is but his looking-glass.

Meditation for the Day

Men are not made unhappy by poverty, but by the thirst for riches.

WHERE there is a cause its effect will appear; and were affluence the cause of immorality, and poverty the cause of degradation, then every rich man would become immoral, and every poor man would come to degradation.

An evil-doer will commit evil under any circumstances, whether he be rich or poor, or midway between the two conditions. A right-doer will do right howsoever he be placed. Extreme circumstances may help to bring out the evil which is already there awaiting its opportunity, but they cannot cause the evil, cannot create it.

Poverty is more often in the mind than in the purse. So long as a man thirsts for more money he will regard himself as poor, and in that sense he is poor, for covetousness is poverty of mind.

A miser may be a millionaire, but he is as poor as when he was penniless.

Thought for the Evening

Calmness of mind is one of the beautiful jewels of wisdom. A man becomes calm in the measure that he understands himself as a thought-evolved being... and he as he develops a right understanding, and sees more and more clearly the internal relations of things by the action of cause and effect, he ceases to fret and fume, and worry and grieve, and remains poised, steadfast, serene.

September Third

Thought for the Morning

To follow, under all circumstances, the highest promptings within you; to be always true to the divine self; to reply upon the inward voice, the inward light, and to pursue your purpose with a fearless and restful heart, believing that the future will yield unto you the need of every thought and effort; knowing that the laws of the universe can never fail, and that your own will come back to you with mathematical exactitude—this is faith and the living of faith.

Meditation for the Day

A man is great in knowledge, great in himself,
and great in his influence in the world,
in the measure that he is great in self-control.

WONDERFUL as are the forces in nature, are vastly inferior to that combination of intelligent forces which comprise the mind of man, and which dominate and direct the blind mechanical forces of nature. Therefore, it follows that to understand, control, and direct the inner forces of passion, desire, will, and intellect, is to be in possession of the destinies of men and nations.

He who understands and dominates the forces of external nature is the natural scientist; but he who understands and dominates the internal forces of the mind is the divine scientist; and the laws which operate in gaining a knowledge of external appearances operate also in gaining a knowledge of internal verities.

The end of knowledge is use, service, the increase

of the comfort and happiness of the world.

Thought for the Evening

Have a thorough understanding of your work, and let it be your own; and as you proceed, ever following the inward guide, the infallible voice, you will pass on from victory to victory, and will rise step by step to higher resting-places, and your ever broadening outlook will gradually reveal to you the essential beauty and purpose of life. Self-purified, health will be yours; self-governed, power will be yours, and all that you do will prosper.

And I may stand where health, success, and power await my coming, if, each fleeting hour, I cling to love and patience; and abide with stainlessness; and never step aside from high integrity; so shall I see at last the land of immortality.

September Fourth

Thought for the Morning

When the tongue is well controlled and wisely subdued; when selfish impulses and unworthy thoughts no longer rush to the tongue demanding utterance; when the speech has become harmless, pure, gracious, gentle, and purposeful, and no word is uttered but in sincerity and truth—then are the five steps in virtuous speech accomplished, then is the second great lesson in Truth learned and mastered. Make pure thy heart, and thou wilt make thy life rich, sweet and beautiful.

Meditation for the Day

*All things, whether visible or invisible, are subservient to,
and fall within the scope of, the infinite and eternal law and causation.*

PERFECT justice upholds the universe; perfect justice regulates human life and conduct. All the varying conditions of life, as they obtain in the world today, are the results of this law reacting on human conduct. Man can (and does) choose what causes he shall set in operation, but he cannot change the nature of effects; he can decide what thoughts he shall think, and what deeds he shall do, but he has no power over the *results* of those thoughts and deeds; these are regulated by the over-ruling law.

Man has all power to act, but his power ends with the act committed. The result of the act cannot be altered, annulled, or escaped; it is irrevocable.

*Evil thoughts and deeds produce conditions of suffering;
good thoughts and deeds determine conditions of blessedness.*

Thought for the Evening

Having clothed himself with humility, the first questions a man asks himself are:—

"How am I acting towards others?"
"What am I doing to others?"
"How am I thinking of others?"
"Are my thoughts of, and acts towards others prompted by unselfish love?"

As a man, in the silence of his soul, asks himself these searching questions, he will unerringly see where he has hitherto failed.

September Fifth

Thought for the Morning

To dwell in love always and towards all is to live the true life, is to have Life itself. Knowing this, the good man gives up himself unreservedly to the Spirit of Love, and dwells in Love towards all, contending with none, condemning none, but loving all.

The Christ Spirit of Love puts an end, not only to all sin, but to all division and contention.

Meditation for the Day

*Man's power is limited to, and his blessedness
or misery is determined by, his own conduct.*

LIFE may be likened to a sum in arithmetic. It is bewilderingly difficult and complex to the pupil who has not yet grasped the key to its correct solution, but once this is perceived and laid hold of it becomes as astonishingly simple as it was formerly profoundly perplexing. Some idea of this relative simplicity and complexity of life may be grasped by fully recognizing and realizing the fact that, while there are scores, and perhaps hundreds, of ways in which a sum may be done wrong, *there is only one way by which it can be done right*, and that when the right way is found *the pupil knows it to be right*; his perplexity vanishes, and he knows that he has mastered the problem.

*In life there can be no falsifying of results;
the eye of the Great Law reveals and exposes.*

Thought for the Evening

When sin and self are abandoned, the heart is restored to its imperishable Joy. Joy comes and fills the self-emptied heart; it abides with the peaceful; its reign is with the pure. Joy flees from the selfish, it deserts the quarrelsome; it is hidden from the impure. Joy cannot remain with the selfish; it is wedded to Love.

September Sixth

Thought for the Morning

In the pure heart there is no room left where personal judgments and hatreds can find lodgement, for it is filled to overflowing with tenderness and love; it sees no evil, and only as men succeed in seeing no evil in others will they become free from sin, and sorrow, and suffering. If men only understood that the heart that sins must sorrow, that the hateful mind tomorrow reaps its barren harvest, weeping, starving, resting not, nor sleeping; tenderness would fill their being, they would see with pity's seeing, if they only understood.

Meditation for the Day

*Selfish thoughts and bad deeds
will not produce a useful and beautiful life.*

LIFE is like a piece of doth, and the threads of which it is composed are individual lives. The threads, while being independent, are not confounded one with the other. Each follows its own course. Each individual suffers and enjoys the consequences of his own deeds, and not the deeds of another. The course of each is simple and definite; the whole forming a complicated, yet harmonious, combination of sequences. There are action and reaction, deed and consequence, cause and effect, and the counterbalancing reaction, consequence, and effect is always in exact ratio with the initiatory impulse.

Each man makes or mars his own life.

Thought for the Evening

To stand face to face with truth; to arrive, after innumerable wanderings and pains, at wisdom and bliss; not to be finally defeated and cast out, but to ultimately triumph over every inward foe—such is man's divine destiny, such his glorious goal; and this, every saint, sage, and saviour has declared. A man only begins to be a man when he ceases to whine and revile, and commences to search for the hidden justice which regulates his life. And as he adapts his mind to that regulating factor, he ceases to accuse others as the cause of his condition, and builds himself up in strong and noble thoughts; ceases to kick against circumstances, but begins to use them as aids to his more rapid progress, and as a means of discovering the hidden power and possibilities within himself.

September Seventh

Thought for the Morning

The will to evil and the will to good are both within thee, which wilt thou employ? Thou knowest what is right and what is wrong, which wilt though love and foster, which destroy?

Thou art the chooser of thy thoughts and deeds; thou art the maker of thine inward state; the power is thine to be what thou wilt be; thou buildest Truth and Love, or lies and hate.

Meditation for the Day

Man is responsible only for his own deeds;
he is the custodian of his own actions.

THE "problem of evil" subsists in a man's own evil deeds, and it is solved when those deeds are purified. Says Rousseau:

"Man, seek no longer the origin of evil; thou thyself art its origin."

Effect can never be divorced from cause; it can never be of a different nature from cause. Emerson says:

"Justice is not postponed; a perfect equity adjusts the balance in all parts of life."

And there is a profound sense in which cause and effect are simultaneous, and form one perfect whole. Thus, upon the instant that a man thinks, say, a cruel deed, that same instant *he has injured his own mind*; he is not the same man he was the previous instant; he is a little viler and a little more unhappy; and a number of successive thoughts and deeds would produce a cruel and wretched man.

*An immediate nobility and happiness attend
the thinking of a kind thought, or doing a kind deed.*

Thought for the Evening

The teaching of Jesus brings men back to the simple truth that righteousness, or *right-doing*, is entirely a matter of individual conduct, and not a mystical something apart from a man's thoughts and deeds.

Calmness and patience can become habitual by first grasping, through effort, a calm and patient thought, and then continuously thinking it, and living in it, until "use becomes second nature," and anger and impatience pass away for ever.

September Eighth

Thought for the Morning

Man is made or unmade by himself; in the armoury of thought he forges the weapons by which he destroys himself; he also fashions the tools with which he builds for himself heavenly mansions of joy and strength and peace. By the right choice and true application of thought man ascends to the Divine Perfection; by the abuse and wrong application of thought he descends below the level of the beast. Between these two extremes are all the grades of character and man is their maker and master.

As a being of Power, Intelligence, and Love, and the lord of his own thoughts, man holds the key to every situation.

Meditation for the Day

Without strength of mind, nothing worthy of accomplishment can be done.

THE cultivation of that steadfastness and stability of character which is commonly called "will-power" is one of the foremost duties of man, for its possession is essentially necessary both to his temporal and external well-being. Fixedness of purpose is at the root of all successful efforts, whether in things worldly or spiritual, and without it man cannot be otherwise than wretched, and dependent upon others for that support which should be found within himself.

The true path of will-cultivation is only to be found in the common everyday life of the individual, and so obvious and simple is it that the majority, looking for something complicated and mysterious, pass it by unnoticed.

*The direct and only way to greater strength
is to assail and conquer weaknesses.*

Thought for the Evening

Whatsoever you harbour in the inmost chambers of your heart will, sooner or later, by the inevitable law of reaction, shape itself in your outward life.

Every soul attracts its own, and nothing can possibly come to it that does not belong to it. To realize this is to recognize the universality of Divine Law.

If thou would'st right the world, and banish all its evils and its woes, make its wild places bloom, and its drear deserts blossom as the rose—then right thyself.

September Ninth

Thought for the Morning

Whatever conditions are rendering your life burdensome, you may pass out of and beyond them by developing and utilizing within you the transforming power of self-purification and self-conquest.

Before the divine radiance of a pure heart all darkness vanishes and all clouds melt away, and he who has conquered self has conquered the universe.

He who sets his foot firmly upon the path of self-conquest, who walks, aided by the staff of faith, the highway of self-sacrifice, will assuredly achieve the highest prosperity, and will reap abounding and enduring joy and bliss.

Meditation for the Day

In the training of the will the first step is the breaking away from bad habits.

HE who has succeeded in grasping this simple, preliminary truth will perceive that the whole science of will-cultivation is embodied in the following seven rules:

1. Break off bad habits.
2. Form good habits.

3. Give scrupulous attention to the duty of the present moment.
4. Do vigorously, and at once, whatever has to be done.
5. Live by rule.
6. Control the tongue.
7. Control the mind.

Anyone who earnestly meditates upon, and diligently practises, the above rules will not fail to develop that purity of purpose and power of will which will enable him to successfully cope with every difficulty, and pass triumphantly through every emergency.

Thought for the Evening

It is the silent and conquering thought forces which bring all things into manifestation. The universe grew out of thought.

To adjust all your thoughts to a perfect and unswerving faith in the omnipotence and supremacy of Good is to co-operate with that Good, and to realize within yourself the solution and destruction of all evil.

September Tenth

Thought for the Morning

Every thought you think is a force sent out. Whatever your position in life may be, before you can hope to enter into any measure of success, usefulness, and power, you must learn how to focus your thought forces by cultivating calmness and repose.

There is no difficulty, however great, but will yield before a calm and purposeful concentration of thought, and no legitimate object but may be speedily actualized by the intelligent use and direction of one's soul forces.

Think good thoughts, and they will quickly become actualized in your outward life in the form of good conditions.

Meditation for the Day

By submitting to a bad habit one forfeits the right to rule over himself.

HE who thus avoids self-discipline, and looks about for some "occult secrets" for gaining will-power at the expenditure of little or no effort on his part, is deluding himself, and is weakening the willpower which he already possesses.

The strength of will which is gained by success in overcoming bad habits enables one to initiate good habits; for, while the conquering of a bad habit requires merely strength of purpose, the forming of a new one necessitates the *intelligent direction of purpose*. To do this, a man must be mentally active and energetic, and must keep a constant watch upon himself. Thoroughness is a step in the development of the will which cannot be passed over.

Slipshod work is an indication of weakness.

Thought for the Evening

That which you would be and hope to be, you may be now. Non-accomplishment resides in your perpetual postponement, and, having the power to postpone, you also have the power to accomplish—to perpetually accomplish: realize this truth, and you shall be today, and every day, the ideal being of whom you dreamed.

Say to yourself, "I will live in my Ideal now; I will manifest my ideal now; I will be my Ideal now; and all that tempts me away from my Ideal I will not listen to; I will listen only to the voice of my Ideal."

September Eleventh

Thought for the Morning

Be as a flower; content to be, to grow in sweetness day by day. If thou would'st perfect thyself in knowledge, perfect thyself in Love. If thou would'st reach the Highest, ceaselessly cultivate a loving and compassionate heart.

To him who chooses Goodness, sacrificing all, is given that which is more than, and includes, all.

Meditation for the Day

Perfection should be aimed at, even in the smallest task.

BY not dividing the mind, but giving the whole attention to each separate task as it presents itself, singleness of purpose and intense concentration of mind are gradually gained two mental powers which give weight and worth of character, and bring repose and joy to their possessor.

Doing vigorously, and at once, whatever has to be done is equally important. Idleness and a strong will cannot go together, and procrastination is a total barrier to the acquisition of purposeful action. Nothing should be "put off" until another time, not even for a few minutes. That which ought to be done now should be done now. This seems a little thing, but it is of far-reaching importance. It leads to strength, success, and peace.

Live according to principle, and not according to passion.

Thought for the Evening

The Great Law never cheats any man of his just due.

Human life, when rightly lived, is simple with a beautiful simplicity.

He who comprehends the utter simplicity of life, who obeys its laws, and does not step aside into the dark paths and complex mazes of selfish desire, stands where no harm can reach him.

Then there is fullness of joy, abounding plenty, and rich and complete blessedness.

September Twelfth

Thought for the Morning

Every man reaps the results of his own thoughts and deeds, and suffers for his own wrong.

He who begins right, and continues right, does not need to desire, and search for felicitous results; they are already at hand; they follow as consequences; they are the certainties, the realities, of life.

Sweet is the rest and deep is the bliss of him who has freed his heart from its lusts and hatreds and dark desires.

Meditation for the Day

*Thoroughness consists in doing little things
as though they were the greatest things in the world.*

THE little things of life are of primary importance is a truth not generally understood, and the thought that little things can be neglected, thrown aside, or slurred over is at the root of that lack of thoroughness which is so common, and which results in imperfect work and unhappy lives.

When one understands that the great things of the world and of life consist of a combination of small things, and that without this aggregation of small things the great things would be non-existent, then he begins to pay careful attention to those things which he formerly regarded as insignificant.

He who acquires the quality of thoroughness
becomes a man of usefulness and influence.

Thought for the Evening

You are the creator of your own shadows; you desire, and then you grieve; renounce, and then you shall rejoice.

Of all the beautiful truths pertaining to the soul. . . none is more gladdening or fruitful of divine promise and confidence than this—that man is the master of thought, the moulder of character, and the maker and shaper of character, environment, and destiny.

September Thirteenth

Thought for the Morning

As darkness is a passing shadow, and light is a substance that remains, so sorrow is fleeting, but joy abides for ever. No true thing can pass away and become lost; no false thing can remain and be preserved. Sorrow is false, and it cannot live; joy is true, and it cannot die. Joy may become hidden for a time, but it can always be recovered; sorrow may remain for a period, but it can be transcended and dispersed.

Do not think your sorrow will remain; it will pass away like a cloud. Do not believe that the torments of sin are ever your portion; they will vanish like a hideous nightmare. Awake! Arise! Be holy and joyful.

Meditation for the Day

The cause of the common lack of thoroughness lies in the thirst for pleasure.

EVERY employer of labour knows how difficult it is to find men and women who will put thought and energy into their work, and do it completely and satisfactorily. Bad workmanship abounds. Skill and excellence are acquired by few. Thoughtlessness, carelessness, and laziness are such common vices that it should cease to appear strange that, in spite of "social reform", the ranks of the unemployed should continue to swell, for those who scamp their work today will, another day, in the hour of deep necessity, look and ask for work in vain.

The law of "the survival of the fittest" is not based on cruelty, it is based on justice; it is one aspect of that divine equity which everywhere prevails. Vice is "beaten with many stripes"; if it were not so, how could virtue be developed? The thoughtless and lazy cannot take precedence of, or stand equally with, the thoughtful and industrious.

The mind that is occupied with pleasure cannot also
be concentrated upon the perfect performance of duty.

Thought for the Evening

Tribulation lasts only so long as there remains some chaff of self which needs to be removed. The *tribulum*, or threshing machine, ceases to work when all the grain is separated from the chaff; and when the last impurities are blown away from the soul, tribulation has completed its work, and there is no more need for it; then abiding joy is realized.

The sole and supreme use of suffering is to purify, to burn out all that is useless and impure. Suffering ceases for him who is pure. There could be no object in burning gold after the dross had been removed.

September Fourteenth

Thought for the Morning

In speaking of self-control, one is easily misunderstood. It should not be associated with a destructive repression, but with a constructive expression.

A man is happy, wise and great in the measure that he controls himself; he is wretched, foolish, and mean in the measure that he allows his animal nature to dominate his thoughts and actions.

He who controls himself, controls his life, his circumstances, his destiny; and wherever he goes he carries his happiness with him as an abiding possession.

Renunciation precedes regeneration. The permanent happiness which men seek in dissipation, excitement, and abandonment to unworthy pleasures, is found only in the life which reverses all this—the life of self-control.

Meditation for the Day

*He who lacks thoroughness in his worldly duties
will also lack the same in spiritual things.*

THOROUGHNESS is completeness, perfection; it means doing a thing so well that there is nothing left to be desired; it means doing one's work, if not better than anyone else can do it, at least not worse than the best that others do. It means the exercise of much thought, the putting forth of great energy, the persistent application of the mind to its task, the cultivation of patience, perseverance, and a high sense of duty. An ancient teacher said, "If anything has to be done, let a man do it, let him attack it vigorously"; and another teacher said, "Whatsoever thy hand findeth to do, do it with thy might."

*It is better to be a whole-souled worldling
than a halfhearted religionist.*

Thought for the Evening

Law, not confusion, is the dominating principle in the universe; justice, not injustice is the soul and substance of life; and righteousness, not corruption, is the moulding and moving force in the spiritual government of the world. This being so, man has but the right himself to find that the universe is right.

When I am pure, I shall have solved the mystery of life; I shall be sure, when I am free from hatred, lust and strife, I am in Truth, and Truth abides in me; I shall be safe, and sane, and wholly free, when I am pure.

September Fifteenth

Thought for the Morning

If men only understood that their hatred and resentment slays their peace and sweet contentment, hurts themselves, helps not another, does not cheer one lonely brother, they would seek the better doing of good deeds which leaves no ruing:—

If they only understood.

If men only understood how Love conquers; how prevailing is its might, grim hate assailing; how compassion endeth sorrow, maketh wise, and doth not borrow pain of passion, they would ever live in Love, in hatred never:—

If they only understood.

Meditation for the Day

*He who has not learned how to be gentle,
loving, and happy has learned very little.*

DESPONDENCY, irritability, anxiety, complaining, condemning, and grumbling all these are thought-cankers, mind-diseases; they are the indications of a wrong mental condition, and those who suffer therefrom would do well to remedy their thinking and conduct. It is true there is much sin and misery in the world, so that all our love and compassion are needed, *but our misery is not needed*—there is already too much of that. No, it is our cheerfulness and our happiness that are needed, for there is too little of that. We can give nothing better to the world than beauty of life and character; without this, all other things are vain; this is pre-eminently excellent; it is enduring, real, and not to be overthrown, and it includes all joy and blessedness.

*A man's surroundings are never against him;
they are there to aid him.*

Thought for the Evening

The grace and beauty that were in Jesus can be of no value to you—cannot be understood by you—unless they are also *in you*, and they can never be in you, until you practice them, for, apart from *doing*, the qualities which constitute goodness do not, as far as you are concerned, exist.

To adore Jesus for his good qualities is a long step towards Truth, but to practice those qualities is Truth itself; and he who fully adores the perfection of another will not rest content in his own imperfection, but will fashion his soul after the likeness of that other.

Therefore thou who adorest Jesus for his divine qualities, practice those qualities thyself, and thou too shalt be divine.

September Sixteenth

Thought for the Morning

Let a man realize that life in its totality proceeds from the mind, and lo, the way of blessedness is opened up to him! For he will then discover that he possesses the power to rule his mind and to fashion it in accordance with his Ideal.

So will he elect to strongly and steadfastly walk those pathways of thought and action which are altogether excellent; to him life will become beautiful and sacred; and, sooner or later, he will put to flight all evil, confusion, and suffering; for it is impossible for a man to fall short of liberation, enlightenment, and peace, who guards with unwearying diligence the gateway of his heart.

Meditation for the Day

*You can transform everything around you
if you will transform yourself.*

UNBROKEN sweetness of conduct in the face of all outward antagonism is the infallible indication of a self-conquered soul, the witness of wisdom, and the proof of the possession of Truth.

A sweet and happy soul is the ripened fruit of wisdom, and it sheds abroad the invisible aroma of its influence, gladdening the hearts of others, and purifying the world.

If you would have others true, be true; if you would have the world emancipated from misery and sin, emancipate yourself; if you would have your home and your surroundings happy, be happy.

And this you will naturally and spontaneously do as you realize the good in yourself.

Commence to live free from all wrong and evil.

*Commence to live free from all wrong and evil.
Peace of mind and true reform lie this way.*

Thought for the Evening

By constantly overcoming self, a man gains a knowledge of the subtle intricacies of his mind; and it is this divine knowledge which enables him to become established in calmness.

Without self-knowledge there can be no abiding peace of mind, and those who are carried away by tempestuous passions, cannot approach the holy place where calmness reigns.

The weak man is like one who, having mounted a fiery steed, allows it to run away with him, and carry him withersoever it wills; the strong man is like one who, having mounted the steed, governs it with a masterly hand and makes it go in whatever direction and at whatever speed he commands.

September Seventeenth

Thought for the Morning

There is no strife, no selfishness, in the Kingdom; there is perfect harmony, equipoise, and rest.

Those who live in the Kingdom of Love, have all their needs supplied by the Law of Love.

As self is the root cause of all strife and suffering, so Love is the root cause of all peace and bliss. Those who are at rest in the Kingdom do not look for happiness in any outward possessions. They are freed from all anxiety and trouble and, resting in Love, they are the embodiment of happiness.

Meditation for the Day

*Immortality is here and now,
and is not a speculative something beyond the grave.*

IMMORTALITY does not belong to time, and will never be found in time: it belongs to Eternity; and just as time is here and now, so is Eternity here and now, and a man may find that Eternity and establish himself in it, if he will overcome the self that derives its life from the unsatisfying and perishable things of time.

Whilst a man remains immersed in sensation, desire, and the passing events of his day-by-day existence, and regards those sensations, desires, and passing events as of the essence of himself, he can have no knowledge of immortality. The thing which such a man desires, and which he mistakes for immortality, is *persistence*; that is, a continuous succession of sensations and events of time.

Persistence is the antithesis of immortality.

Thought for the Evening

Let it not be supposed that the children of the Kingdom live in ease and indolence (these two sins are the first that have to be eradicated when the search for the Kingdom is entered upon); they live in a peaceful activity; in fact, they only truly live, for the life of self, with its train of worries, griefs, and fears, is not *real life*.

The children of the Kingdom are *known by their life*, they manifest the fruits of the Spirit—"Love, joy, peace, long-suffering, kindness, goodness, faithfulness, meekness, temperance, and self-control"—under all circumstances and vicissitudes.

September Eighteenth

Thought for the Morning

The gospel of Jesus is a gospel of *living and doing*. If it were not this it would not voice the Eternal Truth. Its Temple is *Purified Conduct*, the entrance-door to which is *Self-Surrender*. It invites men to shake off sin, and promises, as a result, joy and blessedness and perfect peace.

The Kingdom of Heaven is perfect trust, perfect knowledge, perfect peace. . . no sin can enter therein, no self-born thought or deed can pass its golden gates; no impure desire can defile its radiant robes. . . all may enter it who will, but all must pay the price—*the unconditional abandonment of self*.

Meditation for the Day

The death of the body can never bestow upon a man immortality.

SPIRITS are not different from men, and live their little feverish life of broken consciousness, and are still immersed in change and mortality. The mortal man, he who thirsts for the persistence of his pleasure-loving personality, is still mortal after death, and only lives another life with a beginning and an end, without memory of the past or knowledge of the future.

The immortal man is he who has detached himself from the things of time by having ascended into that state of consciousness which is fixed and unvariable, and is not affected by passing events and sensations. He is as one who has awakened out of his dream, and he knows that his dream was not an enduring reality, but a passing illusion. He is a man with knowledge, the knowledge of both states that of persistence, and that of immortality.

The immortal man is in full possession of himself.

Thought for the Evening

I say this—and know it to be truth—*that circumstances can only affect you in so far as you allow them to do so.* You are swayed by circumstances because you have not a right understanding of the nature, use, and power of thought. You believe (and upon this little word *belief* hang all our joys and sorrows) that outward things have the power to make or mar your life; by so doing you submit to those outward things, confess that you are their slave, and they your unconditional master. By so doing you invest them with a power which they do not of themselves possess, and you succumb, in reality not to the circumstances, but to the gloom or gladness, the fear or hope, the strength of weakness, which your thought-sphere has thrown around them.

September Nineteenth

Thought for the Morning

If you are one of those who are praying for, and looking forward to a happier world beyond the grave, here is a message of gladness for you—you may enter into and realize that happy world now; it fills the whole universe, and it is within you, waiting for you to find, acknowledge, and possess.

Said one who understood the inner laws of Being—"When men shall say, lo here, or lo there, go not after them. The Kingdom of God is within you."

Meditation for the Day

The mortal man lives in the time or world

state of consciousness which begins and ends.

THE immortal man remains poised and steadfast under all changes, and the death of his body will not in any way interrupt the eternal consciousness in which he abides. Of such a one it is said, "He shall not taste of death," because he has stepped out of the stream of mortality, and established himself in the abode of Truth. Bodies, personalities, nations, and worlds pass away, but Truth remains, and its glory is undimmed by time. The immortal man, then, is he who has conquered himself; who no longer identifies himself with the self-seeking forces of the personality, but who has trained himself to direct those forces with the hand of a master, and so has brought them into harmony with the causal energy and source of all things.

*The immortal man lives in the cosmic
or heaven state of consciousness,
in which there is neither beginning nor end,
but an eternal now.*

Thought for the Evening

Heaven and hell are inward states. Sink into self and all its gratifications, and you sink into hell; rise above self into that state of consciousness which is the utter denial and forgetfulness of self, and you enter heaven.

So long as you persist in selfishly seeking for your own personal happiness, so long will happiness elude you, and you will be sowing the seeds of wretchedness. In so far as you succeed in losing yourself in the service of others, in that measure will happiness come to you, and you will reap a harvest of bliss.

September Twentieth

Thought for the Morning

Sympathy given can never be waste.

One aspect of sympathy is that of pity—pity for the distressed or pain stricken, with a desire to alleviate or help them in their sufferings. The world needs more of this divine quality.

"For pity makes the world soft to the weak, and noble for the strong."

Another form of sympathy is that of rejoicing with others who are more successful than ourselves, and though their success were our own.

Meditation for the Day

*The overcoming of self is the annihilation
of all the sorrow-producing elements.*

THE doctrine of the overcoming or annihilation of self is simplicity itself; indeed, so simple, practical, and close at hand is it that a child of five, whose mind has not yet become clouded with theories, theological schemes, and speculative philosophies, would be far more likely to comprehend it than many older people who have lost their hold upon simple and beautiful truths by the adoption of complicated theories.

The annihilation of self consists in weeding out and destroying all those elements in the soul which lead to division, strife, suffering, disease, and sorrow. It does not mean the destruction of any good and beautiful and peace-producing quality.

The overcoming of self is the cultivation of all the divine qualities.

Thought for the Evening

Sweet are companionships, pleasures, and material comforts, but they change and fade away. Sweeter still are Purity, Wisdom, and the knowledge of Truth, and these never change nor fade away.

He who attained to the possession of spiritual things can never be deprived of his source of happiness; he will never have to part company with it, and wherever he goes in the whole universe, he will carry his possessions with him. His spiritual end will be the fullness of joy.

September Twenty-first

Thought for the Morning

Let your heart grow and expand with ever broadening love, until, freed from all hatred, and passion, and condemnation, it embraces the whole universe with thoughtful tenderness.

As the flower opens its petals to receive the morning light, so open your soul more and more to the glorious light of Truth.

Soar upward on the wings of aspiration; be fearless and believe in the loftiest possibilities.

Meditation for the Day

*He who would overcome his enemy the tempter
must discover his stronghold and place of concealment,*

*and must also find out the unguarded gates in his own fortress
where the enemy effects so easy an entrance.*

TEMPTATION, with all its attendant torments, *can* be overcome here and now, but it can only be overcome with knowledge. It is a condition of darkness, or of semi-darkness. The fully enlightened soul is proof against all temptation. When a man fully understands the source, nature, and meaning of temptation, in that hour he will conquer it, and will rest from his long travail; but whilst he remains in ignorance, attention to religious observances and much praying and reading of Scripture will fail to bring him peace.

This is the holy warfare of the saints.

Thought for the Evening

Mind clothes itself in garments of its own making. Mind is the arbiter of life; it is the creator and shaper of conditions, and the recipient of its own results. It contains within itself both the power to create illusion and to perceive reality.

Mind is the infallible weaver of destiny; thought is the thread, good and evil deeds are the warp and woof, and the web, woven upon the loom of life, is character. Make pure thy heart, and thou wilt make thy life, rich, sweet, and beautiful, unmarred by strife.

September Twenty-second

Thought for the Morning

Cherish your visions; cherish your ideals; cherish the music that stirs in your heart, the beauty that forms in your mind, the loveliness that drapes your purest thoughts, for out of them will grow all delightful conditions, all heavenly environment; of these, if you will remain true to them, your world will at last be built.

Guard well thy mind, and, noble, strong, and free, nothing shall harm, disturb or conquer thee; for all thy foes are in thy heart and mind, there also thy salvation thou shalt find.

Meditation for the Day

All temptation comes from within.

MEN fail to conquer, and the fight is indefinitely prolonged, because they labour, almost universally, under two delusions; first, that all temptations come from without; and second, that they are tempted because of their goodness. Whilst a man is held in bondage by these delusions, he will make no progress; when he has shaken them off, he will pass on rapidly from victory to victory, and will taste of spiritual joy and rest.

The source and cause of all temptation is in the *inward desire*; that being purified and eliminated, outward objects and extraneous powers are utterly powerless to move the soul to sin or to temptation. The outward object is merely the *occasion* of the temptation, *never the cause*; this is in the desire of the one tempted.

*A man is tempted because there are certain desires
or states of mind which he has come to regard as unholy.*

Thought for the Evening

Dream lofty dreams, and as you dream so shall you become. Your vision is the promise of what you shall one day be; your Ideal is the prophecy of what you shall at last unveil.

The greatest achievement was at first and for a time a dream. The oak sleeps in the acorn; the bird waits in the egg; and in the highest vision of the soul a waking angel stirs.

Your circumstances may be uncongenial, but they shall not long remain so when you perceive an Ideal and strive to reach it.

September Twenty-third

Thought for the Morning

He who has conquered doubt and fear has conquered failure. His every thought is allied with power, and all difficulties are bravely met and wisely overcome. His purposes are seasonably planted, and they bloom and bring forth fruit which does not fall prematurely to the ground.

Thought allied fearlessly to purpose becomes creative force: he who knows this is ready to become something higher and stronger than a mere bundle of wavering thoughts and fluctuating sensations; he who does this has become the conscious and intelligent wielder of his mental powers.

Meditation for the Day

The good in a man is never tempted. Goodness destroys temptation.

IT is the evil in a man that is aroused and tempted. The measure of a man's temptations is the exact register of his own unholiness. As a man purifies his heart, temptation ceases, for when a certain unlawful desire has been taken out of the heart the object which formerly appealed to it can no longer do so, but becomes dead and powerless, for there is nothing left in the heart that can respond to it. The honest man cannot be tempted to steal, let the occasion be ever so opportune; the man of purified appetites cannot be tempted to gluttony and drunkenness; he whose mind is calm in the strength of inward virtue can never be tempted to anger, and the wiles and charms of the wanton fall upon the purified heart as empty, meaningless shadows.

Temptation shows a man just where he is.

Thought for the Evening

Man's true place in the Cosmos is that of a king, not a slave, a commander under the Law of Good, and not a helpless tool in the region of evil.

I write for men, not for babes; for those who are eager to learn, and earnest to achieve; for those who will put away (for the world's good) a petty personal indulgence, a selfish desire, a mean thought, and live on as though it were not, sans craving and regret.

Man is a master. If he were not, he could not act contrary to law.

Evil and weakness are self destructive. The universe is girt with goodness and strength, and it protects the good and the strong.

The angry man is the weak man.

September Twenty-fourth

Thought for the Morning

Not by learning will a man triumph over evil; not by much study will he overcome sin and sorrow. Only by conquering himself will he conquer evil; only by practicing righteousness will he put an end to sorrow.

Not for the clever, nor the learned, nor the self-confident is the Life Triumphant, but for the pure, the virtuous and wise. The former achieve their particular success in life, but the latter alone achieve the great success so invincible and complete that even in apparent defeat it shines with added victory.

Meditation for the Day

*The Great Law is good the man of integrity is superior
to fear and failure, and poverty, and shame, and disgrace.*

THE man who, fearing the loss of present pleasures or material comforts, denies the truth within him can be injured, and robbed, and degraded, and trampled upon, because he has first injured, robbed, and degraded, and trampled upon his own nobler self; but the man of steadfast virtue, of unblemished integrity, cannot be subject to such conditions, because he has denied the craven self within him and has taken refuge in Truth. It is not the scourge and the chains which make a man a slave, but the fact that he *is* a slave.

*Slander, accusation, and malice cannot affect the righteous man,
nor call from him any bitter response, nor does he need to go about
to defend himself and prove his innocence. Innocence and integrity
alone are a sufficient answer to all that hatred may attempt.*

Thought for the Evening

The true silence is not merely a silent tongue; it is a silent mind. To merely *hold one's tongue*, and yet to carry about a disturbed and rankling mind, is no remedy for weakness, and no source of power.

Silentness, to be powerful, must envelop the whole mind, must permeate every chamber of the heart; it must be the silence of peace.

To this broad, deep, abiding silentness a man attains only in the measure that he conquers himself.

September Twenty-fifth

Thought for the Morning

By curbing his tongue, a man gains possession of his mind.

The fool babbles, gossips, argues, and bandies words. He glories in the fact that he has had the last word, and has silenced his opponent. He exults in his own folly, is ever on the defensive, and wastes his energies in unprofitable channels. He is like a gardener who continues to dig and plant in unproductive soil.

The wise man avoids idle words, gossips, vain argument, and self-defence. He is content to appear defeated; rejoices when he is defeated; knowing that, having found and removed another error in himself, he has thereby become wiser.

Blessed is he who does not strive for the last word.

Meditation for the Day

The man of integrity turns all evil things to good account.

LET the man of integrity rejoice and be glad when he is severely tried; let him be thankful that he has been given an opportunity of proving his loyalty to the noble principles which he has espoused; and let him think, "Now is the hour of holy opportunity! Now is the day of triumph for Truth! Though I lose the whole world, I will not desert the right." So thinking, he will return good for evil, and will think compassionately of the wrong-doer.

The slanderer, the backbiter, and the wrongdoer may seem to succeed for a time, but the Law of Justice prevails; the man of integrity may seem to fail for a time, but he is invincible, and in none of the worlds, visible or invisible, can there be a forged weapon that shall prevail against him.

The man of integrity can never be subdued by the forces of darkness, having subdued all those forces within himself.

Thought for the Evening

Desire is the *craving for possession*; aspiration is the *hunger of the heart for peace*.

The craving for things leads ever farther and farther from peace, and not only ends in deprivation, but is in itself a state of perpetual want. Until it comes to an end, rest and satisfaction are impossible.

The hunger for things can never be satisfied, but the hunger for peace can, and the satisfaction of peace is found—is fully possessed, when all selfish desire is abandoned. Then there is fullness of joy, abounding plenty, and rich and complete blessedness.

September Twenty-sixth

Thought for the Morning

A man will reach the Kingdom by purifying himself, and he can only do this by pursuing a process of self-examination and self-analysis.

The selfishness must be discovered and understood before it can be removed. It is powerless to remove itself, neither will it pass away of itself. Darkness ceases only when light is introduced; so ignorance can only be dispersed by knowledge, selfishness by love.

A man must first of all be willing to lose himself (his self-seeking) before he can find himself (his Divine Self). He must realize that selfishness is not worth clinging to, that it is a master altogether unworthy of his service, and that divine goodness alone is worthy to be enthroned in his heart, as the supreme master of his life.

Meditation for the Day

Without discrimination a man is mentally blind.

A MAN'S mind and life should be free from confusion. He should be prepared to meet every mental, material, and spiritual difficulty, and should not be intricately caught (as many are) in the meshes of doubt, indecision, and uncertainty when troubles and so-called misfortunes come along. He should be fortified against every emergency that can come against him; but such mental preparedness and strength cannot be attained in any degree without discrimination, and discrimination can only be developed by bringing into play and constantly exercising the analytical faculty.

Mind, like muscle, is developed by use.

Thought for the Evening

Be still, my soul, and know that peace is thine. Be steadfast, heart, and know that strength divine Belongs to thee; cease from thy turmoil, mind, and thou the Everlasting Rest shalt find.

If a man would have peace, let him exercise the spirit of peace; if he would find Love, let him dwell in the spirit of Love; if he would escape suffering, let him cease to inflict it; if he would do noble things for humanity, let him cease to do ignoble things for himself. If he will but quarry the mine of his own soul, he shall find there all the materials for building whatsoever he will, and he shall find there also the Central Rock on which to build in safety.

September Twenty-seventh

Thought for the Morning

Men go after much company, and seek out new excitements, but they are not acquainted with peace; in divers paths of pleasure they search for happiness, but they do not come to rest; through divers ways of laughter and feverish delirium they wander after gladness and life, but their tears are many and grievous, and they do not escape death.

Drifting upon the ocean of life in search of selfish indulgences, men are caught in its storms, and only after many tempests and much privation do they fly to the Rock of Refuge which rests in the deep silence of their own being.

Meditation for the Day

Confusion, suffering, and spiritual darkness follow the thoughtless.

THE man who is afraid to think searchingly upon his opinions, and to reason critically upon his position, will have to develop moral courage before he can acquire discrimination.

A man must be true to himself, fearless with himself, before he can perceive the pure principles of Truth, before he can receive the all-revealing Light of Truth.

The more Truth is inquired of, the brighter it shines; it cannot suffer under examination and analysis.

The more error is questioned, the darker it grows; it cannot survive the entrance of pure and searching thought.

To "prove all things" is to find the good and to throw away the evil.

He who reasons and meditates learns to discriminate; he who discriminates discovers the eternally True.

Harmony, blessedness, and the Light of Truth attend upon the thoughtful.

Thought for the Evening

Meditation centred upon divine realities is the very essence and soul of prayer. It is the silent reaching upward of the soul toward the Eternal.

Meditation is the intense dwelling, in thought, upon an idea or theme with the object of thoroughly comprehending it; and whatsoever you constantly meditate upon, you will not only come to understand, but will grow more and more into its likeness, for it will become incorporated with your very being, will become, in fact, your very self.

If, therefore, you constantly dwell upon that which is selfish and debasing, you will ultimately become selfish and debased; if you ceaselessly think upon that which is pure and unselfish, you will surely become pure and unselfish.

September Twenty-eighth

Thought for the Morning

There is no difficulty, however great, but will yield before a calm and powerful concentration of thought and no legitimate object but may be speedily actualized by the intelligent use and direction of one's soul forces.

Whatever your task may be, concentrate your whole mind upon it; throw into it all the energy of which you are capable. The faultless completion of small tasks, leads inevitably to larger tasks.

See to it that you rise by steady climbing, and you will never fall.

Meditation for the Day

Belief is an attitude of mind determining the whole course of one's life.

BELIEF is the basis of all action, and, this being so, the belief which dominates the heart or mind is shown in the life. Every man acts, thinks, lives in exact accordance with the belief which is rooted in his innermost being, and such is the mathematical nature of the laws which govern mind that it is absolutely impossible for anyone to believe in two opposing conditions at the same time. For instance, it is impossible to believe in justice and injustice, hatred and love, peace and strife, self and truth. Every man believes in one or the other of these opposites, *never in both*, and the daily conduct of every man indicates the nature of his belief.

Belief and conduct are inseparable, for the one determines the other.

Thought for the Evening

He who knows that Love is at the heart of all things, and has realized the all-sufficing power of that Love, has no room in his heart for condemnation.

If you love people and speak of them with praise, until they in some way thwart you, or do something of which you disapprove, and then you dislike them and speak of them with dispraise, you are not governed by the Love which is of God. If, in your heart, you are continually arraigning and condemning others, selfless love is hidden from you.

Train your mind in strong, impartial, and gentle thought; train your heart in purity and compassion; train your tongue to silence, and to true and stainless speech; so shall you enter the way of holiness and peace, and shall ultimately realize the immortal Love.

September Twenty-ninth

Thought for the Morning

If you would realize true prosperity, do not settle down, as many have done, into the belief that if you do right everything will go wrong. Do not allow the word "competition" to shake your faith in the supremacy of righteousness. I care not what men say about the "laws of competition," for do not I know the Unchangeable Law which shall one day put them all to rout, and which puts them to rout even now in the heart and life of the righteous man? And knowing this law I can contemplate all dishonesty with undisturbed repose, for I know where certain destruction awaits it.

Under all circumstances *do that which you believe to be right*, and trust the Law; trust the Divine Power which is immanent in the universe, and it will never desert you, and you will always be protected.

Meditation for the Day

Justice reigns, and all that is called injustice is fleeting and illusory.

THE man who is continually getting enraged over the injustice of his fellow men, who talks about himself being badly treated, or who mourns over the lack of justice in the world around him, shows by his conduct, his attitude of mind, that he believes in injustice. However he may protest to the contrary, in his inmost heart he believes that confusion and chaos are dominant in the universe, the result being that he dwells in misery and unrest, and his conduct is faulty.

Again, he who believes in love, in its stability and power, *practises it under all circumstances*, never deviates from it, and bestows it alike upon enemies as upon friends.

*The man who believes in justice remains calm
through all trials and difficulties.*

Thought for the Evening

Forget yourself entirely in the sorrows of others, and in ministering to others, and divine happiness will emancipate you from all sorrow and suffering. "Taking the first step with a good thought, the second with a good word, and the third with a good deed, I entered Paradise." And you also enter Paradise by pursuing the same course.

Lose yourself in the welfare of others; forget yourself in all that you do—this is the secret of abounding happiness. Ever be on the watch to guard against selfishness and learn faithfully the divine lessons of inward sacrifice; so shall you climb the highest heights of happiness, and shall remain in the never-clouded sunshine of universal joy, clothed in the shining garment of immortality.

September Thirtieth

Thought for the Morning

When the farmer has tilled and dressed his land and put in the seed, he knows that he has done all that he can possibly do, and that now he must trust to the elements, and wait patiently for the course of time to bring about the harvest, and that no amount of expectancy on his part will affect the result.

Even so, he who has realized Truth, goes forth as a sower of the seeds of goodness, purity, love, and peace, without expectancy and never looking for results, knowing that there is the Great Over-ruling Law which brings about its own harvest in due time, and which is alike the source of preservation and destruction.

Meditation for the Day

Every thought, every act, every habit, is the direct outcome of belief.

MEN are saved from error by belief in the supremacy of Truth. They are saved from sin by belief in Holiness or Perfection. They are saved from evil by belief in Good, for every belief is manifested in the life. It is not necessary to inquire as to a man's theological belief, for that is of little or no account, for what can it avail a man to believe that Jesus died for him, or that Jesus is God, or that he is "justified by faith", if he continues to live in his lower, sinful nature? All that is necessary to ask is this: "How does a man live?" "How does he conduct himself under trying circumstances?" The answer to these questions will show whether a man believes in the power of evil or in the power of Good.

When our belief in a thing ceases, we can no longer cling to or practise it.

Thought for the Evening

The virtuous put a check upon themselves, and set a watch upon their passions and emotions; in this way they gain possession of the mind, and gradually acquire calmness; and as they acquire influence, power, greatness, abiding joy, and fullness and completeness of life.

He only finds peace who conquers himself, who strives, day by day, after greater self-possession, greater self-control, and greater calmness of mind.

Where the calm mind is there is strength and rest, there is love and wisdom; there is one who has fought successfully innumerable battles against self, who, after long toil in secret against his own failings, has triumphed at last.

October First

Thought for the Morning

In aiming at the life of blessedness, one of the simplest beginnings to be considered, and rightly made, is that which we all make every day—namely, the beginning of each day's life. There is a sense in which every day may be regarded as the beginning of a new life, in which one can think, act, and live newly, and in a wiser and better spirit. The right beginning of the day will be followed by a cheerfulness permeating the household with a sunny influence, and the tasks and duties of the day will be undertaken in a strong and confident spirit, and the whole day will be well lived.

Meditation for the Day

A man cannot cling to anything unless he believes in it;
belief always precedes action,
therefore a man's deeds and life are the fruits of his belief.

HE who believes in all those things that are good will love them, and live in them; he who believes in those things that are impure and selfish will love Them, and cling to them. The tree is known by its fruits.

A man's beliefs about God, Jesus, and the Bible are one thing; his life, as bound up in his actions, is another; therefore a man's theological belief is of no consequence; but the thoughts which he harbours, his attitude of mind towards others, and his actions these, and these only, determine and demonstrate whether the belief of a man's heart is fixed in the false or the true.

There are only two beliefs which vitally affect the life,
and they are: belief in good and belief in evil.

Thought for the Evening

There can be no progress, no achievement, without sacrifice, and a man's worldly success will be in the measure that he sacrifices his confused animal thoughts, and fixes his mind on the development of his plans, and the strengthening of his resolution and self-reliance. And the higher he lifts his thoughts, the more manly, upright, and righteous he becomes, the greater will be his success, the more blessed and enduring will be his achievements.

October Second

Thought for the Morning

None but right acts can follow right thoughts; none but a right life can follow right acts; and by living a right life all blessedness is achieved. Mind is the Master-power that moulds and makes. And Man is Mind, and evermore he takes the tool of thought, and, shaping what he wills, brings forth a thousand joys, a thousand ills;—He thinks in secret, and it comes to pass: environment is but his looking-glass.

Meditation for the Day

As the fruit to the tree and the water to the spring, so is action to thought.

THE sudden falling, when greatly tempted, into some grievous sin by one who was believed, and who believed himself, to stand firm, is seen neither to be a *sudden* nor a causeless thing when the hidden processes of thought which led up to it are revealed. The *falling* was merely the end, the outworking, the finished result of what commenced in the mind probably years before. The man had allowed a wrong thought to enter his mind; and a second and a third time he had welcomed it, and allowed it to nestle in his heart. Gradually he became accustomed to it, and cherished and fondled, and tended it; and so it grew until at last it attained such strength and force that it attracted to itself the opportunity which enabled it to burst forth and ripen into act.

*All sin and temptation are the natural outcome
of the thoughts of the individual.*

Thought for the Evening

Calmness of mind is one of the beautiful jewels of wisdom. A man becomes calm in the measure that he understands himself as a thought-evolved being... and he as he develops a right understanding, and sees more and more clearly the internal relations of things by the action of cause and effect, he ceases to fret and fume, and worry and grieve, and remains poised, steadfast, serene.

October Third

Thought for the Morning

To follow, under all circumstances, the highest promptings within you; to be always true to the divine self; to reply upon the inward voice, the inward light, and to pursue your purpose with a fearless and restful heart, believing that the future will yield unto you the need of every thought and effort; knowing that the laws of the universe can never fail, and that your own will come back to you with mathematical exactitude—this is faith and the living of faith.

Meditation for the Day

Guard well your thoughts, reader, for what you really are
in your secret thoughts today you will become in actual deed.

THERE is nothing hidden that shall not be revealed, and every thought that is harboured in the mind must, by virtue of the impelling force which is inherent in the universe, at last blossom into act good or bad, according to its nature. The divine Teacher and the sensualist are both the product of their own thoughts, and have become what they are as the result of the seeds of thought which they have implanted, or allowed to fall, into the garden of the heart, and have afterwards watered, tended, and cultivated. Let no man think he can overcome sin and temptation by wrestling with opportunity; he can only overcome them by purifying his thoughts.

A man can only attract that to him which is in harmony with his nature.

Thought for the Evening

Have a thorough understanding of your work, and let it be your own; and as you proceed, ever following the inward guide, the infallible voice, you will pass on from victory to victory, and will rise step by step to higher resting-places, and your ever broadening outlook will gradually reveal to you the essential beauty and purpose of life. Self-purified, health will be yours; self-governed, power will be yours, and all that you do will prosper.

And I may stand where health, success, and power await my coming, if, each fleeting hour, I cling to love and patience; and abide with stainlessness; and never step aside from high integrity; so shall I see at last the land of immortality.

October Fourth

Thought for the Morning

When the tongue is well controlled and wisely subdued; when selfish impulses and unworthy thoughts no longer rush to the tongue demanding utterance; when the speech has become harmless, pure, gracious, gentle, and purposeful, and no word is uttered but in sincerity and truth—then are the five steps in virtuous speech accomplished, then is the second great lesson in Truth learned and mastered. Make pure thy heart, and thou wilt make thy life rich, sweet and beautiful.

Meditation for the Day

As a being of thought, your dominant mental attitude will determine your condition in life.

YOU are the thinker of your thoughts, and as such you are the maker of yourself and condition. Thought is causal and creative, and appears in your character and life in the form of *results*. There are no accidents in your life. Both its harmonies and antagonisms are the responsive echoes of your thoughts. A man thinks, and his life appears.

If your dominant mental attitude is peaceable and lovable, bliss and blessedness will follow you; if it be resistant and hateful, trouble and distress will cloud your pathway. Out of ill-will will come grief and disaster; out of good-will, healing and reparation.

The boundary lines of your thoughts are self-erected fences.

Thought for the Evening

Having clothed himself with humility, the first questions a man asks himself are:—

"How am I acting towards others?"
"What am I doing to others?"
"How am I thinking of others?"
"Are my thoughts of, and acts towards others prompted by unselfish love?"

As a man, in the silence of his soul, asks himself these searching questions, he will unerringly see where he has hitherto failed.

October Fifth

Thought for the Morning

To dwell in love always and towards all is to live the true life, is to have Life itself. Knowing this, the good man gives up himself unreservedly to the Spirit of Love, and dwells in Love towards all, contending with none, condemning none, but loving all.

The Christ Spirit of Love puts an end, not only to all sin, but to all division and contention.

Meditation for the Day

Pain, grief, sorrow, and misery are the fruits of which passion is the flower.

WHERE the passion-bound soul sees only injustice, the good man, he who has conquered passion, sees cause and effect, sees the Supreme Justice. It is impossible for such a man to regard himself as treated unjustly, because he has ceased to see injustice. He knows that no one can injure or cheat him, having ceased to injure or cheat himself. However passionately or ignorantly men may act towards him, it cannot possibly cause him any pain, for he knows that whatever comes to him (it may be abuse and persecution) can only come as the effect of what he himself has formerly sent out. He therefore regards all things as good, rejoices in all things, loves his enemies, blesses them that curse him, regarding them as the blind but beneficent instruments by which he is enabled to pay his moral debts to the Great Law.

The Supreme Justice and the Supreme Love are one.

Thought for the Evening

When sin and self are abandoned, the heart is restored to its imperishable Joy. Joy comes and fills the self-emptied heart; it abides with the peaceful; its reign is with the pure. Joy flees from the selfish, it deserts the quarrelsome; it is hidden from the impure. Joy cannot remain with the selfish; it is wedded to Love.

October Sixth

Thought for the Morning

In the pure heart there is no room left where personal judgments and hatreds can find lodgement, for it is filled to overflowing with tenderness and love; it sees no evil, and only as men succeed in seeing no evil in others will they become free from sin, and sorrow, and suffering. If men only understood that the heart that sins must sorrow, that the hateful mind tomorrow reaps its barren harvest, weeping, starving, resting not, nor sleeping; tenderness would fill their being, they would see with pity's seeing, if they only understood.

Meditation for the Day

The history of a nation is the building of its deeds.

A BODY is built of cells, and a house of bricks, so a man's mind is built of thoughts. The various characters of men are none other than compounds of thoughts of varying combinations. Herein we see the deep truth of the saying, "As a man thinketh in his heart, so is he." Individual characteristics are *fixed processes of thought*; that is, they are fixed in the sense that they have become an integral part of the character, that they can be only altered or removed by a protracted effort of the will, and by much self-discipline. Character is built in the same way as a tree or a house is built—namely, by the ceaseless addition of new material, and that material is *thought*.

By the aid of millions of bricks a city is built;
by the aid of millions of thoughts a character, a mind, is built.

Thought for the Evening

To stand face to face with truth; to arrive, after innumerable wanderings and pains, at wisdom and bliss; not to be finally defeated and cast out, but to ultimately triumph over every inward foe—such is man's divine destiny, such his glorious goal; and this, every saint, sage, and saviour has declared. A man only begins to be a man when he ceases to whine and revile, and commences to search for the hidden justice which regulates his life. And as he adapts his mind to that regulating factor, he ceases to accuse others as the cause of his condition, and builds himself up in strong and noble thoughts; ceases to kick against circumstances, but begins to use them as aids to his more rapid progress, and as a means of discovering the hidden power and possibilities within himself.

October Seventh

Thought for the Morning

The will to evil and the will to good are both within thee, which wilt thou employ? Thou knowest what is right and what is wrong, which wilt though love and foster, which destroy?

Thou art the chooser of thy thoughts and deeds; thou art the maker of thine inward state; the power is thine to be what thou wilt be; thou buildest Truth and Love, or lies and hate.

Meditation for the Day

Every man is a mind-builder.

PURE thoughts, wisely chosen and well placed, are so many durable bricks which will never crumble away, and from which a finished and beautiful building, and one which affords comfort and shelter for its possessor, can be rapidly erected. Bracing thoughts of strength, of confidence, of duty; inspiring thoughts of a large, free, unfettered, and unselfish life, are useful bricks with which a substantial mind-temple can be raised; and the building of such a temple necessitates that old and useless habits of thought be broken down and destroyed.

"Build thee more stately mansions, O my soul, As the swift seasons roll."

Each man is the builder of himself.

Thought for the Evening

The teaching of Jesus brings men back to the simple truth that righteousness, or *right-doing*, is entirely a matter of individual conduct, and not a mystical something apart from a man's thoughts and deeds.

Calmness and patience can become habitual by first grasping, through effort, a calm and patient thought, and then continuously thinking it, and living in it, until "use becomes second nature," and anger and impatience pass away for ever.

October Eighth

Thought for the Morning

Man is made or unmade by himself; in the armoury of thought he forges the weapons by which he destroys himself; he also fashions the tools with which he builds for himself heavenly mansions of joy and strength and peace. By the right choice and true application of thought man ascends to the Divine Perfection; by the abuse and wrong application of thought he descends below the level of the beast. Between these two extremes are all the grades of character and man is their maker and master.

As a being of Power, Intelligence, and Love, and the lord of his own thoughts, man holds the key to every situation.

Meditation for the Day

Build like a true workman.

A MAN is to build up a successful strong, and exemplary life a life that will stoutly resist the fiercest storms of I adversity and temptation it must be framed on a few, simple, undeviating moral principles. Four of these principles are: *Justice*, *Rectitude*, *Sincerity*, and *Kindness*. These four ethical truths are to the making of a life what the four lines of a square are to the building of a house. If a man ignores them and thinks to obtain success and happiness by injustice, trickery, and selfishness, he is in the position of a builder who imagines he can build a strong and durable habitation while ignoring the relative arrangement of mathematical lines, and he will, in the end, obtain only disappointment and failure.

Working in harmony with the fundamental laws of the universe.

Thought for the Evening

Whatsoever you harbour in the inmost chambers of your heart will, sooner or later, by the inevitable law of reaction, shape itself in your outward life.

Every soul attracts its own, and nothing can possibly come to it that does not belong to it. To realize this is to recognize the universality of Divine Law.

If thou would'st right the world, and banish all its evils and its woes, make its wild places bloom, and its drear deserts blossom as the rose—then right thyself.

October Ninth

Thought for the Morning

Whatever conditions are rendering your life burdensome, you may pass out of and beyond them by developing and utilizing within you the transforming power of self-purification and self-conquest.

Before the divine radiance of a pure heart all darkness vanishes and all clouds melt away, and he who has conquered self has conquered the universe.

He who sets his foot firmly upon the path of self-conquest, who walks, aided by the staff of faith, the highway of self-sacrifice, will assuredly achieve the highest prosperity, and will reap abounding and enduring joy and bliss.

Meditation for the Day

It is a common error to suppose that little things can be passed by, and that the greater things are more important.

HE who adopts the four ethical principles as the law and base of his life, who raises the edifice of character upon them, who in his thoughts and words and actions does not wander from them, whose every duty and every passing transaction is performed in strict accordance with their exactions, such a man, laying down the hidden foundations of integrity of heart securely and strongly, cannot fail to raise up a structure which shall bring him honour; and he is building a temple in which he can repose in peace and blessedness even the strong and beautiful Temple of his life.

He who would have a life secure and blessed must carry the practice of the moral principles into every detail of it.

Thought for the Evening

It is the silent and conquering thought forces which bring all things into manifestation. The universe grew out of thought.

To adjust all your thoughts to a perfect and unswerving faith in the omnipotence and supremacy of Good is to co-operate with that Good, and to realize within yourself the solution and destruction of all evil.

To mentally deny evil is not sufficient; it must, by daily practice, be risen above and understood. To affirm the Good mentally is inadequate; it must, by unswerving endeavour, be entered into and comprehended.

October Tenth

Thought for the Morning

Every thought you think is a force sent out. Whatever your position in life may be, before you can hope to enter into any measure of success, usefulness, and power, you must learn how to focus your thought forces by cultivating calmness and repose.

There is no difficulty, however great, but will yield before a calm and purposeful concentration of thought, and no legitimate object but may be speedily actualized by the intelligent use and direction of one's soul forces.

Think good thoughts, and they will quickly become actualized in your outward life in the form of good conditions.

Meditation for the Day

When aspiration is united to concentration, the result is meditation.

WHEN a man intensely desires to reach and realize a higher, purer, and more radiant life than the merely worldly and pleasure-loving life, he engages in *aspiration*; and when he earnestly concentrates his thoughts upon the finding of that life, he practises meditation.

Without intense aspiration there can be no meditation. Lethargy and indifference are fatal to its practice. The more intense the nature of the man, the more readily will he find meditation and the more successfully will he practise it. A fiery nature will most rapidly scale the heights of Truth in meditation, when its aspirations have become sufficiently awakened.

Meditation is necessary to spiritual success.

Thought for the Evening

That which you would be and hope to be, you may be now. Non-accomplishment resides in your perpetual postponement, and, having the power to postpone, you also have the power to accomplish—to perpetually accomplish: realize this truth, and you shall be today, and every day, the ideal being of whom you dreamed.

Say to yourself, "I will live in my Ideal now; I will manifest my ideal now; I will be my Ideal now; and all that tempts me away from my Ideal I will not listen to; I will listen only to the voice of my Ideal."

October Eleventh

Thought for the Morning

Be as a flower; content to be, to grow in sweetness day by day. If thou would'st perfect thyself in knowledge, perfect thyself in Love. If thou would'st reach the Highest, ceaselessly cultivate a loving and compassionate heart.

To him who chooses Goodness, sacrificing all, is given that which is more than, and includes, all.

Meditation for the Day

*When a man aspires to know and realize the Truth,
he gives attention to conduct, to self-purification.*

BY concentration a man can scale the highest heights of genius, but he cannot scale the heavenly heights of Truth; to accomplish this he must meditate. By concentration a man may acquire the wonderful comprehension and vast power of a Caesar; by meditation he may reach the divine wisdom and perfect peace of a Buddha. The perfection of concentration is *power*; the perfection of meditation is *wisdom*. By concentration men acquire skill in the doing of the things of life in science, art, trade, etc. but by meditation they acquire skill in *life* itself; in right living, enlightenment, wisdom, etc. Saints, sages, saviours—wise men and divine teachers—are the finished products of holy meditation.

Love Truth so fully and intensely as to become wholly absorbed in it.

Thought for the Evening

The Great Law never cheats any man of his just due.

Human life, when rightly lived, is simple with a beautiful simplicity.

He who comprehends the utter simplicity of life, who obeys its laws, and does not step aside into the dark paths and complex mazes of selfish desire, stands where no harm can reach him.

Then there is fullness of joy, abounding plenty, and rich and complete blessedness.

October Twelfth

Thought for the Morning

Every man reaps the results of his own thoughts and deeds, and suffers for his own wrong.

He who begins right, and continues right, does not need to desire, and search for felicitous results; they are already at hand; they follow as consequences; they are the certainties, the realities, of life.

Sweet is the rest and deep is the bliss of him who has freed his heart from its lusts and hatreds and dark desires.

Meditation for the Day

The object of meditation is divine enlightenment.

WHILE, at first, the time spent in actual meditation is short perhaps only half an hour in the early morning the knowledge gained in that half-hour of vivid aspiration and concentrated thought is embodied in practice during the whole day. In meditation, therefore, the entire life of a man is involved; and as he advances in its practice he becomes more and more fitted to perform the duties of life in the circumstances in which he may be placed, for he becomes stronger, holier, calmer, and wiser.

The principle of meditation is twofold, namely:

1. Purification of the heart by repetitive thought on pure things.
2. Attainment of divine knowledge by embodying such purity in practical life.

Man is a thought-being, and his life and character are determined by the thoughts in which he habitually dwells.

Thought for the Evening

You are the creator of your own shadows; you desire, and then you grieve; renounce, and then you shall rejoice.

Of all the beautiful truths pertaining to the soul. . . none is more gladdening or fruitful of divine promise and confidence than this—that man is the master of thought, the moulder of character, and the maker and shaper of character, environment, and destiny.

October Thirteenth

Thought for the Morning

As darkness is a passing shadow, and light is a substance that remains, so sorrow is fleeting, but joy abides for ever. No true thing can pass away and become lost; no false thing can remain and be preserved. Sorrow is false, and it cannot live; joy is true, and it cannot die. Joy may become hidden for a time, but it can always be recovered; sorrow may remain for a period, but it can be transcended and dispersed.

Do not think your sorrow will remain; it will pass away like a cloud. Do not believe that the torments of sin are ever your portion; they will vanish like a hideous nightmare. Awake! Arise! Be holy and joyful.

Meditation for the Day

By practice, association, and habit, thoughts tend to repeat themselves.

BY daily dwelling upon pure thoughts, the man of meditation forms the habit of pure and enlightened thinking which leads to pure and enlightened actions and well-performed duties. By the ceaseless repetition of pure thoughts, he at last becomes one with those thoughts, and is a purified being, manifesting his attainment in pure actions, in a serene and wise life.

The majority of men live in a series of conflicting desires, passions, emotions, and speculations, and there are restlessness, uncertainty, and sorrow; but when a man begins to train his mind in meditation, he gradually gains control over this inward conflict by bringing his thoughts to a focus upon a central principle.

It is easy to mistake reverie for meditation.

Thought for the Evening

Tribulation lasts only so long as there remains some chaff of self which needs to be removed. The *tribulum*, or threshing machine, ceases to work when all the grain is separated from the chaff; and when the last impurities are blown away from the soul, tribulation has completed its work, and there is no more need for it; then abiding joy is realized.

The sole and supreme use of suffering is to purify, to burn out all that is useless and impure. Suffering ceases for him who is pure. There could be no object in burning gold after the dross had been removed.

October Fourteenth

Thought for the Morning

In speaking of self-control, one is easily misunderstood. It should not be associated with a destructive repression, but with a constructive expression.

A man is happy, wise and great in the measure that he controls himself; he is wretched, foolish, and mean in the measure that he allows his animal nature to dominate his thoughts and actions.

He who controls himself, controls his life, his circumstances, his destiny; and wherever he goes he carries his happiness with him as an abiding possession.

Renunciation precedes regeneration. The permanent happiness which men seek in dissipation, excitement, and abandonment to unworthy pleasures, is found only in the life which reverses all this—the life of self-control.

Meditation for the Day

Selfishness, the root of the tree of evil and of all suffering, derives its Nourishment from the dark soil of ignorance.

THE rich and the poor alike suffer for *their own selfishness*; and none escape. The rich have their particular sufferings as well as the poor. Moreover, the rich are continually losing their riches; the poor are continually acquiring them. The poor man of today is the rich man of tomorrow, and *vice versa*. Fear, also, follows men like a great shadow, for the man who obtains and holds by selfish force will always be haunted by a feeling of insecurity, and will continually fear its loss; whilst the poor man, who is selfishly seeking or coveting material riches, will be harassed by the fear of destitution. And one and all who live in this under-world of strife are overshadowed by one great fear the fear of death.

Each individual suffers by virtue of his own selfishness.

Thought for the Evening

Law, not confusion, is the dominating principle in the universe; justice, not injustice is the soul and substance of life; and righteousness, not corruption, is the moulding and moving force in the spiritual government of the world. This being so, man has but the right himself to find that the universe is right.

When I am pure, I shall have solved the mystery of life; I shall be sure, when I am free from hatred, lust and strife, I am in Truth, and Truth abides in me; I shall be safe, and sane, and wholly free, when I am pure.

October Fifteenth

Thought for the Morning

If men only understood that their hatred and resentment slays their peace and sweet contentment, hurts themselves, helps not another, does not cheer one lonely brother, they would seek the better doing of good deeds which leaves no ruing:—

If they only understood.

If men only understood how Love conquers; how prevailing is its might, grim hate assailing; how compassion endeth sorrow, maketh wise, and doth not borrow pain of passion, they would ever live in Love, in hatred never:—

If they only understood.

Meditation for the Day

The spirit is strengthened and renewed by meditation upon spiritual things.

MAN must pass through three *Gateways of Surrender*. The first is the *Surrender of Desire*; the second is the *Surrender of Opinion*; the third is the *Surrender of Self*. Entering into meditation, he will commence to examine his desires, tracing them out in his mind, and following up their effects in his life and upon his character; and he will quickly perceive that, without the renunciation of desire, a man remains a slave both to himself and to his surroundings and circumstances. Having discovered this, the first Gate, that of the *Surrender of Desire*, is entered. Passing through this Gate, he adopts a process of self-discipline which is the first step in the purification of the soul.

The lamp of faith must be continually fed and assiduously trimmed.

Thought for the Evening

The grace and beauty that were in Jesus can be of no value to you—cannot be understood by you—unless they are also *in you*, and they can never be in you, until you practice them, for, apart from *doing*, the qualities which constitute goodness do not, as far as you are concerned, exist.

To adore Jesus for his good qualities is a long step towards Truth, but to practice those qualities is Truth itself; and he who fully adores the perfection of another will not rest content in his own imperfection, but will fashion his soul after the likeness of that other.

Therefore thou who adorest Jesus for his divine qualities, practice those qualities thyself, and thou too shalt be divine.

October Sixteenth

Thought for the Morning

Let a man realize that life in its totality proceeds from the mind, and lo, the way of blessedness is opened up to him! For he will then discover that he possesses the power to rule his mind and to fashion it in accordance with his Ideal.

So will he elect to strongly and steadfastly walk those pathways of thought and action which are altogether excellent; to him life will become beautiful and sacred; and, sooner or later, he will put to flight all evil, confusion, and suffering; for it is impossible for a man to fall short of liberation, enlightenment, and peace, who guards with unwearying diligence the gateway of his heart.

Meditation for the Day

The loss of today will add to the gain of tomorrow
for him whose mind is set on the conquest of self.

LET a man, therefore, press on courageously, heeding neither the revilings of his friends without, nor the clamouring of his enemies within; aspiring, searching, striving; looking ever towards his Ideal with eyes of holy love; day by day ridding his mind of selfish motive, his heart of impure desire; stumbling sometimes, sometimes falling, but ever travelling onward and rising higher; and recording each night in the silence of his own heart the journey of the day, let him not despair if but each day, in spite of all its failures and falls, records some holy battle fought, though lost, some silent victory attempted, though unachieved.

Learn to distinguish between the real and the unreal,
the shadow and the substance.

Thought for the Evening

By constantly overcoming self, a man gains a knowledge of the subtle intricacies of his mind; and it is this divine knowledge which enables him to become established in calmness.

Without self-knowledge there can be no abiding peace of mind, and those who are carried away by tempestuous passions, cannot approach the holy place where calmness reigns.

The weak man is like one who, having mounted a fiery steed, allows it to run away with him, and carry him withersoever it wills; the strong man is like one who, having mounted the steed, governs it with a masterly hand and makes it go in whatever direction and at whatever speed he commands.

October Seventeenth

Thought for the Morning

There is no strife, no selfishness, in the Kingdom; there is perfect harmony, equipoise, and rest.

Those who live in the Kingdom of Love, have all their needs supplied by the Law of Love.

As self is the root cause of all strife and suffering, so Love is the root cause of all peace and bliss. Those who are at rest in the Kingdom do not look for happiness in any outward possessions. They are freed from all anxiety and trouble and, resting in Love, they are the embodiment of happiness.

Meditation for the Day

Acquire the priceless possession of spiritual discernment.

CLOTHING his soul with the colourless Garment of Humility, a man bends all his energies to the uprooting of those opinions which he has hitherto loved and cherished. He now learns to distinguish between Truth, which is one and unchangeable, and his own and others' *opinions* about Truth, which are many and changeable. He sees that his opinions about Goodness, Purity, Compassion, and Love, are very distinct from those qualities themselves, and that he must stand upon those divine Principles, and not on his own opinions. Hitherto he has regarded his own opinions as of great value, but now he ceases so to elevate his own opinions, and to defend them against those of others, and comes to regard them as utterly worthless.

Stand upon the divine Principles
of Purity, Wisdom, Compassion, and Love.

Thought for the Evening

Let it not be supposed that the children of the Kingdom live in ease and indolence (these two sins are the first that have to be eradicated when the search for the Kingdom is entered upon); they live in a peaceful activity; in fact, they only truly live, for the life of self, with its train of worries, griefs, and fears, is not *real life*.

The children of the Kingdom are *known by their life*, they manifest the fruits of the Spirit—"Love, joy, peace, long-suffering, kindness, goodness, faithfulness, meekness, temperance, and self-control"—under all circumstances and vicissitudes.

October Eighteenth

Thought for the Morning

The gospel of Jesus is a gospel of *living and doing*. If it were not this it would not voice the Eternal Truth. Its Temple is *Purified Conduct*, the entrance-door to which is *Self-Surrender*. It invites men to shake off sin, and promises, as a result, joy and blessedness and perfect peace.

The Kingdom of Heaven is perfect trust, perfect knowledge, perfect peace. . . no sin can enter therein, no self-born thought or deed can pass its golden gates; no impure desire can defile its radiant robes. . . all may enter it who will, but all must pay the price—*the unconditional abandonment of self.*

Meditation for the Day

Find the Divine Center within.

HE who resolves that he will not rest satisfied with appearances, shadows, illusions shall, by the piercing light of that resolve, disperse every fleeting phantasy, and shall enter into the substance and reality of life. He shall learn how to live, and he shall live. He shall be the slave of no passion, the servant of no opinion, the votary of no fond error. Finding the Divine Centre within his own heart, he shall be pure and calm and strong and wise, and will ceaselessly radiate the Heavenly Life in which he lives—which is himself.

Not to know that within you that is changeless,
and defiant of time and death,
is not to know anything, but is to play vainly
with unsubstantial reflections in the Mirror of Time.

Thought for the Evening

I say this—and know it to be truth—*that circumstances can only affect you in so far as you allow them to do so.* You are swayed by circumstances because you have not a right understanding of the nature, use, and power of thought. You believe (and upon this little word *belief* hang all our joys and sorrows) that outward things have the power to make or mar your life; by so doing you submit to those outward things, confess that you are their slave, and they your unconditional master. By so doing you invest them with a power which they do not of themselves possess, and you succumb, in reality not to the circumstances, but to the gloom or gladness, the fear or hope, the strength of weakness, which your thought-sphere has thrown around them.

October Nineteenth

Thought for the Morning

If you are one of those who are praying for, and looking forward to a happier world beyond the grave, here is a message of gladness for you—you may enter into and realize that happy world now; it fills the whole universe, and it is within you, waiting for you to find, acknowledge, and possess.

Said one who understood the inner laws of Being—"When men shall say, lo here, or lo there, go not after them. The Kingdom of God is within you."

Meditation for the Day

*Having betaken himself to the Divine Refuge within,
and remaining there, a man is free from sin.
No doubt shall shake his trust, no uncertainty shall rob him of repose.*

MEN love their desires, for gratification seems sweet to them, but its end is pain and vacuity; they love the argumentations of the intellect, for egotism seems most desirable to them, but the fruits thereof are humiliation and sorrow. When the soul has reached the end of gratification and reaped the bitter fruits of egotism, it is ready to receive the Divine Wisdom and to enter into the Divine Life. Only the crucified can be transfigured; only by the death of self can the Lord of the heart rise again into the Immortal Life, and stand radiant upon the Olivet of Wisdom.

Where self is not, there is the Garden of the Heavenly Life.

Thought for the Evening

Heaven and hell are inward states. Sink into self and all its gratifications, and you sink into hell; rise above self into that state of consciousness which is the utter denial and forgetfulness of self, and you enter heaven.

So long as you persist in selfishly seeking for your own personal happiness, so long will happiness elude you, and you will be sowing the seeds of wretchedness. In so far as you succeed in losing yourself in the service of others, in that measure will happiness come to you, and you will reap a harvest of bliss.

October Twentieth

Thought for the Morning

Sympathy given can never be waste.

One aspect of sympathy is that of pity—pity for the distressed or pain stricken, with a desire to alleviate or help them in their sufferings. The world needs more of this divine quality.

"For pity makes the world soft to the weak, and noble for the strong."

Another form of sympathy is that of rejoicing with others who are more successful than ourselves, and though their success were our own.

Meditation for the Day

Life is more than motion, it is Music; more than rest, it is Peace;
more than work, it is Duty; more than labor, it is Love.

LET the impure turn to Purity, and they shall be pure; let the weak resort to Strength, and they shall be strong; let the ignorant fly to Knowledge, and they shall be wise. All things are man's, and he chooses that which he will have. Today he chooses in ignorance, tomorrow he shall choose in wisdom. He shall "work out his own salvation", whether he believe it or not, for he cannot escape himself, nor transfer to another the eternal responsibility of his own soul. By no theological subterfuge shall he trick the Law of his being, which shall shatter all his selfish makeshifts and excuses for right thinking and right doing. Nor shall God do for him that which it is destined his soul shall accomplish for itself.

Life is more than enjoyment, it is Blessedness.

Thought for the Evening

Sweet are companionships, pleasures, and material comforts, but they change and fade away. Sweeter still are Purity, Wisdom, and the knowledge of Truth, and these never change nor fade away.

He who attained to the possession of spiritual things can never be deprived of his source of happiness; he will never have to part company with it, and wherever he goes in the whole universe, he will carry his possessions with him. His spiritual end will be the fullness of joy.

October Twenty-first

Thought for the Morning

Let your heart grow and expand with ever broadening love, until, freed from all hatred, and passion, and condemnation, it embraces the whole universe with thoughtful tenderness.

As the flower opens its petals to receive the morning light, so open your soul more and more to the glorious light of Truth.

Soar upward on the wings of aspiration; be fearless and believe in the loftiest possibilities.

Meditation for the Day

He who would find Blessedness, let him find himself.

MEN fly from creed to creed, and find unrest; they travel in many lands, and discover—disappointment; they build themselves beautiful mansions, and plant pleasant gardens, and reap—ennui and discomfort. Not until a man falls back upon the Truth within himself does he find rest and satisfaction; not until he builds the inward Mansion of Faultless Conduct does he find the endless and incorruptible Joy, and, having obtained that, he will infuse it into all his doings and possessions.

When a man can no longer carry the weight of his many sins, let him fly to the Christ, whose throne is the centre of his own heart, and he shall become light-hearted, entering the glad company of the Immortals.

The spiritual Heart of man is the Heart of the universe.

Thought for the Evening

Mind clothes itself in garments of its own making. Mind is the arbiter of life; it is the creator and shaper of conditions, and the recipient of its own results. It contains within itself both the power to create illusion and to perceive reality.

Mind is the infallible weaver of destiny; thought is the thread, good and evil deeds are the warp and woof, and the web, woven upon the loom of life, is character. Make pure thy heart, and thou wilt make thy life, rich, sweet, and beautiful, unmarred by strife.

October Twenty-second

Thought for the Morning

Cherish your visions; cherish your ideals; cherish the music that stirs in your heart, the beauty that forms in your mind, the loveliness that drapes your purest thoughts, for out of them will grow all delightful conditions, all heavenly environment; of these, if you will remain true to them, your world will at last be built.

Guard well thy mind, and, noble, strong, and free, nothing shall harm, disturb or conquer thee; for all thy foes are in thy heart and mind, there also thy salvation thou shalt find.

Meditation for the Day

All power, all possibility, all action is now.

WHILST a man is dwelling upon the past or future he is missing the present; he is forgetting to live now. All things are possible now, and *only* now. Without wisdom to guide him, and mistaking the unreal for the real, a man says, "If I had done so-and-so last week, last month, or last year, it would have been better with me today"; or, "I know what is best to be done, and I will do it tomorrow." The selfish cannot comprehend the vast importance and value of the present, and fail to see it as the substantial reality of which past and future are the empty reflections. It may truly be said that past and future do not exist except as negative shadows, and to live in them—that is, in the regretful and selfish contemplation of them—is to miss the reality in life.

To put away regret, to anchor anticipation,
to do and work now, this is wisdom.

Thought for the Evening

Dream lofty dreams, and as you dream so shall you become. Your vision is the promise of what you shall one day be; your Ideal is the prophecy of what you shall at last unveil.

The greatest achievement was at first and for a time a dream. The oak sleeps in the acorn; the bird waits in the egg; and in the highest vision of the soul a waking angel stirs.

Your circumstances may be uncongenial, but they shall not long remain so when you perceive an Ideal and strive to reach it.

October Twenty-third

Thought for the Morning

He who has conquered doubt and fear has conquered failure. His every thought is allied with power, and all difficulties are bravely met and wisely overcome. His purposes are seasonably planted, and they bloom and bring forth fruit which does not fall prematurely to the ground.

Thought allied fearlessly to purpose becomes creative force: he who knows this is ready to become something higher and stronger than a mere bundle of wavering thoughts and fluctuating sensations; he who does this has become the conscious and intelligent wielder of his mental powers.

Meditation for the Day

Virtue consists in fighting sin day after day.

CEASE to tread every byway of dependence, every winding sideway that tempts thy soul into the shadowland of the past and the future, and manifest thy native and divine strength now. Come out into "the open road."

That which you would be, and hope to be, you may be now. Non-accomplishment resides in your perpetual postponement, and, having the power to postpone, you also have the power to accomplish—to perpetually accomplish; realize this truth, and you shall be today, and every day, the ideal man of whom you dreamed.

Act now, and lo! all things are done; live now, and behold! thou art in the midst of Plenty; *be now*, *and know* that thou art perfect.

*Holiness consists in leaving sin,
unnoticed and ignored, to die by the wayside.*

Thought for the Evening

Man's true place in the Cosmos is that of a king, not a slave, a commander under the Law of Good, and not a helpless tool in the region of evil.

I write for men, not for babes; for those who are eager to learn, and earnest to achieve; for those who will put away (for the world's good) a petty personal indulgence, a selfish desire, a mean thought, and live on as though it were not, sans craving and regret.

Man is a master. If he were not, he could not act contrary to law.

Evil and weakness are self destructive. The universe is girt with goodness and strength, and it protects the good and the strong.

The angry man is the weak man.

October Twenty-fourth

Thought for the Morning

Not by learning will a man triumph over evil; not by much study will he overcome sin and sorrow. Only by conquering himself will he conquer evil; only by practicing righteousness will he put an end to sorrow.

Not for the clever, nor the learned, nor the self-confident is the Life Triumphant, but for the pure, the virtuous and wise. The former achieve their particular success in life, but the latter alone achieve the great success so invincible and complete that even in apparent defeat it shines with added victory.

Meditation for the Day

Say not unto thy soul, "Thou shalt be purer tomorrow;
but rather say, "Thou shalt be pure now."

TOMORROW is too late for anything, and he who sees help and salvation; in tomorrow shall continually fail and fall today.

Thou didst fall yesterday! Didst sin grievously! Having realized this, leave it instantly and forever, and watch that thou sinnest not now. The while thou art bewailing the past every gate of thy soul remains unguarded against the entrance of sin now.

The foolish man, loving the boggy side of procrastination rather than the firm highway of Present Effort, says, "I will rise early tomorrow; I will get out of debt tomorrow; I will carry out my intentions tomorrow." But the wise man, realizing the momentous import of the Eternal Now, rises early today; keeps out of debt today; carries out his intentions today; and so never departs from strength and peace and ripe accomplishment.

Thou shalt not rise by grieving over the irremediable past,
but by remedying the present.

Thought for the Evening

The true silence is not merely a silent tongue; it is a silent mind. To merely *hold one's tongue*, and yet to carry about a disturbed and rankling mind, is no remedy for weakness, and no source of power.

Silentness, to be powerful, must envelop the whole mind, must permeate every chamber of the heart; it must be the silence of peace.

To this broad, deep, abiding silentness a man attains only in the measure that he conquers himself.

October Twenty-fifth

Thought for the Morning

By curbing his tongue, a man gains possession of his mind.

The fool babbles, gossips, argues, and bandies words. He glories in the fact that he has had the last word, and has silenced his opponent. He exults in his own folly, is ever on the defensive, and wastes his energies in unprofitable channels. He is like a gardener who continues to dig and plant in unproductive soil.

The wise man avoids idle words, gossips, vain argument, and self-defence. He is content to appear defeated; rejoices when he is defeated; knowing that, having found and removed another error in himself, he has thereby become wiser.

Blessed is he who does not strive for the last word.

Meditation for the Day

*Looking back to happy beginnings, and forward to mournful endings,
a man's eyes are blinded so that he beholds not his own immortality.*

It is wisdom to leave that which has not arrived, and to attend to that which is; and to attend to it with such a consecration of soul and concentration of effort as shall leave no loophole for regret to creep in.

A man's spiritual comprehension being clouded by the illusions of self, he says, "I was born on such a day, so many years ago, and shall die at my allotted time." But he was not born, neither will he die, for how can that which is immortal, which eternally is, be subject to birth and death? Let a man throw off his illusions, and then he will see that the birth and death of the *body* are the mere incidents of a journey, and not its beginning and end.

The universe, with all that it contains, is now.

Thought for the Evening

Desire is the *craving for possession*; aspiration is the *hunger of the heart for peace*.

The craving for things leads ever farther and farther from peace, and not only ends in deprivation, but is in itself a state of perpetual want. Until it comes to an end, rest and satisfaction are impossible.

The hunger for things can never be satisfied, but the hunger for peace can, and the satisfaction of peace is found—is fully possessed, when all selfish desire is abandoned. Then there is fullness of joy, abounding plenty, and rich and complete blessedness.

October Twenty-sixth

Thought for the Morning

A man will reach the Kingdom by purifying himself, and he can only do this by pursuing a process of self-examination and self-analysis.

The selfishness must be discovered and understood before it can be removed. It is powerless to remove itself, neither will it pass away of itself. Darkness ceases only when light is introduced; so ignorance can only be dispersed by knowledge, selfishness by love.

A man must first of all be willing to lose himself (his self-seeking) before he can find himself (his Divine Self). He must realize that selfishness is not worth clinging to, that it is a master altogether unworthy of his service, and that divine goodness alone is worthy to be enthroned in his heart, as the supreme master of his life.

Meditation for the Day

Let a man put away egotism, and he will see the universe
in all the beauty of its pristine simplicity.

LET life cease to be lived as a fragmentary thing, and let it be lived as a perfect Whole; the simplicity of the Perfect will then be revealed. How shall the fragment comprehend the Whole? Yet how simple that the Whole should comprehend the fragment. How shall sin perceive Holiness? Yet how plain that Holiness should understand sin. He who would become the Greater let him abandon the lesser. In no form is the circle contained, but in the circle all forms are contained. In no colour is the radiant light imprisoned, but in the radiant light all colours are embodied. Let a man destroy all the forms of self, and he shall apprehend the Circle of Perfection.

When a man succeeds in entirely forgetting (annihilating)
his personal self, he becomes a mirror in which
the universal Reality is faultlessly reflected.

Thought for the Evening

Be still, my soul, and know that peace is thine. Be steadfast, heart, and know that strength divine Belongs to thee; cease from thy turmoil, mind, and thou the Everlasting Rest shalt find.

If a man would have peace, let him exercise the spirit of peace; if he would find Love, let him dwell in the spirit of Love; if he would escape suffering, let him cease to inflict it; if he would do noble things for humanity, let him cease to do ignoble things for himself. If he will but quarry the mine of his own soul, he shall find there all the materials for building whatsoever he will, and he shall find there also the Central Rock on which to build in safety.

October Twenty-seventh

Thought for the Morning

Men go after much company, and seek out new excitements, but they are not acquainted with peace; in divers paths of pleasure they search for happiness, but they do not come to rest; through divers ways of laughter and feverish delirium they wander after gladness and life, but their tears are many and grievous, and they do not escape death.

Drifting upon the ocean of life in search of selfish indulgences, men are caught in its storms, and only after many tempests and much privation do they fly to the Rock of Refuge which rests in the deep silence of their own being.

Meditation for the Day

*In the perfect chord of music the single note, though forgotten,
is indispensably contained, and the drop of water
becomes of supreme usefulness by losing itself in the ocean.*

THINK thyself compassionately in the heart of humanity, and thou shalt reproduce the harmonies of Heaven; lose thyself in unlimited love toward all, and thou shalt work enduring works and shalt become one with the eternal Ocean of Bliss.

Man evolves outward to the periphery of complexity, and then involves backward to the Central Simplicity. When a man discovers that it is mathematically impossible for him to know the universe before knowing himself, he then starts upon the Way which leads to Original Simplicity. He begins to unfold from within, and as he unfolds himself, he enfolds the universe.

Cease to speculate about God, and find the all-embracing Good within thee.

Thought for the Evening

Meditation centred upon divine realities is the very essence and soul of prayer. It is the silent reaching upward of the soul toward the Eternal.

Meditation is the intense dwelling, in thought, upon an idea or theme with the object of thoroughly comprehending it; and whatsoever you constantly meditate upon, you will not only come to understand, but will grow more and more into its likeness, for it will become incorporated with your very being, will become, in fact, your very self.

If, therefore, you constantly dwell upon that which is selfish and debasing, you will ultimately become selfish and debased; if you ceaselessly think upon that which is pure and unselfish, you will surely become pure and unselfish.

October Twenty-eighth

Thought for the Morning

There is no difficulty, however great, but will yield before a calm and powerful concentration of thought and no legitimate object but may be speedily actualized by the intelligent use and direction of one's soul forces.

Whatever your task may be, concentrate your whole mind upon it; throw into it all the energy of which you are capable. The faultless completion of small tasks, leads inevitably to larger tasks.

See to it that you rise by steady climbing, and you will never fall.

Meditation for the Day

The pure man knows himself as pure being.

HE who will not give up his secret lust, his covetousness, his anger, his opinion about this or that, can see nor know nothing; he will remain a dullard in the school of Wisdom, though he be accounted learned in the colleges.

If a man would find the key of Knowledge, let him find himself. Thy sins are not thyself; they are not any part of thyself; they are diseases which thou hast come to love. Cease to cling to them, and they will no longer cling to thee. Let them fall away, and thyself shall stand revealed. Thou shalt know thyself as Comprehensive Vision, Invincible Principle, Immortal Life, and Eternal Good.

Purity is extremely simple, and needs no argument to support it.

Thought for the Evening

He who knows that Love is at the heart of all things, and has realized the all-sufficing power of that Love, has no room in his heart for condemnation.

If you love people and speak of them with praise, until they in some way thwart you, or do something of which you disapprove, and then you dislike them and speak of them with dispraise, you are not governed by the Love which is of God. If, in your heart, you are continually arraigning and condemning others, selfless love is hidden from you.

Train your mind in strong, impartial, and gentle thought; train your heart in purity and compassion; train your tongue to silence, and to true and stainless speech; so shall you enter the way of holiness and peace, and shall ultimately realize the immortal Love.

October Twenty-ninth

Thought for the Morning

If you would realize true prosperity, do not settle down, as many have done, into the belief that if you do right everything will go wrong. Do not allow the word "competition" to shake your faith in the supremacy of righteousness. I care not what men say about the "laws of competition," for do not I know the Unchangeable Law which shall one day put them all to rout, and which puts them to rout even now in the heart and life of the righteous man? And knowing this law I can contemplate all dishonesty with undisturbed repose, for I know where certain destruction awaits it.

Under all circumstances *do that which you believe to be right*, and trust the Law; trust the Divine Power which is immanent in the universe, and it will never desert you, and you will always be protected.

Meditation for the Day

Truth lives itself.

MEEKNESS, Patience, Love, Compassion, and Wisdom—these are the dominant qualities of Original Simplicity; therefore the imperfect cannot understand it. Wisdom only can apprehend Wisdom, therefore the fool says, "No man is wise." The imperfect man says, "No man can be perfect," and he therefore remains where he is. Though he live with a perfect man all his life, he shall not behold his perfection. Meekness he will call cowardice; Patience, Love, Compassion he will see as weakness; and Wisdom will appear to him as folly. Faultless discrimination belongs to the Perfect Whole, and resides not in any part, therefore men are exhorted to refrain from judgment until they have themselves manifested the Perfect Life.

A blameless life is the only witness of Truth.

Thought for the Evening

Forget yourself entirely in the sorrows of others, and in ministering to others, and divine happiness will emancipate you from all sorrow and suffering. "Taking the first step with a good thought, the second with a good word, and the third with a good deed, I entered Paradise." And you also enter Paradise by pursuing the same course.

Lose yourself in the welfare of others; forget yourself in all that you do—this is the secret of abounding happiness. Ever be on the watch to guard against selfishness and learn faithfully the divine lessons of inward sacrifice; so shall you climb the highest heights of happiness, and shall remain in the never-clouded sunshine of universal joy, clothed in the shining garment of immortality.

October Thirtieth

Thought for the Morning

When the farmer has tilled and dressed his land and put in the seed, he knows that he has done all that he can possibly do, and that now he must trust to the elements, and wait patiently for the course of time to bring about the harvest, and that no amount of expectancy on his part will affect the result.

Even so, he who has realized Truth, goes forth as a sower of the seeds of goodness, purity, love, and peace, without expectancy and never looking for results, knowing that there is the Great Over-ruling Law which brings about its own harvest in due time, and which is alike the source of preservation and destruction.

Meditation for the Day

He who has found the indwelling Reality of his own being
has found the original and universal Reality.

KNOWING the Divine Heart within, all hearts are known, and the thoughts of all men become his who has become master of his own thoughts; therefore the good man does not defend himself, but moulds the minds of others to his own likeness.

As the problematical transcends crudity, so Pure Goodness transcends the problematical. All problems vanish when Pure Goodness is reached; therefore the Good man is called "The Slayer of illusions". What problem can vex where sin is not? O thou who strivest loudly and resteth not! retire into the holy silence of thine own being, and live therefrom. So shalt thou, finding Pure Goodness, rend in twain the Veil of the Temple of Illusion, and shalt enter into the Patience, Peace, and transcendent Glory of the Perfect, for Pure Goodness and Original Simplicity are one.

So extremely simple is Original Simplicity
that a man must let go his hold of everything
before he can perceive it.

Thought for the Evening

The virtuous put a check upon themselves, and set a watch upon their passions and emotions; in this way they gain possession of the mind, and gradually acquire calmness; and as they acquire influence, power, greatness, abiding joy, and fullness and completeness of life.

He only finds peace who conquers himself, who strives, day by day, after greater self-possession, greater self-control, and greater calmness of mind.

Where the calm mind is there is strength and rest, there is love and wisdom; there is one who has fought successfully innumerable battles against self, who, after long toil in secret against his own failings, has triumphed at last.

October Thirty-first

Thought for the Morning

Sympathy bestowed increases its store in our own heart and enriches and fructifies our own life. Sympathy given is blessedness received; sympathy withheld is blessedness forfeited.

In the measure that a man increases and enlarges his sympathy so much nearer does he approach the ideal life, the perfect blessedness; and when his heart has become so mellowed that no hard, bitter, or cruel thought can enter, and detract from its permanent sweetness, then indeed is he richly and divinely blessed.

Meditation for the Day

Great will be his pain and unrest who seeks
to stand upon the approbation of others.

TO detach oneself from every outward thing, and to rest securely upon the inward virtue, this is the Unfailing Wisdom. Having this Wisdom, a man will be the same whether in riches or poverty. The one cannot add to his strength, nor the other rob him of his serenity. Neither can riches defile him who has washed away all the inward defilement, nor the lack of them degrade him who has ceased to degrade the temple of his soul.

To refuse to be enslaved by any outward thing or happening, regarding all such things and happenings as for your use, for your education, this is Wisdom. To the wise all occurrences are *good*, and, having no eye for evil, they grow wiser every day. They utilize all things, and thus put all things under their feet. They see all their mistakes as soon as made, and accept them as lessons of intrinsic value, knowing that there are no mistakes in the Divine Order.

To love where one is not loved;
herein lies the strength which shall never fail a man.

Thought for the Evening

Sweet is the rest and deep the bliss of him who has freed his heart from its lusts and hatreds and dark desires; and he who, without any shadow of bitterness resting upon him, and looking out upon the world with boundless compassion and love, can breathe, in his inmost heart, the blessing: Peace unto all living things, making no exceptions or distinctions—such a man has reached that happy ending which can never be taken away, for this is the perfection of life, the fullness of peace, the consummation of perfect blessedness.

November First

Thought for the Morning

In aiming at the life of blessedness, one of the simplest beginnings to be considered, and rightly made, is that which we all make every day—namely, the beginning of each day's life. There is a sense in which every day may be regarded as the beginning of a new life, in which one can think, act, and live newly, and in a wiser and better spirit. The right beginning of the day will be followed by a cheerfulness permeating the household with a sunny influence, and the tasks and duties of the day will be undertaken in a strong and confident spirit, and the whole day will be well lived.

Meditation for the Day

The wise man is always anxious to learn, but never anxious to teach.

ALL strength and wisdom and power and knowledge a man will find within himself, but he will not find it in egotism; he will only find it in obedience, submission, and willingness to learn. He must obey the higher and not glorify himself in the lower. He who stands upon egotism, rejecting reproof, instruction, and the lessons of experience, will surely fall; yea, he is already fallen. Said a great teacher to his disciples, "Those who shall be a lamp unto themselves, relying upon themselves only, and not relying upon any external help, but holding fast to the Truth as their lamp, and, seeking their salvation in the Truth alone, shall not look for assistance to any beside themselves, it is they among my disciples who shall reach the very topmost height! *But they must be willing to learn.*

The true Teacher is in the heart of every man.

Thought for the Evening

There can be no progress, no achievement, without sacrifice, and a man's worldly success will be in the measure that he sacrifices his confused animal thoughts, and fixes his mind on the development of his plans, and the strengthening of his resolution and self-reliance. And the higher he lifts his thoughts, the more manly, upright, and righteous he becomes, the greater will be his success, the more blessed and enduring will be his achievements.

November Second

November Third

Thought for the Morning

None but right acts can follow right thoughts; none but a right life can follow right acts; and by living a right life all blessedness is achieved. Mind is the Master-power that moulds and makes. And Man is Mind, and evermore he takes the tool of thought, and, shaping what he wills, brings forth a thousand joys, a thousand ills;—He thinks in secret, and it comes to pass: environment is but his looking-glass.

Meditation for the Day

Dispersion is weakness; concentration is power.

THINGS are useful and thoughts are powerful in the measure that their parts are strongly and intelligently concentrated. Purpose is highly concentrated thought. All the mental energies are directed to the attainment of an object, and obstacles which intervene between the thinker and the object are, one after another, broken down and overcome. Purpose is the keystone in the temple of achievement. It binds and holds together in a complete whole that which would otherwise lie scattered and useless. Empty whims, ephemeral fancies, vague desires, and half-hearted resolutions have no place in purpose. In the sustained determination to accomplish there is an invincible power which swallows up all inferior considerations and marches direct to victory.

All successful men are men of purpose.

Thought for the Evening

Calmness of mind is one of the beautiful jewels of wisdom. A man becomes calm in the measure that he understands himself as a thought-evolved being... and he as he develops a right understanding, and sees more and more clearly the internal relations of things by the action of cause and effect, he ceases to fret and fume, and worry and grieve, and remains poised, steadfast, serene.

Thought for the Morning

To follow, under all circumstances, the highest promptings within you; to be always true to the divine self; to reply upon the inward voice, the inward light, and to pursue your purpose with a fearless and restful heart, believing that the future will yield unto you the need of every thought and effort; knowing that the laws of the universe can never fail, and that your own will come back to you with mathematical exactitude—this is faith and the living of faith.

Meditation for the Day

Know this thou makest and unmakest thyself.

DOUBT, anxiety, and worry are unsubstantial shades in the underworld of self, and shall no more trouble him who will climb the serene altitudes of his soul. Grief, also, will be forever dispelled by him who will comprehend the Law of his being. He who so comprehends shall find the Supreme Law of Life, and he shall find that it is Love, that it is imperishable Love. He shall become one with Love, and loving all, with mind freed from all hatred and folly, he shall receive the invincible protection which Love affords. Claiming nothing, he shall suffer no loss; seeking no pleasure, he shall find no grief; and employing all his powers as instruments of service, he shall evermore live in the highest state of blessedness and bliss.

Thou art a slave if thou preferrest to be;
thou art a master if thou wilt make thyself one.

Thought for the Evening

Have a thorough understanding of your work, and let it be your own; and as you proceed, ever following the inward guide, the infallible voice, you will pass on from victory to victory, and will rise step by step to higher resting-places, and your ever broadening outlook will gradually reveal to you the essential beauty and purpose of life. Self-purified, health will be yours; self-governed, power will be yours, and all that you do will prosper.

And I may stand where health, success, and power await my coming, if, each fleeting hour, I cling to love and patience; and abide with stainlessness; and never step aside from high integrity; so shall I see at last the land of immortality.

November Fourth

Thought for the Morning

When the tongue is well controlled and wisely subdued; when selfish impulses and unworthy thoughts no longer rush to the tongue demanding utterance; when the speech has become harmless, pure, gracious, gentle, and purposeful, and no word is uttered but in sincerity and truth—then are the five steps in virtuous speech accomplished, then is the second great lesson in Truth learned and mastered. Make pure thy heart, and thou wilt make thy life rich, sweet and beautiful.

Meditation for the Day

He who has found Meekness has found divinity.

THE mountain bends not to the fiercest storm, but it shields the fledgling and the lamb; and though all men tread upon it, yet it protects them, and bears them up upon its deathless bosom. Even so is it with the meek man who, though shaken and disturbed by none, yet compassionately bends to shield the lowliest creature, and, though he may be despised, lifts up all men, and lovingly protects them.

As glorious as the mountain in its silent might is the divine man in his silent Meekness; like its form, his loving compassion is expansive and sublime. Truly his body, like the mountain's base, is fixed in the valleys and the mists; but the summit of his being is eternally bathed in cloudless glory, and lives with the Silence.

The meek man has realized the divine consciousness
and knows himself as divine.

Thought for the Evening

Having clothed himself with humility, the first questions a man asks himself are:—

"How am I acting towards others?"
"What am I doing to others?"
"How am I thinking of others?"
"Are my thoughts of, and acts towards others prompted by unselfish love?"

As a man, in the silence of his soul, asks himself these searching questions, he will unerringly see where he has hitherto failed.

November Fifth

Thought for the Morning

To dwell in love always and towards all is to live the true life, is to have Life itself. Knowing this, the good man gives up himself unreservedly to the Spirit of Love, and dwells in Love towards all, contending with none, condemning none, but loving all.

The Christ Spirit of Love puts an end, not only to all sin, but to all division and contention.

Meditation for the Day

He who lives in Meekness is without fear,
knowing the Highest, and having the lowest under his feet.

THE meek man shines in darkness, and flourishes in obscurity. Meekness cannot boast, nor advertise itself, nor thrive on popularity. It is *practised*, and is seen and not seen; being a spiritual quality it is perceived only by the eye of the spirit. Those who are not spiritually awakened see it not, nor do they love it, being enamoured of, and blinded by, worldly shows and appearances. Nor does history take note of the meek man. Its glory is that of strife and self-aggrandizement; his is the glory of peace and gentleness. History chronicles the earthly, not the heavenly acts. Yet though he lives in obscurity, he cannot be hidden (how can light be hid?); he continues to shine after he has withdrawn himself from the world, and is worshipped by the world which knew him not.

The meek man is found in the time of trial;
when other men fall he stands.

Thought for the Evening

When sin and self are abandoned, the heart is restored to its imperishable Joy. Joy comes and fills the self-emptied heart; it abides with the peaceful; its reign is with the pure. Joy flees from the selfish, it deserts the quarrelsome; it is hidden from the impure. Joy cannot remain with the selfish; it is wedded to Love.

November Sixth

Thought for the Morning

In the pure heart there is no room left where personal judgments and hatreds can find lodgement, for it is filled to overflowing with tenderness and love; it sees no evil, and only as men succeed in seeing no evil in others will they become free from sin, and sorrow, and suffering. If men only understood that the heart that sins must sorrow, that the hateful mind tomorrow reaps its barren harvest, weeping, starving, resting not, nor sleeping; tenderness would fill their being, they would see with pity's seeing, if they only understood.

Meditation for the Day

The meek man resists none, and thereby conquers all.

HE who imagines he can be injured by others, and who seeks to justify and defend himself against them, does not understand Meekness, does not comprehend the essence and meaning of life. "He abused me, he beat me, he defeated me, he robbed me. In those who harbour such thoughts hatred will never cease . . . for hatred ceases not by hatred at any time; hatred ceases by love." What sayest thou? Thy neighbour has spoken thee falsely? Well, what of that? Can a falsity hurt thee? That which is false is false, and there is an end of it. It is without life, and without power to hurt any but him who seeks to be hurt by it. It is nothing to thee that thy neighbour should speak falsely of thee, but it is much to thee that thou shouldst resist him, and seek to justify thyself, for, by so doing, thou givest life and vitality to thy neighbour's falseness, so that thou art injured and distressed.

Take all evil out of thine own heart,
then shall thou see the folly of resisting it in another.

Thought for the Evening

To stand face to face with truth; to arrive, after innumerable wanderings and pains, at wisdom and bliss; not to be finally defeated and cast out, but to ultimately triumph over every inward foe—such is man's divine destiny, such his glorious goal; and this, every saint, sage, and saviour has declared. A man only begins to be a man when he ceases to whine and revile, and commences to search for the hidden justice which regulates his life. And as he adapts his mind to that regulating factor, he ceases to accuse others as the cause of his condition, and builds himself up in strong and noble thoughts; ceases to kick against circumstances, but begins to use them as aids to his more rapid progress, and as a means of discovering the hidden power and possibilities within himself.

November Seventh

November Eighth

Thought for the Morning

The will to evil and the will to good are both within thee, which wilt thou employ? Thou knowest what is right and what is wrong, which wilt though love and foster, which destroy?

Thou art the chooser of thy thoughts and deeds; thou art the maker of thine inward state; the power is thine to be what thou wilt be; thou buildest Truth and Love, or lies and hate.

Meditation for the Day

Great is the power of purpose.

PURPOSE goes with intelligence. There are lesser and greater purposes, according with degrees of intelligence. A great mind will always be great of purpose. A wreak intelligence will be without purpose. A drifting mind argues a measure of undevelopment.

The men who have melded the destinies of humanity have been men mighty of purpose. Like the Roman laying his road, they have followed along a well-defined path, and have refused to swerve aside even when torture and death confronted them. The Great Leaders of the race are the mental road-makers, and mankind follows in the intellectual and spiritual paths which they have carved out and beaten.

Inert matter yields to a living force,
and circumstance succumbs to the power of purpose.

Thought for the Evening

The teaching of Jesus brings men back to the simple truth that righteousness, or *right-doing*, is entirely a matter of individual conduct, and not a mystical something apart from a man's thoughts and deeds.

Calmness and patience can become habitual by first grasping, through effort, a calm and patient thought, and then continuously thinking it, and living in it, until "use becomes second nature," and anger and impatience pass away for ever.

Thought for the Morning

Man is made or unmade by himself; in the armoury of thought he forges the weapons by which he destroys himself; he also fashions the tools with which he builds for himself heavenly mansions of joy and strength and peace. By the right choice and true application of thought man ascends to the Divine Perfection; by the abuse and wrong application of thought he descends below the level of the beast. Between these two extremes are all the grades of character and man is their maker and master.

As a being of Power, Intelligence, and Love, and the lord of his own thoughts, man holds the key to every situation.

Meditation for the Day

*All things at last yield to the silent,
irresistible all-conquering energy of purpose.*

THE weak man, who grieves because he is misunderstood, will not greatly achieve; the vain man, who steps aside from his resolve in order to please others and gain their approbation, will not highly achieve; the double-minded man, who thinks to compromise his purpose, will fail.

The man of fixed purpose who, whether misunderstandings and foul accusations, or flatteries and fair promises, rain upon him, does not yield a fraction of his resolve is the man of excellence and achievement; of success, greatness, and power.

Hindrances stimulate a man of purpose; difficulties nerve him to renewed exertion; mistakes, losses, pains, do not subdue him; and failures are steps in the ladder of success, for he is ever conscious of the certainty of final achievement.

*The intensity of the purpose increases with the
growing magnitude of the obstacles encountered.*

Thought for the Evening

Whatsoever you harbour in the inmost chambers of your heart will, sooner or later, by the inevitable law of reaction, shape itself in your outward life.

Every soul attracts its own, and nothing can possibly come to it that does not belong to it. To realize this is to recognize the universality of Divine Law.

If thou would'st right the world, and banish all its evils and its woes, make its wild places bloom, and its drear deserts blossom as the rose—then right thyself.

November Ninth

Thought for the Morning

Whatever conditions are rendering your life burdensome, you may pass out of and beyond them by developing and utilizing within you the transforming power of self-purification and self-conquest.

Before the divine radiance of a pure heart all darkness vanishes and all clouds melt away, and he who has conquered self has conquered the universe.

He who sets his foot firmly upon the path of self-conquest, who walks, aided by the staff of faith, the highway of self-sacrifice, will assuredly achieve the highest prosperity, and will reap abounding and enduring joy and bliss.

Meditation for the Day

Joy is always the accompaniment of a task successfully accomplished.

OF all miserable men, the shirker is the most miserable. Thinking to find ease and happiness in avoiding difficult tasks, which require the expenditure of labour and exertion, his mind is always uneasy and disturbed, he becomes burdened with an inward sense of shame, and forfeits manliness and self-respect. "He who will not work according to his faculty, let him perish according to his necessity," says Carlyle; and it is a moral law that the man who avoids duty, and does not work to the full extent of his capacity, does actually perish, first in his character, and last in his body and circumstances. Life and action are synonymous, and immediately a man tries to escape exertion, either physical or mental, he has commenced to decay.

An undertaking completed, or a piece of work done,
always brings rest and satisfaction.

Thought for the Evening

It is the silent and conquering thought forces which bring all things into manifestation. The universe grew out of thought.

To adjust all your thoughts to a perfect and unswerving faith in the omnipotence and supremacy of Good is to co-operate with that Good, and to realize within yourself the solution and destruction of all evil.

To mentally deny evil is not sufficient; it must, by daily practice, be risen above and understood. To affirm the Good mentally is inadequate; it must, by unswerving endeavour, be entered into and comprehended.

November Tenth

Thought for the Morning

Every thought you think is a force sent out. Whatever your position in life may be, before you can hope to enter into any measure of success, usefulness, and power, you must learn how to focus your thought forces by cultivating calmness and repose.

There is no difficulty, however great, but will yield before a calm and purposeful concentration of thought, and no legitimate object but may be speedily actualized by the intelligent use and direction of one's soul forces.

Think good thoughts, and they will quickly become actualized in your outward life in the form of good conditions.

Meditation for the Day

The price of life is effort.

EVERY successful accomplishment, even in worldly things, is repaid with its own measure of joy; and in spiritual things the joy which supervenes upon the perfection of purpose is sure, deep, and abiding. Great is the heartfelt joy (albeit ineffable) when, after innumerable and apparently unsuccessful attempts, some ingrained fault of character is at last cast out, to trouble its erstwhile victim and the world no more. The striver after virtue—he who is engaged in the holy task of building up a noble character—tastes, at every step of conquest over self, a joy which does not leave him again, but which becomes an integral part of his spiritual nature.

The reward of accomplishment is joy.

Thought for the Evening

That which you would be and hope to be, you may be now. Non-accomplishment resides in your perpetual postponement, and, having the power to postpone, you also have the power to accomplish—to perpetually accomplish: realize this truth, and you shall be today, and every day, the ideal being of whom you dreamed.

Say to yourself, "I will live in my Ideal now; I will manifest my ideal now; I will be my Ideal now; and all that tempts me away from my Ideal I will not listen to; I will listen only to the voice of my Ideal."

November Eleventh

Thought for the Morning

Be as a flower; content to be, to grow in sweetness day by day. If thou would'st perfect thyself in knowledge, perfect thyself in Love. If thou would'st reach the Highest, ceaselessly cultivate a loving and compassionate heart.

To him who chooses Goodness, sacrificing all, is given that which is more than, and includes, all.

Meditation for the Day

Everything that happens is just.

AS you think, you travel; as you love, you attract. You are today where your thoughts have brought you; I you will be tomorrow where your thoughts take you. You cannot escape the results of your thoughts, but you can endure and learn, can accept and be glad.

You will always come to the place where your *love* (your most abiding and intense thought) can receive its measure of gratification. If your love be base, you will come to a base place; if it be beautiful, you will come to a beautiful place.

You can alter your thoughts, and so alter your condition. You are powerful, not powerless.

Nothing is fated, everything is formed.

Thought for the Evening

The Great Law never cheats any man of his just due.

Human life, when rightly lived, is simple with a beautiful simplicity.

He who comprehends the utter simplicity of life, who obeys its laws, and does not step aside into the dark paths and complex mazes of selfish desire, stands where no harm can reach him.

Then there is fullness of joy, abounding plenty, and rich and complete blessedness.

November Twelfth

Thought for the Morning

Every man reaps the results of his own thoughts and deeds, and suffers for his own wrong.

He who begins right, and continues right, does not need to desire, and search for felicitous results; they are already at hand; they follow as consequences; they are the certainties, the realities, of life.

Sweet is the rest and deep is the bliss of him who has freed his heart from its lusts and hatreds and dark desires.

Meditation for the Day

The man whose thoughts, words, and acts
are sincere is surrounded by sincere friends;
the insincere man is surrounded by insincere friends.

EVERY fact and process in Nature contains a moral lesson for the wise man. There is no law in the world which is not to be found operating with the same mathematical certainty in the mind of man and in human life. All the parables of Jesus are illustrative of this truth, and are drawn from the simple facts of Nature. There is a process of seed-sowing in the mind and life, a spiritual sowing which leads to a harvest according to the kind of seed sown. Thoughts, words, and acts are seeds sown, and, by the inviolable law of things, they produce after their kind.

The man who thinks hateful thoughts brings hatred upon himself. The man who thinks loving thoughts is loved.

When you know yourself you will perceive that every event
in your life is weighed in the faultless balance of equity.

Thought for the Evening

You are the creator of your own shadows; you desire, and then you grieve; renounce, and then you shall rejoice.

Of all the beautiful truths pertaining to the soul... none is more gladdening or fruitful of divine promise and confidence than this—that man is the master of thought, the moulder of character, and the maker and shaper of character, environment, and destiny.

November Thirteenth

Thought for the Morning

As darkness is a passing shadow, and light is a substance that remains, so sorrow is fleeting, but joy abides for ever. No true thing can pass away and become lost; no false thing can remain and be preserved. Sorrow is false, and it cannot live; joy is true, and it cannot die. Joy may become hidden for a time, but it can always be recovered; sorrow may remain for a period, but it can be transcended and dispersed.

Do not think your sorrow will remain; it will pass away like a cloud. Do not believe that the torments of sin are ever your portion; they will vanish like a hideous nightmare. Awake! Arise! Be holy and joyful.

Meditation for the Day

He who would be blessed, let him scatter blessings.

THE farmer must scatter all his seed upon the land, and then leave it to the elements. Were he to covetously hoard his seed, he would lose both it and his produce, for his seed would perish. It perishes when he sows it, but in perishing it brings forth a greater abundance. So in life, we get by giving; we grow rich by scattering. The man who says he is in possession of knowledge which he cannot give out because the world is incapable of receiving it either does not possess such knowledge, or, if he does, will soon be deprived of it—if he is not already deprived of it. To hoard is to lose; to exclusively retain is to be dispossessed.

He who would be happy, let him consider the happiness of others.

Thought for the Evening

Tribulation lasts only so long as there remains some chaff of self which needs to be removed. The *tribulum*, or threshing machine, ceases to work when all the grain is separated from the chaff; and when the last impurities are blown away from the soul, tribulation has completed its work, and there is no more need for it; then abiding joy is realized.

The sole and supreme use of suffering is to purify, to burn out all that is useless and impure. Suffering ceases for him who is pure. There could be no object in burning gold after the dross had been removed.

November Fourteenth

Thought for the Morning

In speaking of self-control, one is easily misunderstood. It should not be associated with a destructive repression, but with a constructive expression.

A man is happy, wise and great in the measure that he controls himself; he is wretched, foolish, and mean in the measure that he allows his animal nature to dominate his thoughts and actions.

He who controls himself, controls his life, his circumstances, his destiny; and wherever he goes he carries his happiness with him as an abiding possession.

Renunciation precedes regeneration. The permanent happiness which men seek in dissipation, excitement, and abandonment to unworthy pleasures, is found only in the life which reverses all this—the life of self-control.

Meditation for the Day

Men reap that which they sow.

IF a man is troubled, perplexed, sorrowful, or unhappy, let him ask:
"What mental seeds have I been sowing?"
"What seeds am I sowing?"
"What is my attitude towards others?"
"What seeds of trouble and sorrow and unhappiness have I sown that I should thus reap these bitter weeds?"

Let him seek within and find, and having found, let him abandon all the seeds of self, and sow, henceforth, only the seeds of Truth.

Let him learn of the farmer the simple truths of wisdom, and sow broadcast the seeds of kindness, gentleness, and love.

The way to obtain peace and blessedness is to scatter
peaceful and blessed thoughts, words, and deeds.

Thought for the Evening

Law, not confusion, is the dominating principle in the universe; justice, not injustice is the soul and substance of life; and righteousness, not corruption, is the moulding and moving force in the spiritual government of the world. This being so, man has but the right himself to find that the universe is right.

When I am pure, I shall have solved the mystery of life; I shall be sure, when I am free from hatred, lust and strife, I am in Truth, and Truth abides in me; I shall be safe, and sane, and wholly free, when I am pure.

November Fifteenth

Thought for the Morning

If men only understood that their hatred and resentment slays their peace and sweet contentment, hurts themselves, helps not another, does not cheer one lonely brother, they would seek the better doing of good deeds which leaves no ruing:—

If they only understood.

If men only understood how Love conquers; how prevailing is its might, grim hate assailing; how compassion endeth sorrow, maketh wise, and doth not borrow pain of passion, they would ever live in Love, in hatred never:—

If they only understood.

Meditation for the Day

*Destroying the idols of self,
we draw nearer to the great, silent Heart of Love.*

WE have reached one of those epochs in the world's progress which witnesses the passing of the false gods; the gods of human selfishness and human illusion. The new-old revelation of one universal impersonal Truth has again dawned upon the world, and its searching light has carried consternation to the perishable gods who take shelter under the shadow of self.

Men have lost faith in a god who can be cajoled, who rules arbitrarily and capriciously, subverting the whole order of things to gratify the wishes of his worshippers, and are turning, with a new light in their hearts, to the *God of Law*. And to Him they turn, not for personal happiness and gratification, but for knowledge, for understanding, for wisdom, for liberation from the bondage of self.

Enter the Path of obedience to the Law.

Thought for the Evening

The grace and beauty that were in Jesus can be of no value to you—cannot be understood by you—unless they are also *in you*, and they can never be in you, until you practice them, for, apart from *doing*, the qualities which constitute goodness do not, as far as you are concerned, exist.

To adore Jesus for his good qualities is a long step towards Truth, but to practice those qualities is Truth itself; and he who fully adores the perfection of another will not rest content in his own imperfection, but will fashion his soul after the likeness of that other.

Therefore thou who adorest Jesus for his divine qualities, practice those qualities thyself, and thou too shalt be divine.

November Sixteenth

Thought for the Morning

Let a man realize that life in its totality proceeds from the mind, and lo, the way of blessedness is opened up to him! For he will then discover that he possesses the power to rule his mind and to fashion it in accordance with his Ideal.

So will he elect to strongly and steadfastly walk those pathways of thought and action which are altogether excellent; to him life will become beautiful and sacred; and, sooner or later, he will put to flight all evil, confusion, and suffering; for it is impossible for a man to fall short of liberation, enlightenment, and peace, who guards with unwearying diligence the gateway of his heart.

Meditation for the Day

Perfection, which is knowledge of the Perfect Law,
is ready for all who earnestly seek it.

ENTERING that Path—the Path of the Supreme Law—men no longer accuse, no longer doubt, no longer fret and despond, for they know now that God is right, the universal laws are right, the cosmos is right, and that they *themselves* are wrong, if wrong there is, and that their salvation depends upon themselves, upon their own efforts, upon their personal acceptance of that which is good, and deliberate rejection of that which is evil. No longer merely hearers, they become *doers* of the Word, and they acquire knowledge, they receive understanding, they grow in wisdom, and they enter into the glorious life of liberation from the bondage of self.

Adopt the life of self-obliteration.

Thought for the Evening

By constantly overcoming self, a man gains a knowledge of the subtle intricacies of his mind; and it is this divine knowledge which enables him to become established in calmness.

Without self-knowledge there can be no abiding peace of mind, and those who are carried away by tempestuous passions, cannot approach the holy place where calmness reigns.

The weak man is like one who, having mounted a fiery steed, allows it to run away with him, and carry him withersoever it wills; the strong man is like one who, having mounted the steed, governs it with a masterly hand and makes it go in whatever direction and at whatever speed he commands.

November Seventeenth

Thought for the Morning

There is no strife, no selfishness, in the Kingdom; there is perfect harmony, equipoise, and rest.

Those who live in the Kingdom of Love, have all their needs supplied by the Law of Love.

As self is the root cause of all strife and suffering, so Love is the root cause of all peace and bliss. Those who are at rest in the Kingdom do not look for happiness in any outward possessions. They are freed from all anxiety and trouble and, resting in Love, they are the embodiment of happiness.

Meditation for the Day

God does not alter for man, for this would mean that the perfect
must become imperfect; man must alter for God.

THE Children of Truth are in the world today; they are thinking, writing, speaking, acting; yea, even prophets are amongst us, and their influence is pervading the whole earth. An undercurrent of holy joy is gathering force in the world, so that men and women are moved with new aspirations and hopes, and even those who neither see nor hear, feel within them strange yearnings after a better and fuller life.

The Law reigns, and it reigns in men's hearts and lives; they have come to understand the reign of Law who have sought out the Tabernacle of the true God by the fair pathway of unselfishness.

The Law cannot be broken for man,
otherwise confusion would ensue;
this is in accordance with harmony, order, justice.

Thought for the Evening

Let it not be supposed that the children of the Kingdom live in ease and indolence (these two sins are the first that have to be eradicated when the search for the Kingdom is entered upon); they live in a peaceful activity; in fact, they only truly live, for the life of self, with its train of worries, griefs, and fears, is not *real life*.

The children of the Kingdom are *known by their life*, they manifest the fruits of the Spirit—"Love, joy, peace, long-suffering, kindness, goodness, faithfulness, meekness, temperance, and self-control"—under all circumstances and vicissitudes.

November Eighteenth

Thought for the Morning

The gospel of Jesus is a gospel of *living and doing*. If it were not this it would not voice the Eternal Truth. Its Temple is *Purified Conduct*, the entrance-door to which is *Self-Surrender*. It invites men to shake off sin, and promises, as a result, joy and blessedness and perfect peace.

The Kingdom of Heaven is perfect trust, perfect knowledge, perfect peace. . . no sin can enter therein, no self-born thought or deed can pass its golden gates; no impure desire can defile its radiant robes. . . all may enter it who will, but all must pay the price—*the unconditional abandonment of self*.

Meditation for the Day

*There is no more painful bondage
than to be at the mercy of one's inclinations.*

THE Law is that the heart shall be purified, the mind regenerated, and the whole being brought in subjection to Love, till self be dead and Love is all in all, for the reign of Law is the reign of Love. And Love waits for all, rejecting none. Love may be claimed and entered into now, for it is the heritage of all.

Ah, beautiful Truth! To know that *now* man may accept his divine heritage, and enter the Kingdom of Heaven!

Oh, pitiful error! To know that man rejects it because of love of self!

Obedience to one's selfish inclinations means the drawing about one's soul clouds of pain and sorrow which darken the light of Truth; the shutting out of oneself from all real blessedness; for "whatsoever a man sows that shall he also reap."

There is no greater liberty than utmost obedience to the Law of Being.

Thought for the Evening

I say this—and know it to be truth—*that circumstances can only affect you in so far as you allow them to do so*. You are swayed by circumstances because you have not a right understanding of the nature, use, and power of thought. You believe (and upon this little word *belief* hang all our joys and sorrows) that outward things have the power to make or mar your life; by so doing you submit to those outward things, confess that you are their slave, and they your unconditional master. By so doing you invest them with a power which they do not of themselves possess, and you succumb, in reality not to the circumstances, but to the gloom or gladness, the fear or hope, the strength of weakness, which your thought-sphere has thrown around them.

November Nineteenth

Thought for the Morning

If you are one of those who are praying for, and looking forward to a happier world beyond the grave, here is a message of gladness for you—you may enter into and realize that happy world now; it fills the whole universe, and it is within you, waiting for you to find, acknowledge, and possess.

Said one who understood the inner laws of Being—"When men shall say, lo here, or lo there, go not after them. The Kingdom of God is within you."

Meditation for the Day

The moral universe is sustained and protected
by the perfect balance of its equivalents.

IS there, then, no injustice in the universe? There is injustice, and there is not. It depends upon the kind of life and the state of consciousness from which a man looks out upon the world and judges. The man who lives in his passions sees injustice everywhere; the man who has overcome his passions, sees the operations of Justice in every department of human life.

Injustice is the confused feverish dream of passion, real enough to those who are dreaming it; Justice is the permanent reality in life, gloriously visible to those who have wakened out of the painful nightmare of self.

As in the physical world Nature abhors a vacuum,
so in the spiritual world disharmony is annulled.

Thought for the Evening

Heaven and hell are inward states. Sink into self and all its gratifications, and you sink into hell; rise above self into that state of consciousness which is the utter denial and forgetfulness of self, and you enter heaven.

So long as you persist in selfishly seeking for your own personal happiness, so long will happiness elude you, and you will be sowing the seeds of wretchedness. In so far as you succeed in losing yourself in the service of others, in that measure will happiness come to you, and you will reap a harvest of bliss.

November Twentieth

Thought for the Morning

Sympathy given can never be waste.

One aspect of sympathy is that of pity—pity for the distressed or pain stricken, with a desire to alleviate or help them in their sufferings. The world needs more of this divine quality.

"For pity makes the world soft to the weak, and noble for the strong."

Another form of sympathy is that of rejoicing with others who are more successful than ourselves, and though their success were our own.

Meditation for the Day

The Divine Order cannot be perceived until passion and self are transcended.

THE man who thinks, "I have been slighted, I have been injured, I have been insulted, I have been treated unjustly; cannot know what justice is; blinded by self, he cannot perceive the pure Principles of Truth, and, brooding upon his wrongs, he lives in continual misery.

In the region of passion there is a ceaseless conflict of forces causing suffering to all who are involved in them. There is action and reaction, deed and consequence, cause and effect; and within and above all is the divine Justice regulating the play of forces with the utmost mathematical accuracy, balancing cause and effect with the finest precision.

Justice is not perceived, cannot be perceived
by those who are engaged in conflict.

Thought for the Evening

Sweet are companionships, pleasures, and material comforts, but they change and fade away. Sweeter still are Purity, Wisdom, and the knowledge of Truth, and these never change nor fade away.

He who attained to the possession of spiritual things can never be deprived of his source of happiness; he will never have to part company with it, and wherever he goes in the whole universe, he will carry his possessions with him. His spiritual end will be the fullness of joy.

November Twenty-first

Thought for the Morning

Let your heart grow and expand with ever broadening love, until, freed from all hatred, and passion, and condemnation, it embraces the whole universe with thoughtful tenderness.

As the flower opens its petals to receive the morning light, so open your soul more and more to the glorious light of Truth.

Soar upward on the wings of aspiration; be fearless and believe in the loftiest possibilities.

Meditation for the Day

*Having no knowledge of cause and effect in the moral sphere,
men do not see the exacting process which is momentarily proceeding.*

MEN blindly inflict suffering upon themselves, living in passion and resentment, and not finding the true way of life. Hatred is met with hatred, passion with passion, strife with strife. The man who kills is himself killed; the thief who lives by depriving others, is himself deprived; the beast that preys on others is hunted and killed; the accuser is accused, the condemner is condemned, the denouncer is persecuted.

> "By this the slayer's knife doth stab himself,
> The unjust judge has lost his own defender,
> The false tongue dooms its lie, the creeping thief
> And spoiler rob to render.
>
> "Such is the Law."

Ignorance keeps alive hatred and strife.

Thought for the Evening

Mind clothes itself in garments of its own making. Mind is the arbiter of life; it is the creator and shaper of conditions, and the recipient of its own results. It contains within itself both the power to create illusion and to perceive reality.

Mind is the infallible weaver of destiny; thought is the thread, good and evil deeds are the warp and woof, and the web, woven upon the loom of life, is character. Make pure thy heart, and thou wilt make thy life, rich, sweet, and beautiful, unmarred by strife.

November Twenty-second

Thought for the Morning

Cherish your visions; cherish your ideals; cherish the music that stirs in your heart, the beauty that forms in your mind, the loveliness that drapes your purest thoughts, for out of them will grow all delightful conditions, all heavenly environment; of these, if you will remain true to them, your world will at last be built.

Guard well thy mind, and, noble, strong, and free, nothing shall harm, disturb or conquer thee; for all thy foes are in thy heart and mind, there also thy salvation thou shalt find.

Meditation for the Day

Cause and effect cannot be avoided; consequence cannot be escaped.

THE good man, having put away all resentment, retaliation, self-seeking, and egotism, has arrived at a state of equilibrium, and has thereby become identified with the Eternal and Universal Equilibrium. Having lifted himself above the blind forces of passion, he understands those forces, contemplates them with a calm penetrating insight, like the solitary dweller on a mountain who looks down upon the conflict of the storms beneath his feet. For him, injustice has ceased, and he sees ignorance and suffering on the one hand, and enlightenment and bliss on the other. He sees that not only do the fool and the slave need his sympathy, but that the fraud and the oppressor are equally in need of it, and so his compassion is extended towards all.

Unerring Justice presides over all.

Thought for the Evening

Dream lofty dreams, and as you dream so shall you become. Your vision is the promise of what you shall one day be; your Ideal is the prophecy of what you shall at last unveil.

The greatest achievement was at first and for a time a dream. The oak sleeps in the acorn; the bird waits in the egg; and in the highest vision of the soul a waking angel stirs.

Your circumstances may be uncongenial, but they shall not long remain so when you perceive an Ideal and strive to reach it.

November Twenty-third

Thought for the Morning

He who has conquered doubt and fear has conquered failure. His every thought is allied with power, and all difficulties are bravely met and wisely overcome. His purposes are seasonably planted, and they bloom and bring forth fruit which does not fall prematurely to the ground.

Thought allied fearlessly to purpose becomes creative force: he who knows this is ready to become something higher and stronger than a mere bundle of wavering thoughts and fluctuating sensations; he who does this has become the conscious and intelligent wielder of his mental powers.

Meditation for the Day

*They who refuse to trim their lamps of reason
will never perceive the Light of Truth.*

HE who will use the light of reason as a torch to search for Truth, will not be left at last in comfortless darkness.

"Come now, and let us reason together, saith the Lord; though your sins be as scarlet, they shall be as white as snow."

Many men and women pass through untold sufferings, and at last die in their sins, *because they refuse to reason*; because they cling to those dark delusions which even a faint glimmer of the light of reason would dispel; and all must use their reason freely, fully, and faithfully, who would exchange the scarlet robe of sin and suffering for the white garment of blessedness and peace.

They who despise the light of reason, despise the Light of Truth.

Thought for the Evening

Man's true place in the Cosmos is that of a king, not a slave, a commander under the Law of Good, and not a helpless tool in the region of evil.

I write for men, not for babes; for those who are eager to learn, and earnest to achieve; for those who will put away (for the world's good) a petty personal indulgence, a selfish desire, a mean thought, and live on as though it were not, sans craving and regret.

Man is a master. If he were not, he could not act contrary to law.

Evil and weakness are self destructive. The universe is girt with goodness and strength, and it protects the good and the strong.

The angry man is the weak man.

November Twenty-fourth

Thought for the Morning

Not by learning will a man triumph over evil; not by much study will he overcome sin and sorrow. Only by conquering himself will he conquer evil; only by practicing righteousness will he put an end to sorrow.

Not for the clever, nor the learned, nor the self-confident is the Life Triumphant, but for the pure, the virtuous and wise. The former achieve their particular success in life, but the latter alone achieve the great success so invincible and complete that even in apparent defeat it shines with added victory.

Meditation for the Day

A man does not live until he begins to discipline himself; he merely exists.

BEFORE a man can accomplish anything of an enduring nature in the world he must first of all acquire some measure of success in the management of his own mind. This is as mathematical a truism as that two and two are four, for "out of the heart are the issues of life." If a man cannot govern the forces within himself, he cannot long hold a firm hand upon the outer activities which form the visible life. On the other hand, as a man succeeds in governing himself he rises to higher and higher levels of power and usefulness and success in the world. Hitherto his life has been without purpose or meaning, but now he begins to consciously mould his own destiny; he is "clothed and in his right mind."

With the practice of self-discipline a man begins to live.

Thought for the Evening

The true silence is not merely a silent tongue; it is a silent mind. To merely *hold one's tongue*, and yet to carry about a disturbed and rankling mind, is no remedy for weakness, and no source of power.

Silentness, to be powerful, must envelop the whole mind, must permeate every chamber of the heart; it must be the silence of peace.

To this broad, deep, abiding silentness a man attains only in the measure that he conquers himself.

November Twenty-fifth

Thought for the Morning

By curbing his tongue, a man gains possession of his mind.

The fool babbles, gossips, argues, and bandies words. He glories in the fact that he has had the last word, and has silenced his opponent. He exults in his own folly, is ever on the defensive, and wastes his energies in unprofitable channels. He is like a gardener who continues to dig and plant in unproductive soil.

The wise man avoids idle words, gossips, vain argument, and self-defence. He is content to appear defeated; rejoices when he is defeated; knowing that, having found and removed another error in himself, he has thereby become wiser.

Blessed is he who does not strive for the last word.

Meditation for the Day

*In the process of self-discipline there are three stages—
control, purification, and relinquishment.*

MAN begins to discipline himself by controlling those passions which have hitherto controlled him; he resists temptation, and guards himself against all those tendencies to selfish gratifications which are so easy and natural, and which have formerly dominated him. He brings his appetite into subjection, and begins to eat as a reasonable and responsible being, practising moderation and thoughtfulness in the selection of his food, with the object of making his body a pure instrument through which he may live and act as becomes a man, and no longer degrading that body by pandering to gustatory pleasure. He puts a check upon his tongue, his temper, and, in fact, his every animal desire and tendency.

There is in the heart of every man and woman a selfless center.

Thought for the Evening

Desire is the *craving for possession*; aspiration is the *hunger of the heart for peace.*

The craving for things leads ever farther and farther from peace, and not only ends in deprivation, but is in itself a state of perpetual want. Until it comes to an end, rest and satisfaction are impossible.

The hunger for things can never be satisfied, but the hunger for peace can, and the satisfaction of peace is found—is fully possessed, when all selfish desire is abandoned. Then there is fullness of joy, abounding plenty, and rich and complete blessedness.

November Twenty-sixth

Thought for the Morning

A man will reach the Kingdom by purifying himself, and he can only do this by pursuing a process of self-examination and self-analysis.

The selfishness must be discovered and understood before it can be removed. It is powerless to remove itself, neither will it pass away of itself. Darkness ceases only when light is introduced; so ignorance can only be dispersed by knowledge, selfishness by love.

A man must first of all be willing to lose himself (his self-seeking) before he can find himself (his Divine Self). He must realize that selfishness is not worth clinging to, that it is a master altogether unworthy of his service, and that divine goodness alone is worthy to be enthroned in his heart, as the supreme master of his life.

Meditation for the Day

The Rock of Ages, the Christ within, the divine and immortal in all men!

AS a man practises self-control he approximates more and more to the inward reality, and is less and less swayed by passion and grief, pleasure and pain, and lives a steadfast and virtuous life, manifesting manly strength and fortitude. The restraining of the passions, however, is merely the initial stage in self-discipline, and is immediately followed by the process of *Purification*. By this a man so purifies himself as to take passion out of the heart and mind altogether; not merely restraining it when it rises within him, but preventing it from rising altogether. By merely restraining his passions a man can never arrive at peace, can never actualize his ideal; he must purify these passions.

*It is in the purification of his lower nature
that a man becomes strong and godlike.*

Thought for the Evening

Be still, my soul, and know that peace is thine. Be steadfast, heart, and know that strength divine Belongs to thee; cease from thy turmoil, mind, and thou the Everlasting Rest shalt find.

If a man would have peace, let him exercise the spirit of peace; if he would find Love, let him dwell in the spirit of Love; if he would escape suffering, let him cease to inflict it; if he would do noble things for humanity, let him cease to do ignoble things for himself. If he will but quarry the mine of his own soul, he shall find there all the materials for building whatsoever he will, and he shall find there also the Central Rock on which to build in safety.

November Twenty-seventh

Thought for the Morning

Men go after much company, and seek out new excitements, but they are not acquainted with peace; in divers paths of pleasure they search for happiness, but they do not come to rest; through divers ways of laughter and feverish delirium they wander after gladness and life, but their tears are many and grievous, and they do not escape death.

Drifting upon the ocean of life in search of selfish indulgences, men are caught in its storms, and only after many tempests and much privation do they fly to the Rock of Refuge which rests in the deep silence of their own being.

Meditation for the Day

Purification is effected by thoughtful care,
earnest meditation, and holy aspiration.

TRUE strength and power and usefulness are born of self-purification, for the lower animal forces are not lost, but are transmuted into intellectual and spiritual energy. The pure life (pure in thought and deed) is a life of conservation of energy; the impure life (even should the impurity not extend beyond thought) is a life of dissipation of energy. The pure man is more capable, and therefore more fit to succeed in his plans and to accomplish his purposes than the impure. Where the impure man fails, the pure man will step in and be victorious, because he directs his energies with a calmer mind and a greater definiteness and strength of purpose.

With the growth in purity, all the elements which constitute
a strong and virtuous manhood are developed.

Thought for the Evening

Meditation centred upon divine realities is the very essence and soul of prayer. It is the silent reaching upward of the soul toward the Eternal.

Meditation is the intense dwelling, in thought, upon an idea or theme with the object of thoroughly comprehending it; and whatsoever you constantly meditate upon, you will not only come to understand, but will grow more and more into its likeness, for it will become incorporated with your very being, will become, in fact, your very self.

If, therefore, you constantly dwell upon that which is selfish and debasing, you will ultimately become selfish and debased; if you ceaselessly think upon that which is pure and unselfish, you will surely become pure and unselfish.

November Twenty-eighth

Thought for the Morning

There is no difficulty, however great, but will yield before a calm and powerful concentration of thought and no legitimate object but may be speedily actualized by the intelligent use and direction of one's soul forces.

Whatever your task may be, concentrate your whole mind upon it; throw into it all the energy of which you are capable. The faultless completion of small tasks, leads inevitably to larger tasks.

See to it that you rise by steady climbing, and you will never fall.

Meditation for the Day

By self-discipline a man rises higher and higher,
approximating more and more nearly to the divine.

As a man grows purer, he perceives that all evil is powerless, unless it receives his encouragement, and so he ignores it, and lets it pass out of his life. It is by pursuing this aspect of self-discipline that a man enters into and realizes the divine life, and manifests those qualities which are distinctly divine, such as wisdom, patience, non-resistance, compassion, and love. It is here, also, where a man becomes consciously immortal, rising above all the fluctuations and uncertainties of life, and living in an intelligent and unchangeable peace.

By self-discipline a man attains to every degree of virtue and holiness,
and finally becomes a purified son of God,
realizing his oneness with the central heart of all things.

Thought for the Evening

He who knows that Love is at the heart of all things, and has realized the all-sufficing power of that Love, has no room in his heart for condemnation.

If you love people and speak of them with praise, until they in some way thwart you, or do something of which you disapprove, and then you dislike them and speak of them with dispraise, you are not governed by the Love which is of God. If, in your heart, you are continually arraigning and condemning others, selfless love is hidden from you.

Train your mind in strong, impartial, and gentle thought; train your heart in purity and compassion; train your tongue to silence, and to true and stainless speech; so shall you enter the way of holiness and peace, and shall ultimately realize the immortal Love.

November Twenty-ninth

Thought for the Morning

If you would realize true prosperity, do not settle down, as many have done, into the belief that if you do right everything will go wrong. Do not allow the word "competition" to shake your faith in the supremacy of righteousness. I care not what men say about the "laws of competition," for do not I know the Unchangeable Law which shall one day put them all to rout, and which puts them to rout even now in the heart and life of the righteous man? And knowing this law I can contemplate all dishonesty with undisturbed repose, for I know where certain destruction awaits it.

Under all circumstances *do that which you believe to be right*, and trust the Law; trust the Divine Power which is immanent in the universe, and it will never desert you, and you will always be protected.

Meditation for the Day

A life without resolution is a life without aims,
and a life without aims is a drifting and unstable thing.

WHEN a man makes a resolution, it means that he is dissatisfied with his condition, and is commencing to take himself in hand, with a view to producing a better piece of workmanship out of the mental materials of which his character and life are composed, and in so far as he is true to his resolution he will succeed in accomplishing his purpose.

The vows of the saintly ones are holy resolutions directed toward some victory over self, and the beautiful achievements of holy men and the glorious conquests of the Divine Teachers were rendered possible and actual by unswerving resolution.

Resolution the companion of noble aims and lofty ideals.

Thought for the Evening

Forget yourself entirely in the sorrows of others, and in ministering to others, and divine happiness will emancipate you from all sorrow and suffering. "Taking the first step with a good thought, the second with a good word, and the third with a good deed, I entered Paradise." And you also enter Paradise by pursuing the same course.

Lose yourself in the welfare of others; forget yourself in all that you do—this is the secret of abounding happiness. Ever be on the watch to guard against selfishness and learn faithfully the divine lessons of inward sacrifice; so shall you climb the highest heights of happiness, and shall remain in the never-clouded sunshine of universal joy, clothed in the shining garment of immortality.

November Thirtieth

Thought for the Morning

When the farmer has tilled and dressed his land and put in the seed, he knows that he has done all that he can possibly do, and that now he must trust to the elements, and wait patiently for the course of time to bring about the harvest, and that no amount of expectancy on his part will affect the result.

Even so, he who has realized Truth, goes forth as a sower of the seeds of goodness, purity, love, and peace, without expectancy and never looking for results, knowing that there is the Great Over-ruling Law which brings about its own harvest in due time, and which is alike the source of preservation and destruction.

Meditation for the Day

True resolution is the crisis of long thought.

HALF-HEARTED and premature resolution is no resolution at all, and is shattered at the first difficulty.

A man should be slow to form a resolution. He should searchingly examine his position and take into consideration every circumstance and difficulty with his decision, and should be fully prepared to meet them. He should be sure that he completely understands the nature of his resolution, that his mind is finally made up, and that he is without doubt in the matter. With the mind thus prepared, the resolution that is formed will not be departed from, and by the aid of it a man will, in due time, accomplish his strong purpose.

Hasty resolutions are futile.

Thought for the Evening

The virtuous put a check upon themselves, and set a watch upon their passions and emotions; in this way they gain possession of the mind, and gradually acquire calmness; and as they acquire influence, power, greatness, abiding joy, and fullness and completeness of life.

He only finds peace who conquers himself, who strives, day by day, after greater self-possession, greater self-control, and greater calmness of mind.

Where the calm mind is there is strength and rest, there is love and wisdom; there is one who has fought successfully innumerable battles against self, who, after long toil in secret against his own failings, has triumphed at last.

December First

Thought for the Morning

In aiming at the life of blessedness, one of the simplest beginnings to be considered, and rightly made, is that which we all make every day—namely, the beginning of each day's life. There is a sense in which every day may be regarded as the beginning of a new life, in which one can think, act, and live newly, and in a wiser and better spirit. The right beginning of the day will be followed by a cheerfulness permeating the household with a sunny influence, and the tasks and duties of the day will be undertaken in a strong and confident spirit, and the whole day will be well lived.

Meditation for the Day

*Indolence is the twin sister of indifference,
but ready action is the friend of contentment.*

CONTENTMENT is a virtue which becomes lofty and spiritual, as the mind is trained to perceive and the heart to receive the guidance, in all things, of a merciful law.

To be contented does not mean to forgo effort; it means to *free effort from anxiety*; it does not mean to be satisfied with sin and ignorance and folly, but to rest happily in duty done, and work accomplished.

A man may be said to be content to lead a grovelling life, to remain in sin and in debt, but such a man's true state is one of indifference to his duty, his obligations, and the just claims of his fellow-men. He cannot truly be said to possess the virtue of contentment; he does not experience the pure and abiding joy which is the accompaniment of active achievement.

True contentment is the outcome of honest effort and true living.

Thought for the Evening

There can be no progress, no achievement, without sacrifice, and a man's worldly success will be in the measure that he sacrifices his confused animal thoughts, and fixes his mind on the development of his plans, and the strengthening of his resolution and self-reliance. And the higher he lifts his thoughts, the more manly, upright, and righteous he becomes, the greater will be his success, the more blessed and enduring will be his achievements.

December Second

Thought for the Morning

None but right acts can follow right thoughts; none but a right life can follow right acts; and by living a right life all blessedness is achieved. Mind is the Master-power that moulds and makes. And Man is Mind, and evermore he takes the tool of thought, and, shaping what he wills, brings forth a thousand joys, a thousand ills;—He thinks in secret, and it comes to pass: environment is but his looking-glass.

Meditation for the Day

The truly contented man works energetically and faithfully, and accepts all results with an untroubled spirit.

THERE are three things with which a man should be content: With whatever happens; with his friendships and possessions; and with his pure thoughts. Contented with whatever happens, he will escape grief; with his friendships and possessions, he will avoid anxiety and wretchedness; and with his pure thoughts, he will never go back to suffer and grovel in impurities.

There are three with which a man should not be content: With his opinions; with his character; and with his spiritual condition. Not content with his opinions, he will continually increase in intelligence; not content with his character, he will ceaselessly grow in strength and virtue; and not content with his spiritual condition, he will, every day, enter into a larger wisdom and a fuller blessedness.

Results exactly correspond with efforts.

Thought for the Evening

Calmness of mind is one of the beautiful jewels of wisdom. A man becomes calm in the measure that he understands himself as a thought-evolved being. . . and he as he develops a right understanding, and sees more and more clearly the internal relations of things by the action of cause and effect, he ceases to fret and fume, and worry and grieve, and remains poised, steadfast, serene.

December Third

December Fourth

Thought for the Morning

To follow, under all circumstances, the highest promptings within you; to be always true to the divine self; to reply upon the inward voice, the inward light, and to pursue your purpose with a fearless and restful heart, believing that the future will yield unto you the need of every thought and effort; knowing that the laws of the universe can never fail, and that your own will come back to you with mathematical exactitude—this is faith and the living of faith.

Meditation for the Day

Universal Brotherhood is the supreme Ideal of Humanity, and towards that Ideal the world is slowly but surely moving.

BROTHERHOOD as a human organization cannot exist so long as any degree of self-seeking reigns in the hearts of men and women who band themselves together for any purpose, as such self-seeking must eventually rend the Seamless Coat of loving unity. But although organized Brotherhood has so largely failed, any man may realize Brotherhood in its perfection, and know it in all its beauty and completion, if he will make himself a wise, pure, loving spirit, removing from his mind every element of strife, and learning to practise those divine qualities without which Brotherhood is but a mere theory, opinion, or illusive dream.

In whatsoever heart discord rules, Brotherhood is not realized.

Thought for the Evening

Have a thorough understanding of your work, and let it be your own; and as you proceed, ever following the inward guide, the infallible voice, you will pass on from victory to victory, and will rise step by step to higher resting-places, and your ever broadening outlook will gradually reveal to you the essential beauty and purpose of life. Self-purified, health will be yours; self-governed, power will be yours, and all that you do will prosper.

And I may stand where health, success, and power await my coming, if, each fleeting hour, I cling to love and patience; and abide with stainlessness; and never step aside from high integrity; so shall I see at last the land of immortality.

Thought for the Morning

When the tongue is well controlled and wisely subdued; when selfish impulses and unworthy thoughts no longer rush to the tongue demanding utterance; when the speech has become harmless, pure, gracious, gentle, and purposeful, and no word is uttered but in sincerity and truth—then are the five steps in virtuous speech accomplished, then is the second great lesson in Truth learned and mastered. Make pure thy heart, and thou wilt make thy life rich, sweet and beautiful.

Meditation for the Day

*Brotherhood is at first spiritual, and its outer manifestation
in the world must follow as a natural result.*

FROM the spirit of Humility proceed meekness and peacefulness; from Self-surrender come patience, wisdom, and true judgment; from Love spring kindness, joy, harmony; and from Compassion proceed gentleness and forgiveness.

He who has brought himself into harmony with these four qualities is divinely enlightened; he sees whence the actions of men proceed and whither they tend, and therefore can no longer live in the exercise of the dark tendencies. He has realized Brotherhood in its completion, as freedom from malice, from envy, from bitterness, from contention, from condemnation. All men are his brothers, those who live in the dark tendencies as well as those who live in the enlightening qualities. He has but one attitude of mind towards all, that of goodwill.

*Where pride, self-love, hatred, and condemnation are
there can be no Brotherhood.*

Thought for the Evening

Having clothed himself with humility, the first questions a man asks himself are:—

"How am I acting towards others?"
"What am I doing to others?"
"How am I thinking of others?"
"Are my thoughts of, and acts towards others prompted by unselfish love?"

As a man, in the silence of his soul, asks himself these searching questions, he will unerringly see where he has hitherto failed.

December Fifth

Thought for the Morning

To dwell in love always and towards all is to live the true life, is to have Life itself. Knowing this, the good man gives up himself unreservedly to the Spirit of Love, and dwells in Love towards all, contending with none, condemning none, but loving all.

The Christ Spirit of Love puts an end, not only to all sin, but to all division and contention.

Meditation for the Day

Brotherhood consists, first of all, in the abandonment of self by the individual.

THEORIES and schemes for propagating Brotherhood are many, but Brotherhood itself is one and unchangeable, and consists in the complete cessation from egotism and strife, and in practising goodwill and peace; for Brotherhood is a practice and not a theory. Self-surrender and Goodwill are its guardian angels, and peace is its habitation.

Where two are determined to maintain an opposing opinion, the clinging of self and ill-will are there, and Brotherhood is absent.

Where two are prepared to sympathize with each other, to see no evil in each other, to serve and not to attack each other, the love of Truth and Good-will are there and Brotherhood is present.

Brotherhood is only practised and known by him
whose heart is at peace with all the world.

Thought for the Evening

When sin and self are abandoned, the heart is restored to its imperishable Joy. Joy comes and fills the self-emptied heart; it abides with the peaceful; its reign is with the pure. Joy flees from the selfish, it deserts the quarrelsome; it is hidden from the impure. Joy cannot remain with the selfish; it is wedded to Love.

December Sixth

Thought for the Morning

In the pure heart there is no room left where personal judgments and hatreds can find lodgement, for it is filled to overflowing with tenderness and love; it sees no evil, and only as men succeed in seeing no evil in others will they become free from sin, and sorrow, and suffering. If men only understood that the heart that sins must sorrow, that the hateful mind tomorrow reaps its barren harvest, weeping, starving, resting not, nor sleeping; tenderness would fill their being, they would see with pity's seeing, if they only understood.

Meditation for the Day

Prejudice and cruelty are inseparable.

SYMPATHY is not required towards those who are purer and more enlightened than one's self, as the purer one lives above the necessity for it. In such a case reverence should be exercised, with a striving to lift one's self up to the purer level, and so enter possession of the larger life. Nor can a man fully understand one who is wiser than himself, and before condemning, he should earnestly ask himself whether he is, after all, better than the man whom he has singled out as the object of his bitterness. If he is, let him bestow sympathy. If he is not, let him exercise reverence.

When a man is prone to harshly judge and condemn others,
he should inquire how far he falls short himself.

Thought for the Evening

To stand face to face with truth; to arrive, after innumerable wanderings and pains, at wisdom and bliss; not to be finally defeated and cast out, but to ultimately triumph over every inward foe—such is man's divine destiny, such his glorious goal; and this, every saint, sage, and saviour has declared. A man only begins to be a man when he ceases to whine and revile, and commences to search for the hidden justice which regulates his life. And as he adapts his mind to that regulating factor, he ceases to accuse others as the cause of his condition, and builds himself up in strong and noble thoughts; ceases to kick against circumstances, but begins to use them as aids to his more rapid progress, and as a means of discovering the hidden power and possibilities within himself.

December Seventh

Thought for the Morning

The will to evil and the will to good are both within thee, which wilt thou employ? Thou knowest what is right and what is wrong, which wilt though love and foster, which destroy?

Thou art the chooser of thy thoughts and deeds; thou art the maker of thine inward state; the power is thine to be what thou wilt be; thou buildest Truth and Love, or lies and hate.

Meditation for the Day

Dislike, resentment, and condemnation are all forms of hatred, and evil cannot cease until these are taken out of the heart.

THE obliterating of injuries from the mind is merely one of the beginnings in wisdom. There is a still higher and better way. And that way is to purify the heart and enlighten the mind that, far from having to forget injuries, there will be none to remember. For it is only pride and self that can be injured and wounded by the actions and attitudes of others; and he who takes pride and self out of his heart can never think the thought, "I have been injured by another," or, "I have been wronged by another."

From a purified heart proceeds the right comprehension of things; and from the right comprehension of things proceeds the life that is peaceful, freed from bitterness and suffering, calm and wise.

He who is troubled and disturbed about the sins of others is far from the Truth.

Thought for the Evening

The teaching of Jesus brings men back to the simple truth that righteousness, or *right-doing*, is entirely a matter of individual conduct, and not a mystical something apart from a man's thoughts and deeds.

Calmness and patience can become habitual by first grasping, through effort, a calm and patient thought, and then continuously thinking it, and living in it, until "use becomes second nature," and anger and impatience pass away for ever.

December Eighth

Thought for the Morning

Man is made or unmade by himself; in the armoury of thought he forges the weapons by which he destroys himself; he also fashions the tools with which he builds for himself heavenly mansions of joy and strength and peace. By the right choice and true application of thought man ascends to the Divine Perfection; by the abuse and wrong application of thought he descends below the level of the beast. Between these two extremes are all the grades of character and man is their maker and master.

As a being of Power, Intelligence, and Love, and the lord of his own thoughts, man holds the key to every situation.

Meditation for the Day

He who is troubled and disturbed about his own sins is very near to the Gate of Wisdom.

HE in whose heart the flames of resentment burn, cannot know peace nor understand Truth; he who will banish resentment from his heart, will know and understand.

He who has taken evil out of his own heart, cannot resent or resist it in others, for he is enlightened as to its origin and nature, and knows it as a manifestation of the mistakes of ignorance. With the increase of enlightenment, sin becomes impossible. He who sins, does not understand; he who understands, does not sin.

The pure man maintains his tenderness of heart toward those who ignorantly imagine that they can do him harm. The wrong attitude of others toward him does not trouble him; his heart is at rest in Compassion and Love.

Let those who aim at the right life, calmly and wisely understand.

Thought for the Evening

Whatsoever you harbour in the inmost chambers of your heart will, sooner or later, by the inevitable law of reaction, shape itself in your outward life.

Every soul attracts its own, and nothing can possibly come to it that does not belong to it. To realize this is to recognize the universality of Divine Law.

If thou would'st right the world, and banish all its evils and its woes, make its wild places bloom, and its drear deserts blossom as the rose—then right thyself.

December Ninth

Thought for the Morning

Whatever conditions are rendering your life burdensome, you may pass out of and beyond them by developing and utilizing within you the transforming power of self-purification and self-conquest.

Before the divine radiance of a pure heart all darkness vanishes and all clouds melt away, and he who has conquered self has conquered the universe.

He who sets his foot firmly upon the path of self-conquest, who walks, aided by the staff of faith, the highway of self-sacrifice, will assuredly achieve the highest prosperity, and will reap abounding and enduring joy and bliss.

Meditation for the Day

A pure heart and a righteous life are the great and all important things.

THE deeds and thoughts that lead to suffering are those that spring from self-interest and self-seeking; the thoughts and deeds that produce blessedness are those that spring from Truth. The process by which the mind is thus changed and transmuted is two-fold; it consists of *meditation and practice.* By silent meditation, the ground and reason of right conduct is sought, and by practice, right-doing is accomplished in daily life.

For Truth is not a matter of book learning, or subtle reasoning, or disputation, or controversial skill; it consists in right-doing.

Truth is not something that can be gleaned from a book;
it can be learned and known by practice only.

Thought for the Evening

It is the silent and conquering thought forces which bring all things into manifestation. The universe grew out of thought.

To adjust all your thoughts to a perfect and unswerving faith in the omnipotence and supremacy of Good is to co-operate with that Good, and to realize within yourself the solution and destruction of all evil.

To mentally deny evil is not sufficient; it must, by daily practice, be risen above and understood. To affirm the Good mentally is inadequate; it must, by unswerving endeavour, be entered into and comprehended.

December Tenth

Thought for the Morning

Every thought you think is a force sent out. Whatever your position in life may be, before you can hope to enter into any measure of success, usefulness, and power, you must learn how to focus your thought forces by cultivating calmness and repose.

There is no difficulty, however great, but will yield before a calm and purposeful concentration of thought, and no legitimate object but may be speedily actualized by the intelligent use and direction of one's soul forces.

Think good thoughts, and they will quickly become actualized in your outward life in the form of good conditions.

Meditation for the Day

He only has Truth who has found it by practice.

HE who wishes to acquire Truth must practise it. He must begin at the very first lesson in self-control, thoroughly master it, and then pass on to the next and the next, until he attains to the moral perfection at which he aims. It is common with men to imagine that Truth consists in holding certain ideas or opinions. They read a number of treatises, and then form an opinion which they call "Truth", and then they go about disputing with their fellow-men in order to try to prove that their opinion is the Truth. In worldly matters men are wise, for they *do* things in order to achieve their ends, but in spiritual things they are foolish, for they merely read, and do not do things, and then imagine they have acquired Truth.

He only has Truth whose life shows it forth in pure and blameless conduct.

Thought for the Evening

That which you would be and hope to be, you may be now. Non-accomplishment resides in your perpetual postponement, and, having the power to postpone, you also have the power to accomplish—to perpetually accomplish: realize this truth, and you shall be today, and every day, the ideal being of whom you dreamed.

Say to yourself, "I will live in my Ideal now; I will manifest my ideal now; I will be my Ideal now; and all that tempts me away from my Ideal I will not listen to; I will listen only to the voice of my Ideal."

December Eleventh

Thought for the Morning

Be as a flower; content to be, to grow in sweetness day by day. If thou would'st perfect thyself in knowledge, perfect thyself in Love. If thou would'st reach the Highest, ceaselessly cultivate a loving and compassionate heart.

To him who chooses Goodness, sacrificing all, is given that which is more than, and includes, all.

Meditation for the Day

Love, all inclusive.

BY its very nature, Love can never be the exclusive possession of any religion, sect, school, or brotherhood. The common claim, therefore, of such sections of the community to the exclusive possession of Truth in their particular religious doctrine is a denial of Love. Truth is a spirit and a life, and though it may manifest through manifold doctrines, it can never be confined to any one particular form of doctrine. Love is a winged angel that refuses to be chained to any letter doctrine whatsoever. Love is above and beyond, outside and greater than all the opinions, doctrines, and philosophies of men; yet Love includes all—the righteous and the unrighteous, the fair and foul, the clean and the unclean. He whose Love is so deep and wide as to envelop all men of all creeds is he who has most of religion, and most of wisdom, and also most of insight, for he knows and sees men as they are.

Hatred is absence of Love, and therefore absence of all that is included in Love.

Thought for the Evening

The Great Law never cheats any man of his just due.

Human life, when rightly lived, is simple with a beautiful simplicity.

He who comprehends the utter simplicity of life, who obeys its laws, and does not step aside into the dark paths and complex mazes of selfish desire, stands where no harm can reach him.

Then there is fullness of joy, abounding plenty, and rich and complete blessedness.

December Twelfth

Thought for the Morning

Every man reaps the results of his own thoughts and deeds, and suffers for his own wrong.

He who begins right, and continues right, does not need to desire, and search for felicitous results; they are already at hand; they follow as consequences; they are the certainties, the realities, of life.

Sweet is the rest and deep is the bliss of him who has freed his heart from its lusts and hatreds and dark desires.

Meditation for the Day

Love broadens and expands the mind of a man
until it embraces in its kindly folds
all mankind without distinction.

THE way of Love is the way of Life—Immortal Life—and the beginning of that way consists in getting rid of our carpings, quarrellings, fault-findings, and suspicions. If these petty vices possess us, let us not deceive ourselves, but let us confess that we have not Love. To be thus honest with ourselves is to be prepared to find Love; but to be self-deceived is to be shut out from Love. If we are to grow in Love, we must begin at the beginning, and remove from our minds all mean and suspicious thoughts about our fellow-workers and fellow-men. We must learn to treat them with large-hearted freedom, and to perceive the right reason for their actions, to excuse them on grounds of personal right and personal freedom when their opinions, methods, or actions are contrary to us; thus shall we come at last to love them with that Love of which St. Paul speaks, a Love that is a permanent principle.

He who has Love of whatsoever creed or none
is enlightened with the Light of Truth.

Thought for the Evening

You are the creator of your own shadows; you desire, and then you grieve; renounce, and then you shall rejoice.

Of all the beautiful truths pertaining to the soul. . . none is more gladdening or fruitful of divine promise and confidence than this—that man is the master of thought, the moulder of character, and the maker and shaper of character, environment, and destiny.

December Thirteenth

Thought for the Morning

As darkness is a passing shadow, and light is a substance that remains, so sorrow is fleeting, but joy abides for ever. No true thing can pass away and become lost; no false thing can remain and be preserved. Sorrow is false, and it cannot live; joy is true, and it cannot die. Joy may become hidden for a time, but it can always be recovered; sorrow may remain for a period, but it can be transcended and dispersed.

Do not think your sorrow will remain; it will pass away like a cloud. Do not believe that the torments of sin are ever your portion; they will vanish like a hideous nightmare. Awake! Arise! Be holy and joyful.

Meditation for the Day

The Life of Truth is that in which wrong-thinking and wrong-doing are abandoned, and right-thinking and right-doing are embraced.

IT is the wrong deeds of men which bring all the unhappiness into the world. It will be right deeds which will transform all its misery into happiness. By wrong deeds we come to sorrow; by right deeds we come to bliss.

But a man must not think the thought:

"It is the wrong deeds of others which have made me unhappy," for such a thought produces bitterness towards others and increases hatred. He must understand that his unhappiness is from something wrong within himself; he must regard it as a sign that he is yet imperfect, that there is some weak spot within which must be strengthened. He must never accuse others for his lapses of conduct, or for his troubles, but must gain more steadfastness of heart, must establish himself more firmly in the Truth.

Walk with lowly footsteps the holy way of Truth.

Thought for the Evening

Tribulation lasts only so long as there remains some chaff of self which needs to be removed. The *tribulum*, or threshing machine, ceases to work when all the grain is separated from the chaff; and when the last impurities are blown away from the soul, tribulation has completed its work, and there is no more need for it; then abiding joy is realized.

The sole and supreme use of suffering is to purify, to burn out all that is useless and impure. Suffering ceases for him who is pure. There could be no object in burning gold after the dross had been removed.

December Fourteenth

Thought for the Morning

In speaking of self-control, one is easily misunderstood. It should not be associated with a destructive repression, but with a constructive expression.

A man is happy, wise and great in the measure that he controls himself; he is wretched, foolish, and mean in the measure that he allows his animal nature to dominate his thoughts and actions.

He who controls himself, controls his life, his circumstances, his destiny; and wherever he goes he carries his happiness with him as an abiding possession.

Renunciation precedes regeneration. The permanent happiness which men seek in dissipation, excitement, and abandonment to unworthy pleasures, is found only in the life which reverses all this—the life of self-control.

Meditation for the Day

The principles of Truth are fixed and eternal,
and cannot be made or unmade by anyone.

THE principles of Truth were discovered by searching and practice, and are so stated and arranged as to make the path plainer for other feet to tread; and it is the path along which every being has travelled who has passed from sin to sinlessness, from error to Truth. It is the ancient Way along which every saint, every Buddha, every Christ has walked to divine perfection, and along which every imperfect being in the future will pass to reach this glorious goal. It matters not what religion a man professes, if he is daily striving with his own sins, and purifying his heart, he is walking this path; for while opinions, theologies, and religions differ, sin does not differ, the overcoming of sin does not differ, and Truth does not differ.

Religions change from age to age,
but the principles of divine virtue are eternally the same.

Thought for the Evening

Law, not confusion, is the dominating principle in the universe; justice, not injustice is the soul and substance of life; and righteousness, not corruption, is the moulding and moving force in the spiritual government of the world. This being so, man has but the right himself to find that the universe is right.

When I am pure, I shall have solved the mystery of life; I shall be sure, when I am free from hatred, lust and strife, I am in Truth, and Truth abides in me; I shall be safe, and sane, and wholly free, when I am pure.

December Fifteenth

Thought for the Morning

If men only understood that their hatred and resentment slays their peace and sweet contentment, hurts themselves, helps not another, does not cheer one lonely brother, they would seek the better doing of good deeds which leaves no ruing:—

If they only understood.

If men only understood how Love conquers; how prevailing is its might, grim hate assailing; how compassion endeth sorrow, maketh wise, and doth not borrow pain of passion, they would ever live in Love, in hatred never:—

If they only understood.

Meditation for the Day

Truth is one, though it has a variety of aspects,
and is adaptable to men in various stages of growth.

I HAVE sat at the feet of all the Great Teachers, and have learned of them. Unspeakable has been our rejoicing to have found, in the lives and precepts of gentle Indian and Chinese Teachers, the same divine qualities and the same perceptive truths which adorn the character of Jesus Christ. To us they are all wonderful and adorable, and so great and good and wise that we can but reverence and learn of them. They have also had the same marvellous influence for good over the various races among which they have appeared, and have all equally called forth the undying worship of millions of human beings.

Great Teachers are perfected flowers of humanity,
types of what all men will one day be.

Thought for the Evening

The grace and beauty that were in Jesus can be of no value to you—cannot be understood by you—unless they are also *in you*, and they can never be in you, until you practice them, for, apart from *doing*, the qualities which constitute goodness do not, as far as you are concerned, exist.

To adore Jesus for his good qualities is a long step towards Truth, but to practice those qualities is Truth itself; and he who fully adores the perfection of another will not rest content in his own imperfection, but will fashion his soul after the likeness of that other.

Therefore thou who adorest Jesus for his divine qualities, practice those qualities thyself, and thou too shalt be divine.

December Sixteenth

Thought for the Morning

Let a man realize that life in its totality proceeds from the mind, and lo, the way of blessedness is opened up to him! For he will then discover that he possesses the power to rule his mind and to fashion it in accordance with his Ideal.

So will he elect to strongly and steadfastly walk those pathways of thought and action which are altogether excellent; to him life will become beautiful and sacred; and, sooner or later, he will put to flight all evil, confusion, and suffering; for it is impossible for a man to fall short of liberation, enlightenment, and peace, who guards with unwearying diligence the gateway of his heart.

Meditation for the Day

Perfect purity of heart is a condition of emancipation
from all the cravings and indulgences of self.

THERE is a distinction between a worldly life and a religious life. He who is daily following his impure inclinations, with no wish to give them up, is irreligious; while he who is daily controlling and purging away his impure inclinations is religious.

The religious man should curb his passions and the indulgence of his desires, for that is what constitutes religion. He must learn to see men and things *as they are*, and must perceive that they are living in accordance with their nature, and their right of choosing their path as intelligent human beings. He must never intrude his rules of life upon them; and never presume to be, or even think of himself as being, on a "higher plane" than they are. He must learn to put himself in their place, and to see from their standpoint.

A lover of Truth must be a lover of all men.
He must let his love go out without restraint or stint.

Thought for the Evening

By constantly overcoming self, a man gains a knowledge of the subtle intricacies of his mind; and it is this divine knowledge which enables him to become established in calmness.

Without self-knowledge there can be no abiding peace of mind, and those who are carried away by tempestuous passions, cannot approach the holy place where calmness reigns.

The weak man is like one who, having mounted a fiery steed, allows it to run away with him, and carry him withersoever it wills; the strong man is like one who, having mounted the steed, governs it with a masterly hand and makes it go in whatever direction and at whatever speed he commands.

December Seventeenth

Thought for the Morning

There is no strife, no selfishness, in the Kingdom; there is perfect harmony, equipoise, and rest.

Those who live in the Kingdom of Love, have all their needs supplied by the Law of Love.

As self is the root cause of all strife and suffering, so Love is the root cause of all peace and bliss. Those who are at rest in the Kingdom do not look for happiness in any outward possessions. They are freed from all anxiety and trouble and, resting in Love, they are the embodiment of happiness.

Meditation for the Day

The ground of certainty on which we can securely
rest amid all the incidents of life,
is the mathematical exactitude of the moral law.

THE unceasing change, the insecurity and the mystery of life make it necessary to find some basis of certainty on which to rest if happiness and peace of mind are to be maintained. This basic principle, a knowledge of which the whole race will ultimately acquire, is best represented by the term *Divine Justice*. Human justice differs with every man according to his own light or darkness, but there can be no variation in that Divine Justice by which the universe is eternally sustained. Divine Justice is spiritual mathematics. As with figures and objects, so with the thoughts and deeds of men, two and two equally make four.

Given the same cause, there will always be the same effect.

Thought for the Evening

Let it not be supposed that the children of the Kingdom live in ease and indolence (these two sins are the first that have to be eradicated when the search for the Kingdom is entered upon); they live in a peaceful activity; in fact, they only truly live, for the life of self, with its train of worries, griefs, and fears, is not *real life*.

The children of the Kingdom are *known by their life*, they manifest the fruits of the Spirit—"Love, joy, peace, long-suffering, kindness, goodness, faithfulness, meekness, temperance, and self-control"—under all circumstances and vicissitudes.

December Eighteenth

Thought for the Morning

The gospel of Jesus is a gospel of *living and doing*. If it were not this it would not voice the Eternal Truth. Its Temple is *Purified Conduct*, the entrance-door to which is *Self-Surrender*. It invites men to shake off sin, and promises, as a result, joy and blessedness and perfect peace.

The Kingdom of Heaven is perfect trust, perfect knowledge, perfect peace. . . no sin can enter therein, no self-born thought or deed can pass its golden gates; no impure desire can defile its radiant robes. . . all may enter it who will, but all must pay the price—*the unconditional abandonment of self.*

Meditation for the Day

*All the spiritual laws with which men are acquainted have,
and must have, the same infallibility in their operations.*

GIVEN the same thought or deed in a like circumstance, the result will always be the same. Without this fundamental ethical justice there could be no human society, for it is the just reactions of the deeds of individuals which prevents society from tottering to its fall.

It thus follows that the inequalities of life, as regards the distribution of happiness and suffering, are the outworking of moral forces operating along lines of flawless accuracy. This flawless accuracy, this perfect law, is the one great fundamental certainty in life, the finding of which insures a man's perfection, makes him wise and enlightened, and fills him with rejoicing and peace.

*The moral order of the universe is not,
cannot be disproportionate,
for if it were, the universe would fall.*

Thought for the Evening

I say this—and know it to be truth—*that circumstances can only affect you in so far as you allow them to do so.* You are swayed by circumstances because you have not a right understanding of the nature, use, and power of thought. You believe (and upon this little word *belief* hang all our joys and sorrows) that outward things have the power to make or mar your life; by so doing you submit to those outward things, confess that you are their slave, and they your unconditional master. By so doing you invest them with a power which they do not of themselves possess, and you succumb, in reality not to the circumstances, but to the gloom or gladness, the fear or hope, the strength of weakness, which your thought-sphere has thrown around them.

December Nineteenth

December Twentieth

Thought for the Morning

If you are one of those who are praying for, and looking forward to a happier world beyond the grave, here is a message of gladness for you—you may enter into and realize that happy world now; it fills the whole universe, and it is within you, waiting for you to find, acknowledge, and possess.

Said one who understood the inner laws of Being—"When men shall say, lo here, or lo there, go not after them. The Kingdom of God is within you."

Meditation for the Day

Nothing can transcend right.

TAKE away a belief in this certainty from a man's consciousness, and he is adrift on a self-created ocean of chance, without rudder, chart, or compass. He has no ground on which to build a character or life, no incentive for noble deeds, no centre for moral action; he has no island of peace and no harbour of refuge. Even the crudest idea of God as of a great man whose mind is perfect, who cannot err, and who has "no variableness nor shadow of turning," is a popular expression of a belief in this basic principle of Divine Justice.

According to this principle there is neither favour nor chance, but unerring and unchangeable right. Thus all the sufferings of men are right as *effects*, their causes being the mistakes of ignorance; but as effects they will pass away.

Man cannot suffer for something which he has never done,
or never left undone,
for this would be an effect without a cause.

Thought for the Evening

Heaven and hell are inward states. Sink into self and all its gratifications, and you sink into hell; rise above self into that state of consciousness which is the utter denial and forgetfulness of self, and you enter heaven.

So long as you persist in selfishly seeking for your own personal happiness, so long will happiness elude you, and you will be sowing the seeds of wretchedness. In so far as you succeed in losing yourself in the service of others, in that measure will happiness come to you, and you will reap a harvest of bliss.

Thought for the Morning

Sympathy given can never be waste.

One aspect of sympathy is that of pity—pity for the distressed or pain stricken, with a desire to alleviate or help them in their sufferings. The world needs more of this divine quality.

"For pity makes the world soft to the weak, and noble for the strong."

Another form of sympathy is that of rejoicing with others who are more successful than ourselves, and though their success were our own.

Meditation for the Day

Talent, genius, goodness, greatness, are not launched upon the world ready-made. They are the result of a long train of causes and effects.

THE process of growth is seen in the flower, but though not seen in the mental growth, it is nevertheless there.

I said the process of mental growth was not seen; but this is only true in a general sense. The true thinker and sage does see, with his spiritual eye, the process of spiritual growth. Just as the natural scientist has made himself acquainted with natural causes and effects—as, indeed, the ordinary observer is so acquainted—so he has made himself familiar with spiritual causes and effects. He sees the process by which characters, like plants, come into being; and when he sees the flowers of genius and virtue appear, he knows from what mental seeds they sprang, and how they gradually came to perfection through long periods of silent growth. Nothing appears ready-made.

There is always a changing, a growing, a becoming.

Thought for the Evening

Sweet are companionships, pleasures, and material comforts, but they change and fade away. Sweeter still are Purity, Wisdom, and the knowledge of Truth, and these never change nor fade away.

He who attained to the possession of spiritual things can never be deprived of his source of happiness; he will never have to part company with it, and wherever he goes in the whole universe, he will carry his possessions with him. His spiritual end will be the fullness of joy.

December Twenty-first

Thought for the Morning

Let your heart grow and expand with ever broadening love, until, freed from all hatred, and passion, and condemnation, it embraces the whole universe with thoughtful tenderness.

As the flower opens its petals to receive the morning light, so open your soul more and more to the glorious light of Truth.

Soar upward on the wings of aspiration; be fearless and believe in the loftiest possibilities.

Meditation for the Day

An awakened vision calls us to a nobler life.

As a man cannot live in two countries at the same time, but must leave the one before he can settle in the other, so a man cannot inhabit two spiritual countries at the same time, but must leave behind the land of sin before he can live at peace in the land of truth. When one leaves his native land, that he may begin anew in an adopted country, he leaves behind all beloved associations, sweet companionships, dear friends and relatives, yea, all upon which his heart has been ever set must be parted with and left behind. So when one resolves to live in the new world of Truth, the old world of error, with its loved pleasures, cherished sins, and vain associations, must be renounced. By such renunciation the individual gains, humanity gains, and the universe becomes a brighter and more beautiful habitation.

We must shake the mud of the valley from our feet
if we are to commune with the mountain silence.

Thought for the Evening

Mind clothes itself in garments of its own making. Mind is the arbiter of life; it is the creator and shaper of conditions, and the recipient of its own results. It contains within itself both the power to create illusion and to perceive reality.

Mind is the infallible weaver of destiny; thought is the thread, good and evil deeds are the warp and woof, and the web, woven upon the loom of life, is character. Make pure thy heart, and thou wilt make thy life, rich, sweet, and beautiful, unmarred by strife.

December Twenty-second

Thought for the Morning

Cherish your visions; cherish your ideals; cherish the music that stirs in your heart, the beauty that forms in your mind, the loveliness that drapes your purest thoughts, for out of them will grow all delightful conditions, all heavenly environment; of these, if you will remain true to them, your world will at last be built.

Guard well thy mind, and, noble, strong, and free, nothing shall harm, disturb or conquer thee; for all thy foes are in thy heart and mind, there also thy salvation thou shalt find.

Meditation for the Day

*Right thoughts spring from a right mental attitude,
and lead to right actions.*

THAT is the right mental attitude which seeks the good in all the occurrences of life, and extracts strength, knowledge, and wisdom from them. Right thoughts are thoughts of cheer, of joy, of hope, of confidence, of courage, of constant love, of large generosity, of abounding faith and trust. These are the affirmations that make strong characters and useful and noble lives, and that build up those personal successes which make the progress of the world. Such thoughts are inevitably followed by right action, by the putting forth of energy and effort in work, in the accomplishment of some legitimate object; and as the climber at last reaches the hill-top, so the earnest, cheerful, and untiring worker at last accomplishes his end.

*All the successful people, through all time,
have reached their particular success by laboring for it.*

Thought for the Evening

Dream lofty dreams, and as you dream so shall you become. Your vision is the promise of what you shall one day be; your Ideal is the prophecy of what you shall at last unveil.

The greatest achievement was at first and for a time a dream. The oak sleeps in the acorn; the bird waits in the egg; and in the highest vision of the soul a waking angel stirs.

Your circumstances may be uncongenial, but they shall not long remain so when you perceive an Ideal and strive to reach it.

December Twenty-third

Thought for the Morning

He who has conquered doubt and fear has conquered failure. His every thought is allied with power, and all difficulties are bravely met and wisely overcome. His purposes are seasonably planted, and they bloom and bring forth fruit which does not fall prematurely to the ground.

Thought allied fearlessly to purpose becomes creative force: he who knows this is ready to become something higher and stronger than a mere bundle of wavering thoughts and fluctuating sensations; he who does this has become the conscious and intelligent wielder of his mental powers.

Meditation for the Day

Suffering is a purifying and perfecting process.
"We become obedient by the things which we suffer."

TO inflict suffering upon others is to become more deeply involved in ignorance; but to suffer ourselves is to come nearer to enlightenment. Pain teaches men how to be kind and compassionate. It at last makes them tender-hearted and thoughtful for the sufferings of others. When a man does a cruel deed, he thinks, in his ignorance, that that is the end of it, but it is only the beginning. Attached to the deed is a train of consequences which will plunge him in a tormenting hell of pain. For every wrong thought we think, or unkind deed we do, we must suffer some form of mental or bodily pain; and the kind of pain will be in accordance with the initiative thought or act.

By acquainting man with suffering,
it enables him to feel for the sufferings of others.

Thought for the Evening

Man's true place in the Cosmos is that of a king, not a slave, a commander under the Law of Good, and not a helpless tool in the region of evil.

I write for men, not for babes; for those who are eager to learn, and earnest to achieve; for those who will put away (for the world's good) a petty personal indulgence, a selfish desire, a mean thought, and live on as though it were not, sans craving and regret.

Man is a master. If he were not, he could not act contrary to law.

Evil and weakness are self destructive. The universe is girt with goodness and strength, and it protects the good and the strong.

The angry man is the weak man.

December Twenty-fourth

Thought for the Morning

Not by learning will a man triumph over evil; not by much study will he overcome sin and sorrow. Only by conquering himself will he conquer evil; only by practicing righteousness will he put an end to sorrow.

Not for the clever, nor the learned, nor the self-confident is the Life Triumphant, but for the pure, the virtuous and wise. The former achieve their particular success in life, but the latter alone achieve the great success so invincible and complete that even in apparent defeat it shines with added victory.

Meditation for the Day

Every resource is already with you and within you.

JUST as the strong doing of small tasks leads to greater strength, so the doing of those tasks weakly leads to greater weakness. What a man is in his fractional duties that he is in the aggregate of his character. Weakness is as great a source of suffering as sin, and there can be no true blessedness until some measure of strength of character is evolved. The weak man becomes strong by attaching value to little things and doing them accordingly. The strong man becomes weak by falling into looseness and neglect concerning small things, thereby forfeiting his simple wisdom and squandering his energy.

*There is no way to strength and wisdom
but by acting strongly and wisely in the present moment.*

Thought for the Evening

The true silence is not merely a silent tongue; it is a silent mind. To merely *hold one's tongue*, and yet to carry about a disturbed and rankling mind, is no remedy for weakness, and no source of power.

Silentness, to be powerful, must envelop the whole mind, must permeate every chamber of the heart; it must be the silence of peace.

To this broad, deep, abiding silentness a man attains only in the measure that he conquers himself.

December Twenty-fifth

Thought for the Morning

By curbing his tongue, a man gains possession of his mind.

The fool babbles, gossips, argues, and bandies words. He glories in the fact that he has had the last word, and has silenced his opponent. He exults in his own folly, is ever on the defensive, and wastes his energies in unprofitable channels. He is like a gardener who continues to dig and plant in unproductive soil.

The wise man avoids idle words, gossips, vain argument, and self-defence. He is content to appear defeated; rejoices when he is defeated; knowing that, having found and removed another error in himself, he has thereby become wiser.

Blessed is he who does not strive for the last word.

Meditation for the Day

*The year is passing, and blessed are they who can let
its mistakes, its injuries, and wrongs pass away forever,
and be remembered no more.*

THE past is dead and unalterable; let it sink into oblivion, but extract and retain its divine lessons; let those lessons be strength to you now, and make them the starting-points of a nobler, purer, more perfect life in the coming years. Let all thoughts of hatred, resentment, strife, and ill-will die with the dying years; erase from the tablet of your heart all malicious memories, all unholy grudges. Let the cry, "Peace on earth and good-will to men!" which at this season re-echoes through the world from myriads of lips, be to you something more than an oft-reiterated platitude. Let its truth be practised by you; let it dwell in your heart; and do not mar its harmony and peace by thoughts of ill-will.

*Blessed is he who has no wrongs to remember, no injuries to forget;
in whose pure heart no hateful thought about another
can take root and flourish.*

Thought for the Evening

Desire is the *craving for possession*; aspiration is the *hunger of the heart for peace*.

The craving for things leads ever farther and farther from peace, and not only ends in deprivation, but is in itself a state of perpetual want. Until it comes to an end, rest and satisfaction are impossible.

The hunger for things can never be satisfied, but the hunger for peace can, and the satisfaction of peace is found—is fully possessed, when all selfish desire is abandoned. Then there is fullness of joy, abounding plenty, and rich and complete blessedness.

December Twenty-sixth

Thought for the Morning

A man will reach the Kingdom by purifying himself, and he can only do this by pursuing a process of self-examination and self-analysis.

The selfishness must be discovered and understood before it can be removed. It is powerless to remove itself, neither will it pass away of itself. Darkness ceases only when light is introduced; so ignorance can only be dispersed by knowledge, selfishness by love.

A man must first of all be willing to lose himself (his self-seeking) before he can find himself (his Divine Self). He must realize that selfishness is not worth clinging to, that it is a master altogether unworthy of his service, and that divine goodness alone is worthy to be enthroned in his heart, as the supreme master of his life.

Meditation for the Day

*No man can be confronted with a difficulty which he
has not the strength to meet and subdue.*

DO not regard your difficulties and perplexities as portentous of ill; by so doing you will make them ill; but regard them as prophetic of good, which, indeed, they are. Do not persuade yourself that you can evade them: you cannot. Do not try to run away from them; this is impossible, for wherever you go they will still be there with you—but meet them calmly and bravely; confront them with all the dispassion and dignity which you can command; weigh up their proportions; measure their strength; understand them; attack them, and finally vanquish them. Thus will you develop strength and intelligence; thus will you enter one of those byways of blessedness which are hidden from the superficial gaze.

There is no peace in sin, no rest in error, no final refuge but in wisdom.

Thought for the Evening

Be still, my soul, and know that peace is thine. Be steadfast, heart, and know that strength divine Belongs to thee; cease from thy turmoil, mind, and thou the Everlasting Rest shalt find.

If a man would have peace, let him exercise the spirit of peace; if he would find Love, let him dwell in the spirit of Love; if he would escape suffering, let him cease to inflict it; if he would do noble things for humanity, let him cease to do ignoble things for himself. If he will but quarry the mine of his own soul, he shall find there all the materials for building whatsoever he will, and he shall find there also the Central Rock on which to build in safety.

December Twenty-seventh

Thought for the Morning

Men go after much company, and seek out new excitements, but they are not acquainted with peace; in divers paths of pleasure they search for happiness, but they do not come to rest; through divers ways of laughter and feverish delirium they wander after gladness and life, but their tears are many and grievous, and they do not escape death.

Drifting upon the ocean of life in search of selfish indulgences, men are caught in its storms, and only after many tempests and much privation do they fly to the Rock of Refuge which rests in the deep silence of their own being.

Meditation for the Day

*Go to your task with love in your heart
and you will go to it light-hearted and cheerful.*

WHAT heavy burden is a man weighted with which is not made heavier and more unendurable by weak thoughts or selfish desires? If your circumstances are "trying" it is because you need them, and can evolve the strength to meet them. They are trying because there is some weak spot in you, and they will continue to be trying until that spot is eradicated. Be glad that you have the opportunity of becoming stronger and wiser. No circumstances can be trying to wisdom; nothing can weary love. Stop brooding over your own trying circumstances and contemplate the lives of some of those about you.

*The duty which you shirk is your reproving angel;
the pleasure which you race after is your flattering enemy.*

Thought for the Evening

Meditation centred upon divine realities is the very essence and soul of prayer. It is the silent reaching upward of the soul toward the Eternal.

Meditation is the intense dwelling, in thought, upon an idea or theme with the object of thoroughly comprehending it; and whatsoever you constantly meditate upon, you will not only come to understand, but will grow more and more into its likeness, for it will become incorporated with your very being, will become, in fact, your very self.

If, therefore, you constantly dwell upon that which is selfish and debasing, you will ultimately become selfish and debased; if you ceaselessly think upon that which is pure and unselfish, you will surely become pure and unselfish.

December Twenty-eighth

Thought for the Morning

There is no difficulty, however great, but will yield before a calm and powerful concentration of thought and no legitimate object but may be speedily actualized by the intelligent use and direction of one's soul forces.

Whatever your task may be, concentrate your whole mind upon it; throw into it all the energy of which you are capable. The faultless completion of small tasks, leads inevitably to larger tasks.

See to it that you rise by steady climbing, and you will never fall.

Meditation for the Day

Animal indulgence is alien to the perception of Truth.

THERE are little selfish indulgences, some of which appear harmless, and are commonly fostered; but no selfish indulgence can be harmless, and men and women do not know what they lose by repeatedly and habitually succumbing to effeminate and selfish gratifications. If the God in man is to rise strong and triumphant, the beast in man must perish. The pandering to the animal nature, even when it appears innocent and seems sweet, leads away from truth and blessedness. Each time you give way to the animal within you, and feed and gratify him, he waxes stronger and more rebellious, and takes firmer possession of your mind, which should be in the keeping of Truth.

Live superior to the craving for sense-excitement,
and you will live neither vainly nor uncertainly.

Thought for the Evening

He who knows that Love is at the heart of all things, and has realized the all-sufficing power of that Love, has no room in his heart for condemnation.

If you love people and speak of them with praise, until they in some way thwart you, or do something of which you disapprove, and then you dislike them and speak of them with dispraise, you are not governed by the Love which is of God. If, in your heart, you are continually arraigning and condemning others, selfless love is hidden from you.

Train your mind in strong, impartial, and gentle thought; train your heart in purity and compassion; train your tongue to silence, and to true and stainless speech; so shall you enter the way of holiness and peace, and shall ultimately realize the immortal Love.

December Twenty-ninth

Thought for the Morning

If you would realize true prosperity, do not settle down, as many have done, into the belief that if you do right everything will go wrong. Do not allow the word "competition" to shake your faith in the supremacy of righteousness. I care not what men say about the "laws of competition," for do not I know the Unchangeable Law which shall one day put them all to rout, and which puts them to rout even now in the heart and life of the righteous man? And knowing this law I can contemplate all dishonesty with undisturbed repose, for I know where certain destruction awaits it.

Under all circumstances *do that which you believe to be right*, and trust the Law; trust the Divine Power which is immanent in the universe, and it will never desert you, and you will always be protected.

Meditation for the Day

Sacrifice all hatred, slay it upon the altar of devotion—devotion to others.

WHATEVER others may say of you, whatever they may do to you, *never take offence*. Do not return hatred with hatred. If another hates you perhaps you have, consciously or unconsciously, failed somewhere in your conduct, or there may be some misunderstanding which the exercise of a little gentleness and reason may remove; but under all circumstances "Father, forgive them" is infinitely better than "I will have nothing more to do with them." Hatred is so small and poor, so blind and wretched. Love is so great and rich, so far-seeing and blissful.

Open the floodgates of your heart for the inpouring
of that sweet, great, beautiful love which embraces all.

Thought for the Evening

Forget yourself entirely in the sorrows of others, and in ministering to others, and divine happiness will emancipate you from all sorrow and suffering. "Taking the first step with a good thought, the second with a good word, and the third with a good deed, I entered Paradise." And you also enter Paradise by pursuing the same course.

Lose yourself in the welfare of others; forget yourself in all that you do—this is the secret of abounding happiness. Ever be on the watch to guard against selfishness and learn faithfully the divine lessons of inward sacrifice; so shall you climb the highest heights of happiness, and shall remain in the never-clouded sunshine of universal joy, clothed in the shining garment of immortality.

December Thirtieth

Thought for the Morning

When the farmer has tilled and dressed his land and put in the seed, he knows that he has done all that he can possibly do, and that now he must trust to the elements, and wait patiently for the course of time to bring about the harvest, and that no amount of expectancy on his part will affect the result.

Even so, he who has realized Truth, goes forth as a sower of the seeds of goodness, purity, love, and peace, without expectancy and never looking for results, knowing that there is the Great Over-ruling Law which brings about its own harvest in due time, and which is alike the source of preservation and destruction.

Meditation for the Day

Inside the gateway of unselfishness lies the Elysium of Abiding Joy.

KNOWING this—that selfishness leads to misery, and unselfishness to joy, not merely for one's self alone—for if this were all how unworthy would be our endeavours!—but for the whole world, and because all with whom we live and come in contact will be the happier and the truer for unselfishness; because Humanity is one, and the joy of one is the joy of all—knowing this, let us scatter flowers and not thorns in the common ways of life—yea, even in the highway of our enemies let us scatter the blossoms of unselfish love—so shall the pressure of their footprints fill the air with the perfume of holiness and gladden the world with the aroma of joy.

Seek the highest Good, and you will taste the deepest, sweetest joy.

Thought for the Evening

The virtuous put a check upon themselves, and set a watch upon their passions and emotions; in this way they gain possession of the mind, and gradually acquire calmness; and as they acquire influence, power, greatness, abiding joy, and fullness and completeness of life.

He only finds peace who conquers himself, who strives, day by day, after greater self-possession, greater self-control, and greater calmness of mind.

Where the calm mind is there is strength and rest, there is love and wisdom; there is one who has fought successfully innumerable battles against self, who, after long toil in secret against his own failings, has triumphed at last.

December Thirty-first

Thought for the Morning

Sympathy bestowed increases its store in our own heart and enriches and fructifies our own life. Sympathy given is blessedness received; sympathy withheld is blessedness forfeited.

In the measure that a man increases and enlarges his sympathy so much nearer does he approach the ideal life, the perfect blessedness; and when his heart has become so mellowed that no hard, bitter, or cruel thought can enter, and detract from its permanent sweetness, then indeed is he richly and divinely blessed.

Meditation for the Day

*The universe has no favorites; it is supremely just,
and gives to every man his rightful earnings.*

HAPPY in the Eternal Happiness is he who has come to that Life from which the thought of self is abolished. Already, even now and in this life, he has entered the Kingdom of Heaven. He is at rest on the bosom of the Infinite.

Sweet is the rest and deep the bliss of him who has freed his heart from its lusts and hatreds and dark desires; and he who, without any shadow of bitterness or selfishness, can breathe, in his heart, the blessing:

Peace unto all living things, making no exceptions or distinctions—such a man has reached that happy ending which can never be taken away, the fullness of peace, the consummation of Perfect Blessedness.

*Man can find the right way in life, and,
having found it, can rejoice and be glad.*

Thought for the Evening

Sweet is the rest and deep the bliss of him who has freed his heart from its lusts and hatreds and dark desires; and he who, without any shadow of bitterness resting upon him, and looking out upon the world with boundless compassion and love, can breathe, in his inmost heart, the blessing: Peace unto all living things, making no exceptions or distinctions—such a man has reached that happy ending which can never be taken away, for this is the perfection of life, the fullness of peace, the consummation of perfect blessedness.

Made in the USA
Lexington, KY
24 November 2014